As Time Goes By

JUDITH DUPONT

Translated by Agnes Jacob

As Time Goes By

JUDITH DUPONT

Translated by Agnes Jacob

International Psychoanalytic Books (IPBooks)
New York • IPBooks.net

Copyright © 2019 Judith Dupont and IPBooks

International Psychoanalytic Books (IPBooks)
Queens, New York
United States
Online at: www.IPBooks.net

All rights reserved. This book may not be reproduced, transmitted, or stored in whole or in part by any means, including graphic, electronic, or mechanical without the express permission of the publisher except in the case of brief quotations embodied in critical articles and reviews.

Book design by Dan Williams

ISBN: 978-1-949093-19-3

Printed in the United States of America

INTRODUCTION
EVA BRABANT

"I can't tell anyone, so I tell everyone", wrote Frigyes Karinthy[1] in one of his poems, lending his voice to all those who hide silently behind their actions before deciding to take up a pen and expose their thoughts. To be able to do this, to "tell everyone", one has to ignore the time-honoured adage: "A secret life is a happy life". But the desire to "have one's say" triumphs over the fear of confronting the world with all its dangers, real or imaginary.

A psychoanalyst who undertakes to go over the course of her professional life and presents the ideas connected with it will, of course, revive certain memories. To be able to speak about herself, the analyst, like everyone else, must overcome some resistance. Analytic practice is based on the ability to listen, to remain attentive to the other. However, an analyst can only listen to those who come to him in search of themselves if he listens to himself. Immersion into the patient's past causes his own past to resurface. By changing the internal narration, the analysis makes it possible to carve out a place for oneself in the world. The psychoanalyst chooses this practice out of a desire to understand, but as the author of the present work points out, at times he must also be able to accept his own inability to understand, or the fact that he may misunderstand. The practice of psychoanalysis gives rise to questions formulated in discussions with colleagues.

Certain exchanges become publications. The analyst's way of thinking, expressed in writing, reveals his or her position in the essential historical debates of the discipline, and throws light on his particular way of being. Acquiring the ability to face conflict is one of the aims of analysis. For an analyst, private and professional life are intertwined. In her reflections on the profession and on her own experiences, Judith Dupont follows the path traced by its creator and by certain eminent figures, controversial or not. Sigmund Freud wrote his "Autobiographical Study"[2] in 1924, the year when he felt the need to provide an account of the foundation and development of psychoanalysis, and reveal to the world, with great reserve and modesty, the

---

1   Hungarian author, humorist, poet and philosopher (1887–1938).
2   Freud, S. (1924), "An Autobiographical Study", S.E., Vol. 20, Hogarth Press.

man who had the courage to face the human in himself. Another example of self-revelation made by a psychoanalyst is Sándor Ferenczi's *Clinical Diary*[3]. His approach is entirely different. He divests himself gradually of all his protective layers, in order to experience what the patient feels, by living in two subjective worlds at the same time. His story shows the perils of this exercise.

As Freud pointed out in 1917[4], of the three major discoveries that changed man's vision, the first being gravity, the second the evolution of the species, and the third the existence of the unconscious, it is the third that caused the most profound and lasting shock. The misfortunes suffered by the discipline ever since its inception continue to testify to this.

While the founding ideas of the first two discoveries became widely accepted, the truth of the third is difficult to prove without being experienced personally. Since its creation, psychoanalysis has given rise to criticism, mainly because it is based less on its theories than on an experience. The experience in question is personal, and therefore difficult, or even impossible, for anyone who has not gone through it to understand. The desire to share this experience nonetheless is one of the reasons psychoanalysts try to express themselves in writing. In their texts, they attempt to develop an idea that has remained in suspense, add commentary to their colleagues' theories, or contest the validity of certain of their concepts. Indeed, the diversity of theories reinforces the ever-uncertain, always arguable character of the discipline.

Certain psychoanalysts who had a stone, a pebble or a grain of sand to contribute to the construction of the edifice created by the founding father have supplemented his ideas, while others opposed them, keeping controversy alive. Just as in other disciplines, psychoanalytic theories evolve through disagreement and disputes. Some theories survive because they open a new perspective, and others because they refute previous theories. Once analytic institutions were created, their members had to follow the one and only "right" theoretical approach to the exclusion of all others. Certain analysts who were exploring "different" approaches ended up creating their own institutions. Others initiated

---

3   Ferenczi, S., *The Clinical Diary of Sándor Ferenczi*, Harvard University Press, 1995.
4   Freud, S., "A Difficulty in the Path of Psycho-Analysis" (1917a), in *Introductory Lectures on Psycho-Analysis*, S.E., Vol. 17, Hogarth Press.

divisions which led to the creation of groups and subgroups, each one developing not only its own theory, but also its own language. Some of these languages have become the *schibboleth* serving to select the privileged few who can gain entry to a group.

Conflict surrounding Ferenczi's ideas caused a rift between him and Freud. Ferenczi was fully aware that Freud did not approve of his ideas, and of the fact that many of their colleagues also found them disturbing. But this rift did not create a scission in their lifetime. After Freud's death, Ernest Jones, the self-proclaimed official historian of psychoanalysis, labeled Ferenczi psychotic in order to discredit his ideas. This procedure, invented by totalitarian regimes, allowed him to persuade many of his colleagues, for several decades, that the dissemination of the ideas of this *enfant terrible* of psychoanalysis would place the Freudian theory and institutions in jeopardy. As Judith Dupont points out, to comply with the attitude of "benevolent neutrality" prevailing at that time, the analyst was supposed to attribute the origin of the patient's suffering exclusively to the repression of infantile desires. Because he considered that our lives are not shaped solely by our own desires, but also by what others do to us, Ferenczi became extremely critical of this attitude. An analyst who takes into account the crucial power of trauma cannot simply apply the theory to the patients' narratives, because these narratives cannot be reduced to riddles that can be solved if only one has the right key. Ferenczi reasoned that analysts use the theory as a defence to avoid questioning their personal therapeutic methods. And many patients resign themselves to this dismissal on the part of their analysts, considering it, like their past traumas, unavoidable. An analyst who adopts the Ferenczian approach does not consider his practice a purely intellectual task; instead, he recognises the role of his own desire to help patients suffer less, and even to live a better life.

Although for half a century Ferenczi, who advocated constant self-scrutiny, was regarded as the enemy of the psychoanalytic "cause", fortunately today we are no longer forced to choose between his way of thinking and that of Freud, his friend and teacher. Most analysts recognise that subjective truth is determined neither by Oedipus alone nor by trauma alone, but by a combination of both. The fact that henceforth most analysts refuse to opt for one of these visions of the human over the other is due in great part to the efforts of Michael Balint, Alice Balint, Nicolas Abraham,

Maria Torok and Judith Dupont. But the task is never completed once and for all. Freud's theories brought us a better understanding of the functioning of the human mind, but they do not represent a construction for all eternity. Theories can offer a better understanding of living only if they remain living themselves. This can only be achieved if the next generation of practitioners is free to supplement them, examine them closely, introduce a change of perspective — in short, make their own contribution.

Judith Dupont wrote her book with this objective in mind. She gives the reader an account of her life, a life in which psychoanalysis was present from the start, as it were. Born in a family counting several psychoanalysts among its members, she stresses the importance of these ties, without trying to minimise the role of her parents, as is done, according to Charles Rycroft, by psychoanalysts who attempt to erase the past in order to legitimise the present[5].

Judith Dupont contributed to the task of bringing about a radical change in our understanding of the conflict between Freud and Ferenczi. Having recognised its fundamental role in the history of psychoanalysis, she was ready to devote the time and energy needed necessary to make Ferenczi's writings available to her French colleagues. By translating his texts and letters, by giving lectures, by taking part in debates, she supported the ideas of this thinker some had declared mad. By fighting against the injustices and biases created by a half-century of ostracism, she rejected this one-sided image of our discipline, an image that could only drive it into an impasse.

The readers of Judith Dupont's book encounter a person ready to do battle without being violent, someone who promotes her ideas through recourse to her own work, rather than by attacking others, who may find the reasoning of others inspiring, but keeps pursuing her own. Her style clearly illustrates that one can use a comprehensible language and still remain a psychoanalyst.

Her commitment to this historic combat has made Judith Dupont an important figure in the history of psychoanalysis. She describes the evolution of a tradition, that of the Middle Group created in England by Michael Balint[6] and a few others, who had refused to adopt "truths" legitimated only

---

5   Rycroft, C., "On Ablation of the Parental Images", in *Psychoanalysis and Beyond*, London: Hogarth Press, 1985.
6   Balint, M., *The Basic Fault: Therapeutic Aspects of Regression*, Northwestern University Press, 1992.

by the exclusion of all others. It is probably not a matter of chance that the analysts who followed this "third path" were people transplanted from one culture to another. Despite its traumatic consequences, exile can offer certain benefits. Having left behind his native language and culture, the immigrant can only take his place in a new culture by reconciling the old with the new. His intermediary position impels him to reject rigid attitudes and to accept differences, between eras and between cultures. When confronted with conflict between individuals, he attempts to understand each person's point of view. In this book, Judith Dupont presents in writing, as she rarely did orally, her ideas about Freud, Ferenczi, the history of psychoanalysis and her own practice. Her thinking is entirely free of dualistic attitudes, and she presents her own way of proceeding without ever giving "instructions" to others.

She recounts the origin and the history of the only psychoanalytic journal that survived all the scissions — *Le Coq-Héron* — and whose continued existence is probably closely tied to an attitude she shares: remaining open to the ideas of others, even when we find them disturbing. This journal, which does not belong to any analytic school, accepts the work of psychoanalysts with the most diverse perspectives. Readers of all kinds have remained loyal to it since its creation. Could this be because its image resembles that of its founder?

FOREWORD

I am not a writer. I have been working as a psychoanalyst for over fifty years, and this is the sphere that has inspired me to express certain ideas, fantasies, daydreams... and to tell a few stories. I always wrote during my years of practice, and now that those years are coming to an end, I realise when I reread my texts that they have a certain coherence. Even though they were written for different reasons and were published in different places, they spring from the same source and attempt to convey the same vision of the profession, of human beings in general and of my own particular involvement.

Unfortunately, I am not the most orderly person, and there is disarray in my writings, as in all the other areas of my life. Once an article is written, and possibly published, I forget about it. As a result, manuscripts of all my articles—except those stored safely in my computer — are scattered in various drawers and filing cabinets, between my office and my home. Some are probably lost. So I am unable to say when each article was written, and where it was published. I apologise to journals in France and abroad, which did me the honour of publishing my texts, for not being able to mention them all here. I have therefore decided to refrain from any such mentions. But my carelessness will perhaps be forgiven, given that almost all the texts were rewritten, and the articles are no longer identical to those previously published.

To highlight the reasons which impelled me to gather these texts together in a book, the section "Itinerary and Analytic Reflections" presents the texts in which I speak of my origins, my career path and my opinions.

Then, given that I had written extensively about two authors who inspired me greatly, Sándor Ferenczi and Michael Balint, I dedicated a chapter of the book to each of them. These two chapters are composed of articles about them as individuals, about their work and about my perspective on their lives and accomplishments.

A fourth chapter is composed of articles on various subjects. But despite this diversity, the author's perspective and focus lends them coherence.

Finally, a few very short articles deal with specific points which, for some reason, caught my interest particularly, or are topics I was asked to discuss.

Thus, I have tried to bring together a collection of writings which, despite their diversity, are linked together in some way. Although they were written at different epochs in my life, they are included here in rewritten form because they express my current point of view.

Two of my texts are not included in this book: the first, *Manuel à l'usage des enfants qui ont des parents difficiles* (Instruction Manual for Children with Difficult Parents), was published by Seuil in 1980, under the pseudonym Jeanne Van den Brouck; the second is a children's story, *Une nuit mouvementée* (A Toilsome Night), written for my two grandsons, and unpublished.

CHAPTER 1
ITINERARY AND ANALYTIC REFLECTIONS

MY ENCOUNTERS WITH PSYCHOANALYSIS

PREAMBLE

At a psychoanalytic conference, while standing with a cup of coffee in my hand during the pause between two presentations, I was approached by a courteous gentleman who introduced himself as a German publisher. He had just published a volume of "psychoanalytic autobiographies" of several of our colleagues, and wanted to publish another volume. He invited me to contribute a text to this work. This would be a difficult task, I thought, but I promised to try.

To write my autobiography, even "psychoanalytic", seems too pretentious an undertaking. I will try to write what I remember about my encounters — numerous and varied — with psychoanalysis. Indeed, psychoanalysis made its appearance in my family long before I did. This being so, I must start my story by telling the stories of different members of my family, for their stories influenced mine very deeply. Of course, all these factors had a role to play, but I don't consider them essential in defining who I am. I am the child of an era, but I feel that I am above all the child of my parents, the wife of my husband, the mother of the daughter and the son I was fortunate enough to have, and the friend of my friends. My relationships with people have influenced me more than events and ideas. These relationships form the fabric of my life and the foundation of my work as a psychoanalyst.

ORIGINS

I must begin by saying a few words about my origins. My distant origins are quite vague, as is the case in many Jewish migrant families. I know that my father's ancestors were Jews who had settled in Alsace, and arrived in Hungary after passing through Germany and Bohemia. In the course of this journey, they certainly changed their name (to comply with the law), replacing their Hebrew name — which I never knew — with the name "Engel". My great-grandfather was a printer in Bohemia; his son Peter was a landowner, and his son, Lajos, my paternal grandfather, settled on a farm in Dormánd, in Hungary. He is said to have been a very shy man, so shy that he looked for a bride by consulting the lonely hearts advertisements, according to my father. He married Irene Beck, a beautiful, rather distant woman, an excellent housekeeper who ran the household with a firm hand and had four children, two boys and two girls. The younger son, László, was going to become my father.

On my mother's side, the roots of the family go back to Spain. I presume that the family had to leave Spain during the reign of Queen Isabella, expelled from the country like most Jews. I don't know how certain members of the family ended up first in Vienna, then in Hungary, in Szeged, calling themselves Prosnitz. In Jewish families, it is particularly difficult to establish family lineage because of numerous changes of name, and the absence of official documents. Births were registered at the synagogue, and as we know, many synagogues were destroyed in Europe. In addition, a decree obliged Jews, at least in German-speaking countries, to give up their Hebrew family names and take, or rather buy, German-sounding names. The richest families were able to buy "brilliant" names like Gold, Silber, Diamant. The others settled for names designating occupations, places, colours. The poorest Jews were even given laughable names. Later, many Hungarian Jews, very attached to their country and having fought in wars of liberation, wanted to change their German names to typical Hungarian names. This is how the Fraenkels became Ferenczis, and Frigyes (Frédéric) Spitzer, my grandmother's husband, became Frédéric Kovács.

From that point on, I know my maternal family's history quite well; its members played an essential role in the direction my life took, and in the choice of my profession.

My grandmother, Vilma Prosnitz, had a difficult start in life. Her mother was widowed very early, and left to raise three daughters alone; Vilma was the youngest. The family became destitute, for the customs of the era did not approve of a bourgeois woman working. In any case, Vilma's mother had no training of any kind. The oldest sister, Irene, married her beloved, Vilmos Székely, who was a lawyer or a notary. The second sister, Margit, died of tuberculosis. To escape utter poverty, 15-year-old Vilma, a pretty young girl, was married to the cousin of her brother-in-law Székely, a man 22 years older than her. She told him frankly that she did not love him, but he insisted that they try being married, promising her that if she met a man she loved, he would grant her a divorce. Vilma Prosnitz, now Székely, had three children in three years: two girls, Alice and Olga, and then a boy, Ferenc (Francis). The three pregnancies exhausted her so much that she fell ill with tuberculosis. She was sent to a sanatorium in the mountains and the children went to live with their aunt Irene.

Against all expectations, Vilma started to recover. At the sanatorium, she met a young man her own age, Frédéric Kovács, a young architect who had come to visit his brother. Later, he would often tell the story of his amazement when he first set eyes on this stunning woman in a yellow blouse, with whom he fell in love instantly.

Once she was cured and returned home, Vilma told her husband that she had met a man she loved and wanted a divorce. But her husband would not hear of a divorce. Vilma then left her husband's home to join Frédéric; her husband went through with the divorce, naming her the party at fault. He obtained custody of the children and their mother was forbidden to see them.

This separation lasted six or seven years. The children, including my mother Olga, suffered greatly from it, as did their mother. She circumvented the prohibition by going to meet her children when they left school every day, in a closed carriage so no one would see her, and riding alongside them slowly so that she could speak to them regularly for a few minutes. The children's father travelled often, for business and pleasure, and the children were left in the care of a governess, entrusted with their instruction. The governess, not a very stable person herself, had a sister who was a patient in a psychiatric hospital. On Sundays, the children were taken to visit this mentally-ill sister in the hospital. It was a disturbing and unforgettable experience.

In the meantime, Vilma had married Frédéric, who had a magnificent villa built for them, with a big garden, on one of the hills of Buda, the Naphegy (Hill of the Sun). Illness, divorce and separation from her children had taken their toll, and Vilma started to suffer from agoraphobia. Seeking a solution to this problem, she started psychoanalysis with Dr. Sándor Ferenczi. Not only did he cure her of agoraphobia, but he realised in the course of the analysis that she was exceptionally intelligent, talented and sensitive, in short, that she had all the qualities that would make her a good psychoanalyst.

I do not know exactly when this analysis took place, nor when and how my grandmother completed her analytic training. It appears that it was before the First World War, and therefore before Ferenczi started analysis with Freud.

The three children were so unhappy living with their

father and being looked after by their governess, that one day Alice, the oldest, who had a strong character, decided to run away. She was 11 or 12. When the governess was not there, she took her younger siblings by the hand and went to her mother's house with them. Their father did nothing to try to get them back, or even to see them. Frédéric Kovács raised his wife's children as if they were his own, and adopted them legally as soon as it was possible to do so. The children never saw their father again, and never even knew when and where he died.

The frequent separations, due to death, illness, divorce, and then the children who ran away, marked the family profoundly, up to my own generation. Vilma and her three children, particularly the two girls, huddled very close together under Frédéric's protective wing. One might even say that they were clinging to each other.

Despite Frédéric's solid presence — physical and moral — the family was in truth a matriarchy: Vilma was no doubt more talented and cultured than her husband. She seemed to be closer to her daughters than to her son. Of course, Frédéric was the head of the family, but Vilma was now working as a psychoanalyst and her income contributed to the family income. Both daughters were remarkable people. Alice in her studies, and Olga in the art of drawing and painting. Ferenc, the youngest, was a more fragile child who had had heart problems since early childhood. He later became an architect, like his adoptive father. Frédéric was a real *pater familias* who, after adopting his wife's three children, also offered his protection to his future sons-in-law. He spent much time with his adoptive daughters' children, and felt responsible for the whole family.

Alice continued to distinguish herself in her studies. She was the classmate of a girl named Emmi Bergsmann, whose brother Michael would later change his name to the more Hungarian-sounding Balint. Another of their brilliant classmates was Margit Schönberger, who later became Margaret Mahler. After her secondary-school studies, Alice studied mathematics, like her classmate Emmi, and then went on to ethnology. It was at university that she became better acquainted with Michael, still called Bergsmann then[1]. She lent him *Three Essays on the Theory of Sexuality* and *Totem and Taboo*, by Freud. Balint was seduced by Freud's thought, and was very taken with Alice and her

---

1   See Moreau-Ricaud, M., Balint, M., *Le renouveau de l'École de Budapest*, Érès, 2000.

family. Michael and Alice married and left for Berlin, to receive training in psychoanalysis from Hanns Sachs.

Vilma's second daughter, Olga, my mother, was particularly gifted in drawing and painting from an early age. She stopped her secondary studies before graduating and entered the Frischauf Art School. She continued her training with Robert Berény, a renowned painter whose works are displayed at Hungary's National Gallery, and who was one of Sándor Ferenczi's friends. Her first exhibition, when she was nineteen, was very successful, as newspaper clippings of the era attest. The Ernst Museum bought one of her paintings, and many people commissioned portraits.

She was a young woman of twenty when her step-father made her the gift of a trip to Paris. On the train, she met a young man who, like her, was on his way to discover the West; his name was László (Ladislas) Engel. They got along well and decided to see each other in Paris. They married a few years later, in 1924.

My father and his older brother Paul were expected to take over the management of the family farm after their father died of Spanish influenza in 1917. But my father had no interest in agriculture. When he was 23, and a year later, a publisher named Pan published two of his stories, "The Tempest" and "The Fire Dragon", written under the pen name László Dormándi, after Dormánd, the name of his native village.

MY CHILDHOOD IN BUDA

After my parents married, they took up residence in Budapest, in a building constructed by Frédéric Kovács, where Michael and Alice Balint lived as well, after their return from Berlin, where they started their psychoanalytic training. Thanks to a loan from Frédéric Kovács, my father bought the Pan publishing house, and renamed it Éditions Panthéon. Now, he could look after a family. And so, I was born on September 22, 1925. The three names my parents chose for me were those of famous female figures: Judith, Eve and Marie.

Around this time, my father changed his name officially from Engel to Dormándi, his pen name. At the same time, or perhaps a little earlier, like many Hungarian Jews, my parents also changed their religion, to prevent their future children from being subjected to the *numerus clausus* imposed on Jews when entering university. They considered it absurd to suffer, and cause their children to suffer, the disadvantages of a religion in which they did not believe, any more than they believed in any other. Therefore, my father became Protestant and my mother, for reasons unknown to me, became Catholic.

As I said earlier, my grandfather — for I always considered Frédéric Kovács my true and my only grandfather — had a very strong sense of family loyalty. In the building at 12 Mészáros Street in Buda, which he had built and owned, my parents and I lived on the fifth floor; Irene Székely, my grandmother's widowed sister, lived on the same floor; the Balints lived on the fourth floor; my uncle Ferenc on the third; my father's sister Nora and her family on the second; and my grandmother's cousin, Elisabeth Bér, had a studio on the ground floor. In addition, Fraulein Mimi Kiefel, the German governess who looked after my cousin John Balint and myself, also had a room on the fifth floor. The ground floor housed the Psychoanalytic Clinic, the first of its kind, under the direction of Sándor Ferenczi. Most psychoanalysts provided their services free of charge one or two times a week; Michael Balint and my aunt Alice were among them.

My grandfather Frédéric was tall and heavy, and his weight occasioned some health problems which required treatment. In 1927, he went to Baden-Baden for a stay of several months in Georg Groddeck's sanatorium. Each day, he wrote his wife long letters in which he related in detail what life was like at the sanatorium, and the treatments he received there. Social events held an important place at Groddeck's clinic, and Frédéric took part in them enthusiastically[2].

My cousin John Balint and I were always together: at each other's homes, or visiting our grandparents, the Kovács. We were classmates at the same primary school, a pilot project whose director, Martha Nemes, was using an experimental method of education. Classes were mixed and were composed of ten to twelve pupils. We called our teacher "aunt Eva" and were very fond of her. Thanks to her methods, we learned quickly, well and with pleasure.

In addition to my cousin John, who was my best friend, I had another very dear friend, Maria — our friendship lasted until she died — ; she was the second of the three daughters

---

[2] Long excerpts of these letters are presented at the end of *The Sándor Ferenczi-Georg Groddeck Correspondence, 1921–1933*, Fortune, C. (Ed.), London: Open Gate Press, 2002.

of psychoanalyst Imre Hermann. We saw each other very often, at her home or mine, or at my grandparent's home.

Whenever I speak of my grandparents, I am referring to the Kovács. I also had my paternal grandmother, who was in Budapest all year except for the summer months, which she spent on her farm in Dormánd. But I got along with her less well; she was a self-centered woman who had no interests other than the game of bridge and needlework, activities in which she excelled. I would visit her for a few hours, as rarely as possible, out of a sense of duty, and that suited both of us. I never knew my paternal grandfather, of course; he died long before I was born.

My childhood, which was very pleasant in many ways, included two circumstances of a difficult nature.

Each year, my mother went abroad for two or three months, to paint undisturbed. She took her first trip, which lasted six months, when I was nine months old. She went to the United States, travelling on the same ship as Sándor and Gizella Ferenczi, to try her luck as a painter. The trip was a success. She had several exhibitions and many orders for portraits, including that of a publishing magnate, and that of dancer Margaret Severn, daughter of Elizabeth Severn, Ferenczi's famous patient. After that, there were trips to Paris every year, lasting two or three months. Each time, I went to stay with my grandparents, whom I loved, but I was separated from my father and my cousin John, seeing them only in the weekends. I felt very alone. I played or I read in my grandparents' large sitting room, while Vilma saw her patients on the first floor, and Frédéric worked in his architect's office on the second floor. I learned very quickly that when patients arrived or left, I must not go into the hall, and, above all, must not make any noise.

Between sessions, my grandmother would come down to say hello to me, but it was Elisabeth, the housekeeper, who kept me company most often, along with Mihály, the valet and Molnár, the chauffeur (Elisabeth's husband). I was very attached to them, and they to me. They all stayed with my grandparents until they both died.

The second difficulty of my childhood was my chronic kidney disease. I suffered from colibacillosis, a condition for which there was no cure at the time; during my febrile episodes, which could last for months, I could not leave my bed. Our loyal family physician, Dr. Kármán, did everything in his power to help me, but to no avail. When I was about twelve, sulfamide drugs were discovered and I was cured in two weeks of an illness that had caused me years of suffering. I am tempted to say that this illness was a means I had found to try to prevent my mother from travelling. But it was clearly a counter-productive method, for she needed to get away to paint all the more because at home her daughter's health problems took up much of her time and energy.

VACATIONS

My mother liked the countryside, and my father liked luxury hotels. As a result, we almost never took vacations together. My father went to Juan-les-Pins, while my mother and I spent almost all our vacations in Austria, in the village of Tragöss, with my grandparents and the Balints. In Tragöss, we always met a Viennese family, the Millers, whose daughter Erika was the same age I was.

Probably as a reaction to my mother's absences and to my illness, I developed a form of anorexia at that time, but my grandfather found an efficient way to cure it. He created a club, the Tragösser Tourist Club; he was its president and John Balint was the vice-president. All the members of the family were presidents of something, except my father, who played the role of member of the club. As for me, I could become a vice-president also, if I ate everything on my plate for three days in a row. I had to try several times, but finally I succeeded. My mother made name plates for each of us, and one large family name plate, which Mr. Seidl, the innkeeper, framed and hung above our table. After the war, when Michael Balint passed through Austria on his way to Hungary, he visited Tragöss and found the club's nameplate in its usual place. The Seidls were awaiting our return. But Austria had changed and we had no desire to go back there.

In the last years when we vacationed there, walls and public benches gradually became covered with swastikas sketched in chalk. My mother also had a piece of chalk with her wherever she went, and she transformed the swatiskas into little windows with curtains and geranium boxes. But, as we all know, her vision was not the one that prevailed.

THE PROTESTANT SECONDARY SCHOOL

I started my secondary education at the Protestant school Baar-Madas. This beginning was not easy, for a number of reasons.

At the time, religious courses were compulsory in

Hungarian schools. Up until that time, I had not received any religious education, so my parents found a young woman who agreed to teach me the basic principles of the Calvinist Protestant religion. Still, when I started secondary school my perspective was very different from that of most of my schoolmates.

In addition, because of my illness, I started my classes several weeks after the other girls. By then, they all knew each other, and I knew no one. My uniform, also compulsory, was makeshift to say the least. All this, as well as the contrast with the perfectly harmonious years I had experienced in primary school, made me feel different and even marginal. The fact that my father was a writer and editor, and my mother a painter, added to my strangeness among these girls, many of whom were daughters of ministers (in the government of Admiral Horthy, whom my parents hated), people in the military or members of the nobility. I think it was then that I started to define myself by my difference rather than my similarity — an attitude that often helped me and was harmful on occasion.

Strangely, my favourite teacher taught religion. She was an imposing lady named Olga, like my mother. Kind and well-meaning, she succeeded in awakening my interest in God and religious faith, for a time. The teacher I hated the most taught physical education. I was small, fragile and very bad at athletic endeavours. I remember standing helplessly with a pole or a gym rope while the others climbed effortlessly, with the teacher looking at me scornfully, without bothering to explain what I should do.

I, who had learned so quickly and easily in primary school, was now having more and more trouble concentrating and understanding anything at all. My parents saw that there was a problem and suggested that I change schools, but I refused — I don't know why... perhaps because I felt it would have been admitting defeat or running away from the problem.

BOOKS

My cousin John and I were not as close now; he was going to a boys' secondary school and, unlike me, was a very good student. Indeed, his father, who had also been a brilliant student, kept a close watch on his studies and was very demanding and ambitious for his son. I envied him a little, because my parents were not too concerned with my studies; in fact, neither of them had been particularly brilliant in school. They just consoled me when I had poor marks, telling me that I would do better next time.

At that time in my life, my greatest pleasure came from reading: Kipling's *Jungle Book*, Mark Twain's *Tom Sawyer and Huckleberry Finn*, Fenimore Cooper's *Great Indian Stories*, Jack London, Alexandre Dumas, Charles Dickens, the Hungarian classic writers, and everything I happened to find.

My father had an impressive book collection. He let me take any book I wanted, saying that if it interested me, it meant that I was ready to read it. If I was not interested, I was not ready yet. From time to time, he took me to his office with him. While he was busy with his work, I went into the room where the books were stored on wide shelves along the four walls, and I read everything within my reach. Ever since those wonderful moments, I have loved the smell of paper, of printing ink and of binder's glue, as well as books themselves — their feel, their weight in my hand — things that electronic versions will never be able to replace for me.

SOCIAL LIFE

My parents had many friends and they often came to see us. But the hub of our social life was my grandparents' home. Not only was this the place of our family reunions, but we also had visitors who were well-known people: Sándor Ferenczi, our neighbour, with his wife Gizella, and sometimes Elma, Gizella's eldest daughter; composer Leo Weiner, a grouchy but amusing man; painter Robert Berény and his wife Eta, a very beautiful dark-haired woman whose portrait appears in her husband's painting *Woman Playing Cello*, in the National Gallery in Budapest. There was also Grete Varró, the director of a renowned music school, and other, less well-known but just as well-loved people.

Their subjects of conversation included psychoanalysis, art, literature, music and, of course, politics. Some guests listened to records in one of the sitting rooms, or were gathered around the radio listening reverently to a concert conducted by Arturo Toscanini; some played bridge in another room, others were in the middle of a discussion or were taking a walk in the garden. It was a lively, colourful world, very enriching for the mind. Curiosity, originality and independent thinking were appreciated and encouraged. This created an even greater rift with the attitude required

CHAPTER 1: MY ENCOUNTERS WITH PSYCHOANALYSIS

in my school, where the most cherished values were conformity, discretion and obeying the rules.

MY FIRST ENCOUNTER WITH PSYCHOANALYSIS

This encounter occurred early, for as I said, psychoanalysis was part of my family well before I came along.

In 1930, the Ferenczis took up residence in a villa, at 11 Lisznyai Street, two minutes away from the Kovács. We often visited them on Sundays. I was not eager to make these visits, because I was afraid of their dog Bandi, a tiny Pekingese that never stopped barking.

The day of Ferenczi's death has remained etched in my memory. On that day, May 22, 1933, I was at my grandparents' house. Everyone was upset, my grandmother was crying, there was a constant back-and-forth between Kovács residence and the Ferenczi residence. People whispered: "The Doctor is dead", or repeated this phrase when they answered the telephone. As for me, I was just as upset by the illness of my grandmother's little fox-terrier Bell, who was dying of distemper. He died the same morning as Ferenczi. And so I was crying like everyone else in the house, but I didn't know exactly if it was for the Doctor, for the dog, or because everyone was crying. I did not dare speak to anyone and I felt a little frightened by the density of feeling that assailed me from the outside and the inside.

A few years later, I remember going with my family to the psychoanalytic congress in Marienbad: John Balint and I were in the hotel room, very bored, waiting for someone to have some time for us. We were playing with toy cars in the long hotel corridors that I still see in my dreams sometimes.

For me, psychoanalysis was connected with the need to be quiet because a patient was arriving or leaving. I also remember my grandmother's office well, with its drop leaf desk and several levels of shelves; on the top shelf there was a bust of Freud made by my mother. It was a unique piece, destroyed at the same time as my grandparents' house, at the end of the war. Above the head end of the couch, near the armchair, there was a New-Zealand batik wall hanging, brought back from Australia by Géza Róheim, when he returned from his extended field research, as a gift to my grandmother, his psychoanalyst.

But my true encounter with psychoanalysis occurred

much later. We shall come to that in due time.

WORLD EVENTS

The whole family followed with great concern the rise of the Nazi regime in Germany and Austria, the fascist system rising to power in Italy, and Italy's devastating war in Ethiopia. In Hungary, the atmosphere became menacing. In 1937, the Germans invaded Austria. On the morning of the annexation of Austria, the Balint and Dormándi families had a meeting in Michael Balint's office. It was obvious that the Nazis were too close to Hungary, and that as Jews, baptised or not, we would soon be in danger. We had to prepare to leave. It was not an easy decision to make, particularly because the family would be split apart, which was almost inconceivable for Vilma and her two daughters.

The Balints were thinking of immigrating to England, where Michael could count on the help of his psychoanalytic milieu; my parents planned to go to Paris, where my mother travelled regularly and had many friends, and where my father's best friend, Paul Winkler, lived. Winkler was the director of a press agency; he was also the representative in Western Europe of the American "King Features Syndicate", the distributor of Walt Disney's cartoons and other strips. My father was the representative of the same agency in the Balkan countries. He believed he could run his publishing house from Paris, leaving the Assistant Director of Éditions Panthéon to take charge of operations in Hungary.

Our families began to organise our emigration. John started to learn English, and I started to learn French.

MY FIRST VISIT TO PARIS

In the summer of 1937, my mother left for Paris, as she did every year. As soon as school was over, I took a train to join her, with Juliette, a beautiful, charming Swiss lady who was my French teacher. In Paris, my mother always stayed at a residence for women, at 4 rue de Chevreuse, in the 6th arrondissement. She had a second bed placed in her room for me. That year, Paris was hosting a Universal Exposition. I remember the colonial pavilions, people wearing clothes like I had never seen... everything was colourful, new, surprising. My only clear memory is of my visit to the Palais de la Découverte, which opened its doors that year, as part of the Universal Exposition; an electric organ played Schubert's Serenade. The scientific content of the Exposition was fascinating, but the music was terrible. It took me a long time to be able to enjoy Schubert's Serenade again. My mother also took me to Saint-Cloud to visit Marie Bonaparte, whose portrait she was drawing in colour. The Princess did not pay much attention to me, or I to her, because I was completely fascinated with her enormous birdhouse full of all kinds of birds.

EMIGRATION

After the summer holidays, my parents organised our departure. For our very close family, being uprooted like this was heartbreaking. I tried not to think about it too much, but in the spring, when all the contents of the house were packed up, when I saw the furniture empty and bare, my bookshelf without any books, I started to understand what a great change was awaiting us.

We left in my grandparents' Daimler. All our things and our furniture had been shipped by rail. I remember turning around to look at our house one more time, so that I would not forget it.

We crossed Italy and stayed in Venice a day or two with the Balints. Then we stopped for a few days in Lavarone, where the Balints and my grandmother were meeting some of their colleagues. I remember meeting a little girl named Doris, whose family were German Jews, who told me that one day, in her city, while she was pushing her baby brother in his pram, Nazis attacked them. They took the baby out of the pram and broke his arm. I was very shaken by this story, because in Hungary we had not yet seen this level of brutality. Now, it was clear that the worst was yet to come.

We now drove north towards Paris. There, my grandmother and the Balints attended a psychoanalytic congress. In the meantime, my parents, my grandfather, John and I drove through the city in the Daimler looking for an apartment. We visited quite a number before my grandfather, the expert architect, finally approved of one, located on the fifth floor, at 20 Breteuil Avenue, in the 7th arrondissement, near Les Invalides. Much renovation work had to be done. In the meantime, my parents rented a furnished apartment on Raspail Boulevard, where we lived in two small, poorly-lit rooms.

The Kovács and the Balints went back to Hungary. We accompanied them as far as Nevers, and then took the train back to Paris. Despite being a psychoanalyst, my grandmother was very superstitious; when she left us at Nevers (a name which reminded her of "never"), she cried a flood of tears, taking the name as an omen predicting that we would never see each other again. The Balints had to return to Hungary also, because they did not yet have entry visas for England. They were not the only Jewish psychoanalysts from Central Europe who wanted to go to Western countries, and Ernest Jones, who reigned over British psychoanalysis at the time, did not want to see too great a number of his foreign colleagues invade his domain. He therefore strongly recommended that they immigrate to Australia, where psychoanalysts were scarce. Michael Balint firmly refused, and it was thanks to John Rickman that Balint and his family finally obtained a visa and settled in Manchester.

OUR NEW HOME IN FRANCE

At long last, we were able to move into our apartment on Breteuil Avenue, after taking back our furniture and other things we had placed in storage. Unfortunately, the storage facility had been flooded during a storm, and many of our precious books arrived looking like little bricks, their pages solidly stuck together.

We went on vacation that summer. My father went to Juan-les-Pins with his friend Arthur Koestler and Arthur's sweetheart, in their car, a little two-seater convertible, with a third seat behind, outside the car. One of the doors was tied with string so the passenger would not fall out, and therefore could not be opened. To enter the car, one had to climb in. The three of them squeezed in on two seats, the baggage was piled on the third, and off they went.

My mother and I had been invited to Brittany by Anne Berman, Princess Bonaparte's secretary. Doctor Louis Codet and his wife had a house named Ker Codet in Saint-Guénolé, a small fishing port; they lent it to Anne Berman, who spent her vacations there with her friend Jacqueline.

THE FOREIGNERS' CLASS

In September 1938, I enrolled in the Victor-Duruy secondary school. Given the large number of refugees of all origins, the school opened a special class called the "foreigners' class", for students between 12 and 18. There were newcomers from Spain, a girl from Czechoslovakia, one from Austria, one from Romania, a Chinese girl... and also the children of diplomats stationed in Paris: some British students, an American girl and a Swedish girl. About a dozen girls entrusted to a brilliant teacher, Mlle Blanchard, who succeeded in teaching these adolescents of different ages and speaking different languages enough French and a solid enough foundation in French culture to enable them to attend a grade appropriate for their age.

That winter, my Kovács grandparents came to stay with us for a few months. They were thinking about emigrating, to be with us, because the separation was very difficult for us all. Princess Bonaparte promised my grandmother to send her sufficient patients so that she would be able to earn a living for herself and her husband. But for my grandfather, a respectable bourgeois from Central Europe, being "kept" by his wife was simply unthinkable, so that they finally decided to return to Hungary.

At the end of the school year, I took an exam that allowed me to enter a normal class of the Victor-Duruy secondary school.

That summer we went to Saint-Guénolé again with Anne Berman, but this time my father stayed in Paris, to run the operations of the publishing house from his new location. An old friend of my father's had joined us, the writer and journalist François Fejtö, with his wife Rose. The holidays, which had started out well despite the threatening world situation, were interrupted brutally by a double shock. One day, when my mother had gone out to sea with her fishermen friends, a telegram arrived from England, where the Balints had finally been able to immigrate at the start of 1939. Since my mother was not there, I opened the telegram, whose content was so shocking that I simply could not believe it: "Alice died suddenly. Michael." I wondered if it might not be a secret code the family had agreed on, for transmitting very confidential information. When my mother came back, I gave her the telegram, hoping she would confirm my theory. But, of course, this was not the case. She burst into tears; we ran to the post office to call my father, who already knew; then we packed up and returned to Paris. As soon as we were there, my mother took the necessary steps to be able to leave for Manchester, to be with Michael and John. She obtained the papers in record time and left two days later. The next day war broke out.

WAR

Because we were of Hungarian nationality, and Hungary, though neutral, was not an allied country, my mother was unable to obtain a visa to return to France. We had to appeal to everyone we knew who had any influence for her to be able to come back to France after several months.

In the first months of the war — this period that came to be called the "Phony War" — no one knew what turn events would take. Paul Winkler, who had a castle on a property in Chartrettes, about fifty kilometres from Paris, moved his press agency there, along with all his personnel. He persuaded my father to join him there, with me. Life was very boring for me there. My only diversion was the weekly arrival of magazines published by Opera Mundi, hot off the press, smelling of paper and fresh ink. After three months, my father had enough of life in the country and, since all was quiet for the moment, we went back to Paris.

My mother finally returned. It had not been easy for her to leave Michael and John. Michael was devastated. Not only were he and Alice very close as a couple, but they had been friends since adolescence. They had studied together, they had received their psychoanalytic training from the same analysts, and they had developed all their ideas together. My mother explained the reason for Alice's sudden death: after she had John, she had been pregnant again, but the fetus died *in utero*; her condition was not diagnosed and she developed severe septicemia, with endocarditis. An aortic aneurysm was diagnosed. No one knew about this except Alice and Michael. I think that immigration, and above all separation from her mother and her sister, were more than Alice could bear. One morning, while she was getting dressed, she felt unwell and asked Michael for a glass of water. When he came back with it, Alice was dead.

Michael's whole universe collapsed. John was about to enter the Abbotsholme boarding school. Michael would be alone in a foreign country, far from his family, his friends and everything familiar to him.

THE CATASTROPHE

Everything remained unchanged until May 1940. On May 10th, the German army invaded Belgium. The "Phony War" was now real war. Soon, Belgian refugees started to arrive in France, and teaching was suspended because the school premises were requisitioned for housing refugees.

CHAPTER 1: MY ENCOUNTERS WITH PSYCHOANALYSIS

A few weeks earlier we had learned that my grandmother Vilma was ill; she had a gallbladder problem. Doctors were hesitant to perform surgery. It was a mistake. She had a large stone in her gallbladder and when they finally operated on her, it was too late: the stone had perforated the gallbladder. A telegram arrived announcing her death. My mother fell into a deep depression. It was hard for me to realise that my whole familiar world was disintegrating.

Then the flash war began. The German troops were closer to Paris. People were panicked and started to leave. My mother wanted to leave Paris also. One morning, we packed a few things in knapsacks and took the underground to Austerlitz station. The lineup of passengers waiting for the train started in the station corridors. My father thought that the situation was hopeless and we went back home.

There was an atmosphere of impending doom in the city. But my father stayed so calm, trying to solve problems as they came up, that I don't have the impression of having been afraid. We listened to the radio from morning 'til night. My father and I wandered through the streets trying to find something to eat. This is how we found ourselves on Place de l'Opéra, completely alone. The city was empty, silent, covered by a black cloud of smoke: gasoline reserves and all kinds of archives were being burned. As for my mother, she was lost in her grief. To console herself, she kept finding striking resemblances between me and her sister Alice. They were imaginary, but I was aware of how much she needed them. I think that this was the first indirect prompting leading to the choice of my future profession.

LIFE UNDER THE OCCUPATION

One morning we were awakened by the heavy clanking of metal. We rushed out on the balcony: it was German tanks passing in front of the house. Paris was occupied. The rest of the country soon would be as well. Philippe Pétain became head of the French State; France was no longer a republic. Pétain soon introduced the anti-Jewish laws, even before the Germans requested it. Jews had to declare themselves to their local police prefecture, and turn in their radios, which they no longer had the right to own. In France, my parents were not known, and our family name, Dormándi, had no undesirable connotation. My father, who used to hunt, remembered that the hunter always shoots the rabbit when it leaps up. He therefore decided that we must definitely not leap, meaning not declare ourselves to the police. So we did not go to the prefecture and we kept our radio, an invaluable treasure at the time.

For the next four years, there was something surrealistic about our situation. We lived in our apartment, under our own name, I went to secondary school, we went on vacation to Vendée. And we were cold and hungry like everyone else. My father lost 20 kilograms in one year, and my mother about fifteen. In our circle of friends, some people disappeared, either because they were arrested, or because they left for unknown destinations in the so-called "free zone", or to live in clandestinity.

We were completely cut off from the Balints, because in France England had become an "enemy" country; but it was not an "enemy" country in Hungary. Therefore, we sometimes had news of Michael and John through my grandfather Kovács, or uncle Ferenc and his wife.

My father could no longer stay in touch with his publishing house, and certainly not with the American agency King Features Syndicate. My parents looked for other means to earn a living. My mother made ceramic objects, and my father founded a modest cartoon publication. He also wrote. One of his novels, *On the Other Shore*, was published in Hungary by Éditions Panthéon, and three others were published in French by the Belgian publisher Maréchal.

All things considered, we lived as normally — that is, abnormally — as most people in France. We had frostbite in winter, we exchanged recipes requiring few ingredients, we learned to walk in wooden sole shoes. Several events made a strong impression on me during this crucial period of my life. One of them was the so-called Vel' d'Hiv (winter velodrome) roundup. My father, who was a Freemason, had friends among "brothers" employed in police prefectures, who knew what the police was preparing. One day, he was warned that foreign Jews would be arrested. Huguette, one of my friends, whose family were Greek Jews, lived on rue de Rivoli with her parents and her deaf-and-dumb sister, right in the area where the raid would take place. So my mother and I left at five in the morning, as soon as the curfew was over, to go and warn them that they had to leave right away. But the raid had been carried out during the night. We found only the concierge in tears, who told us the family had been taken away, but the younger sister had escaped the raid because she was in an institution for the deaf and dumb.

One day, friends of ours sent a young man to see us,

a cartoonist who wanted to create a cartoon series for my father's publication. His name was Jean Bruller, later known as Vercors. We got along right away. Soon afterwards, Jean told us about the Éditions de Minuit, an underground publishing house that he had founded with Pierre de Lescure. He showed us a few of its little books with white covers, including *The Silence of the Sea*, which he had written. My father offered right away to distribute the books published by Éditions de Minuit.

We listened to Radio London, which was strictly forbidden, but it was the only relatively reliable source of news.

A friend, the actress Isabelle Anderson, the wife of the painter Jean Duval, had put us in touch with the Protestant Temple of the Oratory of the Louvre, so that I could join the girl scouts of the Oratory, now called the Oratory Youth Group, since scouting was also forbidden. This experience revived my interest in religion, because the pastors of this temple behaved remarkably during this difficult period, and they saved many lives. One of them, Pastor Vergara, headed a social centre, *La Clairière*, where he hid many Jewish children before having them transferred to the "free zone". My mother worked with him there.

The day when wearing the yellow star became compulsory, four of our classmates came to school wearing this badge; but many of our classmates had had the idea of putting a yellow handkerchief in their jacket pocket, to show solidarity with their Jewish schoolmates.

THE LIBERATION OF PARIS

Paris was liberated in August 1944, as a result of an organised uprising. During the fight for Paris, there was gunfire everywhere, especially in our neighbourhood, since we lived between École Militaire and the Invalides; the residents fought to liberate the city until the very end. One morning, it was the sound of tanks that drew us out into the street; American tanks were filing past on the Boulevard des Invalides, to drive back the last pockets of resistance. It was only then, when it was ending, that I realised what extreme tension we had lived under for the past four years.

At last, we could contact the Balint family again. And my mother started to travel again; she would spend weeks at a time in England, at Michael's home, to paint. There, she painted the portrait of Melanie Klein and her grandchildren, of Paula Heimann's daughter, of Dr. Gillespie's daughter, and of many other people.

We were all very worried about relatives who were still in Hungary, whom we were unable to contact, and of whom we had no news since early 1944. We knew that my grandfather, Frédéric Kovács, died before things became disastrous in Hungary. It was lucky, in a manner of speaking.

At last, we were able to locate my uncle Ferenc and his wife Alice (whom we called "Alice 2", to distinguish her from Alice Balint, "Alice 1"). They had been able to hide and to survive the persecutions and the battle of Budapest, but the beautiful house on Naphegy and all its contents were destroyed in a fire. Many of my mother's works were among these, including the portrait of Frédéric Kovács and the bust of Freud.

It was around this time that I decided to become a psychoanalyst. I remember the exact moment when I told my mother of my decision: we were in the kitchen and she was taking cooked potatoes out of a big pot, one by one. I was watching her, as I sat on a stool, and I told her that I had chosen my profession. She was delighted. I knew she would be, and this had no doubt influenced my decision. But there were other reasons. Since I was born, and even after we left Hungary, I had heard people around me talk about psychoanalysis. Even my parents, who were not analysts, were very interested in the psychological aspects of people, relationships, situations and world events. When my mother was about to paint a portrait, she first had long conversations with her models, to get to know them and be able to take into account their personalities, as much as their physical features.

MY STUDIES

To prepare for my future studies, I chose, in the last year of my secondary studies, a philosophy/science class. Then, when I had my undergraduate degree, I went into the Physics/Chemistry/Biology program, which was the prerequisite for studying medicine.

Now that we could easily reach the Balints again in England, I had discussed these things with Michael, who was convinced that a medical degree was essential to be able to practice psychoanalysis safely. He felt that too many lay analysts had administrative problems that seriously disturbed their professional practice. He did not argue that medical knowledge was necessary for practicing psychoanalysis. He was in favour of non-physicians practicing psychoanalysis, and had great respect for many of them, starting with his wife Alice. But I suspect he believed in the usefulness of scientific rigour, and I know he had great respect for diplomas. He himself had earned several of them. He was an ambitious man, not indifferent to honours bestowed on him or on members of his family. Yet he was not a man of power. It was not the power that went with leading others that interested him, but rather the respect he could earn. And he did not want to earn it easily. He made it a point to truly deserve it. His ambition was sometimes hard to take for those close to him, who did not necessarily share it. I remember his pride in every success obtained by his son John in his medical career and later his academic career. And his great happiness, much later, when he was elected President of the British Psychoanalytical Society — him, "the son of a little Jewish doctor from the suburbs of Budapest", as he liked to say.

Personally, I appreciated his advice and I often followed it, although my vision of life, or at least my life, was a little more playful, less sombre.

I embarked, accordingly, upon the study of medicine. I felt rather lost in that environment. At the hospital, in my first year, I didn't seem to know what to do, and I suspected that the department heads responsible for us didn't really know what to do with us either. Some of them even called us, with undisguised disdain, "the lithiasis of the corridors". At the beginning of the second year, the dissection room horrified me: the smell, those poor bodies on the tables, torn apart, the jokes in bad taste made by certain students, and particularly what we were expected to do there — all this made me want to escape. In fact, I learned to use a scalpel quite skillfully, an ability which later served me mostly to open envelopes and cut the pages of new books.

But I had a training period in a Department of Pediatrics, and what I saw there interested me greatly — not so much the children's diseases as the children themselves. I spent much time with a little boy who had a bone-related problem whose nature I don't remember exactly. I and two other trainees took turns caring for him. It turned out that this little boy, in addition to the disease for which he was treated, also had pulmonary tuberculosis which no one noticed. All three of us, who had been assigned to him, contracted primary tuberculosis and had to interrupt our studies.

MY TWO YEARS OF ILLNESS

This period of illness was beneficial to me in many respects. It proved to be an important turning point in my life. For the first time in a long time, I had time for a social life, for my own internal development, without worrying about anything else. I was not very ill, I did not feel in danger, and so I lived a carefree life far from the whirlwind of ordinary activity.

I was sent to the Sancellemoz sanatorium. It had a fantastic library and we could take out as many books as we wanted. I came upon Freud; his books had just started to be re-edited. At the time, I didn't understand very much.

At the sanatorium, there was a young girl from Oran, with her mother. This woman took me, and another young girl who had just returned from Auschwitz, under her wing. She taught me to put on makeup, to arrange my hair, in short, all the futile things no one in my family had had time for during the years of privation and worry under the Occupation. Many years later, I was surprised to meet this young girl's brother; he had become a doctor and was president of the Balint Society in France.

A little after the end of the war, my parents realised that we would never go back to Hungary. So we applied for French citizenship. To our great surprise, my parents were granted it quite easily, but not me. We made some enquiries and found out that it was the Order of Physicians (created by the Vichy government) which had opposed my request, based on the *numerous clausus* for medical students. When I applied again during my illness, I was granted citizenship at once. Because I was no longer enrolled in Medical School, the Order did not have to be consulted.

THE TRIP TO HUNGARY

As soon as we became French citizens, we divested ourselves of our Hungarian citizenship and decided to make a trip to Hungary. Michael Balint had gone there before us, sent by the British Psychoanalytical Society to find out what became of the psychoanalysts who had stayed there. Of course, he also wanted to find out what happened to his parents. It was a sad trip. He found out that his parents committed suicide when they were on the point of being arrested and deported. Losses among analysts were considerable as well. Among the survivors, there was Istvan Hollos and his wife, and to my great relief, Imre Hermann and his whole family. My oldest friend, Maria, was alive and well.

My parents and I went to Hungary in the fall of 1947. The trip was charged with emotion. Budapest was devastated. Ruins everywhere, shell holes and traces of gunfire. My uncle Ferenc lived in an apartment with a door blocked shut, because the room that had been on the other side had been obliterated by a bomb; there was nothing there but a hole now. We went to see the place where my grandparents' villa had been: it was a vacant field which, now that it was bare, seemed very small. One asked oneself how it could have held a big house, a garden, a hothouse, a tennis court. Among the clumps of earth, we found fragments of my grandmother's best dinner service. It was all that was left of our little family paradise.

A number of family friends also survived. We saw Robert Berény, the painter, again. We went to a concert to listen to Annie Fischer play the piano, and Leo Weiner, the composer came with us. Both were friends of my grandparents and of the Ferenczis. But above all, I was reunited with my old friend Maria Hermann again; she had just met the love of her life, the mathematician István Vincze, whom she was to marry soon afterwards.

My father learned that his employees at Panthéon had continued to run the publishing house during the war, until the Arrow Cross Party came to power. They then divided up among themselves the supply of books, money and administrative papers, and went underground. After the liberation of the country, they reappeared with the books, the money and the papers, and started operations again, even before contacting my father. Only one person was missing, Mr. Sömlyén, the assistant director, who had been arrested and deported. He never came back. Afterwards, the Panthéon did not survive long, because all publishing houses were nationalised and integrated into the National Press.

Although I was happy to be reunited with people dear to me in Hungary, I felt like a stranger in that country. It had only been a few years, but the language had evolved, given the intervening events and all the new notions that had to be named. My vocabulary, however, was still the one I had when I was twelve. The language of my adult life was French. And I had become mistrustful of this population that had forced us to flee and had persecuted and killed so many of our friends and acquaintances. I had projected some of this aversion onto the language. Although in France I liked to speak it with my parents as a special private language we shared, I did not like to hear it spoken around me by absolutely everyone. So I made no effort to improve my Hungarian or update my vocabulary.

Many years later, I remember having to prepare a short talk in Hungarian. I wrote the text as best I could and asked a Hungarian colleague to correct it. But presenting it was a strange and distressing experience for me. I understood all the words, but I didn't recognise myself in them. As I was reading the text, I felt none of the emotion I had put into the writing of it. I never wanted to do this again. Now, even when I am in Hungary I prefer to speak in my broken English which at least has the advantage of being a truly foreign language. I don't really understand this hostility towards my mother tongue, but I must admit that it is there.

VISITING LONDON

At the end of the 1940s, during the period of rest imposed by my illness, we spent one Christmas in London, visiting Michael Balint. He had just divorced Edna, the woman he married after Alice's death. It was an unhappy marriage that ended after two years. Now, Michael was living alone. After Christmas my parents returned to France and I stayed with Michael for a few months, to keep him company and look after the house. He had a lively social life and frequent affairs, but he was still very alone and not very happy.

The National Health Service had just been introduced in England, and heated debates between doctors who were "for" and those who were "against" were going on. Michael organised a great reception to which he invited about twenty physicians, men and women. During the meal, he asked the question of the day: "What do you think of the National Health Service?" There followed an awkward silence. The guests were dismayed. Obviously, it was against the rules of British etiquette to bring up such a subject in the middle of a reception. Finally, one of the ladies broke the silence by asking a colleague seated across the table: "How do you manage to grow such magnificent wallflowers in your garden?" There was a sigh of relief and the conversation continued, within the boundaries of social conventions. After dinner, the men gathered in a room to talk about the problem foremost in their minds, while the ladies, all of them doctors as well, gathered in another room to chat about less serious subjects. Michael, who liked to be provocative sometimes, was delighted to have thrown a spanner in the works, provoking such a typically British reaction.

Another time, he took me to a meeting of the British Psychoanalytical Society. I tried to understand the presentation and the discussion that followed, but my English and my knowledge of psychoanalysis were insufficient to allow me to benefit from what I was hearing. After the meeting, I saw the president call Michael to speak to him in private. When we left, Michael told me, very amused, what they had said to each other. The president told him: "You can have as many lady friends as you like, but please don't bring them to the meetings". Michael replied: "But she is my niece". And the president insisted: "Alright, I know you have many nieces, but still, don't bring them to the meetings of the Society". I don't know which one of us felt more flattered: he or I.

Indeed, Michael Balint was a very charming and interesting man. We had many discussions and he often used provocation to back me into a corner, never accepting a poorly constructed argument, or one made in bad faith, nor any preconceived idea. In a conversation with him, passion was not forbidden, but it was not enough. He demanded that his interlocutor really think.

GOING BACK TO MEDICAL SCHOOL

In September of that year I was completely well again and I started my second year of medical studies, interrupted two years earlier.

My father had found work; he was a radio journalist preparing programs to be broadcast in Hungary. He worked at home in the mornings, and went to the office in the afternoon. This left him plenty of time to write. Nine of his novels were published in French between 1950 and 1962, and many short stories were published in magazines.

As for my mother, she still made and sold ceramic objects, but she was also commissioned to paint several portraits, both in France and in England. She started to have exhibitions again, particularly at the Berheim-Jeune gallery, Charpentier gallery, and a small gallery on rue Dauphine. Galerie Zack no longer existed: Madame Zack had been deported and never came back.

But all this was not enough to feed the family or pay my tuition. So I looked for a way to contribute to the family income. I translated texts, I knitted clothes for private clients and later for shops and a fashion magazine, and I even served tea at bridge parties. This did not bring in a lot of money, but it was enough to pay my tuition and to allow me to buy, once in a while, some fabric from which I could make a dress for my mother or myself. Our clothes had become very worn during the four years of Occupation and the years of scarcity that followed; and I had grown out of my old clothes. I remember that when I was 18 or 19, I felt frustrated that I could never buy anything new.

In medical school, I made a few friends, and above all I became friends with Jacques Dupont. He was also working to put himself through school. He had a small print shop on the 7th floor of a building, in a maid's room lent to him by a friend, where he stencil printed course material and all kinds of brochures. During the Occupation, despite his young age, he had been part of the Resistance as a member of the FTP group ("Francs Tireurs et Partisans"), and had printed pamphlets and clandestine bulletins using a stencil. After the Liberation, this had become his occupation. His small business was starting to prosper and he needed help. He asked me to come and work for him; I would definitely earn more money than I earned knitting. This is how I met my future husband. For in the pure tradition of romantic novels, it was not long before I married the man I worked for.

MY TRAINING UNDER PROFESSOR HEUYER

I obtained an internship with Georges Heuyer, head of a department of child psychiatry. He had three assistants: René Diatkine, Serge Lebovici and Cyrille Koupernik. It was the first traineeship that brought me closer to the field in which I wanted to practice. I learned a great deal, especially from Diatkine... and even more from the children who came to be seen or be treated there. Despite his reputation, Professor Heuyer did not seem very psychologically astute. I found Lebovici to be very abrupt, especially with his trainees. The third assistant, Koupernik, was more reassuring and showed great sensitivity, but his approach was the least psychoanalytic.

It was the year when I started to understand psychoanalytic texts, without really assimilating all the concepts. I was aware that my understanding was still superficial and purely intellectual. To arrive at true emotional understanding, I needed to acquire a minimum of clinical experience. When I heard children or parents describe what they were going through, the things I was reading suddenly became meaningful. Perhaps this was so because my first contact with psychoanalysis had occurred through those close to me — it was an emotional connection. I had not encountered psychoanalysis through reading, as many people do. Overall, what I most remember about training under Heuyer are his public consultations, and the lectures given by Lebovici, which were never followed by discussions. Those of us who were in training never had the chance — or the ability — to undertake any action on our own.

The two most memorable internships I had in medical school were the one under Professor Gilbert-Dreyfus, and the one in labour and delivery, with Professor Ravina.

It was in Pr. Gilbert-Dreyfus' endocrinology department that I came across the regular presence of a psychoanalyst in a medical department. His name was Dr. Held. Gilbert-Dreyfus was a sensitive, intelligent man, kind and courteous with patients and trainees. He provided explanations and answered questions, but always tactfully, careful not to offend the sensibilities of patients, or frighten them. We learned a lot from him, not only about endocrinology, but also about how to treat human beings, be they ill, dependent or healthy.

My internship under Pr. Ravina was deeply moving. It was there that I witnessed the birth of a child for the first time. One of the first births I saw was a breach delivery. The blood, the cries, the smell... I almost fainted. I went and sat in a corner of the room to be out of the way, because the others had more urgent things to do than to look after a faint-hearted trainee.

I am always very moved by the birth of a baby. Some are welcomed joyfully, others are rejected at once, and still others are expected to accomplish the impossible task of filling a void no one can fill. And then there are the children born with more or less severe deformities. And those who die at birth, leaving their parents distraught, unable to mourn a being so eagerly awaited, whom they did not have time to know. In Pr. Ravina's department, I learned a great deal about the doctor's responsibility; the responsibility to decide in situations where it is impossible to expect the parents to decide and carry the weight of their decision. I learned never to be simply a technician interested only in evading all possible blame, and concerned above all with avoiding any problems.

The brief training period we had in psychiatry, at the Sainte-Anne Hospital, left me with an uncomfortable feeling. The presentations of patients, where the patient presented had been performing this function for years and played the clown to amuse the audience, were simply unbearable. Even more unbearable were the comments made about them, in their presence. Only one of our professors was an exception to the rule: Pr. Baruch, who treated the patients with respect and demanded that the students show the same respect. This experience certainly contributed to my decision not to undertake a specialisation in psychiatry.

THE DUPONT PRINTING COMPANY

Jacques and I attended our traineeships faithfully, but we seldom attended classes. We both worked at the print shop, in our little maid's room on the 7th floor. A few weeks before final exams we studied hard, and passed all our exams successfully. Working with Jacques taught me excellent learning techniques I had not yet developed. The printing firm prospered and Jacques found and rented larger premises on rue des Haies, in the 20th arrondissement.

THE VALLÉE FOUNDATION

Jacques and I married on October 11, 1952, just before starting our sixth and last year of medical studies, which we chose to spend at the Vallée Foundation, an institution for mentally retarded girls. The residents were children with different degrees of retardation, from slight to profound mental debility. The place was completely demoralising. Not only were the children afflicted by their condition, but they also suffered from inadequate supervision, an almost total lack of care, and unattractive surroundings. The children's meals arrived cold from the kitchens of Bicêtre Hospital, located several hundred metres away. This dismal situation was relieved somewhat by school activities. Very competent teachers taught several classes for the children who were able to learn. In addition, the Director of the Foundation was a remarkable man, Dr. Desclaux, who did everything possible for the children. But his efforts were not always successful, and were not supported by the administration. The weekly showing of films which he wanted to organise for the children was quickly forbidden, because it was not possible to guarantee the officially required presence of a fireman on the premises. The attractive isolation room he had succeeded in setting up was immediately invaded by material never ordered but delivered by mistake, which the delivery men refused to take back. This devoted man experienced moments of real despair. Still, he succeeded in having a beautiful mural painted on one of the walls by the husband of one of his trainees.

One year, during his vacation, he died in a car accident, on a straight road, driving at 30 km an hour. We always wondered if the accident was not disguised suicide. He was replaced by Dr. Soulayrac, who was less interested in the children than in his personal research, conducted in a laboratory on the grounds of the Foundation. The trainees took care of the children, but in the existing conditions no real sustained treatment could be carried out. My worst memory is of the day when someone would come to take away the girls who had reached the age limit for living at the Foundation, and who would now be transferred to an adult psychiatric hospital. They did not want to leave this place that was familiar, at least, where they had their friends and their school. They ran everywhere, tried to hide, and had to be taken away by force. It was unbearable.

Our traineeship ended in a strange manner. Given the lack of personnel, we had suggested to one of our friends, who had dropped out of medical school to become a journalist, that he come and help out with the children. We submitted his application to Soulayrac and it was approved. Our friend worked at the Foundation two or three months, and everyone was happy with his work. Then, with our permission, he published a series of articles in his weekly paper *Samedi soir* (Saturday Night), owned by Paul Winkler. Being careful, he had a psychiatrist reread his articles, to make sure the scientific content was accurate. But this psychiatrist took it upon himself to warn the directors of the Vallée Foundation that somebody was mounting an "attack" against them. A scandal broke out. Luckily for Jacques and me, the news which first arrived was inaccurate, and we quickly had our traineeship validated, before it would have become impossible to do so. The psychoanalyst associated with the Foundation, with whom I had started my thesis, refused to continue working with me.

Jacques worked in an anatomic pathology lab. His supervisor provided me with a thesis subject and the documentation I needed. This is how it came about that in early 1955 I presented a thesis in anatomic pathology, a field very far removed from my interests.

MY PSYCHOANALYTIC TRAINING

I applied for psychoanalytic training before the first scission of the Paris Psychoanalytic Society. I was given a list of nine training analysts with whom I had to meet, so that they could decide if it was suitable for me to have training analysis, therapeutic analysis, or no analysis at all.

I remember some of those meetings. I saw Dr. Berge, whom I knew a little because one of his sons, the schoolmate of a close friend, was taking drawing lessons from my mother. I quite liked Dr. Schlumberger. Dr. Mâle made me ill at ease by criticising my attitude, my voice, my pronunciation. I finally got angry, which great improved his opinion of me, but not my opinion of him. Going to see Dr. Nacht was rather unpleasant: I waited almost two hours because he went to do an errand at the time when he had asked me to come. He did not bother to apologise. It was the kind of thing I don't find acceptable, so I was not going to choose him as my analyst. Despite this regrettable beginning, I came to respect him later, if only for his courage during the war, when he took part in the Resistance. Françoise Dolto was very gracious when I saw her. So was Jacques Lacan, who was friendly, courteous and even a little seductive. After the interview, he escorted me to the waiting room and asked me to write down my contact information on a sheet of paper, saying he would come back to take it in a few minutes. But he never came back. I finally left the sheet of paper on a table and let myself out. Something in this mixture of seduction and neglect repelled me. I decided this was not the right place for me either. Finally, I met Dr. Daniel Lagache. He saw me at the appoint time, he was pleasant and courteous, but reserved. It seemed that this was just the kind of reassuring atmosphere I needed to start analysis. I decided that if my application was accepted, he was the one I would choose. A few weeks later I received a letter saying that I had been accepted for training analysis. I made an appointment with Dr. Lagache and he agreed to start working with me as soon as his schedule would allow it.

It was during this period when I awaited the decision about training that the first scission took place in the French psychoanalytic group. Lagache, Lacan, Dolto and a number of other analysts left the Paris Psychoanalytic Society, to establish the French Psychoanalytical Association. As a result, these analysts lost their affiliation with the International Psychoanalytical Association. Michael Balint advised me to see some analysts on both sides, whom I felt I could trust, to discuss the consequences of my choice of an analyst. I consulted Dr. Berge, who had chosen to be a member of both associations. He told me that for the beginner candidate I was, it made no difference what group I chose, and that there were excellent analysts on both sides. I was happy to conclude that I did not have to change my decision.

I started my analysis on June 4th, 1954. I remember the date for a very specific reason. During our first session, Lagache asked me to tell him about my problems. Being extremely naive, I answered that I did not have any, except perhaps one: that after two years of marriage I was still not pregnant. Exactly nine months to the day after this meeting, my daughter Hélène was born. And my son Pierre came along sixteen months later. My analyst was delighted to see how fertile our exchanges were proving to be.

It is not easy to explain what could have produced a pregnancy before any analysis, based on a simple conversation. I can only offer some hypotheses: during my lengthy childhood illness, our family doctor warned my mother that it would be best, in view of my condition, if I did not marry, and if I did, that I have no children. My mother never stopped worrying about me, despite my obviously complete recovery. Although she was happy to learn that my wish to have a baby was coming true, she could not hide her concern for my health. I managed not to disappoint her: I contracted a short-term kidney infection at the start of my marriage, and at the start of each pregnancy; it was complete cured within a week each time.

To pay for my analysis, I had to find a job, because the income from the print shop was not enough. Paulette Laforgue, the ex-wife of psychoanalyst René Laforgue, was an old friend of my mother's. She worked as a demonstrator in biology at the Palais de la Découverte (a science museum). The psychotechnical demonstrator had just quit, and she got me the job. It was while examining the various devices whose functioning I would have to explain to visitors that I discovered I was slightly colour-blind. I worked about a year at the science museum, until the print shop became profitable enough to provide more than my modest wages as demonstrator.

I started analysis with Daniel Lagache at the same time as my job at the Palais de la Découverte. When I think about those four years of analysis, so emotion-filled and intense, I am surprised to find that aside from a few details I cannot remember their content, or even the crucial moments, as I will explain in a subsequent chapter. Some incidents whose importance is not clear to me today, and some significant dreams, are all I have left of that period I lived so intensely. It was no doubt this experience that made me say that in analysis nothing ever changes, except that once in a while you suddenly realise that you are elsewhere, in a different place. For me, there was neither revelation nor sudden recovery of forgotten events, but rather a slow, imperceptible evolution. At the end of my four years of analysis, some of my old anxieties disappeared, I lost my paralysing shyness... and I was almost completely cured of hay fever.

MY BEGINNINGS AS AN ANALYST

When I started my analysis, I was asked not to read psychoanalytic literature, not to make changes to my family situation — marriage, divorce, children — and not to start practicing until my elders authorised it. I did not completely comply with the first request, not at all with the second, but I completely agreed with the third. I waited for my analyst and a committee of three of his colleagues to give me the go-ahead before I tried to find some patients and look for a job in a clinic or a medical centre offering psychological and education services.

I quickly realised that I could not see patients at our home, because we lived with my parents and we had two small children in the house. Therefore, I rented premises near the house, from a private person, in a building housing a laboratory for medical tests. The plaque with the inscription "Analysis Laboratory" next to the door of the building created some confusion.

At the same time, I started to attend Juliette Favez-Boutonier's group supervision sessions, and a little later, those given by Françoise Dolto. I found group supervision very useful, because the situations recounted by my colleagues under supervision, and the comments they solicited, taught me at least as much as the work with my patients. Thus, I learned that a situation could be handled in different ways, that there was no such thing as the right technique, that each person had to invent his own method, which he knew how to apply, which suited his personality and whose consequences he was ready to assume. I learned that one can never simply copy someone else's method. Any technique had to be adapted first to one's own sensitivity. In addition, each analyst perceives different aspects of what the analysand brings to the process, and approaches the situation in his own way. I have sometimes been asked if I am Freudian, Ferenczian, Lacanian, Jungian or something else; I always answered that I can only be Dupontian, because everything that came from Freud, Ferenczi and the others had to be reshaped in my internal world, so I could use it in my own way. Of course, I can say that the authors who influenced me the most are Ferenczi and Balint. But neither of them built their theories into a school of thought. They offered their ideas freely, to everyone.

As for me, I cannot choose a unique, coherent theory sufficient in itself. I am more familiar with some theories than with others, some suit me more than others, but all of them attempt to explain the same human phenomena. Sometimes, a patient's spontaneous way of expressing himself brings to mind a certain theory which, in that particular case, will offer a better understanding than other theories. Still, the authors I know best, those whose writings I translated, come to my mind more often than other authors. Ferenczi, Balint and Maria Torok certainly had greater influence on me than other analysts whose methods are just as effective.

But when I started, things were different. I read relatively little, and mostly clinical writings rather than theoretical texts. I tended to forget easily what I read, except when the situations described resembled what I had seen myself.

Around this time, I started to work at the Parents' School, founded and directed by Dr. Berge. I administered tests; I was very interested in them. I gave them to all the members of my family, and was delighted to find out that I had married a man endowed with "giftedness". But over time, my interest in tests decreased considerably. These tests were used in most centres where I worked subsequently. My impression was that they produced something like an instant photograph, with all the inherent sources of error that such an image implies. And there was a risk in drawing certain conclusions from these test results, which could have long-term effects on the future of the children involved. For instance, I have had occasion to see over and over again that children with the same intelligence quotient can do very well or very poorly.

A little later, I was hired to work in Jenny Aubry's clinic, where I met remarkable people, both colleagues at the same level as I was, and experienced practitioners from whom I learned a great deal. Georges Favez was one of them; being in supervision with him was enormously enriching. He was a very astute clinician, but never tried to impose his vision, encouraging me to perfect my hypotheses based on my own observations. This was my first individual supervision, and I understood its advantages. It was easier for me to speak about my involvement in the analytic process than it had been in a group, and I had more time with the supervisor. This made me realise that the Hungarian system of supervision was well-founded: this system requires the candidate's first case to be supervised by his own analyst, on the couch. The method was developed by Ferenczi and Vilma Kovács. I know that Michael Balint continued the practice, even after he moved to England. This method allows the analyst to learn to analyse his counter-transference and use it more judiciously, that is, interpret the feelings elicited in him by his patient's subjective experience. The Hungarian method was not adopted in any other country. Could it be because it demands a great deal from both the supervisor and the candidate?

DEVELOPMENT OF MY PROFESSIONAL ACTIVITY

After my first position in Jenny Aubry's clinic, I worked in several therapeutic centres. After a short stint in a clinic in Drancy, a Northern Paris suburb, I was hired by a guidance centre in the Aisne, whose director was Dr. Marcelle Geber. I worked there for about twelve years. This centre, founded by an American association, had three locations in the Aisne region: in Soissons, in Laon and in Saint-Quentin. Each site had a team of psychoanalysts, psychologists, physiotherapists and social workers, and was available to the children in that area. The work was interesting; we could discuss the problems we encountered between us or with Dr. Geber. For all those years, I spent one day a week in Soissons, and the next day in Laon.

Working in a team always generates tension, even when its members get along well. Dissatisfaction can focus on a particular person, or there can be hostility between the therapists and the administration. It was in a situation of this kind that I and several members of the team handed in our resignations. I remember the words of one of the social workers who pleaded with us to stay for the sake of the children who needed us. I now know that she was right. This incident taught me to be wary of being carried away in the heat of passion, in a conflict that with some perspective will appear trivial.

After that I worked in a school for gifted children with emotional problems, in Saint-Maximin, near Chantilly. It was a place "taken over" by analysts from Quebec, who did not yet have a training institute and came to be trained in France. I made strong, durable friendships with some of them. In the school, the work environment was quite strange and unconventional. We saw children for individual therapy or in group therapy. But the treatment was carried out where the children lived. The director, Mme Cassel, together with the principal, served us sumptuous midday meals in her apartment, while the children ate much less well. The atmosphere was not very conducive to a therapeutic relation. Even if we were very discreet about the content of the sessions with the children, our closeness with the management of the school put us in a difficult position. Then, the salutary effect of the May 1968 rebellion gave us the needed support to ask the director to have our meals in the students' refectory, and to share their meals. Mme Cassel saw this as a personal rejection and fired the entire psychological team.

THE ÉTIENNE-MARCEL CENTRE

After leaving the Aisne guidance centre and a little before being fired from Saint-Maximin, I had joined the team at the Étienne-Marcel Centre, on Françoise Dolto's recommendation. She was also working there at the time. This Centre was, and still is, comprised of a medical/psychological/educational centre and a day hospital for severely ill children. The Centre was operated by its four founders, including Bernard This, Thérèse Tremblais and Madeleine Casanova. I met many exceptional people there, with whom discussions were always lively and instructive. We worked in groups composed of a psychoanalyst, a psychologist, a physiotherapist and a social worker. The Centre also organised scientific evenings with very interesting speakers.

In the meantime, my private practice had also grown. My parents had moved into a larger apartment on Île de la Cité, and I could use one of the rooms with a private entrance as my office. At the time, I had as a client a very agitated young girl I had trouble keeping in my office during her visits. She would try to open all the doors and she turned everything upside-down. I decided to continue my sessions with her at the Étienne-Marcel Centre, where the premises were more suitable for such a turbulent patient. But because the money she paid me at the end of each session played an important role in her therapy, I asked her to continue paying for her therapy as before. Because the Centre paid me for my work, I placed the money from this patient in a box, thinking that I would decide what to do with it when her treatment was over. At the end of her therapy, a considerable sum had accumulated in the box. I and my work group decided to use it to create a journal.

THE COQ-HÉRON *JOURNAL*

This is how *Le Coq-Héron* was born. It was named after a small street near Étienne-Marcel Street, because the name amused us. At first, the publication was a modest internal bulletin, mimiographed by my husband fifty copies at a time. Little by little, the journal developed, especially thanks to texts translated for the first time into French. We were able to translate from English, from German, from Hungarian, from Spanish. We were the first to bring to French readers two little articles by Freud, translated from Hungarian: "The Psychology of the Secondary School Student" and "Should Psychoanalysis Be Taught in University?" We also published some articles by Ferenczi and others about him. Authors like Michael and Enid Balint, Masud Khan, Margaret Mahler, Imre Hermann, Gyorgy Vikar and Bryan Bird gave us their texts. We also published some classic Hungarian texts, such as Istvan Hollos' *Mes adieux à la Maison jaune*, and the Complete Works of Alice Balint. We published many French authors as well: Françoise Dolto, Bernard This, Jean-Luc Donnay, Jean Losserand, Jacques Lacan, Pierre Benoît, Alain Didier-Weill. The editorial committee expanded. Soon, *Le Coq-Héron* was printed by offset and sold in bookstores.

The journal was original in part because of one particularity: it brought together analysts from hostile schools. But this hostility was not reflected in the editorial content. On the contrary, it occasioned passionate discussions. One of our rules ensured the smooth functioning of this heterogeneous editorial staff: any article was to be accepted and published if one person on the editorial committee (not the author, of course) had found something worthwhile in it. Articles could only be refused unanimously. Those who disagreed with the content of an article could add their comments in print, but could not prevent the publication of the text. The journal refused to have a "position"; its aim was to offer a forum for discussion. *Le Coq-Héron* continues to be published since 1969; it is now one of the oldest psychoanalytic journals in France. It owes its long life partly to the generosity of the printer, who granted it unlimited credit in difficult times. Today, the journal is published by *Érès* and has had over 220 issues.

MY PRIVATE PRACTICE

From the beginning, I always had a private practice, especially with adult patients. I saw children at the Centres where I worked. I have often asked myself why most psychoanalysts begin their careers by treating children, which is much more difficult than working with neurotic adults. Working with children requires much greater experience. There are innumerable techniques that can be used with children, and they have to be endlessly reinvented. In addition, analysis of a child is inevitably family therapy. In a family, problems are so interconnected that all members of the family have to be considered in one way or another, particularly those living with the patient. This can sometimes be true in therapy with adults as well, but it is rare for family members to involve themselves in the analysis directly. In therapy with children, it is, on the contrary, to be expected.

At first, I provided the children in therapy with abundant material: toys, pencils, paper, modeling clay. After a while, I kept only the paper and pencils, and sometimes the modeling clay. I felt that with less means, the children expressed themselves better.

TRANSLATION

Immigration forces one to acquire a new language. French has become my acquired language in a new culture, but Hungarian is the language of my childhood. I kept going back and forth between these two languages, and I think this is why I always liked translation. I always found it to be a pleasure; it is a bridge-building activity: between two languages, two periods in one's life, sometimes between two parents, between two different groups that might be hostile, between two intellectual and emotional experiences (because different languages express things differently, and at a different level).

Immigration involves all kinds of losses, and particularly that of language. I changed my language of everyday expression in pre-adolescence; this involved a discontinuity between the language of childhood emotions and activities, and the language of my subsequent culture and emotions. I was unable to sing my francophone children the Hungarian nursery rhymes sung to me, and I cannot express a complex idea in my mother tongue.

The mother tongue can act as a ghost, a phantom. Sometimes, a Hungarian expression or a single word springs into my mind, with no apparent connection to the present context; its meaning is not always clear to me. In general, I cannot connect it to anything in the present, be it through its meaning or its sound. But it is there, and probably not without a reason.

The activity of translation is a means of managing the complexity of feelings, of attachments, of rejections, a way to suture the internal severing.

My first translation of some scope was Sándor Ferenczi's *Thalassa, A Theory of Genitality*. I translated it into French from the Hungarian, because the Hungarian edition, published by Panthéon, my father's publishing house, was reviewed and corrected by Ferenczi, after being translated from the original German. In Hungarian, the book was called *Catastrophes in Sexual Development*. I did not translate this work alone; I always preferred translating with a partner or in a group. Each language has its particular "genius", its own way of approaching things, and we know that each translation involves losses or additions to the author's intentions. The translator must make choices, and must decide whether to stay as close as possible to the text wherever possible, and invent terms when an equivalent does not exist, changing the author's style. Or the translator might choose to transmit the spirit of the text in a style similar to that of the author, even if ideas have to be expressed somewhat differently. In a text which is both scientific and personal, the translator goes back and forth between these two methods.

To illustrate, when translating Freud and Ferenczi from German, our translation group often struggled to render the simple and concrete German original into precise, abstract-tending French.

Translating Ferenczi also exposed me to the connections between languages. Not only my mother tongue and my acquired language, but especially German, and then English, Spanish and Latin, since Ferenczi's texts, written in German, contain expressions and quotes in many various languages.

I went over the French version of *Thalassa* with a colleague, and then submitted it to Nicolas Abraham, who later wrote the Preface. Nicolas Abraham and Maria Torok convinced Gérard Mendel, head of the psychoanalysis collection at Payot, to recommend the publication of this little book. It was published in pocket book form, with the title *Thalassa, psychanalyse des origines de la vie sexuelle*, an intriguing title which no doubt contributed to the commercial success of the book.

Later in this book I devote a chapter to Ferenczi's introduction in France, which began with this initial translation.

REPRESENTING FERENCZI'S LITERARY WORKS

Elma Laurvik and Magda Ferenczi, Gizella Ferenczi's two daughters, suggested to Michael Balint, Ferenczi's literary executor, that I should take over this responsibility after him. He agreed. I was touched by his trust and after thinking about it briefly, I accepted.

I remember a heated discussion concerning the publication of Ferenczi's *Clinical Diary*. Michael had me read his English translation of it. He thought that the *Diary* and the *Freud-Ferenczi Correspondence* should be published at the same time, since each one contributes to a better understanding of the other. Given the spurious idea introduced by Jones in volume III of his biography of Freud about an imaginary mental illness afflicting Ferenczi, Balint was afraid that if the *Diary* was published separately, readers whose minds had already been adversely influenced would be disconcerted and tend to agree with Jones. As to the *Freud-Ferenczi Correspondence*, Anna Freud would not agree to have it published unabridged, and Michael Balint refused just as categorically to leave out portions of it. He had even considered starting with the publication of only those years that could be presented in their totality, but Anna Freud did not find any such years. At that point, Balint started to gather material for writing a biography of Ferenczi, to accompany the *Diary* and, he hoped, the *Correspondence*. But he did not have time to write it. He died suddenly in his sleep on December 31, 1970, of a heart attack.

Enid Balint gave me the Ferenczi archives. With the *Coq-Héron* translation group, which had just finished the translation of Volume IV of Ferenczi's *Complete Works*, we decided to continue with the translation of the *Clinical Diary*.

The main obstacle to the publication of the *Freud-Ferenczi Correspondence* was the fact that it revealed the complex story of Ferenczi's relations with Gizella and with Gizella's oldest daughter Elma. As a result, the *Coq-Héron* translation group decided to publish as soon as possible the *Ferenczi-Groddeck Correspondence*, which discusses this episode extensively.

But things were not advancing and we finally decided to publish the *Clinical Diary,* that I consider a major work in the history of psychoanalysis. It is the surprisingly frank testimony of a man who conducts his own analysis with the same rigour as that of his patients. The reader sees him fumbling in the dark, looking for ways to help people with pathologies that the orthodox psychoanalysis of that era did not even attempt to treat. He was wrong many times, started again, tried something else, but never gave up. The *Diary* is also the testimony of a man who feels he suffers from a deadly disease, and tries to understand what is happening to him, to identify the nature of this physical and psychic impasse which is killing him. Finally, he describes his relationship with Freud, which so strongly influenced his life.

The publication of the *Clinical Diary*, first in French, then in English and only lastly in the original German, did not create the scandal that might have been expected. The book was greeted with respect, warmth and interest by the psychoanalytic community, which recognised its importance at once.

THE FREUD-FERENCZI CORRESPONDENCE

The turbulent story of the publication of the *Freud-Ferenczi Correspondence* will be described in detail in the second chapter (see "Introducing Ferenczi in France"). After Anna Freud's death, when this publication became possible, a publisher, editors and funds for the project had to be found. We formed a committee charged with these tasks. Two editors were hired: Ernst Falzeder and Eva Brabant. André Haynal was charged with finalising the editors' comments. Ingeborg Meyer-Paldemo, who worked for Fischer Publishers, revised and made improvements to the transcription of the original letters — work Michael Balint had started to do. In France, the director of Calmann-Levy thought it would be an excellent book, bringing prestige to the publisher, and accepted to publish it.

TRANSLATING BALINT'S WORK

In the meantime, with some other people, I had started to translate Balint's work into French. In my eyes, Balint's writing was the direct continuation of Ferenczi's work. So it was with great pleasure that I started to translate first *Techniques psychothérapeutiques en médecine* (Psychotherapeutic Techniques in Medicine), working with Jean-Paul Valabrega, and then *Le Défaut fundamental* (The Basic Fault: Therapeutic Aspects of Regression) and *Les voies de la régression* (Thrills and Regressions), with Myriam Viliker; *Amour primaire et technique psychanalytique* (Primary Love and Psychoanalytic Technique), with René Gelly and Suzanne Kadar; and *Psychothérapie focale* (Focal Psychotherapy) with René Gelly. I was able to have *Problems of Human Pleasure and Behaviour* be translated into French by Claude Monod, an excellent translator. But although she submitted her translation in time to Payot, the publisher only published the book years later, in 2011, in a revised translation. This collection of articles appeared under the title *Sexe et société. Essai sur le plaisir et la frustration.*

CORBEIL-ESSONNES HOSPITAL

After leaving the Aisne Guidance Centre and the Saint-Maximin school, I worked at the Étienne-Marcel Centre. But my private practice was still modest, so I looked for a second job. My friend and colleague Lucien Mélèse put me in touch with Dr. Jacques Bamberger, head of Pediatrics at the Corbeil-Essonnes Hospital. He assigned me the exciting task of evaluating in what manner a psychoanalyst can best contribute to his department. Dr. Bamberger was a remarkable man; his sensitivity, attitude to the children and the personnel, and his open mind impressed me greatly.

I was free to innovate. At first, I went from one room to another in the department, speaking to the staff, the children, the parents. Then I started conducting therapy with children. Very soon, all my time was filled, and I was not accomplishing everything I wanted. I realised there must be a better way of doing things. There were two of us in the "psychological team", a psychologist/physiotherapist and myself. I therefore suggested to Dr. Bamburger that he should hire more psychologists, psychotherapists, speech therapists, music therapists... Little by little, as new positions were created, the team filled out and soon there were eleven or twelve of us. My main task from then on was to organise coordination meetings where we discussed the problems encountered by the different members of the team, or by the doctors and nurses in the department.

Whenever possible, we tried not to have a therapist assigned to a child treated by a a doctor of the department who was treating him, but rather to work with the doctor in the coordination meetings, to help him conduct the therapy himself, since he was the person familiar to the child. It was not, in fact, psychotherapy in the usual sense of the word, but rather what Balint had in mind when he wrote *Psychotherapeutic Techniques in Medicine*[3]. Thanks to this procedure, a young intern succeeded in giving back the desire to live to a boy with leukemia, who had given up the fight and was not responding to treatment; the intern was also able to have the boy's family rally around him again, after they had considered him lost and had started to mourn him.

Various children's institutes near the hospital soon heard about these coordination meetings where professionals could come to discuss problems they encounter. Soon, the staff of an adoption agency acquired the habit of coming to discuss with us certain difficult problem they encountered; some nearby health centres did the same. It was very exciting work, which I continued to do for about fifteen years.

DEVELOPING MY PRIVATE PRACTICE

Since the beginning, I worked in private practice. Gradually, I acquired enough patients and, above all, enough experience to be able to stop working in psychological/ educational centres and at the hospital. My patients were sometimes referred to me by colleagues, but most often by former patients. I saw less and less children, and after a while worked only with adults.

In this work, I also had to be inventive, to help each patient find a way to feel better, given his own psychic possibilities. I adapted continuously, to suit each situation.

---

[3] Balint, M., *The Doctor, His Patient and the Illness*, Elsevier Canada, 2000; and Balint, M. and Balint, E., *Psychotherapeutic Techniques in Medicine*, Tavistock Publications, 1961.

My fees were set based on the financial means of my patients. But there must be limits to this arrangement. Not only because psychoanalysis is how I earn a living, but also because I noticed that when the fee is inferior to a certain amount the person feels devalued, and not without reason: this means, in fact, that I believe them incapable of doing any better in life.

It has been my custom to see patients for forty-five minutes, and I always start on time. I have had countless discussions with my Lacanian friends about variable-length sessions — usually shorter — without ever coming to an agreement on this point. I tend to think that the important thing is to invent methods that suit the situation, and whose consequences we feel we can handle. Thus, I have had occasion to conclude an analysis, conducted on the couch for a long time, by correspondence and a single session a month.

As I said earlier, what I am most interested in is what goes on between people, between me and my patients, especially from a therapeutic rather than a scientific point of view. I only fully understand a theory if it reminds me of a clinical situation. If not, I am unable to use it.

I have always found it surprising to know that Ferenczi was blamed for his *furor sanandi*. I can understand that some people in the field are more interested in the advancement of knowledge than in the therapeutic effects of psychoanalysis. Their contributions are essential. But reproaching others with their desire to heal seems incomprehensible to me.

As time went by, I started to attend conferences and make presentations more often. As a result, I was able to exchange ideas and to collaborate with colleagues from Canada, the United States, Spain, Belgium, Italy, Hungary and France. I always remained on the fringes of associations. It was not by choice, it was just the way things were, because of my nature... or my pathology. My way of reacting to my emigrant/immigrant situation, to my Hungarian-French and Judeo-Protestant identity has something to do with it. In any case, this way of being allowed me to avoid to a large extent the tensions and conflicts that inevitably arise in any human group.

Over the years, I wrote a number of articles and only one little book on whose content I reflected a long time before writing the book. Its title was *Manuel à l'usage des enfants qui ont des parents difficiles* (Manual for Children with Difficult Parents). The idea came to me while I was giving lectures at the Palais de la Découverte (science museum) on different types of so-called problem children: children who lie, children who steal... These lectures, on the model of those given at Dr. Berge's Parents' School, where I worked for a time at the start of my professional life, made me somewhat ill at ease. Psychoanalysis had lent me a perspective which made me think that children had much greater problems with their parents, and for much longer, than parents had with their children. I thought it was urgent to look at the problem from the opposite perspective, and to offer children some reading material dealing with the most common problems they encounter with their parents. After several failed attempts at writing a serious text on this question, a humoristic style appeared as the obvious choice, and the book was written effortlessly. It seemed to have been the right approach; the little book, written under a pen name, was given a favourable reception.

LIFE GOES ON

Psychoanalysis is a profession that demands much time, reflection and emotional investment. Still, there is ample time for sharing in one's husband's concerns, seeing one's children grow up and orienting their lives, welcoming grandchildren, cultivating friendships. This part of life nourishes the other. Without this support I could not practice my profession, or any other no doubt.

HOW ANALYSTS GET SMART

"Now you," Eliza said, "should name

Through whom it was to you wit came."

"How Girls Get Smart"

Jean de la Fontaine

The profession of analyst, like most others, forces one to think about the way it is taught and practiced, the best way to assess its results, and to evaluate the quality of the professionals who practice it. In the case of psychoanalysis, it seems particularly difficult to find answers to these basic questions, so that this profession eludes classification, despite endless attempts to include it in a pre-existing category. Indeed, it is not medicine, although it can be therapeutic; it is not psychiatry, although it deals with the human psyche; it is not psychology, although it uses it. Neither is it philosophy, although it involves a particular view of the world; nor is it sociology, to which it can be applied; and it is certainly not religion…

To be able to create a university program in psychoanalysis, and to know under what heading to place the taxes paid by these professionals, government agencies try to integrate this occupation in an existing category: Health? Education? Another sector? Despite the good will demonstrated by some professionals who wish to be recognised as working in an established and respectable field, there is always an essential element that escapes all possibility of official regulation.

For this reason, psychoanalysis poses a problem to those who practice it, and who feel responsible for maintaining a high level of quality in the profession: the much discussed and never resolved problem of the training of analysts. Even though suitable candidates are selected, the number of years of compulsory analysis respected, the number of weekly sessions and supervised cases determined, the best professionals carefully chosen to train new analysts, the fact remains that different institutions have different programs. Some candidates do extremely well, no matter what School they belong to, others fall short despite the best efforts of those who train them. Obviously, the profession of analyst cannot be taught, it can only be learned. One cannot "shape" an analyst, but some people succeed in "shaping themselves" to practice this profession.

Thus, we are dealing with an undefinable, unclassifiable, unteachable profession, whose nature is nevertheless clearly understood. Contrary to some opinions, it is not an "impossible" profession, since many people learn it, practice it and are judged capable of exercising it, although it is unclear by what criteria.

Two stories come to mind in this regard. One is very down-to-earth; it concerns my mother's handwritten recipe book, which I inherited. According to her, to make an excellent chocolate cake, one needs flour, butter, just enough sugar, and chocolate. The cake must be baked at the right temperature, for just the right time. Of course, when I tried to follow the recipe for the first time, I was not very successful. When I took the cake out of the oven, it fell and rolled into a corner of the kitchen, without even crumbling. In short, the result was not great. But gradually it started to improve.

The second story is a little more scholarly, and comes from Ancient Greece. A traveller is on his way to Athens. On the road, he comes across Archimedes sitting under a fig tree. He asks Archimedes: "How far is Athens?" Archimedes replies: "Walk!" The traveller tells himself that the old man must be deaf. He repeats his question, speaking louder. Archimedes answers again: "Walk!" Exasperated, the traveller tells himself that there is nothing to be done with the dumb old man, and continues on his way. After he walks a little distance, Archimedes shouts after him: "At this rate, it will take you two and a half hours". It is more or less in this way that analysts get smart, providing their temperament can withstand all the uncertainty, while allowing them to assume their responsibilities fully.

I would like to provide a personal illustration. How I became "smart" in relation to psychoanalysis happened more or less in the following manner. As I already said, I was born in 1925. Ferenczi had just written Thalassa, a book later published in Hungarian by my father's publishing house. My grandmother, my aunt, my uncle, were all analysed by Ferenczi, became his students and then his colleagues. Members of my family who were not part of this process were nevertheless his friends and frequent visitors at his home. They all felt great affection, tenderness and admiration for this sensitive, intelligent, courageous and creative man. I think that despite my young age at the time, all the affection existing in this psychoanalytic circle contributed to how I got smart in this area.

Thus, I was brought up by members of this family. They were loving and attentive to my reactions, even curious about what I had to say. They were the ones who taught me that it is important to listen to people and accept them, even if I don't always understand them, or not altogether. They also taught me that it was possible to be very angry at someone one loves, without causing a disaster to happen. They had many set principles about the upbringing of children, but were ready to change them if what they did was not working. They taught me that when theory and the patient's inner world are not in agreement, it is always the patient who is right, although this might not mean "literally" right. This education certainly contributed to the way in which I became "smart" about analysis.

This harmonious life in a close family came to an end with Austria's annexation by Nazi Germany, which prompted our immigration to France, a country my parents knew well, but still a foreign country. Being cut off from the rest of the family by the German occupation of France, and by the constant danger this represented for us, reinforced the closeness between me and my parents. This unusual closeness between generations must have exerted an influence on all aspects of my life, including my subsequent professional life.

I was about fifteen years old when I told my mother that I intended to become a psychoanalyst. My aunt Alice, a psychoanalyst, died in 1939; my grandmother, another analyst, died in 1940. My mother was profoundly affected by having to be separated from and then losing these two people she loved. I felt very keenly her secret desire to see something of them revive through me. Although this desire was never expressed directly, it influenced in some way the "smartness" we are discussing, just as the atmosphere of my childhood years did. For if world history had not intervened, chances are that I would have chosen to work in my father's publishing house, a place where I spent much time in my childhood. My recurring dreams of libraries and bookstores are still the delight of many of my nights.

But after the war, the Panthéon Publishing House ceased to exist. After a year or two it was nationalised and became part of the official press of the Hungarian People's Republic, whose citizens my parents and I did not want to become. The expression of internal freedom, unknown in Hungary, which I observed in my classmates and among our friends in France, certainly played a role in the way I became psychoanalytically "smart".

And so, when the time came, after the war and after my graduation, I set out to accomplish my psychoanalytic project. On the advice of my uncle Balint, I studied medicine first. I considered it a means, not an end. But I drew a triple benefit from this decision: a body of knowledge, a diploma that allowed me to avoid certain difficulties encountered by lay analysts, and most importantly the fact that I met the man who has been sharing my life for over sixty years.

After meeting with many older practitioners, some of whom I found disconcerting, I was accepted in "training" analysis with Daniel Lagache, whose simple and direct manner made a good impression on me. It was a memorable and fruitful experience, as I recounted earlier: my daughter was born exactly nine months after my first session, and my son not long afterwards.

Towards the end of this four-year analysis, I started to see patients, attend the meetings of the Association and participate in supervisions, which were often collective. I learned a great deal, particularly to listen closely to what the other candidates were doing. I also learned never to borrow a way of doing things, even when I found it brilliant. They did things their way with their patients, and I did things my way with mine. This is how I developed one of the only absolute rules of my practice: that one can always handle the consequences of one's own mistakes better than those of others. This is because an error, a false move, is always based on an internal logic that it is possible to identify and that makes sense in the relation with the patient. A patient knows us, or more accurately, "senses" us, and can deal with our mistakes and misunderstandings, and even forgive them if we are willing to put their criticism and reproaches to good use. A professional technique borrowed from a colleague or a teacher whose talent and skill we admire has no recognisable meaning for the patient, any more than for the analyst.

Supervised work taught me a great deal. The reactions of my supervisor and my colleagues in supervision threw a new and often unexpected light on an analytic situation I brought to the session. Of course, it was up to me to recognise in what was said the things I could use, for which I could take full responsibility.

Now that I often carry out the role of supervisor, I realise that supervision is a particular skill, characterised by the same uncertainty as every other aspect of this equally particular profession. In this activity also, what one does is bring to a clinical discussion something which is not strictly speaking knowledge, but rather a different perspective than that of the patient's analyst. The supervisor must be modest: he is not teaching anything. Rather, the other analyst must determine if he can draw a benefit from the exchange with the supervisor, in his own way and at his own pace. Among my many supervisors, those who played this role most skillfully were Françoise Dolto and Georges Favez.

In addition, I read a great deal, I attended seminars and I translated works from languages I knew. This certainly contributed to my culture and strengthened my intellect, but I cannot say in what way it may have helped me to ''get smart''. What literature offers contributes directly to intelligence, but only indirectly to practical "smartness". Although clinical practice and theory are interdependent, as

Ferenczi and Rank's book *The Development of Psychoanalysis* wisely indicates, they are nevertheless two very different approaches, even contradictory at times. Theory attempts to define ideas and concepts, and to perfect them over time. Clinical practice requires flexibility, adaptation to individuals and situations, and the setting aside of all preconceived ideas. Theory attempts to throw light on the different aspects of observed phenomena, to formulate them, to identify the points that can be generalised. Although imagination has a major role to play here, theorising requires intellectual rigour. Clinical practice, on the other hand, requires above all sensitivity to the being of the other; theory is only useful when it is sufficiently "directed" to intervene silently, even when it does not come to mind specifically at the time things unfold in the session.

In the 1960s, I started to translate into French the works of Ferenczi, followed by those of Balint. There was something very familiar in the methods of these two authors whose affective influence was part of my childhood, even though I was then too young to understand the discussions I heard. Later, their theories seemed particularly easy to understand, and their theories and hypotheses constituted an appropriate pathway for reaching the patients who came to see me. Of course, many other approaches are possible — very different approaches which suit other people much better. But that particular approach suited my own sensitivity best.

Today, I still continue to learn. Each new person I meet initiates a new experience. My previous experience does not bring answers, but only the ability to ask better questions.

Perhaps I am stating the obvious. But the fact is that sometimes those who know the obvious hesitate to make use of it. Proceeding freely, taking risks without any protection or guarantee, requires one to have acquired adequate internal protection earlier in one's life.

In summary, this is how I got "smart" (and continue to get smart) thanks to the influence of those around me. I believe that some of my colleagues will recognise in my story aspects of their own experiences.

PRACTICING PSYCHOANALYSIS

When Francis Martens invited me to go to Brussels to speak of "anything I wanted", I thought it would be interesting to discuss what the work of psychoanalysis is.

Not what psychoanalysis is, or what being an analyst is, but the act — if it is an act — of conducting psychoanalysis: the practice of analysis. I thought it would be an easy subject. After all, psychoanalysing is what I've been doing for fifty years. But as soon as I formulated this comforting thought, I ran out of ideas.

To start with, what kind of *definition* can be given to this activity? Theoretical? Technical? Clinical? Formal? Another sort? How can one define something so multifaceted, with so many aspects to consider? There is the analyst's training, which never ends, to prepare him to analyse others; there are the two protagonists and everything about them; there is the timing of the start of the analysis, the concrete elements of the setting, the diagnosis, absence of a diagnosis or refusal to make a diagnosis; there is knowledge and everything that depends on it, and also everything unrelated to knowledge... the list is endless.

While I was reflecting on how best to describe psychoanalytic practice, I came across a remarkable text by my colleague Jean-Claude Lavie, published in the bulletin of the French Psychoanalytic Society; he writes:

"One should not confuse practice with technique. A practice is a mode of applying a technique specific to the style of the person who uses it, or to the requirements of a case. [...] The practice of psychoanalysis is personal by its very nature and can never consist of imitating or copying even a great teacher. It is the person of the analyst himself, with everything that he is, who constructs the situation and manages it".

I could not give you a better definition.

Having said this, we have not yet said anything concrete about the practice. But we have established that the subject I am about to discuss is somewhat complex. I agree with Jean-Claude Lavie's conclusion: everything related to psychoanalytic practice is so imbued with subjectivity — the analyst's, the patient's, that of those to whom we try to describe this practice — so that we can certainly attempt to discuss the subject, but without knowing exactly what we are saying, or what others will hear.

Nevertheless, I shall undertake this uncertain task, come what may. I can try to start at the beginning, or even a little before.

WHY BECOME A PSYCHOANALYST?

This question elicits the most diverse answers. Some of my colleagues encountered psychoanalysis during their studies, in philosophy courses, or later, and it was a real revelation in some cases. Others undertook an analysis to improve their well-being. Still others, often doctors, psychiatrists, teachers or social workers, thought — rightly, in my opinion — that the practice of their profession would become more interesting and gain in quality. One day, I even met a nun who was in the process of questioning her vocation. But what lies behind all these motives that seem so reasonable? Childish curiosity? The need to be useful? The desire to be respected? A desire for control? Or is it even possible to be clear about one's own motivations?

I can list some of the motives that drove me to choose this occupation, but certainly not all of them. The two most obvious ones, as I said, are that I was born in a milieu steeped in psychoanalysis — psychoanalysis at its beginnings, which generated passionate discussions around me. This world of reflection and research became familiar to me long before I understood the discussions, and before I could take part in it. The second motivation seems lighter, but in fact I wonder if it was not the more powerful of the two: my mother's desire that I become an analyst, like her beloved sister whom she lost too early. Once the decision is made, the modalities of training have to be worked out.

IS TRAINING A UTOPIA OF SORTS?

Psychoanalytic training does not start at the end of one's studies, even in the rare cases where a person has already chosen this profession at that early stage. First, one has to have an occupation, financial independence, and the ability to pay for the training. Most candidates for psychoanalytic training are psychologists, psychiatrists, physicians, philosophers, social workers; but there are also — and among the best known — ministers of various religious faiths, lawyers, an interior decorator, the owner of a brewery and some high society ladies.

A lengthy struggle was necessary to reach more or less general agreement — some fifteen years ago — that non-physicians can practice psychoanalysis as long as they receive training, but untrained physicians are not qualified to practice analysis. Analysts themselves were divided on this question. A memorable discussion held in 1927 (published in its totality in the *Coq-Héron*, issue no. 150) presents the various arguments of the participants. Today, the question is still relevant and is being raised, in a different way, by government agencies...

On the subject of psychoanalytic training, we could add an observation made by Alice Balint, an analyst interested in child development, whose life regretfully ended much too early. She dedicated many articles to factors favouring child development, and factors she considered detrimental. And she added a very reassuring note for parents and teachers facing difficult situations, commenting that in truth there are very few things that a child will not overcome, at least to some extent.

I believe this remark could also be comforting to those who perform the difficult task of training future analysts. Problems related to psychoanalytic training have always generated heated discussions — rarely very rewarding — , and have created violent controversy, and even disputes and scissions. Interestingly, most of these problems were clearly identified as early as 1927 by Siegfried Bernfeld, the following year by Ferenczi, and many times subsequently, especially by Balint and Jean-Paul Valabrega, and recently by Otto F. Kernberg and Daniel Kuperman, but no solution was found. This strange impasse is one of the questions I would like to examine: how is it that a well-known problem, with known causes, can prove to be insoluble?

Freud spoke little of psychoanalytic training. In Volume I of "Minutes", written in 1907, he wrote: "In an analysis, if there is no suffering, there is no cure; this creates a problem in 'training' analyses". But he adds further that "psychoanalysis is teachable". In 1910, in "The Future Prospects of Psycho-Analytic Therapy", he only discusses self-analysis, to be pursued throughout one's professional life. The same year, in "'Wild' Psycho-Analysis", he comments that "[the technique] is to be learnt from those who are already proficient in it. [...] 'wild' analysts do more harm to the cause of psycho-analysis than to individual patients". Finally, in 1912, in "Recommendations to Physicians Practising Psycho-Analysis", Freud concludes that not anyone can become an analyst. Lastly, undergoing prior psychoanalysis proves to be indispensable. Freud confirms this in his 1916–1917 text *A General Introduction to Psychoanalysis*: "Psychoanalysis is learned, first of all, from a study of one's self. [But] one gets much further if one allows himself to be analyzed by a competent analyst." This principle is the one Freud continued to maintain. However, the controversy about lay analysts, arising in the mid 1920s, forced him to consider structured training, controlled and sanctioned by a regulatory institution. But his personal tendency was to favour a "laisser faire" policy.

Indeed, it seems that the training of psychoanalysts became problematic after the International Psychoanalytical Association was established, with all the bureaucratic organisation it brought about, and after the foundation of the first Berlin Psychoanalytic Institute. In the 1910 article in which Ferenczi, at Freud's request, recommends founding the IPA, the dangers of such an organisation are clearly identified. Comparing the structure of the Association to that of a family, Ferenczi pointed out — with great realism — the almost inevitable consequences of attributing power to certain types of individuals rather than others.

To my knowledge, Ferenczi is the only author who started his article about training with the question of "*How to study* psychoanalysis", and not "how *to teach* it" or "how *to train* an analyst". Ferenczi speaks of an "*apprentice analyst*", not a "candidate". This is because the term "candidate" stresses acceptance into a group or to an examination, rather than the acquisition of knowledge or know-how related to a practice. Ferenczi insists on the need for personal analysis as part of the apprenticeship: the only element unanimously agreed upon by all analytic groups. This requirement is so obvious that there is hardly any need to specify it; it is simply something that is needed. Who would think of specifying that a hammer has to be held by the handle to hammer a nail? However, torrents of words have been wasted on the question of whether the analysis should be conducted for such and such a number of years, with such and such a number of weekly sessions, lasting such and such a lapse of time, carried out with such and such a type of analyst.

In other texts, Ferenczi assigns the IPA the task of preserving, as much as possible, the "purity" of analysis, and "furthering its development". The IPA brings together those who share "the basic principles" of psychoanalysis. Ferenczi does not specify shared technical modalities; he himself tried many technical procedures, and then abandoned or modified them when they proved ineffective or excessive.

Michael Balint wrote two articles about training: one in 1947 and another in 1953. By then, most psychoanalytic associations had established training programs. Balint starts by examining them. He is particularly critical of the dogmatism apparent in the training system, which he sees as having a "strikingly similarity with primitive initiation rites":

"On the part of the initators — the training committee and the training analysts — we observe secretiveness about our esoteric knowledge, dogmatic announcements of our demands and the use of authoritative techniques. On the part of the candidates, i.e. those to be initiated, we observe the willing acceptance of the exoteric fables, submissiveness to dogmatic and authoritative treatment without much protest and too respectful behaviour".

This initiation, instead of helping the candidate "develop a strong and critical ego", Balint says, attempts "to force [him] to identify with his initiator, ... to build up a strong super-ego which will influence him all his life." This situation is further aggravated by the efforts of each of the schools to attract as many candidates as possible, who show themselves loyal to its particular principles. It seems that many people in charge of training are aware of this problem. But the subject is so emotionally charged that most proposed changes deal with details, or simply terminology, without changing the content. The only significant change that some associations have dared to make is to admit that training analysis is like any other analysis, and that it is only afterwards that it becomes clear whether or not it succeeded in teaching; consequently, the candidate is free to choose his analyst in any category of practitioners and in any association. Of course, the power to accept a student or not into the training program of the association of his choice is still held by those in charge of the association, so that the restriction removed earlier in the process reappears further along.

But the fact is that the training of an analyst cannot take place under the pressure of a certain power. Indeed, I would even say that the idea of training an analyst is a utopia of sorts. I think that in truth there are some people who succeed in training themselves to become analysts, despite everything. No pre-established program can set out the path a certain person needs to follow to acquire the skills necessary to analyse others. What applies to everyone is personal analysis, which in most cases makes it possible to acquire the psychic flexibility required by analytic work.

But with the exception of this practice, the path followed by each student analyst is unforeseeable. To illustrate: some people need to acquire considerable theoretical knowledge before starting to work with patients. Experience will eventually teach them to adapt and enrich their theoretical foundation. Other people cannot assimilate theoretical information without having had some clinical experience, which gives meaning to the theory.

These personal differences are also influenced, no doubt, by the student analyst's past activities, now that the question of lay analysis has been resolved. A physician or psychologist will probably be less intimidated by contact with patients than a professional who has never worked in such a setting, and who will tend to acquire solid theoretical support first.

For several decades, psychoanalytic associations have continued to search for a solution to this dilemma: how to reconcile the hierarchical structures of the associations with the freedom needed to train as an analyst. For, as we know, it is very difficult to resist the lure of power, and a hierarchical structure always involves a series of superposed powers. For this reason, a series of choices must be made to move across the different levels of power. Today, there may still be associations which select those who will be accepted for training analysis. In others, selection starts once a candidate has been accepted for training. Then there is the selection of those who can practice analysis supervised by a training analyst (because some supervisions undertaken by a student with an analyst of his choice do not count as officially supervised analyses.) After that, another selection will determine if the candidate will be accepted into the Association as a member. In some associations, this is the end of the process. In others, there is another stage: being made a full member. The different categories have different names depending on the Association, but the principle remains more or less the same.

The criteria on which these selections are based are very hard to define and, as far as I know, have never really been clearly defined. There is a great risk that original minds may be turned away in this process — I wonder if Ferenczi would have been accepted into a modern-day Association — , and only those whose path is familiar to the gatekeepers, or who can conceal their particularities enough not to shock anyone, will be accepted. Let us note in passing that this selection process can be traumatising, since the candidate is asked to reveal himself as fully as possible to examiners who do not reveal their impressions, merely announcing their decision with no explanation.

You may say that it is easy to criticise, but much harder to offer a solution. I agree. Therefore, I will present my view of the situation, a view which may be as imperfect as what I described above. I believe that it is very difficult to acquire psychoanalytic training under pressure of any kind, especially the pressure produced by the need to satisfy those who can decide the fate of one's future professional life. This does not mean that I am opposed to the existence of psychoanalytic associations, since only they can organise courses, seminars and professional meetings. I can therefore imagine the possibility that, after a personal analysis, conducted wherever and with whomever one wishes, psychoanalytic societies offer courses and seminars attended by apprentice analysts in the order and for the length of time suitable to each of them, starting when the candidate is ready. Some will doubtless start too early, others too late, but who better to decide when the right time is than the candidate himself?

Every apprentice analyst will no doubt feel the need to have his first analyses supervised, or the ones he feels are the most difficult. I see no need to set a number for these supervised analyses, nor to decide in the apprentice analyst's place who the supervisor should be, or to determine if the supervisions should be individual or collective.

At a certain point, the apprentice analyst will want to join an association. It is then that the members of the association of the candidate's choice can decide if he has the qualities they require. No doubt some original minds will have trouble being accepted and will have to risk working independently (without belonging to any association), but not without contact with other professionals.

Among the many possible objections to such an ultra liberal program, there is, I must admit, a major one. Associations are supposed to guarantee the quality of the professionals they train, in order to ensure the safety of patients, which is highly desirable. But I wonder about the effectiveness of this guarantee of quality promised by the associations, given the dysfunctionality and ethical misconduct we have seen among members of all associations, at all levels of the hierarchy. I have certainly not covered all the failings and problems associated with this troublesome question, but have presented the reader with some of my misgivings.

THE QUESTION OF THEORIES

Many different theories attempt to describe the same phenomena and explain the same mechanisms. Of course, they often contradict each other, for the same phenomenon appears different when seen from a different perspective. A circle seen straight on is clearly a circle, but seen from the side, it is just as clearly a line. Some theories are "open": they don't claim to explain everything, and lead to many questions and uncertainties. They are the ones I most like to work with, because they don't incite the analyst to fit the patient in a particular mold that explains his situation. I am much more mistrustful of theories that are too coherent and monolithic, leaving no opening for other ways to think.

Adhering too closely to a single theory creates too great a temptation to twist everything the patient says, and all his attitudes, so as to be able to fit them into the theory concerned. But it also happens at times that the patient starts to express himself in the language of a specific theory; in that case, that theory is probably particularly suited for work with this patient. In addition, all analysands do not speak the same language; I feel that they should not be pressured into adopting a language other than the one which comes naturally to them.

Indeed, what I said about theories and about the patient also applies to the analyst. Each of us has his own language, or his own way of using language, even if elements of it are borrowed here and there. For each analyst, it is the only means available for establishing a genuine relation with the analysand. We modify this language to come closer to that of the patient, but we never abandon it altogether. In fact, I believe that we elaborate a common language with each patient. This is how the patient/analyst relation is established.

But is this really what can be called a relation? And if it is, what kind of relation is it? There is no consensus on this question either. One of the characteristics of analytic practice is that nothing can be taken for granted, everything can be brought into question, and there are many ways of looking at the same thing. The patient/analyst relation is certainly not symmetrical. They both work together to conduct the analysis of the patient, while the analyst, undoubtedly informed by the patient, conducts his own analysis simultaneously. Nevertheless, a relation exists. If the analyst is not genuinely involved, he can understand a number of things about the patient, but I doubt that he can really help him. I am among those who think that contributing to the advancement of the science is not enough, and I do not think that the desire to help the patient takes anything away from the "purity" of analysis. Even though "the cure comes as a bonus", as Freud said, it remains an essential objective. I would consider it dishonest vis-à-vis the patient not to consider it important. I remember the comment of a colleague who said that the analyst must never be exactly where he is expected. I, on the contrary, do everything I can to make sure the patient finds me where he expects me. We were probably speaking of slightly different things, for I agree that showing that there are other answers than the ones the analysand expects is enriching and can offer him new possibilities. But it is best to be present when the patient wants to connect with us.

I feel that the concept of analysis has evolved over time. In the past, it was essentially *one-person psychology*, where the analyst listened, observed the patient and tried to understand him based on analytic theory, so as to convey this understanding to the patient through correct and clearly formulated interpretations — even brilliant whenever possible. I believe that the term "psychoanalysis" itself was engendered by this rather scientific attitude.

Gradually, and especially thanks to Ferenczi, analysis became *two-person psychology*, where a relation with the patient had to be established, and everything else: transference, counter-transference, interpretations, attitudes, possible errors, silences or words, were part of this relation. The relation is one in which the two protagonists are, and know they are, involved and working with this mutual involvement just as much, if not more, than with theoretical knowledge. I think that in analytic practice theory is only useful if it is completely internalised and functions almost as a reflex — a reflex like that of a driver who is not consciously thinking of the rules of the road, but obeys them automatically.

I know that I could not work in any other way. Of course, at times I find myself adopting the scientific attitude of the observer, particularly when I reflect afterwards on what occurred in an analysis, or when I want to explain it to someone else. But at other times I can be deeply involved through counter-transference, partly conscious and partly unconscious, which also helps me, most often after the session, to understand certain things by interpreting what I feel, in relation to the patient's problem. But if I have no feelings towards the patient, if I maintain the indifference recommended — but perhaps not practiced — by Freud, I can't hear or understand anything. The translation error which introduced the term "neutrality" instead of "indifference" — the term used by Freud — , seems to me to have been fortunate in some respects: neutrality refers to discretion, not to non-involvement in the patient's life, and not to an absence of affect.

I also need to establish a friendly and reassuring atmosphere, because it is in this atmosphere that I understand best the messages addressed to me. I know that this atmosphere makes it harder for the patient to express hostile and negative feelings. Therefore, I am particularly attentive to these negative messages, often coded, because I know that it is not easy to express them in the atmosphere that I create. In addition, I need a balanced atmosphere, not authoritative, which compensates to some degree the effects of the friendly atmosphere. I don't hesitate to use humour and to offer interpretations in the form of funny stories. This makes it possible to be more confrontational, without endangering the underlying smoothness of the relation. Some of my colleagues need more distance, a certain authority, or perhaps a certain prestige. I would not say that they are wrong. To work well, one must create an atmosphere in which it is possible to be oneself.

CREATING THE RIGHT ATMOSPHERE

Organising an analytic practice, the setting, the rules, the payments, the absences of the analysand or the analyst — all these can contribute to establishing the kind of atmosphere in which one works best. The setting can vary greatly: Freud analysed Max Eitington while they walked together through the streets of Vienna; and he analysed Katharina while she sat on the grass on a mountainside. Ferenczi analysed his superior in the army on horseback. But the *traditional setting* is clearly defined: couch or chair. Thus, the setting and the atmosphere are both variable. Of course, the atmosphere created does not depend solely on one's own needs; each patient contributes to it in his own way. But even in this respect attitudes differ. Some analysts only take patients who will adapt to the atmosphere they have created, while others are willing to make changes, whenever possible, to adapt to the needs of each patient. The roots of these two attitudes are to be found in the early history of psychoanalysis: for some, the idea is to select patients considered "suitable for analysis", using traditional or orthodox analytic techniques; for others, like Ferenczi, the idea is to invent each time the techniques that make it possible to help a particular patient.

What factors contribute to creating the atmosphere in which the analysis will be conducted? The setting: some analysts try to make their offices as neutral-looking as possible. They avoid anything that may reveal their tastes or personality. Others want to work in a place where they feel well, and they fill the room with the objects they like to see around them. You will not be surprised to learn that I am part of the second category. Moreover, I am convinced that bareness and neutrality reveal the analyst's personality just as much as an office full of personal objects. But I do not place photographs of my children or husband in my office; I feel this would be a lack of discretion.

Some analysts soundproof their offices as much as possible. Others explain in passing the sounds that might be heard during the session. In fact, it is surprising how deaf an analysand can be to external noise when he is immersed in his thoughts. For instance, one day, in the middle of a session, my analyst stood up suddenly to silence a group of children making noise in the waiting room. I had not heard them at all.

At the start of an analysis, some analysts specify the rules they want respected: so many sessions a week, on such and such days and at such and such a time, for such and such a fee, payable in such and such form; this is what we will do if sessions are missed, and this is the procedure for vacations. Other analysts come to an agreement with the patient regarding the days and times of the sessions, and the fee. Some analysts demand that patients take their vacations at the same time they do. There are even analysts — as I was surprised to learn — who require payments during vacations, including their own.

In this regard, I find it difficult to say what category I am in, because my method varies somewhat depending on my perception of the personality of each patient. With some, I may choose to be very flexible, while I am very strict with others. This could be the effect of experience. I ask patients to pay for missed sessions that were not cancelled, or not cancelled early enough (a week or a few days, depending on the analysand's occupation). At the same time, I consider that a paid session is owed to the analysand. I must be at my office, available and ready to see him, if at the last minute he

CHAPTER 1: MY ENCOUNTERS WITH PSYCHOANALYSIS

finds that he can keep the appointment after all.

I have no rigid principles concerning the method of payment. Some patients pay by cheque, others in cash. I go along with the method they choose, until the question of the patient's relation to money arises. At that time, I may ask that the patient change his method of payment. Often, I decline payment for the first session, which I consider an initial introduction. But if a person goes to the heart of the matter at once and is deeply involved as early as the first session, I may choose to ask that this session be paid, if only to acknowledge the importance of what occurred. In addition to analysing the patient's subjective relation to money, I feel it is useful, in some instances, to underline its real and concrete dimension: it is my income, and the patient is not paying merely to analyse what a financial transaction means to him. It would be hypocritical to say that. I ask him to pay me a reasonable sum because I need to earn a living. I don't believe it would be a good thing to ignore such an important factor — and so foreseeable — as my countertransference and the simple reality of the situation.

I try to establish fees based on what I perceive the financial means of the patient to be, but within a range suitable to me. This is not always easy, and I have made mistakes, sometimes with surprising results. For instance, one day Françoise Dolto sent me two patients; one had comfortable means, and it was important not to ask for less than she had paid Françoise Dolto. The other patient had more limited means, to which I had to adapt my fees. But I confused them with each other. The analysis of the one I charged too little soon came to an end. The other woman didn't say anything, found a second job, paid the fees that were too high without flinching, and benefitted greatly from her analysis. I did not draw a definite conclusion from this, but I never forgot the incident. Neither did I forget the Tunisian student who left because I had taken into account his modest means and asked for a fee that was too low — something he found demeaning for himself, for me and for our work.

Another question arises at the start of an analysis: couch or chair? Most often, the deciding factor is the patient's pathology. But practical factors can also influence the decision. I have never conducted analysis on the couch once a week. I feel that one cannot let the patient access a very emotionally laden problem and then leave him alone with it for a week. But I have often conducted analyses on the couch two times a week if circumstances required it.

Some therapies require major adjustments, like the analysis of a person I saw for three years four times a week, who was transferred to a foreign country before the end of our work together. We continued to the end of the analysis by means of a weekly letter he wrote me always on the same day, at the same time, that I read at exact times, when he could also reach me by telephone. Then the person started coming to Paris one Saturday a month, and we had two sessions that day. Another analysis, carried out on the couch for a long time, was completed by Internet. I could also mention the instant analysis conducted by means of my address and my housekeeper[4], who is particularly brilliant, or the analysis made possible by an umbrella[5].

LENGTH OF THE SESSIONS

The length of the sessions is as controversial a subject as the number of weekly sessions. This duration must be constant for some patients, and variable for others, depending on their content. At first, the established length was 60 minutes, then it became 50 minutes, and finally 45 minutes in most cases. I also have colleagues who have 30-minute sessions.

---

4   A man who was walking on Place Dauphine learned from the restaurant owner at number 24, or from the concierge, that there was an analyst in that house. He came up and rang my bell. I was not there and it was the housekeeper who opened the door. She told him that he had to make an appointment, gave him my phone number and told him what my office hours were. But the man lingered and started to tell her his problems. Then he left. He came back a few days later, when he knew I would not be there. "I forgot to tell you two or three important things", he told my housekeeper. And he had a second session on the landing, while she listened, with kindness and patience. Then he left, saying he felt much better, and that perhaps he did not need to make an appointment with Dr. Dupont...

5   A lady came to see me about her little girl. I gave them an appointment, but she came alone. We spoke for a good while before she left, forgetting her umbrella. She did not call me back and I put the umbrella away without thinking any more about it. About four or five months later, she called me to say that she had been thinking all this time, had understood a lot of things, and wanted to come and take back her umbrella. We made an appointment, she came and she took her umbrella, saying: "As I told you, I have been thinking and I think I understand everything. I have never been able to use this umbrella, which is much too hard to open. But now, I understand. Look! With a triumphant air she opened her umbrella in my office, closed it again, gave me a big smile and left. I never saw her again.

Personally, I could not work with sessions that are too short or variable. I don't feel comfortable with this arrangement, and I would not do it as a matter of principle. For the analyst to decide to interrupt the session, even for very specific reasons, seems to me to be a rather brutal action. I think it is important for an analysand to know how much time he has, to speak or to keep silent, and it may also be important that the analyst and the patient be able to withstand silences, repetitions, even boredom and time experienced as wasted. I believe this mutual tolerance is essential for developing a relationship. But I have friends and colleagues who conduct variable-length sessions, with excellent results for the patients. So I cannot object to this method in general, but can say only that it does not suit me personally.

ANALYTIC TREATMENT

All the elements discussed so far are variable and can be seen from different perspectives. This is especially true for the treatment itself. What happens between an analyst and an analysand is always unique. For a certain patient, working with a different analyst would be completely different; for the analyst, everything is different with each patient.

What is probably constant for each analyst is his way of listening: the things he hears, the things to which he pays particular attention, the things he knows how to use, and the things he simply doesn't hear — his blind spots. When a patient says that I did not understand him, I am always ready to believe him.

But there are also analysands who do not want to be understood at some point in their analysis. Some speak too softly to be heard. If this is pointed out once, or twice at the most, and nothing changes, it means this is what the patient needs to do just then. I am thinking, for example, of a woman whose very possessive mother always wanted to know everything she did and thought. This woman sometimes needed to speak without being heard.

According to the traditional method, the analyst proceeds by making interpretations. I noticed that the more time passed, the less I did this. Most of the time, my interpretations are reformulations, from a different perspective, of the patient's own interpretations. Sometimes I point out the consequences of his discovery. On occasion, I draw a parallel with the situation he describes by using an amusing story. Some interpretations are not accepted, or not heard, because they are not accurate, or are given too early. In the second case, the patient will likely find it himself a little later.

Sometimes, a problem arises: a patient brings us a gift. Should we accept it or not? I feel that a refusal, even when it is explained, is very harsh, almost insulting. So I usually accept, saying that from now on this object is part of what we share, and I place it on a shelf in my office, where it **is** very visible, so that we can talk about it from time to time. The meaning of a gift is not always obvious; it's necessary to be able to talk about it to clarify what it means. I have also refused gifts, especially from a patient who brought them repeatedly, choosing things of a more and more personal nature. I asked him to keep them for the moment and to think about what they mean to him, saying that we will decide later what we should do with them.

KEY MOMENTS

In an analysis, there are sometimes decisive turning points. But not always. Sometimes patients complain that they feel they are not making progress. I ask them if everything is the same as it was at the start of the analysis. Usually, they realise that things have changed. I myself would say that in analysis, most of the time, there is no progress. But suddenly one realises that one is **elsewhere.** Sometimes, the change manifests itself in some way: in the person's appearance, clothing or hairstyle. I remember a man who exclaimed one day, when he came into the office, after years of analysis: "This room is full of colour! It always seemed dull to me until now".

THE END OF ANALYSIS

In most cases, the idea of putting an end to the analysis occurs to me and to the patient about the same time. I usually wait for the patient to talk about it, and then I say that I agree, and that we can start to think about it. Of course, in some cases things happen differently; analyses can be interrupted for all kinds of reasons. Sometimes the patient is running away from a difficulty. I may respond by saying that I would not have stopped the analysis just then, or that this is perhaps the end of a stage, but not necessarily of the analysis. But I want to add that the patient has to decide, and that it is good to recognise and accept this, and to tell him what one thinks of his decision. This allowed some patients to come back and continue the analysis when they were ready to do so.

In this respect too, there are different approaches. Some analysts feel that when an analysis ends, well or not so well, the relationship is over and they must not see the patient again for any reason. They think it is important to separate, and to survive a separation. This argument makes sense. But I prefer to do things differently. I believe that the ability to withstand separation should be a result of analysis, not something imposed on the patient. Most of my patients do not return after the end of their analysis. But some do, and can work on what was left undone, or what has arisen since due to intervening events in their lives. Some patients send me cards with holiday greetings for several years. Is this unacceptable? I don't know, but I don't want to stop them from doing it.

Some analysts don't want to hear it when a patient says he wants to stop. They simply refuse to pay attention to this. They set the next appointment as if the desire to stop was only something to analyse in a future session, rather than a concrete objective. This may indeed be the case when the desire to stop is expressed suddenly, in the middle of the session. But the situation is different when the patient speaks of this, or repeats it, while he is standing, at the end of the session, when he is about to leave. Ignoring it in those circumstances is often seen by the patient as intolerable disregard.

CONCLUSION

The subject of psychoanalytic practice can be discussed endlessly given the diversity of the situations analysts encounter, and the different styles they adopt. Everything I just talked about could be seen as small talk, and there is some truth to this. But at the same time, it is the content of our daily practice, and I feel it could be useful to discuss it elsewhere than in supervisions or between colleagues. In summary, what I can say is that while one analyses with one's head, one treats the patient with everything one is. And it requires everything one is to gain access to the material that requires analysis.

Our theoretical models describe phenomena and mechanisms, but none of them can be applied without adjustments. When the patient and the theory diverge, the patient is the one who is right. This is also what makes it difficult to translate the language of a theory into the language of another theory. For instance, how would Freud, Lacan, Winnicott, Ferenczi, Balint or Maria Torok talk about what Melanie Klein called the "paranoid-schizoid position"? It would be an interesting exercise to try to answer this question.

Theories are elaborated based on clinical work. But theoretical formulations are rarely very useful in clinical work. The most important advice I could give is what Jean-Claude Lavie recommended: never to imitate anyone, not even the most competent and respectable experts, but to do only what one feels is right, the things whose consequences one thinks — or hopes — that **one** can deal with. As popular wisdom says, one can always handle one's own errors better than those of others. There is no problem with admitting to a patient that one was wrong, misunderstood, or took a wrong turn. On the contrary: the patient will trust us that much more, with good reason, as illustrated by the following incident.

One day, a patient told me at the end of the session that he forgot to bring the money to pay me. This had never happened before to this very orderly and disciplined man. I told him it was not a problem, and that he could pay the next time. But the next time, he forgot to come! He called me that evening, very embarrassed. During the following sessions, I had to admit that I had been wrong to tell him that it didn't matter that he forgot the money. I had not heard the message, and had forced him to repeat it by forgetting the next appointment. After this, we were able to embark upon a new stage of our work; this patient, always so courteous, thoughtful and accommodating, became aware of a side of himself which he had been careful not to know until then.

Everything I described here makes me think that the attempts of psychoanalytic regulatory organisations in our various countries to control the competence of psychoanalysts are in vain. This could be unfortunate, but how can we objectively assess factors as subjective as those involved in psychoanalytic practice? I don't know what would be more harmful: establishing arbitrary criteria that could deprive the profession of creative, original minds, or letting patients decide if what they are doing with a particular analyst suits them or not. We know that sometimes patients are helped by any method, while at other times analyses conducted by renowned analysts end in disaster. Freud did not do so badly with his analysis — if it was one — with such a mediocre and unwittingly "analyst" as Fliess, while Ferenczi's therapy with the inventor of psychoanalysis left him helpless in the face of the tremendous task of overcoming emotional disappointments and surviving.

Of course, I am not saying that anyone can do anything, and that this would be psychoanalysis. But I think that it is difficult and dangerous to define set rules for such a diversified practice. Psychoanalysis remains the best guarantee — albeit imperfect — for quality of the psychoanalyst.

In my view, the relationship making psychoanalysis possible relies on the greatest honesty and trustworthiness of which one is capable. I know that many of my colleagues, and some of the best among them, see things differently. We shall continue to exchange ideas...

TRANSLATION

I have always enjoyed translating. When a particular situation, immigration to be specific, creates the opportunity to speak several languages — or indeed forces one to speak them — the act of translating is an attempt to build a bridge: between two languages, two periods in one's life, two parents, two groups of people whose relations might be hostile, two different mental and emotional levels (because different languages express things on different levels).

Emigration always involves losses, especially the loss of a language; but the age at which one leaves a country also matters. And leaving alone, as a family or as a couple are different situations. In my case, I left Hungary in early adolescence, with the linguistic competence of a person that age.

When one changes languages in early adolescence, a rift is created between the language of childhood emotions and activities, and the language of culture. I think that there is an intermediary area where they overlap. If one longs for one's native country, this zone is more extensive; but if the departure was forced, as it would be by persecution for instance, this area of overlap is smaller.

An adult can learn a language perfectly and can come to speak it without an accent; but his manner of expressing certain basic emotions, positive or negative, will be associated with his mother tongue, because these emotions were experienced first in the context of that language.

For some people who emigrated at a very young age, their native language acts like a ghost or a phantom. A young European woman raised in Africa where her father was working, who was cared for by an African nursemaid until the age of two, was recounting a childhood memory. Suddenly, to her great surprise, she pronounced a series of syllables whose meaning she did not know. She asked her parents what these words meant, and they translated the lines of a nursery rhyme her nursemaid used to sing her, in her language.

There is also the story of a scientist of Hungarian origin, who had been living in an English-speaking country for decades and had apparently forgotten his mother-tongue, who was giving a lecture at a university. Suddenly, panic-stricken and covered in cold sweat, he said to himself: "I am speaking to them in Hungarian; they will think I am mad!" Then he realised that in fact this was not so and that he had been speaking in English, the only language he knew well.

This linguistic ghost can also take other forms: a Hungarian philosopher learned perfectly the language of the country where he immigrated, and spoke it without an accent. At a certain point, he undertook psychoanalysis in Hungarian, with a Hungarian analyst. After concluding his analysis, he still spoke the language of his new country perfectly... but with a Hungarian accent, which he had not had previously. People who, in their adulthood, do not know any language other than their mother tongue, often staunchly refuse to acquire even the most rudimentary elements of another language, because they are prisoners of the link between the word and the thing or notion it represents in their own language. Although they understand the culturally enriching effect of a diversity of languages, anything that disturbs this well-established link for them personally is too threatening. This notion is illustrated by the Frenchman who tells his friend: "These English people are crazy. Instead of saying "*pain*", they say "bread". His friend explains patiently that English is a different language, with a different word for the French word "*pain*": the word "bread". "Of course," his friend says, "I understand. But still, it's "*pain*" after all, isn't it?"

There is also the story of the Hungarian man who immigrated to Paris and was living in the Latin Quarter, but refused to learn a single word of French. He would go into a café and give his order in Hungarian. Of course, the waiter didn't understand. So the man would start to shout and insult him, still in Hungarian. The amazing thing is that he usually succeeded in obtaining what he wanted.

The activity of translation is a way to manage this complexity of feelings, attachments, rejection and confusion. The double perspective concerning an idea, the double style and the double rhythm help to heal the internal rift.

Translating Ferenczi's texts added another element to the work of translation: Ferenczi wrote mostly in German. His letters to Freud and most of his articles were written in German, because they were intended for a multilingual audience, and Hungarian is not an international language. For this reason, most cultured Hungarians spoke other languages. Ferenczi's texts, private as well as public, include words and phrases in English, French, Spanish and Latin.

Still, he was brought up in a small town in Hungary, went to a Hungarian school and was surrounded by a Hungarian population. In his letters to Freud, he often quotes Hungarian poems and proverbs. He also uses images and turns of phrase taken directly from the Hungarian language. Many times, our team of translators would translate a German expression used by Ferenczi into Hungarian, in order to reveal all its facets, before finding a French equivalent we found adequate.

Ferenczi travelled a great deal, but did not emigrate. He was very attached to his country, and to the Hungarian culture and language. This is why, when translating his German texts, we also needed to be in contact with his mother tongue, Hungarian. I took great pleasure in this back-and-forth between languages, carried out with different members of the translation team, people of different origins who took part in this project for many years.

FIFTY YEARS LATER

When I was invited to recount what I remember about my own analysis, the first thing I thought of was the masterful account of her analysis given by Marie Cardinal in *The Words to Say It*. How was she able to take the reader on this intimate voyage, and transmit something of this unusual experience to people who have had no experience of this kind?

I myself lived through this experience; my psychoanalysis lasted four years. It was an intense experience which left very few memories: a few images, some subjects that must have been discussed, which I don't remember. It is difficult to speak of such an intimate experience without being indiscreet, and especially for someone like me who does not easily reveal strong emotions.

What I recall about my analysis are a few clear images, some of the subjects discussed, and the certainty of having discussed others which left no vivid impression. Interestingly, the three things I remember clearly are the initial contact, the first session and the session in which we agreed on the date when the analysis would end. The temporal limits of the analysis, one might say.

I undertook the analysis in order to learn the profession of analyst, a profession practiced by several members of my family, the parents of my best friend and many family friends. What I knew so far were certain things connected with this practice: that patients should arrive and leave without crossing anyone's path, that no one should make noise while there are patients in the office, and above all, that no one should interrupt the sessions.

When I was applying to be a candidate for training, I saw several experienced analysts. I chose to work with Daniel Lagache. Nine months after my first session with him, my first child was born. Now, so many years later, I can explain this "miracle" — which was not really one. But I don't remember if the explanation was found during the analysis or later. In any case, after this initial effect was produced, we soon had a second child.

There was much to do and I did my best to keep up. Fortunately, after an unproblematic second pregnancy, a little boy was born without difficulty.

As far as the analysis was concerned, the initial problem was finding the money to pay for it. The money I earned at the science museum and in my husband's printing shop provided the necessary means, and I could start my analysis.

All I remember about the first session was that I was invited to lie on the couch and say anything that came into my mind. Being a trusting and rather disciplined person, I did as I was told. I remember saying as I left: "It's a funny feeling".

About four years later, after two brief interruptions for the birth of each of the children, I brought up the idea of ending the analysis. I still remember the surprising explanation I gave for my desire to stop: "I have had enough of being grateful…" I probably wanted to say something like: "I don't want to be given support anymore, I want to stand on my own two feet". Or perhaps something else, but something related to freedom. Not freedom of thought, which no one had ever asked me to give up and which came naturally to me, but the freedom to organise my own life. Lagache suggested that we take three months to think about ending the analysis, and I accepted. I have no memory of the last session.

I must say that I am somewhat surprised by the light tone with which I speak of an experience that was certainly not light. Perhaps, as I said earlier, this is a defence against strong emotions which might overwhelm me. I no doubt learned this from my father, who was profoundly embarrassed by open displays of emotion. He was a passionate man who strove with all his might to keep strong emotions under control. However, this did not apply to problems affecting his health. His doctors had a hard time dealing with him. My rare emotional outbursts embarrassed him so much that I always attempted to avoid them. It is when I try to speak of something as charged with emotion as my analysis that I realise how strong this prohibition became.

My four years of analysis bear the imprint of the setting in which we worked. I would arrive before the building of my analyst, on Saint-Germain Boulevard; next to it, there was an elegant boutique of man's clothing, whose window I always examined with envy. I hoped to have enough money one day to buy a beautiful pullover for my husband. I believe my wish came true, but it's possible that I am only imagining it.

Upstairs, perhaps on the second floor, I would come into the waiting room: a large Louis XV or XVI room (I know nothing about furniture styles) with two armchairs near the door, on each side of a low table on which there were two bronze lizards I found very attractive. The wait was short: Lagache respected the hour of the appointments and his analysands' time.

The office was longitudinal. I don't remember what decorated the walls when I started my analysis, but after a few months — or years? — three large paintings of cities appeared. They could have been ancient Italian cities. But my inattentive eye saw in them — knowing it was not so — views of Budapest. I imagine that I needed to link my present life in Paris with my past life in Budapest, the world of analysis in Hungary with analysis in France. These paintings were helping me to heal the rift between my two lives.

Sometimes I was eager to go to my sessions, and other times I really had no desire to go, like most analysands, no doubt. But I had been taught to keep my engagements, and I almost never missed a session. My analyst made me pay for unjustified absences, but not those for which there was a reason. It was up to me to decide what the case was. To illustrate, I did not pay when I had influenza, but I paid when I missed a session to go to a concert in Royaumont. My decisions were never brought into question, and did not elicit any comments.

I remember certain incidents: my analyst getting up suddenly, saying: "This noise is becoming unbearable!" while I was immersed in my thoughts. Only when he did this did I realise that children were making noise in the waiting room. I had not heard them. Another thing I remember is that one day he commented on what I was saying by singing Cherubino's aria from *The Marriage of Figaro*. I also remember a dream about a crowded tramway, interpreted by Lagache as a desire to have many children. Another time, I explained something at length and my analyst indicated that he hadn't understood anything. Strangely, I felt very well and very relaxed when this happened, and I said so. He was somewhat surprised. As for me, I concluded that it is not essential for the analyst to understand, as long as the patient understands. I have since shared this observation with my patients. There was another time when I may have surprised my analyst; it was when I told him that thanks to my husband I had made considerable progress: I was now able to be late without being completely panicked, as I used to be. He gave me a puzzled look and asked if I truly consider this progress. I answered that in my case, it certainly was.

These images come to my mind, unaltered by time. I also remember many subjects we discussed, but could not say exactly when.

I know that I often cried during my analysis. But I don't remember for what reason. I suppose that I cried when I could not lift the prohibition I mentioned earlier. I imagine that my analysis must have been characterised by understatements: de-dramatisation through choice of words. But my analyst's hearing was finely tuned. The same phenomenon is no doubt reproduced in my writing. I have to hope that my readers will be as perspicacious as my analyst.

One of the more urgent questions to deal with in my analysis was what Judaism meant to me. What meaning could it have for someone who did not know the traditions, had no religious faith, and was officially Protestant? At the same time, this very small aspect of my identity had served to kill people legally. Something was wrong here. I was guilty of something without knowing it and, in addition, I was guilty of giving consideration to this absurd guilt. The troubling thing was that sometimes people one would not expect, close friends, came out with anti-Jewish expressions unwittingly, not intending any harm. In this respect, I did not even trust my analyst completely, although I had never heard him say anything the least bit suspect. After working on this question for a long time — I don't remember exactly how —, I felt much better. I saw the Jewish problem as being that of anti-Semites, not of Jews, although the former could create serious problems for Jews. I came to understand the mechanisms of this absurdity more clearly, although the absurdity remained unchanged. And one day I told my analyst that I had come to the reassuring conclusion that he could not be anti-Semitic because it would be antithetical to psychoanalysis. This question never troubled me again, so the conclusion I reached must have suited me. Of course, what worked for me might not work for another person.

My analyst and I also spent considerable time talking about my mother's repeated absences, since from the time I was 9 months old she would go to Paris for at least three months every year. For me, this was an eternity. Abandonment is certainly my "basic fault", in the Balintian sense. It's true that my father and I kept my mother very busy when she was there: between the ages of 6 and 11, I was constantly sick with a kidney infection for which there was no cure at the time; my father was also always sick because he smoked too much and had a stomach ulcer. Was this the cause **or** the consequence of my mother's absences? Or was it a little of both? The fear of abandonment has left traces that are still there today, to a lesser degree. I am no longer looking out the window in tears when I wait for someone I love to arrive; I am just a little uneasy.

I know that in analysis we spent much time discussing my parents, and my family in general. The members of this family were not only close, they clung to each other, no doubt as a result of unexpected early separations. This clinging creates complications, despite the warmth and security it provides to each person in the family. But behind this warmth and feeling of protection, one could still sense the tragic past of this family, which was overcome thanks to the courage — for which she paid dearly — of my grandmother Vilma Kovács, and the talent of her analyst, Sándor Ferenczi. This sorely tried and solidly united family was torn apart again by external events, after the annexation of Austria by Germany. Several people lost their lives as a result: Alice Balint, who died of a ruptured aneurysm in 1939, and Vilma Kovács, who died the following the year because a bladder operation had been postponed too long. Her husband died four years later. I missed my grandparents so much that I sometimes thought I saw them on the street, on their way to our home. These losses were certainly discussed in the analysis.

We no doubt talked about immigration. The disappearance of the setting of my early life, the loss of my friends and of my beloved cousin who went to England with his parents, the need to build another life — all this must have taken up a large part of the analysis, but I don't remember it.

I know I talked a great deal about my relationship with my husband who, in a way, recreated my lost family security. It was crucial for me to repair all rifts that might occur between us. The analyst was very supportive of my efforts to do this.

The external events that occurred during my analysis also held an important place. The Algerian War of Independence was being fought. My husband and I couldn't bear to see people treated with contempt and persecuted because of their origin, as I had been, and we were strongly against colonisation. This caused me to find myself in treacherous situations at times; but I hesitated to talk about this to my analyst, because other people were involved. Then I decided (with good reason) that I could trust him completely. My parents were involved as well, and I think that despite the risk it was very satisfying to fight, to the best of my ability, an injustice against which we had been helpless when it was carried out against us.

The other external event to which I could not remain indifferent was the Hungarian Uprising of 1956. General indignation sparked by the actions of the political police and by the intervention of the Soviet army did not prevent those who had fled fascist Hungary from seeing some fascist undertones in the attitudes of some of the brave revolutionaries, despite their courage, the beauty of their objectives of freedom, and the unjust and cruel treatment to which they were subjected afterwards. But it was difficult not to be able to stand entirely in solidarity with our friends whose views we saw as almost completely right. Some of them held my reservations against me, and I regretted it. My ambiguous, ambivalent feelings towards my native country took up many sessions in the analysis, and probably reflected a deeper ambivalence between the desire to remain a little longer in the safety of the family cocoon, and my desire for independence.

As far as the benefits I drew from my analysis, I *feel* them more than I *know* them. Any attempt to put them into words would be inadequate. My impression has always been that in an analysis one does not "progress", or change very much, but after a while one is "in a different place" and sees things differently. One has a different perspective. Any attempt to describe this sort of shift in someone's external as well as internal experience would lead to oversimplification and would distort what is essential. What I have recounted here is what is left after memory has done its work of sorting. Each person has his own way of appeasing his soul, especially if he needs this serenity. Memory and forgetting are the means by which this is done. I think this takes place even for an analysand who becomes an analyst.

Therefore, this story will have no conclusion, since psychoanalysis does not produce one. But it has an end... they say. I myself am tempted to think that once an analysis is started, it continues throughout life, whether it becomes the person's occupation or not. My own analysis was very enriching. But attempting to describe all the ways in which I benefitted from it would take us too far into the most intimate of worlds...

CHAPTER 2
ABOUT FERENCZI

FERENCZI'S PERSPECTIVE

In an article published in Issue No. 6 of the journal *Psychanalyse*, entitled "*Ferenczi: faux problème ou vrai malentendu*" (Ferenczi: False Problem or True Misunderstanding), Wladimir Granoff observed that "if Freud invented psychoanalysis, it was Ferenczi who put it into practice". Indeed, we can say that Ferenczi introduced an essential element in psychoanalysis, an element which did not interest Freud the theoretician, or in any case, was not a priority for him. What this is, is a turn of mind, an attitude, a type of relation, a mode of listening — all of which have theoretical underpinnings: object relations, counter-transference, regression..., but are not defined by theory. The affiliation can be followed in a direct line from Ferenczi to Balint, and then in different directions towards Donald W. Winnicott, Leonard Shengold, Nicolas Abraham, Maria Torok and many others. My intention here is to describe the evolution of this specifically Ferenczian element.

Ferenczi met Freud in February 1908. He had read The Interpretation of Dreams in 1900 and had been asked to write a review of it. But he found the book too disconcerting at the time, so he never actually wrote the review. Yet his numerous texts written before 1900, and in the period before he met Freud, testify to a real interest on the part of Ferenczi, a neurologist at the time, in the psychoanalytic ideas of Sigmund Freud[1].

Before contacting Freud directly, he had met Jung in Switzerland, in Burghölzli's clinic, in 1907[2]. Then, in February 1908, Ferenczi wrote to Freud, went to visit him, and the affinity between the two men was obvious at once, both personally and on the level of ideas. That same year, Ferenczi published the first articles in which he explicitly proclaimed his affiliation with psychoanalysis. He accompanied the Freud family on their vacation, and attended the 1908 Psychoanalytic Congress in Salzburg, where he presented a paper entitled "Psychoanalysis and Education".

---

1 See Claude Lorin, *Le Jeune Ferenczi : Premiers écrits* 1899-1906 (The Young Ferenczi : First Writings, 1899-1906), Paris, Aubier-Montaigne, 1983.

2 After this visit, they exchanged a few letters; three of Jung's letters to Ferenczi were published in Le Coq-Héron, No. 123.

The relationship between the two men and the development of Ferenczi's ideas are closely connected and evolve simultaneously. Ferenczi, who offered ample proof of the autonomy of his ideas in his pre-analytic texts, now becomes an enthusiastic advocate of Freudian theory. But he adds his personal touch, and he never loses sight of his own objectives. Indeed, Ferenczi is first and foremost a physician who wants to heal his patients, while Feud is above all a theoretician, a researcher who wants to understand[3].

In 1909, Freud asked Ferenczi to accompany him and Jung to America, where Freud was to give a series of lectures at Clark University. This trip would be followed by many others the two of them took together, including a memorable voyage in 1910 to Palermo, in Sicily, where they had their first serious disagreement, which had grave consequences for their relationship and greatly influenced Ferenczi's future work.

Thus, between 1908 and 1911, some of Ferenczi's first articles were dedicated to promoting Freud's theories; to mention just a few: "Actual and Psycho-neuroses in the Light of Freud's Investigations and Psycho-analysis" and "The Analytic Interpretation and Treatment of Psychosexual Impotence" in 1908; "Psychoneuroses" in 1909; "The Psychological Analysis of Dreams" in 1910; and "The Psychoanalysis of Wit and the Comical" in 1911. But there are also articles in which Ferenczi presents altogether original ideas.

The first article marking a new stage in his thinking and in psychoanalytic theory (which has not yet yielded all its consequences) is "Introjection and Transference", written in 1909. In this article, Ferenczi defines transference by saying that unconscious phantasies connect persons and events of the subject's present reality with long forgotten psychical experiences, causing the affective energy of unconscious ideational complexes to be displaced onto present ideas, and exaggerating their affective intensity[4]. Thus, Ferenczi does not attribute everything that occurs in analysis to the past; from the start, he inscribes the analytic process in the current relation with the analyst, thereby implicitly rejecting the definition of the analyst as being

---

3   In analytic circles, Ferenczi was referred to as «Doctor», while Freud was called «Professor», so there would be no confusion in anyone's mind.

4   Ferenczi, S. (1916), «Introjection and Transference», in *Contributions to Psychoanalysis*, Jones, E. (trans.), Boston: Richard G. Badger, pp. 30-80.

simply a reflecting mirror. This perspective has considerable consequences: it implies the participation of two people in the analytic situation — the analyst and the patient — , and no longer one person alone, namely the patient, observed by an emotionally "neutral" analyst.

Then Ferenczi introduces the notion of introjection: "The neurotic is constantly seeking for objects [...] whom he can... draw into his circle of interest, i.e., introject[5]."

Subsequently, it became clear that these two mechanisms, transference and introjection, are not the prerogative of neurotics only. In fact, would it not be possible to say that a certain degree of neurosis is not an illness, but rather the normal state of human beings? Ferenczi senses this to be the case when he writes, a little further: "The objection will be raised that extension of the circle of interest [...], and sensitiveness for the stimuli of the outside world, are attributes with which normal persons also [...] are endowed; that one cannot, therefore, designate introjection as the psychical mechanism that is typical and characteristic of [neurotics]. " And he goes on to say that from a psychoanalytic perspective, there are no fundamental differences between normality and neurosis[6].

The notion of introjection was to be taken up later by Nicolas Abraham and Maria Torok, who developed it into a major tool of psychoanalytic theory specifically for understanding the structure of melancholic states.

Even before taking an interest in the psychoanalytic perspective, Ferenczi often wrote and published short clinical observations. He continued to do so throughout his life. The 1912 series includes "Paracelsus to the Physicians": "...And let it be no laughing matter to you, physicians, you know only a small fraction of the power of the will. For the will is a generator of spirits of a kind with which reason has nothing whatever to do." "[A] premonition of the unconscious, which is inaccessible to reason[7]," Ferenczi writes.

That same year, the psychoanalytic community initiated extensive discussions on masturbation, involving almost all of its members. Ferenczi took part in the discussions by writing an article entitled "On Onanism". He still held some of the ideas of his time, which asserted that masturbation

---

    5   ibid.
    6   ibid.
    7   Ferenczi, S., *Final Contributions to the Problems and Methods of Psycho-Analysis*, Karnac, Balint, M. (ed.), 1994, p. 323.

causes psychical and nervous disturbances, but he added that they are much less harmful than the psychoneurotic symptoms caused by rough frightening and repression[8].

In 1913, Ferenczi published a long series of brief observations of a few paragraphs or a few pages each, which were his forte: "Obsessional Etymologizing", "The Kite as a Symbol of Erection", "Childish Ideas of Digestion", "To Whom Does One Relate One's Dreams", etc. But he also published several major articles, which became classic texts of psychoanalytic literature. Two clinical articles are part of this list. In one of them, "Taming of a Wild Horse", he shows how the tamer uses two methods of hypnosis: paternal hypnosis, which is authoritative and employs loud-voiced commands, and maternal hypnosis, induced by affectionate stroking and appealing. The other article, "A Little Chanticleer", tells the story of a little boy who urinated while playing in the hen-house; a roaster had snapped at this penis, or perhaps bitten it. Following this trauma, and after a latent period of one year, the child took on the role of a chicken, crowing and cackling, but terrified of any sort of fowl. Ferenczi's investigations revealed that the child was in the habit of masturbating, had often been punished for this, and even threatened with castration. Ferenczi made use of this case to study the relation between trauma, threats, punishments and the child's Oedipal position between his father and his mother. This situation makes reference to another concept, which Ferenczi was to discuss later: identification with the aggressor.

Freud was very enthusiastic about this story, because it confirmed his theory of the Oedipus complex and the castration complex. He even asked Ferenczi for permission to use the story in his own work. Ferenczi was delighted to be able to provide proof for the two central theories of the master.

In 1913 Ferenczi also published a number of theoretical articles reflecting the original ideas he was developing. These articles included "Belief, Disbelief and Conviction" and "The Ontogenesis of Symbols". The most important and best-known text written in this period was probably "Stages in the Development of the Sense of Reality".

---

8   Ferenczi, S., *First Contributions to Psychoanalysis*, Jones, E. (trans.), Brunner/Mazel, 1980, p. 186.

"STAGES IN THE DEVELOPMENT OF THE SENSE OF REALITY"

In this article, Ferenczi relies on Freudian theory postulating a pleasure principle and a reality principle to describe the different stages leading from functioning based on the pleasure principle, to functioning based on the reality principle.

One passage of this text was to produce considerable consequences. It reads as follows: "[...] there is a stage in human development that realises this ideal of being subservient only to pleasure. [...] I mean the period of human life passed in the womb. In this state the human being lives as a parasite of the mother's body. For the nascent being an "outer world" exists only in a very restricted degree. [...] If, therefore, the human being possesses a mental life when in the womb, although only an unconscious one, — and it would be foolish to believe that the mind begins to function only at the moment of birth — he must get from his existence the impression that he is in fact omnipotent[9]."

This outer world which barely exists for the fetus — but nevertheless exists — brings into question the theory of primary narcissism, which Michael Balint would set aside once and for all, and replace with the idea of primary love. These notions can be seen as ushering in the passage from psychology applying to one person: the patient, to psychology involving two people, that takes into account everything occurring between the patient and the therapist. This two-person psychology postulates that the psychical life of human beings is inscribed from the beginning, from the intra-uterine stage, in a relationship, be it ever so primitive.

But in 1913 Ferenczi had not yet formulated this idea clearly, although it constitutes the foundation of his work. In the article we are discussing, he introduced the idea that the *stage of omnipotence* in the womb is the starting point of the passage from functioning based on the pleasure principle, to functioning based on the reality principle. The second stage occurs after birth, when the child seeks to reconstitute by magic the initial state of omnipotence. This is the period of *magic-hallucinatory omnipotence*. But the conditions necessary to maintain this impression of omnipotence become more and more complex; the simple signals through which the child expresses his needs no longer suffice to bring about their satisfaction "by magic". As a result, the child is impelled to invent specific gestures that will be understood by those around him and will produce the satisfaction he expects. This is the *period of omnipotence through magic gestures*. According to Ferenczi, hysteria is a form of regression to this stage.

Gradually, the child will perceive that in order for his more and more varied and complex desires to be satisfied, more and more varied and complex conditions have to be in place. This is how he comes to differentiate between me and not-me. But before this happens, there is a stage in which all objects are endowed with the qualities of the child's own physical being. This is the *animistic phase*.

After this, the child, whose interest is focused essentially on his primary functions, that is, drinking, eating, urinating, touching his erogenous zones, etc., will perceive in the outer world that which in some way, even very vaguely, resembles his functions. This is how *symbolic relations* come into being.

Now, the distinction between the outer world and the "me" of the child is established. If he is surrounded by loving care, he can maintain, to some extent, the illusion of his omnipotence, by perfecting the signals he used to express his desires. This is when he gradually develops language. Symbolism through gestures is replaced by verbal symbolism.

"[...] conscious thought by means of speech signs is the highest accomplishment of the psychical apparatus, and alone makes adjustment to reality possible...[9]", Ferenczi writes. Even at this stage, the illusion of omnipotence can be maintained in a loving environment. This is the *period of magic thoughts and magic words*. Now, the illusion of omnipotence is mitigated by the awareness that there are greater powers — the people surrounding the child — who must provide their assistance.

The reign of the pleasure principle comes to an end when the child no longer feels psychically dependent on his parents. Ferenczi writes that this is when "the feeling of omnipotence gives way to the full appreciation of the force of circumstances[10]."

As for sexuality, the period of unconditional omnipotence can last as long as there is autoerotic activity.

Ferenczi's 1913 writings end with a series of brief clinical observations, and a short but important article on the ontogenesis of symbols.

---

9   ibid.
10   ibid.

The First World War broke out in 1914. Ferenczi was recruited to work as a military physician. It was also during this period that the three sections of his analysis with Freud were conducted. Ferenczi's writing during those years consisted of numerous clinical notes of varying lengths, some of which announced important future developments; one of these texts, on the psychoanalysis of organic states, refers to the ideas of Georg Groddeck. Another article, based on Ferenczi's experiences as a military doctor is entitled, "Two Types of War Neurosis". Ferenczi treated soldiers who had suffered serious trauma in battle or during bombardments. Afterwards, the question of trauma, its mechanisms and the treatment of its consequences, would become increasingly important in Ferenczi's thought and research.

THE "ACTIVE TECHNIQUE"

During this period, Ferenczi pursued his persistent interest in the technical problems of analytic treatment, and experimented with different techniques throughout his life. The first of these was the so-called "active" technique. In 1919, Ferenczi undertook the first of his major technical experiments, motivated by the difficulties he encountered in some of his analyses with hysterical patients.

Let us remember that Ferenczi was, first and foremost, a physician. He considered that any worthwhile theory must be rooted in clinical practice. Therefore, he never stopped searching for new technical means that would succeed in treating patients who were not helped by classical psychoanalytic technique as defined by Freud. He observed that the hysterics he was treating were able to obtain all sorts of hidden erotic satisfactions during the analysis, and settled into this state so comfortably that the work no longer progressed. Strong transference love for the analyst reinforced this stagnation. Trying to remedy this situation, Ferenczi created a technical procedure intended to reactivate the arrested analytic process.

In the chapter he contributed to Benjamin Wolman's collective work Psychoanalytic Techniques, published by Basic Books in 1967, Michael Balint defines Ferenczi's active technique as follows: "The underlying idea was that in many cases in which the flow of free associations had become stagnant and unproductive; this was caused by the disappearance of libido from the actual analytic work into unconscious fantasies and unconscious bodily gratifications. Naturally, this displacement was provoked by, and represented, a crisis in the transference relationship, and the analytical task thus became that of finding the area into which the libido had been displaced to mobilize it so that it could become available again for productive work. [...] The analyst's active intervention could then take two forms. He could propose that the patient cease to indulge in this particular habit, that is, give up the concealed satisfaction of his repressed wishes; or, on the contrary, he could encourage the patient to enjoy it openly and freely. It was hoped that a successful intervention by the analyst would cause a considerable increase of tension in the patient and that this, in turn, would produce two results: a breakthrough into consciousness of a hitherto repressed instinctual urge or drive, changing an unpleasant symptom into a pleasurable satisfaction, thereby strengthening and extending the rule of the patient's ego; and further, by removing resistances, it would start the patient's dried-up or stagnant associations flowing again."

Ferenczi points out that, in fact, any interpretation made by the analyst is a form of activity as well. So is the state of psychic frustration in which an analysis is generally conducted. The active technique is an extreme form of this type of intervention.

The most important article about the active technique, written in 1925, is entitled "Psychoanalysis of Sexual Habits". Ferenczi starts by examining habits related to primary functions like miction and defecation. Miction, like the evacuation of faeces, can be a source of tension or of pleasure. He demonstrates that the way a person manages these functions is closely linked to character: changes in one can bring about changes in the other. Then Ferenczi goes on to examine the advantages and consequences of sexual abstinence during the analytic process.

At this time, Ferenczi still shared the educative, or rather re-educative, view Freud had of analysis. His own views would progress considerably over time. In his *Clinical Diary*, in 1932, he even reproached Freud with starting education too early in his analyses.

In the article we are discussing, Ferenczi specifies that everything he refers to as "activity" designates "only the patient's actions and behaviour; he alone, therefore, is [...] active, not the analyst[11]." But he realises that this is not altogether the case, and adds: "Nevertheless, [...] in

---

11   Ferenczi, S., *Further Contributions to the Theory and Technique of Psycho-Analysis*, Karnac, 2002, p. 291.

exceptional cases the analyst must employ the familiar educational instruments of friendliness and severity[12]." But he could not yet have the experience psychoanalysts would acquire subsequently; for my part, I would say that activity is present everywhere in psychoanalytic practice, if only due to a pre-established schedule of appointments, the office setting — personalised or neutral — , the payments, the decision to comment or to keep silent. We can also mention the variable-length sessions conducted by some analysts. What Ferenczi tried to do is to view all these situations from the perspective of activity, and to try to determine the elements that justify its use.

One person who played an important role in Ferenczi's personal and professional life was the German physician Georg Groddeck.

GEORG GRODDECK'S INFLUENCE

Ferenczi and Groddeck became acquainted in 1921. When Groddeck met Freud in 1917, the latter was very impressed with this doctor's innovative ideas. Today, Groddeck is considered the precursor or inventor of what we call psychosomatic medicine. Ferenczi was less enthusiastic. Then, little by little, there was a reversal in the opinions of Freud and Ferenczi. Freud realised that Groddeck would never adopt his own conception of psychoanalysis. At some point, Freud must have understood that Groddeck followed his own ideas, which seemed somewhat fanciful to Freud's rigorous mind. From then on, he always spoke of Groddeck in a friendly but ironic tone.

In contrast, Ferenczi became more and more interested in Groddeck's refusal to consider physical and psychical pathologies as distinct phenomena. He adopted Groddeck's conception of medicine that deals with a mind/body unit, which Ferenczi's successor, Michael Balint, later theorised and developed as medicine for the whole person. Indeed, from the beginning Ferenczi sought the means of placing psychoanalytic discoveries in the service of doctors, and particularly general practitioners. The same objective later motivated Balint to create groups of physicians whose members, including a psychoanalyst, discussed their cases from the perspective of their counter-transference and its effects, to better understand the patient and his pathology.

---

12   ibid.

CRITIQUE OF THE ACTIVE TECHNIQUE

Throughout the 1920s, Ferenczi continued to apply his active technique to various types of cases; finally, in 1926, he concluded that in some cases this technique was contraindicated. Then, little by little, he had to admit that this rather authoritative method created a situation in which the analyst became an authority figure in reality, not only in the transference. And this situation was not conducive to the development of the friendly and mutually respectful atmosphere he wanted to create.

Among the many brief clinical observations written during this period, I would like to mention a one-page article called "The Dream of the Clever Baby". The figure of the "wise baby" holds an important place, explicitly or implicitly, in Ferenczi's thinking concerning the considerable aptitude for comprehension and adaptation seen in some children, an aptitude that sometimes allows them to survive in extremely difficult situations, such as having a psychotic mother. In these situations, in order to cope, the child matures prematurely, "like a fruit injured by a bird".

THE CONFLICT WITH OTTO RANK

Ferenczi also worked and was on friendly terms with Otto Rank, an independent thinker like himself, and another of Freud's close collaborators and faithful friends.

In 1924, they published together a work entitled *The Development of Psycho-Analysis*. They both insisted on the fact that theory must always be rooted in clinical practice, not the other way around. They pointed out the danger of trying to fit the patient into the framework of psychoanalytic theory, instead of listening to him; or of attributing to him the difficulties or failures for which the analyst is responsible. Ferenczi and Rank also pointed out the need to find technical means making it possible to reduce the duration of the treatment, so as to make it accessible to a larger number of people. They listed several errors to avoid. The book was given a poor reception by the psychoanalytic community. Ferenczi and Rank were criticised for publishing the book without having consulted the secret committee first. Freud was not happy with the content of the book either; he feared it may constitute a dilution or distortion of psychoanalysis.

Shortly after this book was published, Rank published another book, *The Trauma of Birth*. The psychoanalytic community was thunderstruck. Freud initially found the book to have some merit, but later rejected it. Among English and German analysts, with Ernest Jones and Karl Abraham in the lead, there was outrage. Indeed, for the first time, Rank pointed out the central role of the mother in human development, maintaining that the Oedipus complex is not the source of every neurosis, but that many crucial events and situations occur in the pre-Oedipal period; moreover, Rank claimed that birth itself is a trauma that leaves traces. Freud conceded the existence of this trauma, but saw it as strictly biological. For Rank, the essential point was separation from the mother and from the security she represents. This notion threatened the central position held by the Oedipus complex, a key concept of Freudian theory. Rank tried to convince Freud, to no avail, that he was not questioning the importance of the Oedipus complex, but was only thinking that many things of crucial importance can also occur before this complex comes into play. Prompted by certain of his followers, Freud finally rejected Rank's idea completely, and soon rejected Rank himself. The latter came to be considered as deviant and mentally unstable. Just as Ferenczi would be in his turn. But, as with Ferenczi later, the psychoanalytic community greatly exaggerated the violence of this break, whereas in fact Freud tried to maintain certain ties with Rank whenever possible, and continued to manifest his friendship to Ferenczi despite their disagreements. This is how it came about that Ferenczi and Rank were excluded from the community for several decades, and their writings ignored by most analysts.

At first, Ferenczi tried to defend Rank, but not being able to bear Freud's possible disapproval, he ultimately rejected Rank and his ideas, which were not very different from his own. But from then on it became more and more obvious that Ferenczi was following his own path. He was not any more successful than Rank in having his most innovative and important ideas accepted. One work constituted the exception to this rule: *Thalassa*, which Freud saw as Ferenczi's greatest achievement.

THALASSA

In 1924, Ferenczi wrote *Thalassa. A Theory of Genitality*, subsequently translated into Hungarian under the title *Catastrophes in Sexual Life*. This "bio-analytical" fantasy impressed Freud and became world-famous; I shall not attempt to summarise it here. It draws a parallel between the phylogenetic development of animal — and therefore human — life, and the ontogenetic development of the individual, through a series of "catastrophes" which trigger a process of adaptation each time.

ACCEPTANCE OF UNPLEASANT IDEAS

In 1926, Ferenczi wrote an interesting article entitled "The Problem of Acceptance of Unpleasant Ideas". He had been struck by the contradiction between the sense of reality on the one hand, and the avoidance of displeasure as well as repression on the other. To resolve this contradiction, Ferenczi made use of one of Freud's latest discoveries, the phenomenon of negation, which he considered a transition stage between denial and acceptance of reality. Repression and negative hallucination make it possible to ignore unpleasant aspects of reality. Negation brings them into consciousness, but in reverse. According to Ferenczi, recognition of unpleasant things is the result of a double negation: the denial of unpleasantness, and the denial of this denial.

In analysis, the support provided by transference love allows the patient to recognise displeasure. And later, satisfactions in his real life allow him to give up the transference. Ferenczi thought that the so-called liquidation of transference corresponds to identification with the analyst. I prefer to say that it corresponds to identification with the human in the analyst. In other words, the patient stops overestimating the analyst's power, beneficial or harmful, and comes to see him simply as a human companion.

Then Ferenczi established a sort of principle of lesser evil: something unpleasant can be accepted if it makes it possible to avoid even greater unpleasantness. He assumed that an unconscious mechanism assesses degrees of unpleasantness.

To illustrate the process, Ferenczi gives the example of the baby who, having always found the maternal breast at the right moment — a breast which for him was merely an indifferent thing — one day encounters frustration and hunger. From that point on, the breast which is sometimes there and sometimes not there becomes an object of love and hate, depending on the situation. Thus, reality testing does not consist in finding the satisfactory object, but in finding it again.

This is the situation that Michael Balint would later try to describe using the notion of "primary love". Primary substances, like air for example, are always available to us and we only realise how much we "love" them when they are lacking.

Alternating feelings of love and hate for objects which appear or do not appear at the right moment allow the development of object relations.

In this article, Ferenczi often refers to his 1913 article "Stages in the Development of the Sense of Reality." I feel that today this article raises a number of questions that cast doubt on Ferenczi's concept of primary omnipotence. In recent years, research has shown that the fetus is in contact with the external world, albeit in a very primitive manner; for example, the fetus reacts to sounds, being appeased by some and aggressed y others. It can also experience all sorts of more or less traumatising events in the uterus; it can remember and recognise certain sounds heard while in the uterus, such as his father's voice and even certain pieces of music. There have been cases where a newborn obviously recognised a Mozart quartet he often heard in utero, or where a fetus could not bear the voice of a tenor and forced his mother to leave the concert hall to calm him. Ferenczi himself referred to an intrauterine life, which implies the possibility of the beginnings of a relation with the external world.

Up to this point, Freud had shown interest in Ferenczi's ideas and innovations, even if he did not always agree. He even encouraged Ferenczi to pursue his investigations, which he was not always able to follow because, as he explains in his letters, he found it difficult to follow closely the development of a process in progress when it is not his own. However, the direction taken by Ferenczi seems more and more foreign, mistaken and hopeless to him.

Ferenczi wrote the articles considered today to be his most important between 1928 and 1933. These articles are also the ones that caused his greatest difficulties with Freud and the other members of the psychoanalytic community, who saw in them a deviation, a distancing from the fundamental principles of psychoanalysis. Freud felt betrayed and abandoned by his friend and had harsh words for Ferenczi. This is when the enduring myth claiming that Ferenczi sunk into paranoid delusions was born. Ernest Jones complacently spread this myth and even claimed that this state of affairs had originated years earlier. He also recounted this myth in Volume III of his biography of Freud, prompting protest from those who knew Ferenczi well, with Michael Balint first among them. Ferenczi suffered greatly as a result of the atmosphere all this created, and above all as a result of the disapproval of his friend and master Freud, as can be seen in many passages of his 1932 *Clinical Diary*.

The nine articles written in the last four and a half years of his life deserve to be examined in detail. Almost all of them deal with trauma, its mechanisms, its effects and its treatment. A series of "notes and fragments" from this period deal with the same subjects. I have chosen to study four articles in more depth: "The Adaptation of the Family to the Child", "The Unwelcome Child and His Death-Instinct", "Child-Analysis in the Analysis of Adults" and, the most important article of all, "Confusion of Tongues Between the Adults and the Child".

THE ADAPTATION OF THE FAMILY TO THE CHILD

In this article, which is a critique of child-rearing in Ferenczi's time, the latter is clearly still disturbed by the controversy created by *The Trauma of Birth*. Although he credits Freud with the essential points in Rank's discovery, specifically the anguish produced by the passage from intrauterine life to life outside the womb[13], Ferenczi attempts to show that the child's physiological adaptation to life outside the womb, and parental instinct, compensate and make it possible to forget the shock of the birth trauma. But as the article continues, Ferenczi repeatedly points out how undependable parental instinct really is, and how it fails in difficult situations such as weaning, toilet training, management of "bad" habits, and during adolescence.

All of the last part of Ferenczi's work shows a steady orientation towards his own perspective, which is at least fifty years ahead compared to that of his colleagues, and in many respects even compared to Freud's. The controversy around Otto Rank's book had destabilised him, but he was unable to go against what his own experience, observations and intuition had taught him. The tension between Freud and Ferenczi became more and more distressing. In his letters to Freud, Ferenczi never stopped arguing his case, trying to explain, to convince Freud that despite any possible

---

13   In this article, Ferenczi does not insist on the essential difference between Freud's idea and that of Rank: Freud speaks of a physiological event, while for Rank the trauma is related mainly to separation from the mother.

errors or exaggerations of which he may be guilty, there is something relevant in the direction his investigations had taken.

THE UNWELCOME CHILD AND HIS DEATH-INSTINCT

In this article, Ferenczi points out, not without malice, that in one of his essays which discusses the commonly seen disposition to colds in people, Ernest Jones refers to Rank's concept of birth trauma, which Jones so fiercely opposed; for his own part, Ferenczi accepts and uses Freud's concept of death-instinct, which he would later reject in his *Clinical Diary*. Ferenczi sees this impulse as the equivalent of the self-destructive trends he observes in epilepsy, asthma, anorexia and glottal spasms in children.

Ferenczi's use of the concept of a death-instinct deserves closer scrutiny: let us remember his concept of a 'reckoning-machine" making it possible to choose the lesser of two unpleasant things. Is self-destruction an impulse, or does it represent the choice of a lesser evil? Are we speaking of the seduction of non-being, or of avoidance of something unbearable in life? Ferenczi thinks that the newborn is still so close to non-being that he can easily slip back into it, even very willingly, if he was unwelcome at birth, treated brutally or without love, or welcomed at first, only to be rejected later.

Ferenczi thinks that the child must be cared for with much tenderness and love to forgive his parents for bringing him into the world without any intention on his part. In this respect, his position is totally opposed to that of Françoise Dolto, who believes that if a child is born, it is because he wants to be. Otherwise, as Ferenczi himself concedes, he can have recourse to a miscarriage or be stillborn. Dolto believes that each of us is responsible for having chosen to be born. For my part, I am tempted to side with Dolto on this question.

To treat these individuals who were unwelcome at birth and become pessimistic, skeptical, mistrustful, emotionally infantile, alcoholic (or drug-addicted) adults, Ferenczi advises the use of elasticity and indulgence in the therapeutic technique. The analysis should proceed like child analysis, to reinforce the capacity for life. Only later can the patient be taught to adapt to the frustrations of reality, that is, undergo classical Freudian analysis.

CHILD-ANALYSIS IN THE ANALYSIS OF ADULTS

This text was presented by Ferenczi in 1931, on the occasion of Freud's 75th birthday. The article starts with a plea. Ferenczi refers to his disagreements with Freud and to the harsh criticism of his colleagues, pointing out that, nevertheless, he was the one who was invited to make this celebratory address. It is a discreet manner of asking Freud and his colleagues to show tolerance towards his investigations, which they find so shocking. He reminds them that despite the very individual direction taken by his research, he has remained faithful to the basic principles of psychoanalysis.

One of the key principles presented in this article is the notion that when the therapeutic process stagnates or fails, the person responsible is the analyst, not the patient. It is up to the analyst to invent the techniques, or the necessary changes in technique, allowing the patient to progress. Ferenczi introduces the idea that regression may have therapeutic value; he refuses to consider regression an obstacle to analysis, seeing it rather as a tool in the service of the analytic process. Of course, he agrees with Freud that actions have to be replaced with remembering, but not right from the start of the analysis. In Ferenczi's opinion, some analyses of adults can resemble child analyses, because the analyst indulges the patient and accepts his regressive transference without interpreting it at once. This permissiveness makes it possible to regress to serious traumas suffered in childhood, so that the origin of the subject's illness can be identified.

But Ferenczi is aware that this process can go wrong, and that the regression can become unmanageable. We shall see later how Balint, Ferenczi's disciple, friend and successor, proposed to solve this problem.

Technical considerations were of great concern to Ferenczi and his article discusses them at length. He insists above all on the need to allow the patient to follow his own path. He advises the analyst to ask questions rather than make statements, and never to take advantage of the regression — which in extreme cases can resemble a trance state — to introduce his own ideas and theories into the patient's psyche. The same thing applies to the upbringing of children: rather that instill rigid rules of behaviour, adults should teach children independence and courage.

This article is the first to sketch the Ferenczian theory of the mechanism of reaction to trauma: a splitting of the personality, causing one part to watch over the other; or causing one part to be destroyed, leaving the surviving part to observe events. Ferenczi would elaborate these ideas in his last article, "Confusion of Tongues Between the Adults and the Child".

Ferenczi insists that the analyst must never let a patient leave when the latter has just relived a childhood trauma in analysis, without first helping him regain a certain inner tranquillity, just as a good parent stays with his child at bedtime to discuss the problems and tensions that arose that day, before leaving him alone for the night. This is where Ferenczi advocates variable-length sessions...always longer rather than shorter, based on a theoretical consideration totally different than that of today's proponents of this technique.

Ferenczi calls himself an agnostic monist; he sees no separation between the physical and the psychical. This is one of the reasons for his affinity with Groddeck[14]. In this article, he shows how, in the course of therapeutic regression, the analyst sees with his own eyes the emergence of the physical symptoms the patient developed as a result of trauma. Ferenczi prefers to call these symptoms "autosymbolic representations" rather than hysterical symptoms.

CONFUSION OF TONGUES BETWEEN THE ADULTS AND THE CHILD: THE LANGUAGE OF TENDERNESS AND PASSION

This is one of Ferenczi's major articles, which summarises the themes of his research and the subjects on which he reflected in the last months of his life. However, when he presented this paper at the 12th International Psychoanalytic Congress in Wiesbaden under the title: "The Passions of Adults and Their Influence on the Sexual and Character Development of Children", it created a scandal. Ferenczi had first gone to Vienna to read the paper to Freud; the latter was so shocked that he left the room without even holding out his hand; Ferenczi was deeply hurt. Freud advised Ferenczi not to read the paper at the Congress. Jones, taking a stance not devoid of perfidiousness, thought that Ferenczi should be allowed to present his work, since

---

14 There are a growing number of people who think all illnesses, and therefore all medicines, are « psychosomatic ». See Michael Balint's concept of the « whole person »: he sees the psyche and the body as forming a unit that reacts as one to any attack, regardless of its origin.

it was not significant enough to be remembered by anyone. Twenty years later, he again tried to prevent Balint from including the article in an English edition of Ferenczi's work, pretexting that it might throw a shadow on the latter's image.

All this shows how far ahead of his time Ferenczi's ideas were. Today, no one doubts that this article is an essential text in psychoanalytic literature. Ferenczi took a stand in an ongoing controversy with Feud regarding the origin of traumatic effects: are they the result of real trauma, or of pathogenic fantasies? Freud never entirely rejected the real source of trauma, but thought that most traumatic states originated in fantasy. Ferenczi asserted that *all* traumatic states were caused by real trauma, and that an analysis cannot be considered complete until it goes back as far as this real trauma.

True to his habit, in this article Ferenczi describes his failures, as well as the lessons he drew from them: he admits that he was able to reach the level of the original trauma, and to make the patient relive this trauma repeatedly, adding that this repetition did not lead to a durable cure. The patient sometimes experienced nightmares and anxiety attacks, and even temporary improvement, but nothing more. Ferenczi notes that one of the obstacles to a cure is the anger, hate and contempt the patient feels for the analyst, without being able to express these feelings, which are not merely effects of transference, but are directed at the analyst in response to what Ferenczi calls his professional hypocrisy, his shortcomings and his lack of understanding. Ferenczi thinks that the patient should be able to express his true feelings freely, and the analyst should do the same. Therefore, he recommends that the analyst be very honest with the patient, expressing even his negative feelings and recognising his errors, to earn the confidence of his patient. Without this confidence, without the almost maternal sympathy of the analyst, reproducing the past will have the same effects as the original trauma. Regression into the infantile, splitting and the distress provoked by the reproduction of the trauma induce in the patient a state of hypersensitivity to the analyst's emotional attitude towards him. This is why the analyst must be completely sincere. When the patient is in this state, he reacts only to the analyst's attitude rather than to phrases and intellectual explanations.

The original traumas Ferenczi discusses in his article

are for the most part sexual, inflicted on children by adults in their entourage. He is surprised by the frequency of such events, which at the time were so completely shrouded in silence that most people, including analysts, thought them to be exceptional occurrences. Only today, when prosecutions for pedophilia are numerous — perhaps a little too much so — does society seem to recognise that pedophilic tendencies, whether they are acted out or not, are very widespread. They were certainly just as widespread before children's rights came into existence, at a time when these rights were only protected in extremely severe cases.

Ferenczi describes these traumatic sexual situations as the result of a sort of misunderstanding, a "confusion of tongues": the child seeks closeness with he adult (some adults even speak of "provocation"), inviting him to play a game which "may assume erotic forms but remains, nevertheless, on the level of tenderness", and the adult allows himself "to be carried away" by passion.

Ferenczi describes the mechanism of trauma as follows: the child subjected to such violence is paralysed with fear, does not dare to protest, accepts the "game" of the adult despite his pain and disgust, and ends up identifying with the aggressor, even to the point of introjection of the latter. But, at the same time, the child introjects the aggressor's guilt feelings. All this plunges the child into confusion, and causes the splitting of his personality. He is innocent and guilty at once. The adult perpetrator behaves as if nothing happened; he denies the event in his own thoughts: "Nothing happened, it's only a child, he imagined everything". As a result, the child loses faith in his own senses. He can no longer be conscious of his hatred and anger. In analysis, interpretations related to such reactions remain without effect.

What the child tries to do, by means of a split, is to re-establish in hallucinatory fashion the situation of tenderness existing before the trauma; he tries to undo the event. Sometimes, the need to deal with the internal consequences of trauma triggers in the child the precocious maturation of part of his personality, a traumatic progression as it were. Just as we saw earlier in the case of the wise baby.

Ferenczi's list of possible traumas includes passionate love, passionate sanctions and, finally, what he calls "terrorism by suffering" and constant complaining. When the trauma is repeated, multiple splitting can occur, a veritable fragmentation or atomization of the personality.

Ferenczi presents these theories as hypotheses. He asks his colleagues to think about them and to observe how they apply to their practice, as well as to their children and pupils. Despite all this caution and modesty, the shock is great (except in the Hungarian group). Some analysts think that Ferenczi is rejecting infantile sexuality, because he speaks of the child's innocence. But, of course, Ferenczi's use of the word "innocence" does not imply the absence of sex drives, but the absence of guilt associated with these drives, before adults superimpose passion on infantile eroticism.

A series of five articles written in 1931 and 1932, but published only after Ferenczi's death in 1934 under the title "Trauma Theory", at once prefigure and complete "Confusion of Tongues".

THE CLINICAL DIARY

Ferenczi's *Clinical Diary*, written in 1932, can be said to be the clinical illustration of his investigations on trauma and its effects. In this book, Ferenczi presents, almost day by day, the unfolding of the analyses of four traumatised patients, two of whom were candidates for becoming analysts: Elisabeth Severn (designated as Rn) and Clara Thompson (Dm). But the *Diary* also contains numerous reflections on Ferenczi's latest theories, many of which are self-observations dealing with counter-transference. Most of the *Diary* is typed; Ferenczi no doubt intended to have it published. One fifth of it, however, is handwritten, and concerns Ferenczi's relationship with Freud. This relationship seems to be a perfect illustration of Ferenczi's theories on trauma: passionate love at first, seduction by Freud, and on Ferenczi's part, admiration and dependence. Then, there is the Palermo incident, where Freud excludes Ferenczi for the first time. Concretely, while they are vacationing together in Sicily, Freud asks Ferenczi to work with him on his project on Schreber. Ferenczi thinks that he is invited to exchange ideas with Freud, who is in fact only asking him to write down what he is dictating. Ferenczi objects and Freud decides to work alone. Ferenczi is clearly unhappy and Freud interprets his discontent as a sign of homosexual inclinations and childishness. Then, during the First World War, Ferenczi undergoes three short segments of psychoanalysis with Freud, in which everything that may indicate a hostile or negative reaction remains unanalysed. Later, Ferenczi reproached Freud with this omission, and Freud continued to defend himself years after

Ferenczi's death, as we can see in "Analysis Terminable and Interminable".

When Ferenczi chose to follow his own path, showed interest in curing his patients and in developing techniques in view of achieving a cure, he was subjected to passionate sanctions: his ideas were criticised, rejected and described as errors he would have to correct. His desire to heal patients was called *furor sanandi*. He himself was called the *enfant terrible* of psychoanalysis, and finally labeled as mentally ill and paranoid.

My own impression is that Ferenczi's last articles, and his *Clinical Diary*, illustrate the "traumatic progression" he considered a possible result of trauma. His contemporaries did not understand him because he was fifty years ahead of his time. As for the phenomenon of splitting, Ferenczi might have avoided it by parting with his life.

Once again, this raises the question of whether a trauma is always a misfortune, or are some people able to benefit from it, even if they pay a price? We are reminded of Boris Cyrulnik's theory of resilience, or of the popular saying: "What doesn't kill you makes you stronger".

Although Ferenczi's life ended tragically, his perspective and approach were taken up by a number of analysts, the Hungarians particularly, but others as well, who were interested in the direction taken by his investigations. Ferenczi had many successors, the first of whom was Michael Balint.

Ferenczi left us with a number of questions and unfinished experiments. Despite the scandal provoked by his last investigations, and the rejections he suffered in Berlin, London and America, the Hungarian group continued to support him. Especially Michael Balint, his analysand, pupil, colleague and friend, whose work was a continuation of what Ferenczi had started. The latter confirmed this in a note written during his last vacation in Luchon, in 1932: "Balint picked things up where I had got stumped."

MICHAEL BALINT AND *THE BASIC FAULT*

Balint never had the same type of dependent relationship with Ferenczi as the latter had with Freud. I believe this to be as much due to Ferenczi's priorities — his desire to teach "independence and courage", as we have seen — as it is due to Balint's character. Balint knew Ferenczi before starting his analytic training. His mother-in-law, Vilma Kovacs, his wife Alice's mother, had been Ferenczi' analysand and pupil.

Balint started to publish articles in 1930, and his thinking followed a highly coherent path from his earliest articles to his last book written almost forty years later, *The Basic Fault*, published a few years before his death. It was during his own research that he came across certain facts that could contribute to solve some of Ferenczi's unanswered dilemmas. Although the vicissitudes of history forced Balint to immigrate to England at the start of 1939, the direction of his research did not change.

I shall now describe the best-developed aspects of his theory, as he presents them in his last writings. The chapter which follows will delve into this subject in greater detail.

In Balint's perspective, the life of the psyche is always relational; primary narcissism does not exist. Narcissism can only be secondary. Starting with this idea of a primary relation, he sees the psychic apparatus as composed of *three areas* of the mind: the *Oedipal area* comprised of three people, the *basic fault area* involving two people, and the *area of creation*, where the subject is alone and tries to draw something out of his own being.

Balint observed that all these areas can be reached in the analytic process. In fact, it was essential to reach them in cases where there had been early trauma. He concluded, as Ferenczi had before him, that *regression* was not a hinderance, but rather a therapeutic tool.

This is where Balint picked up things where Ferenczi's attempts to solve dilemmas created by regression had remained futile. Balint described *two types of regression*: *benign regression*, from which the patient can emerge spontaneously at the right time, and *malignant regression* leading to a desperate and exasperating spiral of repeated demands impossible to satisfy. Emerging from benign regression is a kind of rebirth, a new start that Balint called *new beginning*. Balint came to identify *two extreme forms of regression*: *ocnophilia*, where the subject finds security in objects, and *philobatic regression* where the subject finds security in spaces devoid of any obstacles, in which he will not encounter any dangerous or malevolent objects.

Balint considers love a primary affect which permeates the relation with these pre-objects constituted by *primary substances* such as air or, earlier still, amniotic fluid. The subject lives with these primary substances in a sort of "harmonious mix-up through interpenetration".

In his last published article, ("Trauma and Object Relationship"), which dealt with trauma, Balint asserted that certain "misunderstandings" between the child and his entourage can have an effect just as traumatising as actual mistreatment. This initial trauma, regardless of its cause, determines the form taken by the basic fault, the wound in the psychic structure which cannot heal, which every human being carries, and which determines his particular neurosis.

True to Ferenczian principles, Balint bases his theories on clinical experience. What takes place in the analysis and what he observes in this process is what will prompt him to make changes in the technique.

Ferenczi understood that the "neutrality" and "indifference" recommended by Freud in order not to lock the patient in an unrealistic relation with the analyst was not suitable for all patients, nor at every stage of an analysis. Those we call today "borderline cases", or patients in regression, need something else. Ferenczi thought it best to allow them, through his attitude, to experience the care, security and support of which they were deprived early in life. This required that the analyst give of his own person, to an extent most of his colleagues were unwilling to do. I believe that this demand, which forced analysts to become aware of their technical and emotional limitations, played a role in the impassioned rejection of Ferenczi's views. The latter was certain that he had identified something essential making it possible to treat patients considered unfit for analysis by so-called orthodox analysts, and to break the deadlock in a stagnant analysis, or one that was cut short. His colleagues knew this, which is why he became the analyst of people whose state was considered hopeless, who were sent to him from all over the world. But Ferenczi could see that he was not always able to resolve the situations he created in analysis.

His premature death did not leave him time to find a solution. It was Balint's theory of the basic fault and of the basic fault stage which brought the solution needed in these situations.

I believe that it is thanks to these two people, followed by many others, that we made the transition from one-person psychology, involving mainly the observation of the patient and his intra-psychic mechanisms by an "indifferent" analyst, to a two-person psychology, focused on what transpires between the analyst and the analysand, and by extension, between the analysand and his entourage. Thus, analysis becomes less and less concerned with educating the patient, focusing instead on helping the patient to accept himself as he is. In other words, helping him to accept responsibility for his personality, his desires, his convictions and his actions.

INTRODUCING FERENCZI IN FRANCE

In his lifetime, Ferenczi was considered one of the most important psychoanalysts working with Freud, perhaps even the most important. He was certainly the most imaginative, the most innovative. Towards the end of his life, he explored paths of which Freud disapproved, but which are considered today the foundation of contemporary theory and technique. Ferenczi was not the only person of his era to explore these paths. Otto Rank tended in the same direction when he wrote *The Trauma of Birth* and later, when he formulated his ideas in the United States. Ferenczi and Rank were the two people who pointed out the critical importance of the pre-Oedipal period and the early relationship with the mother, which Freud found so hard to admit, because it tended to reduce the importance of the Oedipus complex as the major cause of any pathology.

Ferenczi and Rank were therefore seen by Freud's orthodox followers as dangerous dissidents. Rank chose to break with Freud and lived for the rest of his life in exile. Ferenczi did not want to sacrifice his friendship with Freud, preferring to give up his relationship with Rank, and continuing his own investigation. After their death, Ernest Jones took revenge on the two rebels by insisting that they were both mentally ill and that, therefore, their work was of no interest. Freud was almost convinced of the same thing. And the entire psychoanalytic community, with few exceptions, accepted this version of things and lost interest in the two authors.

Ferenczi's family, namely Gizella Ferenczi and her two daughters, Elma and Magda, asked Michael Balint, Sándor Ferenczi's friend and closest collaborator, to become his literary executor. Balint acquired access to Ferenczi's unpublished notes, and to his 1932 *Diary*, which no one knew existed at the time. As I said earlier, this diary contained Ferenczi's theoretical and clinical observations and reflections, in typed form, probably intended to be published at the right time. But it also contained some handwritten passages, in which Ferenczi analysed his relationship with Freud in a more disabused tone — passages probably intended for a more intimate circle.

In 1939, Balint took the *Diary*, and the letters Freud had written to his friend over the twenty-five-year period of their friendship, to England. At Gizella's request, Anna Freud consented to give her Ferenczi's letters to Freud; now, Balint had the entire correspondence, but not the right to publish it without the agreement of Anna Freud and her family.

By 1939, many of Ferenczi's writings had been published in German, Hungarian and English, and a few even in Spanish. Indeed, up until 1933, he had published regularly, either in the medical and psychoanalytic press, or in collections of articles in Hungarian or German. It was shortly after his death that the first problem concerning the publication of his work arose.

We know that his article "Confusion of Tongues Between the Adults and the Child", one of his best-known and highly appreciated texts, was violently rejected by Freud and by most of the psychoanalytic community. Nevertheless, Ferenczi presented it at the 1932 Wiesbaden Conference, but after his death Jones prevented its publication in the *International Journal of Psychoanalysis*.

After this, even greater difficulties arose. In 1936, Michael Balint, entrusted with Ferenczi's literary heritage, had Pantheon publish A Brief Presentation of Psychoanalysis (the Hungarian title), containing a series of posthumous articles, specifically the lectures Ferenczi gave in Spain in 1928. Balint was also preparing to have Ferenczi's complete works published in German by the Swiss publisher Hans Huber. The books were printed in Hungary and were to be sent to Bern. But the anti-Jewish laws were becoming more and more strict in Hungary, the Germans had invaded Austria, in Germany books by Jewish authors were being burned, and Balint, who had decided to leave Hungary for England, thought it best to have what was already printed sent to England, even though the work was not complete. Balint arrived in England in 1939. He had time to show Freud Ferenczi's last writings, including those later published under the title Notes and Fragments, and Reflections upon Trauma (published in German in Internationale Zeitschrift für Psychoanalyse, Vol. XX, 1934, p.10. Freud had had time to rethink some of his ideas since 1933; this time, he found Ferenczi's latest investigations much less shocking. He told

Balint: "There are many interesting points there[15]".

Balint lost no time in his efforts to publish Ferenczi's writings. First, he sent the printed portions of *Bausteine zur Psychoanalyse* to Hans Huber in Switzerland. But in the meantime, war had broken out, France was occupied, and the pages he sent had to make a long detour through Spain, a neutral country, then through Italy, to reach Switzerland. The ship carrying the parcel caught fire; the crew put the fire out by pouring tons of water into the hold. At the end of the journey, the printed pages were unusable. All the work had to be redone. The *Bausteine* was only published in 1964.

After lengthy negotiations with Jones, President of the British Psychoanalytical Society, and Director of the *International Journal of Psychoanalysis*, Balint was able to have a special issue of the *Journal* dedicated to Ferenczi in 1947; this issue included *"Confusion of Tongues"*.

Balint also succeeded in having Hogarth Press publish three volumes of Ferenczi's work, representing about three quarters of his writings. These English translations, quite mediocre except for the last volume revised by the Irish author Francis Stuart, were never rewritten; this incomplete edition is till the one used in re-editions by other English-language publishers, especially in the United States.

At the end of the 1950s, after the publication of the third volume of Jones' acclaimed biography of Freud, most of the psychoanalytic community accepted Jones' theory that Ferenczi was psychotic in the last five years of his life, and that his writings were of no interest.

After this, Ferenczi's work was practically forgotten everywhere, including in Hungary. In 1949, Balint was able to have the International Journal of Psychoanalysis publish a special issue dedicated to Ferenczi, which did not cause much of a stir.

One of the first occasions when Ferenczi was mentioned in France was in 1952, when Daniel Lagache wrote an article entitled "Le problème du transfert". He quoted Ferenczi extensively, often associating him with Rank, and showing that these two authors had the same orientation, whether they collaborated as they did to write *The Development of Psycho-Analysis*, or worked on their own. We should mention that Lagache was on friendly terms with Michael Balint and thought highly of his work. Of course, Balint was a disciple of Ferenczi and never missed an opportunity to

---

15   Personal communication by Michael Balint to Judith Dupont.

have the latter's work known.

Jacques Lacan also read Ferenczi. As early as 1953, in his report at the Rome Congress, he quotes "Confusion of Tongues", Ferenczi's most controversial article, dating back to the Wiesbaden Conference. Lacan also refers to Ferenczi in a 1966 article entitled "Du sujet enfin en question" (On the Subject Who is Finally in Question), in order to formulate a criticism. In 1955, he had quoted Ferenczi at length in, "Variante de la cure-type" (Variations of the Standard Treatment), in reference to the analyst's subjective experience during the analytic process. In 1956, in "Situations de la psychoanalyse" (The Situation of Psychoanalysis), Lacan speaks of Jones' resentment towards Ferenczi; in 1958, in "La direction de la cure et les principes de son pouvoir" (The Direction of the Treatment and the Principles of Its Power), Lacan formulates his objections to the concept of introjection.

In 1961, Wladimir Granoff wrote an article about Ferenczi, published in issue No. 6 of La Psychanalyse: "Ferenczi: faux problème ou vrai malentendu" (Ferenczi: False Problem or True Misunderstanding), after reading Vera Granoff's first French translation of "Confusion of Tongues". This article examines the "Ferenczi dilemma" as perceived by the analytic community, studies its historical aspects and recapitulates all the key elements of Ferenczian theory. Granoff speaks of the rivalry between Jones and Ferenczi for Freud's friendship, and for the presidency of the psychoanalytic movement. Then Granoff examines the complex relationship between Freud and Ferenczi; the article provides a lengthy analysis of Thalassa, Ferenczi's work most highly regarded by Freud. Finally, Granoff reviews Ferenczi's concept of trauma, the ways in which it differs from Freudian theory, and the consequences it has on practice.

At the start of the 1960s, Balint very generously gave me a series of texts by Ferenczi in Hungarian — original editions — , of which he had two copies. One of them was *Thalassa*, published in Hungarian by my father's publishing house, Pantheon, under the title *Catastrophies in Sexual Development*. This book delighted me. I was interested, amused; it was a sort of biological-psychological fantasy appealing to the imagination. I decided to translate it. I didn't know that by doing so I would be infringing on the territory of my colleague Ilse Barande, who had just read the book and started to translate it. But because I had submitted my request to Balint first, and thanks to my close relations with him, I obtained the translation rights. As for Ilse Barande, she is the author of the first biography of Ferenczi published in France[16].

At the same time, still with Balint's help, I started to look for a publisher. It was not easy. Why publish Ferenczi, since no one was interested in him? The *Presses universitaires de France* (PUF) considered the project, but finally decided not to take the risk.

This is when two "Franco-Hungarians", Nicolas Abraham and Maria Torok, intervened. They had read Ferenczi and were preparing to integrate his ideas into their theoretical work, in their own way. They knew Gérard Mendel, who was in charge of the psychoanalytic collection at Payot, and convinced him that it was worthwhile to publish *Thalassa*, and perhaps the rest of Ferenczi's work.

Thus, Payot published *Thalassa* at the start of the 1960s, under the intriguing title *Thalassa, psychoanalyse des origines de la vie sexuelle*. It had been agreed that if this book sold well enough, Payot would publish a first volume of the *Complete Works*, then perhaps a second and a third. In fact, *Thalassa*, with an Introduction by Nicolas Abraham, was a great success; its title made it possible for it to be sold even in train stations. *Thalassa* was subsequently retranslated and published in Volume III of the *Complete Works*, under its original title: *Thalassa: A Theory of Genitality*. But the original French translation is still available and has been reedited five times.

In any case, it was decided that Ferenczi's *Complete Works* would be published in four volumes. Michael Balint distributed the articles to be placed in each volume; he also wrote the Preface of the first two volumes. I believe he was wrong to leave out book reviews of books rarely read by that time, as well as some articles which he thought had lost their interest. My colleague Myriam Viliker and myself decided to restore the left-out articles, but not the book reviews. Today, I think we were also wrong. A complete edition should be truly complete.

In the meantime, Gizella's two daughters became aware that, like Michael Balint, they were growing older, and that a successor should be chosen to be Ferenczi's literary executor. They thought that I was well suited to do this job, and Balint agreed. I was very moved to be the one to whom

---

16   Barante, I., *Sándor Ferenczi*, Paris: Payot, 1996.

this responsibility would be entrusted after Balint.

Michael Balint died at the end of December 1970. Enid Balint, his widow, gave me all Ferenczi's papers, texts, correspondence with publishers and with Elma Laurvik, accounts and contracts, but not two of his major writings: the *Clinical Diary* and his correspondence with Freud. She assured me that Balint has wished that she herself be responsible for these writings. Balint had not said anything about this to me, but knowing Enid, I had no reason to doubt her word. Therefore, I accepted this arrangement for a time. Especially since there was still work to do to prepare the last two volumes of the *Complete Works* for publication. Myriam Viliker and I translated volumes II and III; then, the translation group at *Coq-Héron*, the journal I founded in 1969, which published, among other things, French translations previously unavailable, translated the texts in Volume IV. After this, we wanted to start translating the *Clinical Diary*, without even knowing when and how it would be published.

Therefore, I wrote to Enid Balint, saying that it was difficult for me to be the literary executor of an author without access to all his literary production. She agreed with me and sent me the original German version of the *Clinical Diary*, specifying that she would like to submit this text to impartial arbitration, to decide if it could be published. To do this, she contacted two German psychoanalysts, Alexander and Margarete Mitscherlich. Both of them said that the *Diary* was too intimate, too susceptible to attacks from Ferenczi's adversaries, to be published. Nevertheless, we started to translate it so that a French version would be available as soon as publication would seem opportune.

Michael Balint had wanted the *Diary* and the *Freud-Ferenczi Correspondence* to be published simultaneously, because he felt the two texts shed light on each other. But there were two obstacles to this: Anna Freud absolutely refused the publication of the entire correspondence — the only form Balint considered acceptable — , and some of Ferenczi's supporters were afraid to see in print the complexities of Ferenczi's love life, which the correspondence revealed to a great extent. The members of the translation group then came up with the idea of translating and publishing the Ferenczi-Groddeck correspondence, to which there were no obstacles and which revealed the whole story of Ferenczi's loves. The expected scandal did not occur. Ferenczi had become a historical figure whose private life did not excite public passions.

Anna Freud died in 1982 and the rest of the Freud family did not oppose the publication of the correspondence. The two obstacles had been removed, and the Diary as well as the correspondence could be published. But the publication of the enormous Freud-Ferenczi correspondence, comprised of about 1250 letters, was sure to raise problems. We therefore decided to publish the Diary as soon as the translation was ready.

The *Clinical Diary* came out in French in 1985; it was a complete version which included the handwritten passages in which Ferenczi speaks of his relations with Freud. The book solicited interest and was given a warm and respectful reception.

Then we formed a committee for the publication of the *Freud-Ferenczi Correspondence*, charged with finding publishers in the different languages, commentators and financing. To work out how we would proceed, Enid Balint invited all the members of the committee to come to London on a Sunday to examine the correspondence and decide what to do. Arthur Rosenthal, the director of Harvard University Press, came from the United States; André Haynal came from Geneva. Ilse Simitis, who represented Fischer Publishing, came from Germany. Mark Paterson, director of the Sigmund Freud Copyrights, came from the English village of Wivenhoe, and I came from Paris. Enid Balint had brought from her deposit box at the bank the black suitcase which should have held the correspondence. We opened it with solemnity...but the correspondence was not there. Enid called the bank to ask if there was another black suitcase in the deposit box, but was told that there was not. The correspondence was lost. We were dismayed. Enid called all the university libraries to which Michael might have donated the correspondence. None of them had it. Since there was nothing else to do, we examined the contents of the black suitcase, which proved to be very interesting, and we returned to our various countries.

The next day, Enid Balint went to the bank herself and found the second black suitcase in the deposit box: the employee who had answered the telephone had relied on his memory, without going to check. Finding publishers was not easy; Harvard University Press was willing to pay for the translation, but not for the comments. Fischer took the same stance, but wanted to appoint a commentator chosen by them. In France, Payot and Gallimard, which had been solicited to possibly produce a joint publication, decided not to undertake the project given the impressive volume of the correspondence. Finally, an Austrian publisher named Böhlau agreed to publish it. For the French version, the question remained in suspense. The *Coq-Héron* translation group nevertheless decided to start working at once.

A young Austrian, Ernst Falzeder, offered his services to provide comments, was given a test and was accepted, as was Eva Brabant; being of Hungarian origin, she was entrusted with conducting enquiries in Hungary. André Haynal and an Austrian colleague agreed to provide a finalised version of the comments; but Haynal's colleague never provided the promised help and André Haynal did all the work alone. *In extremis*, the two commentators were to be joined by a third, who lived in Vienna and could therefore have been very useful. But she contributed so little that her name in the three volumes where it appears is only a decoration. Funds had to be found to pay Ernst Falzeder and Eva Brabant. André Haynal was able to obtain a grant from the University of Geneva for Falzeder. He was also able to have substantial financial help granted to Eva Brabant, who received donations from different psychoanalytic associations and from a number of colleagues as well. The largest contribution came from two Canadian associations, one French and one English. In France, it was the International Association for the History of Psychoanalysis which offered us the greatest help.

In the meantime, Ingeborg Meyer-Palmedo from Fischer Publishers revised, improved and finished the transcription of the letters, work that had been done by Michael Balint as a first draft. This improved version was the one the translation group used, sometimes referring to photocopies of the originals, which can be seen today at the Freud Museum in London. (The original letters are now at the Austrian National Library.) André Haynal, after solving the difficult question of how to pay the commentators, worked tirelessly with them to complete, structure and ensure the coherence of the comments.

One of our friends, the historian and journalist François Fejtö, had just had a book published by Calmann-Lévy. He thought it opportune to mention the Freud-Ferenczi correspondence, saying that it seemed that in France none of the publishers were interested in it. The Director of Calmann-Lévy thought that it would be a prestigious work, even if it were not profitable, and offered to publish it. The translation was quite advanced, and the first volume of the projected three came out in 1992. Once again, it was the French version that was published first, and it had huge sales. The English version followed, and only much later the original German version.

Certain books contributed to making Ferenczi known in France. We mentioned the first earlier: Ilse Barande's book entitled simply *Sándor Ferenczi*, published by Payot in 1972. In 1974, Eva Brabant, who would later be a commentator of the Freud-Ferenczi correspondence, had her book *Ferenczi et l'école hongroise de psychoanalyse* published by Harmattan. Then, a French psychoanalyst, Claude Lorin, became interested in Ferenczi's pre-psychoanalytic articles which foretold clearly the path their author was to take. In 1984, Lorin published extensive passages of these articles, with commentary; his book was published by Aubier-Montaigne. French readers only have these passages at their disposal, until the articles will one day be translated in their integrality. In 1985, Pierre Sabourin's book *Ferenczi, paladin et grand vizir secret* was published by *Éditions universitaires*; a second, enhanced edition was published in 2013 by CampagnePremière. It was Freud who had called Ferenczi by these grandiose names in one of his letters. Sabourin, a member of the *Coq-Héron* translation group, was the first author who had access, for his biography, to the *Clinical Diary* and the Freud-Ferenczi correspondence. André Haynal had access to the same sources when he wrote *LaTechnique en question. Controverses en psychoanalyse* (Debate on Psychoanalytic Technique) published by Payot in 1987. The book centres on Freud, Ferenczi and Balint. In 1997, Thierry Bokanowski's *Sándor Ferenczi*[17] was published by PUF in the series "Psychanalystes d'aujourd'hui". Finally, in 2001 Delachaux & Niestlé published André Haynal's most recent book about Ferenczi, entitled *Un psychanalyste pas comme un autre. La renaissance de Sándor Ferenci*[18]. After that, research on Ferenczi's work, and writings about him multiplied. Among the latest books, three were published by CampagnePremière: *Impardonnable Ferenczi* by Yves Lugrin, *L'Île des rêves de Sándor Ferenczi* (The Dream Island of Sándor Ferenczi) by José Jimenez Avello, and *Lire Sándor Ferenczi* by Hélène Oppenheim-Gluckman.

Today, Ferenczi is known and respected in France,

---

17 Bokanowski, T., *The Modernity of Sándor Ferenczi*, Weller, A. (trans.), Routledge, 2017.
18 Haynal, A., *Disappearing and Reviving: Sándor Ferenczi in the History of Psychoanalysis*, Karnac, 2002.

probably more than in other countries. He has taken his rightful place as an essential author of classic texts of psychoanalytic literature, which are particularly timely, since we've realised in the past few decades how relevant his ideas, intuitions, perspective and techniques can be for dealing with the situations and pathologies most frequently seen today, pathologies considered in the past to be unfit for analysis. More and more Ferenczi seminars are held, and the articles that were the most severely criticised in the past are the ones now soliciting the greatest interest, "Confusion of Tongues" first among them. To end this brief summary of Ferenczi's introduction in France, we would like to express, once again, our gratitude to Wladimir Granoff, who was the first to publish this essential text in French.

THAT "CRAZY" FERENCZI

It is very surprising to see how easily almost all of the psychoanalytic community accepted Ernest Jones' assertion that Ferenczi was crazy in the last months of his life. He was supposedly suffering from a mental illness whose signs Jones claimed to have noticed much earlier, and which culminated in paranoia. Jones said that he based his assertion on what was described to him by someone who witnessed the events of Ferenczi's last days, but he never revealed the name of this witness, who remained unidentified. Those who are known to have witnessed Ferenczi's last days firmly deny Jones' claims.

However, as Raymond Aron said, "a false idea is a real fact". Indeed, such a unanimous acceptance of Jones' thesis can be seen as a symptom: the symptom of the resistance of the psychoanalytic world to something Ferenczi would have wanted to introduce in psychoanalysis.

Jones asserted that Ferenczi's mental illness affected him during the last months of his life; consequently, all the ideas he developed during this period should be discarded as the product of a deranged mind, and therefore worthless. This work is essentially comprised of five articles:

- The Unwelcome Child and His Death-Instinct (1929)
- The Principles of Relaxation and Neocatharsis (1930)
- Child Analysis in the Analysis of Adults (1931)
- Confusion of Tongues Between the Adults and the

Child (1933)

- *Reflections upon Trauma* in "Notes and Fragments"; this paper is composed of several notes written in 1931 and 1932, gathered together by Michael Balint and published posthumously.

A sixth major text has been published since then, which had not been available to the analysts of the period: Ferenczi's *Clinical Diary*, written in 1932. Widely studied and published now, we can easily imagine the scandal it would have provoked at the time, confirming the alleged madness of its author.

Today, the five articles listed above are the ones most often quoted, and are considered Ferenczi's major contribution; they triggered subsequent research on trauma, its effects and its treatment. But it is not certain that all of the analytic community has been able to accept and integrate their content. For some people, they may represent an attempt at appropriation and neutralisation, that is, another form of resistance. This time, it would be the resistance society still offers to psychoanalysis, and in general to any disturbing idea that is difficult to refute: first trying to disqualify the author by calling him a heretic, a charlatan or a madman; then ridiculing his ideas, before oversimplifying them to the point where they become flat and colourless. Societies may progress, but they are never progressist. A structure always strives to maintain itself as it is, and only changes if it is forced to do so. This no doubt applies to psychoanalytic societies as well.

But we also know that resistances always arise for a reason; we build defences when we feel the need to protect ourselves against something we cannot tolerate. It appears that Ferenczi's ideas were perceived as intolerable by his colleagues at the time he developed them. And by Freud as well. Indeed, even Freud needed solid defences to elaborate his revolutionary concepts. Given his lucidity, he must have been fully aware of this. In fact, in October 1928, he wrote to István Hollós, a Hungarian psychiatrist and psychoanalyst who had sent him his book *Mes adieux à la Maison Jaune* (published in French translation by *Coq-Héron*), that he did not like psychotic patients: "They make me angry and I find myself irritated to experience them so distant from myself and from all that is human. This is an astonishing intolerance which brands me a poor psychiatrist." And a little further he asks himself:

"Am I not reacting like physicians used to react to

hysterics in the past?"

To try to understand what it was in Ferenczi's thinking that created such resistances, it is interesting to examine these five articles from this point of view. The articles develop the same ideas by degrees, from different perspectives. It is no doubt in certain aspects of these ideas that we can find the source of the unease created in the analytic community. Ferenczi is constantly making a parallel between the parent-child relationship and the analyst-analysand relationship, especially in cases where the patient is in a state of regression. This is, in fact, one of his innovative ideas. He considers that regression during the analysis is not a pitfall to avoid, but rather a useful stage of the treatment. But he encounters a problem, which his pernicious anemia left him no time to solve: how to create an atmosphere that would allow the patient to emerge from his regression, once he had revived, during this regression, the trauma in which his pathology originated. In his attempts to answer this question, Ferenczi created situations which, seen from the outside, reinforced his colleagues' unfavourable opinions.

The parallel he makes between parent-child relations and analyst-analysand relations leads Ferenczi to conclude that every analyst, like the parent, may encounter situations in which he falls short. Both the parent and the analyst have a task impossible to fulfil perfectly. This causes a constant feeling of guilt vis-à-vis the child or the patient. The only thing to do is to be aware of this and manage as best as possible the consequences of such a deficiency.

This conclusion causes Ferenczi to look more closely at the analyst's counter-transference, that is, the spontaneous transference of the feelings originating in his own psychic world, as well as the transference triggered by the words and actions of the patient. Indeed, Ferenczi states unequivocally that the analyst/patient relation is not solely transferred from past experiences, but also exists as a present reality.

Contrary to many analysts of his era, including Freud, Ferenczi did not consider counter-transference a disturbing phenomenon to be neutralised as much as possible, but rather an essential tool in analytic work, delicate to handle but indispensable. This conception brings into question the relatively comfortable position of the analyst as an impartial reflecting mirror. In this perspective, analytic work is no longer scientific observation, but exhausting personal emotional involvement. It is not surprising that analysts are tempted to distance themselves and grant priority to intellectual tools, regardless of the requirements of the process, choosing to place their own emotional balance first. This measure of self-protection goes hand to hand with a degree of more or less conscious guilt.

The fact that Ferenczi insists on highlighting all the situations likely to provoke a feeling of inadequacy, and as a result, the analyst's guilt, is no doubt responsible for the analysts' desire to set aside his thinking and his work, which sorely try their narcissism.

A particular analyst/analysand configuration is that involving training analysis, as it was practiced in Ferenczi's time, and still is today in certain analytic associations. In this situation, the relation between the two protagonists is one of master and pupil, incompatible, some would say, with conducting psychoanalysis properly. This questionable situation is followed by shared membership in the same association. Both analyst and analysand will find it difficult to leave behind the roles they had in relation to each other in the analysis. This will aggravate conflictual situations in the association.

Ferenczi seemed fully aware of this reality. Of course, he was the one to propose that an international psychoanalytic association be created, but he did so at Freud's request, even expressing a certain degree of skepticism as to its future functioning. In the 1910 article where he advocates the creation of such an association, he lists what he calls the "pathologies of organisations", while expressing the hope that awareness of these potential conflicts by people who had received analytic training will help to resolve them, even if they cannot be prevented. Since then, we have all had occasion to discover how well-founded his skepticism was. Phenomena seen in any human collectivity occur exactly in the same way in psychoanalytic groups. Emotions individuals perceive in themselves and are able to control escape their awareness and their control when they are in a group. Perhaps the resistance of the analytic community to Ferenczi's contribution is a phenomenon of this nature.

Another pervasive theme in these five articles is childhood trauma, which Ferenczi considers to lie at the root of all neurosis, and to be accessible if the analysis is pursued far enough. In these articles, he explains in detail what he means by this. He admits, agreeing with Freud, that many narratives of childhood trauma recounted on the couch are fantasies; but he claims that these fictional accounts nevertheless correspond to a psychical reality that was, in fact, traumatising. This means that there is a psychic reality on which hysterical fantasies are founded. These trauma-producing events are not necessarily spectacular. They can consist of "unintelligent, capricious, tactless or actually cruel treatment". In addition, incestuous tendencies in adults can be concealed under a mask of tenderness, but are just as disturbing for the child.

All these events are not necessarily experienced as traumatic, but they sometimes become traumatic when their reality is denied by people who are important in the child's life, especially his mother. If the event is acknowledged in words, and the child has the support of a loving person, the event can be integrated without producing traumatic effects. But if no one listens to the child, if he is scolded or treated roughly when he is stunned, paralysed by a psychic shock, the same event can act as a trauma.

According to Ferenczi, a patient in a state of deep regression, or struggling with a crushing Ego, is as fragile as a child and must be treated with great tact to avoid reproducing the early traumatic situation and triggering the same effects.

It is not hard to imagine that this way of conceiving of the production of trauma seemed disturbing to analysts (or parents) who were certain that they had never aggressed or mistreated their patients (or children). The idea that seemingly harmless attitudes or actions can sometimes cause long-lasting damage is extremely disturbing and guilt-producing.

For Ferenczi, the question of the generation of trauma is closely linked with infantile sexuality, which he has been reproached with wanting to deny. In the five articles cited above, he considers children "innocent" beings, hungry for affection, traumatised by the passionate reaction of adults to an appeal of a totally different nature. This is what he calls "confusion of tongues". Ferenczi is not saying that "innocence" in children means an absence of eroticism, but only an absence of guilt. In his article "The Principles of Relaxation and Neocatharsis", he states explicitly: "[...] children themselves manifest a readiness to engage in genital eroticism more vehemently and far earlier than we used to suppose". But the child's eroticism has the character of play and is a way of seeking affection. The misunderstanding comes when the adult responds with passionate eroticism, triggered by the misunderstood invitation of the child, who was expecting another kind of response. The trauma results from this discrepancy. Punishment as a response to erotic activity such as masturbation or children "playing doctor" can have the same traumatic effect, as can the premature forcing of genital sensations.

In "Child-Analysis in the Analysis of Adults", Ferenczi presents the view that the analyst should let the adult patient regress to a childish level, and respond to him on the same level. In other words, the analyst should create a situation where the child in the patient can express himself in a childish way. But Ferenczi also points out the limits of this game: the adult patient must not try to relive the child's reality through the actions of an adult. Actively aggressive desires, sexual desires and, in general, excessive desires of any kind should not be satisfied. But this was precisely the obstacle upon which Ferenczi's experimental techniques stumbled. Some of the satisfactions he thought he could grant went beyond this limit.

However, Ferenczi was not proposing to replace the technique of frustration by the technique of relaxation and permissiveness. What he wanted was to enrich the therapeutic arsenal by adding a new technique that could be used in cases which could not be treated using the techniques available at the time. Ferenczi was not casting doubt on infantile sexuality. He was only insisting that its specific nature be recognised. This constant alternating between his adult self and identification with the infantile causes the analyst to be endlessly confronted to his countertransference and to his own resistances. This task is exhausting. Ferenczi supposes that to be able to accomplish it, the analyst himself should be "perfectly" analysed. But is such "perfection" possible? Even Ferenczi, the optimist, doubts it. As a result, he tries to invent all sorts of measures allowing the analyst to diminish the effects of the errors he will inevitably commit. The first of these measures is to admit his mistakes to the patient. He recommends that analysts be humble, do not hesitate to call themselves into question when a patient has a reproach to make, instead of hastily interpreting the situation as being a function of the patient's pathology.

Ferenczi's clinical know-how and therapeutic talent were universally recognised. His colleagues from everywhere sent him desperate cases. These were for the most part what we call today borderline cases or psychotic patients, considered unsuited for analysis using the techniques available at the time. Often, these patients could not bear to lie on the couch, with the analyst sitting out of sight. They could barge into the room and place themselves in all kinds of positions relative to the analyst. This raised another problem for Ferenczi: the delicate question of what place to attribute to bodies in this talking cure. Freud had eliminated all physical contact from the analytic process. Many analysts still avoid them as much as possible; in some Anglo-Saxon countries even the handshake at the start and the end of the session is prohibited. Ferenczi believed that often recollections surface when physical gestures take place, and that these gestures then serve as connections by being bodily memory traces. Therefore, he placed great importance on the attitudes, postures, gestures and expressions of his patients. Touching the patient was not scandalous, provided the analyst knew when and how. For example, Ferenczi did not stop his patient called Dm in the Clinical Diary from kissing him occasionally. The kiss was clearly meant to make him uncomfortable, since he comments that being near Dm was unpleasant because of her disagreeable odour. She had boasted in public that she could "kiss papa Ferenczi" whenever she liked. Freud saw this as erotic behaviour, and wrote a critical and ironic letter to Ferenczi (called the "kissing technique" letter), which deeply wounded the latter. A few lines in the Clinical Diary shed some light on this incident.

While working with patients in deep regression — what Ferenczi called a "state of trance", he became more attentive to the reproaches they addressed to him: being insensitive, cold, cruel, or selfish. He also became aware of the latent hostility existing between the analyst and the analysand, a hostility the latter cannot or does not dare express, and of which the analyst is often unaware. Through his interpretations, no matter how relevant, the analysand perceives all his latent feelings. Especially the analyst's resistances, which impede the progress of the analysis. Even if the analyst is aware of these resistances, he never overcomes them completely because, like everyone else, he has blind spots — in other words, an unconscious. Therefore, Ferenczi insists that when the analysis is stalling it is best to reveal to the analysand one's negative countertransferential feelings, because he is certain that anything is better than hypocrisy. In short, Ferenczi is asking analysts to expose themselves, to give up their relatively safe position, a position he likens to that of the adult at the origin of the initial trauma, in which, given his status of authority over the child, he places the responsibility for what occurred on the latter. The *Clinical Diary* shows that Ferenczi was willing to pursue this path relentlessly, since he experimented with mutual analysis, mainly with his patient Rn (Elisabeth Severn), and perhaps briefly with Dm (Clara Thompson) as well. It was a painful and anxiety provoking experience that he ended up interrupting and criticising.

Ferenczi's self-critical attitude made analysts uncomfortable as well. They were forced to admit that beyond the love and devotion of their patients and pupils, the latter had to free themselves of these transferential and identificatory feelings, and that their analysts had to help them achieve this goal. In other words, they had to forfeit their patients' love and gratitude, and their pupils' admiration and loyalty; they had to accept being abandoned by the former, and being criticised and contradicted by the latter. Of course, in theory this is the very aim of analysis and analytic training: to bring patients and trainees to think for themselves and develop critical awareness. But in fact, it is difficult to relinquish the gratitude of a patient one believes one has helped. As for training analysts, especially those who have developed coherent personal theories, they wish to found a new school and to have disciples who will spread and expand these theories. In this respect as well, Ferenczi's expectation can seem unbearably frustrating.

In his "Reflections upon Trauma", Ferenczi describes the mechanisms involved in psychic shock and its consequences: atomization, disintegration and possibly even death. This distressing subject becomes even more poignant given our knowledge that Ferenczi wrote these notes while suffering from a fatal illness, and that he was trying to formulate this personal experience. The uneasiness provoked by these notes is increased by the description of various defence mechanisms against the fear of death, which ultimately prove useless, leaving self-destruction, death or madness as the only possible outcome.

These five articles shed light on all the demands Ferenczi made on his colleagues and, above all, on himself, and on the criticism he addressed to analysts. He confronts them with their cowardice, hypocrisy and inadequacy. Moreover, although he considers these failings inevitable, he does not excuse them: analysts must be constantly aware, be willing to live with this guilt and even admit it to their patients. In addition, no patient should be considered incurable from the start. It is up to the analyst to look tirelessly for the right manner and techniques to help him. When reminded that no one should be expected to do the impossible, Ferenczi replies that the frontier between possible and impossible is very hard to establish. The analyst must constantly fine-tune his listening and his ability to be receptive, all the while knowing that in his profession there is neither perfection nor safety.

One may ask what impelled Ferenczi to follow such a difficult, painful, far from ego-building, and even distressing and dangerous path. His last articles, his *Clinical Diary* and his correspondence with Freud provide two possible answers: on the one hand, a deep feeling of guilt rooted in his childhood, specifically in his relationship with his mother, and the self-punishing tendency resulting from it; on the other hand, the need to express his criticism of Freud and of the rigidity of the analytic process and techniques established by him. Ferenczi also blamed Freud for the inadequate analysis he had as his analysand, because Freud did not perceive and analyse his negative transference. Many of the demands Ferenczi addressed to other analysts were no doubt intended first of all for Freud. In general, Ferenczi blames him for showing little interest in the therapeutic aspect of analysis, for his clear contempt of patients, and for the theoretical and technical rigidity which prevents analysis from being useful in treating certain pathologies.

Criticism of this kind is implicit in Ferenczi's last articles. But most of the analytic community of that period could not bear for any aspect of the new Freudian science, still poorly understood and often under attack, to be questioned. The intangible nature of the doctrine and the technique was precisely what provided the greatest security. The mission of the IPA was to safeguard and ensure the transmission of this Freudian edifice. For many analysts, this doctrine and these techniques constituted the evaluation criteria for their own work; it was thanks to them that these analysts could carry on with their trying daily practice. It is understandable that, overall, they disapproved of this research which upset a sense of security they badly needed.

The fate, or intention, of prestigious masters who create a coherent theoretical and practical system that can be passed on is to acquire the greatest possible number of loyal followers who will adhere to this system as it is. The new school of thought bears their name, and those who deviate from the recommended doctrine are excluded or exclude themselves. Ferenczi never established a new school, and did not provide a coherent, ready-to-use set of tools for theory and practice. He advocated free and continuous research based on clinical practice. He wanted to encourage a critical sense and individual responsibility.

Ferenczi's clinical practice was particularly difficult. The patients most often discussed in the *Clinical Diary* recounted early and violent sexual traumas inflicted by family members, or by their father. Contrary to most of his colleagues, Ferenczi chose to believe these narratives, partly because they emerge gradually, bit by bit, during successive trance-like states; and also because many of his patients admitted in their analysis that they had behaved in similar ways with children.

The bourgeois society of Freud's era — and that of most of his colleagues — found it very hard to admit the truth of these extremely unpleasant stories; it was very tempting to consider them, as a matter of course, crazy inventions that it would be crazy to believe. To believe that such stories are always pure fantasies originating in forbidden and repressed desires would be much more acceptable. In addition, such fantasies would lend themselves to the classical analytic technique. It would be possible to interpret, explain, rid the person of guilt feelings, and at the same time eliminate the guilt feelings of the presumed perpetrator of the abuse, who would thus recover his respectability and authority. But if we admit that the stories told by these very perturbed patients described by Ferenczi are true and testify to real psychic shocks inflicted by another person, the classic methods no longer apply. The therapist would then be dealing with splitting, with deep wounds whose roots descend all the way to the organic; and he would have to suture these wounds, help them heal and reinsert them in psychic functioning.

To reach the level of these deep traumas, Ferenczi tried to guide his patients into the indeterminate zone where the psychical and the organic intermingle and become one. As a result, he had great difficulty linking what he observed with accepted theories, in order to describe and name the phenomena he witnessed, to convey his ideas and impressions to his colleagues in a way they could understand. At the edges of the unconscious, Ferenczi struggled with the elusive and the intangible, to try to forge new therapeutic methods.

But those who approach madness too closely are always regarded with suspicion, even when they do so to better understand it. Unless one defines oneself as radically different from the madman, one is already on the edge of an abyss into which it is easy to fall. Even among psychiatrists, attitudes towards madness vary widely. Some have empathy for their patients, try to understand them, to find structure and meaning in their delusions, give them the reference points they lack, look for the threads that could serve to suture their division. Other psychiatrists "fight" mental illness, which they strive to eliminate rather than heal. They cannot bear the existence of madness, they cannot bear what it tries to express. For madmen bring us into question, they force us to see the price we pay for our balance, and reveal our potential frailties. For these psychiatrists, it is a blessing that we now have drugs which put an end to anxiety-provoking discourses, and bring some relief to patients.

Ferenczi clearly belonged to the first category of psychiatrists. He never stopped trying to invent methods adapted to individual cases, to accompany his patients in their particular worlds and allow them to emerge from these worlds and attain more tolerable states. One of his most objectionable experiments, we might say one of the most "crazy", aimed at providing his patients with the support they needed, was his attempt at mutual analysis, described only in the *Clinical Diary*. Reasons to criticise and reject this technique abound. But this criticism does not eliminate the need to find an answer to the problems Ferenczi wanted to solve. Once again, he brought his colleagues face to face with a situation in which it was very tempting to assert that the pathologies involved did not lend themselves to analytic treatment, and that only Ferenczi's *furor sanandi* impelled him to insist on using this method.

What then was the problem Ferenczi tried to solve through mutual analysis?

As we have seen, the analyst's reaction to the transference of the patient, called counter-transference, is an unavoidable phenomenon, even an indispensable tool for understanding and perceiving what the patient is trying to convey. The term "counter-transference" is somewhat misleading, for it seems to suggest that the analyst is merely reacting to the patient's transference. In fact, the analyst reacts with his whole being, with his past and present experience; therefore, it would be more accurate to speak simply of transference. The analyst is able to become aware and understand part of this transference, but some aspects of it always elude him, and it is precisely these elements which remain unconscious that often play the most active role in the relationship. Despite this, how can they be integrated in the analytic process, especially with patients who are particularly sensitive — perhaps to the point of fragility — , to the unexpressed and the uncontrolled? Those who were never able to build a structured image of the world and of their own place in it, due to the incompetence or instability of their entourage, or those who were destabilised by a more or less early trauma, could be exposed to a repetition of the initial shock because of these uncontrollable elements. They never know what to expect from the analyst, regardless of the latter's desire to be reliable.

In order for an analysis to take place and be carried through with such patients, the analyst must provide a truly stable and reliable environment where they feel safe. They need to know what to expect from their analyst, given the ambivalent feelings they necessarily inspire in him — a fact of which they are perfectly aware. This ambivalence, their own and the analyst's, is what causes the greatest anxiety for them. This is because in the past they had to face it in a situation of emotional instability and total insecurity. In the course of analysis, they should be able to integrate these feelings with the help of stable reference points set in place gradually. Through mutual analysis, Ferenczi tried to give these wounded patients, who were hypersensitive and had fragmented personalities, the opportunity to assess their analyst at the emotional level, to feel in what way and to what degree they could count on him. The analysis of the analyst was meant to supply them with the elements they needed to be able to do this. In particular, letting the patients discover the analyst's mistakes, his oversights, his weaknesses, his negative feelings in a situation in which the analyst admits them and takes responsibility for them. One could think that revealing oneself this way to severely ill people involves taking an insane risk. Ferenczi resolved to take this risk, not without admitting that there was something to fear. From this point of view, mutual analysis can look like an extreme remedy for the patient and a kamikaze strategy on the part of the analyst. The experiment proved to be impossible to apply, but Ferenczi was an innovator. He exposed himself to emotional upheaval without protecting himself, as Marie Curie had exposed herself to radiation. Today, each of us deals as best he can with extremely fragile patients; thanks to Ferenczi, we see the problem more clearly, but as far as a solution is concerned, each of us does what he can, one patient at a time. As far as I know, there is no standardised technique that can be passed on to others. And I doubt that there ever will be. In such situations, each analyst must invent a method to use with each patient, a way of being the analyst finds bearable, and which gives the patient the support he needs.

It is as if Ferenczi had placed all analysts — starting with himself — in a kind of double bind: being perfect, while knowing that there is no such thing, and at the same time recognising one's shortcomings. Taking responsibility for one's shortcomings, but never stopping there. Admitting that the analysis cannot solve everything, but acting as if all problems can be solved by the analyst provided he finds or invents the necessary means.

In his *Clinical Diary*, Ferenczi expresses the thought that it is this conflict which is killing him: "A certain strength in my psychological makeup seems to persist", he writes on October 2, 1932, six months before his death, "so that instead of falling ill psychically, I can only destroy — or be destroyed — in my organic depths". And on the same day he asks: "Is the choice here one between dying and 'rearranging myself' — and this at the age of fifty-nine?"

Can we say, in conclusion, that perfectly sane people can find themselves — and perhaps place themselves — in insane situations? Or situations that seem insane to those who do not understand their underlying reasons. And that these daring innovators can be called insane when they try to describe their experiences to others?

THE FREUD-FERENCZI RELATION IN LIGHT OF THEIR CORRESPONDENCE

People like Freud and Ferenczi, who leave a mark on their era thanks to their personality as much as their ideas, always tend to become legendary, in other words, the object of all kinds of legends. Thus, according to legend, Freud and Ferenczi felt great affection for each other as soon as they met.

There developed between them a warm, intimate, even tender relation, based on what Freud called, in one of his letters, "an intimate community of life, feeling and interest". But in 1930 this relationship came to an abrupt end at Ferenczi's initiative, when he distanced himself in order to pursue experimental paths that led beyond psychoanalysis. Some versions of the legend claim that their correspondence was interrupted in 1930, and that Ferenczi was a dissenter, like Alfred Adler or Wilhelm Stekel.

Like all legends, this is an oversimplified account,

intended to highlight certain aspects of the story rather than others. It testifies to the instant mutual sympathy between them, to their friendship and a few major incidents, but it leaves out the complexity of their friendship. Yet this complexity reflects an important fact about human beings: the ambivalence and, simultaneously, the continuity of feelings ranging between "normalcy", neurosis and psychosis, between sadism and masochism, in short, between black and white. The aim is not to abolish oppositions, but to highlight the existence of a continuous back-and-forth between opposites, which makes it possible to suppose that a human being can understand another human being, even if the latter seems very different, even detestable. All these subtleties were present in the relationship between Freud and Ferenczi, which is therefore worth reconstituting in all its complexity — present from the start — , and which unfolded in a context that allowed the quality of their exchanges to remain constant throughout the duration of their friendship.

But — or as a result — , when Ferenczi decided to undergo analysis, he could not imagine choosing as his analyst anyone but Freud. And the analysis was undertaken, despite the fact that Freud expressed clear reluctance, fearing that this enterprise would make him lose a friend. This analysis triggered an extremely intense and passionate transference on Ferenczi's part. Freud reacted by attempting to subdue the excess of passion by maintaining the analysis at an intellectual level. A large part of the father-son relation, in the transference as well as in the counter-transference, remained unresolved. Ferenczi blamed Freud for not having analysed his negative transference. I believe that, in addition, Freud was not aware of his own negative transference. This experience of the analysis no doubt rendered their subsequent relations even more complex, despite the warm feelings between them and the strength of their friendship. The correspondence between the two men contains indications of these complications, right from the start.

This correspondence covers a period of about twenty-five years, between 1908 and 1933 (not thirty years, as one version of the legend claims). There are 1250 letters, which make it possible to follow the intricacies of their relation, as well as the history of psychoanalysis in the course of that 25-year period. Some commentators, like Ilse Grubrich-Simitis (1980, 1986) or Susanne Hommel (1990), consider this correspondence a sort of epistolary analysis lasting twenty-five years; essentially, the analysis of Ferenczi by Freud, but with some attempts by Ferenczi to analyse Freud — attempts the master was quick to cut short. Ferenczi made a last attempt at analysing Freud in his 1932 *Clinical Diary*, which Freud never read.

The correspondence starts with Ferenczi's letter dated January 18, 1908, in which he expresses his desire to meet Freud, who sets a meeting with him for Sunday, February 2nd. Ferenczi also wrote the last letter of the correspondence, on May 4, 1933, a few weeks before his death on May 22.

This exchange of letters gives us some glimpses into the private life and internal world of the two men, and the development of their relationship. It was an asymmetrical relationship: Freud was looking for a loyal, efficient, affectionate, free-spirited collaborator, who could nevertheless be guided, a kind of son, but one who had already solved his Oedipal conflict with another father; Ferenczi seems to have been looking for a loving, understanding, protective father willing to let him pursue freely his personal undertakings, even when he did not agree. Thus, from the beginning, the ambivalence present on both sides indicates the differences in their deepest motivations, in their way of thinking and their sensitivity. This ambivalence also reveals their way of dealing with these differences.

This means that problems did not emerge suddenly, on a certain occasion; they were there from the start. But obviously, they did not prevent the development of a stable and productive relationship. It is impossible to say how this relationship would have evolved if Ferenczi's premature death would not have cut it short. But we know that in 1939, when Michael Balint, Ferenczi's literary executor, was preparing the latter's unpublished texts for publication, he submitted them to Freud — including "Confusion of Tongues", which Freud had found so shocking seven years earlier — who now made no objection to them. In his introduction to the *Clinical Diary*, Balint wrote: "Freud [...] was sent all the hitherto unpublished material. It can be stated that he followed our work with interest, did not object to any part of the text proposed by us; on the contrary, he expressed his admiration for Ferenczi's ideas, until then unknown to him [...]".

It is impossible to know what direction Ferenczi's research would have taken had he lived. But Ferenczi himself connects the direction of his investigations, his illness and his relationship with Freud. The question of the therapeutic value of regression had run into an impasse. A note written in 1932 attests to this: "Balint takes up things where I got stuck", Ferenczi wrote in Luchon, during his last vacation.

In addition to this analytically-oriented correspondence, Ferenczi convinced Freud — not without difficulty — to become his analyst; Ferenczi's analysis was conducted by Freud in three segments. The first took place in October 1914, and was brutally interrupted when Ferenczi was drafted into service as a military doctor. The second segment was conducted between June 14 and July 5, 1916, and the last in September and October of the same year, over a period of about fifteen days.

This brief analysis had been preceded by preliminary steps. It had a great impact on Ferenczi, and had many future consequences throughout the lives of both men: for Ferenczi, they appear even in his *Clinical Diary*, and for Freud, they are present even after his friend's death, in the famous 1937 article "Analysis Terminable and Interminable".

PRELIMINARIES

The two friends' ambivalent feelings are apparent from the start in their correspondence. As early as the summer of 1908, Freud invited Ferenczi to join him in Berchtesgaden, where he was spending his vacation with his family. On May 9th, Ferenczi wrote: "I [...] request that you inform me [...] when I can avail myself of your permission to spend some time with you in Berchtesgaden. [...] If I could be of assistance to you in some work or other, I would do so with pleasure". Freud answered this offer of assistance on May 10th by sending a polite refusal: "You are welcome at any time [...]. It is understood at the outset that you will not disturb me in my work and that I won't have to take any precautions against you [...]. Now and then you will take a meal with us or climb a mountain with my boys".

Another snag of this type appears in an exchange of letters in January 1909, concerning a paper of Ferenczi's that Freud does not want to present at one of the Wednesday Society meetings:

"[Your paper] deserves [...] efforts on its behalf. You can imagine why I did not favor presenting your ideas in the Wednesday Society. The question of priority would have been confused thereby. I hope that you also know that I am making difficulties with the *Jahrbuch* only in your interest, and that only for the time being as well. I don't have the feeling of being the "benefactor" toward you and others and thus do [not] tie to my actions the otherwise justified fears of which you speak".

In his answer written on January 11th and 12th, Ferenczi insists on calling Freud a benefactor, but points out his slip, that is, the omission of "not" or another negation. Ferenczi writes: "No matter how hard I try, I cannot now remember any fears that I expressed to you. I presume that the sentence is somehow garbled; perhaps a "not" or some other negation is missing there. As a true adherent of your teachings, however, I cannot consider an occasional writing error meaningless [...]".

In his January 17th letter, Freud admits his mistake and "explains" his slip: "You are correct. The sentence lacks a negation. The letter was written on the eve of an inner earthquake, a bad migraine, and at such times I have the bad habit of directly contradicting myself. The attack certainly has no worse significance".

It seems that Ferenczi did not find this far-from-psychoanalytic explanation adequate, and was left harbouring a certain bitterness. This is signalled by the fact that he changed the salutation of his next letter from "Dear Professor" (which he had been using for some time) to the more formal "Very honoured professor" he had used in his first letters.

Very soon, Freud conceived the possibility that his "dear son", as he sometimes addressed him, could become his son-in-law. There are some references to this in the letters. At first, Freud thinks of his eldest daughter Mathilde. When he announces her engagement to Robert Hollitscher in a letter dated October 27, 1908, what he says is: "If I answer your letters so late and inadequately, then one can justifiably conclude that results from an external disruption, because internally nothing has changed between us. In fact, I can inform you that my daughter has become engaged to a young man of her own choosing [...]".

Later, concerning Sophie's marriage, Freud wrote in a letter dated July 20, 1912:

"The young man [Max Halberstadt]'s visit naturally ended with an acknowledgement of the engagement [...]. There you have an at-the-time unintended overdetermination to the motif of the "three sisters" or three daughters [...]."

We might be tempted to interpret this somewhat

cryptic statement as a sign of this secret desire of Freud's. Of his three daughters, only Anna was still available. It may, in fact, have been Freud's secret desire to see Ferenczi become part of his own family that made him take such a critical view of Elma, who had Ferenczi's preference.

On March 12, 1911, Freud, a fervent collector of antiquities, as we know, purchased some valuable objects to celebrate the 25th anniversary of the start of his practice. In a letter to Ferenczi written the same day, he speaks of this, saying: "[...] I can't get very rich this year. That hasn't prevented me from presenting myself with various treasures in honor of the twenty-fifth anniversary of my practice[...]. Your earrings arrived right on the day of the purchase and suffered in comparison". For Freud, this lack of tact was a rare occurrence.

THE "PALERMO INCIDENT"

The first inkling of a request by Ferenczi to be analysed by Freud is to be found in the significant events which constitute the so-called "Palermo incident". In 1910, Freud and Ferenczi spent their vacation together in Sicily. At the time, Ferenczi was immersed in his self-analysis. He had been attempting to draw Freud into a sort of epistolary analysis, but had given up in the face of Freud's very clear reluctance. But despite his best efforts, slips of the pen, double meanings and unintentional references abound in his letters. Freud was also making this trip at a difficult time in his life. He was writing an essay on the Schreber case and was, for the first time, considering the possibility of accepting Ferenczi's help. In fact, he hoped that Ferenczi would prove to be an efficient and loyal secretary who would deal with all the practical matters and transcribe the text as Freud dictated it to him. But this was not what Ferenczi wanted. His wish was that he and Freud establish a relation of complete trust, that they exchange confidences and allow themselves total "analytic honesty" — in short, that they have an almost symbiotic relationship. Ferenczi would have liked to take part in the elaboration of ideas, and discuss them in an atmosphere of mutual sincerity and trust, as had been the case a year earlier when they travelled together to the United States. But Freud no longer wanted such a degree of openness after his experience with Fliess. Freud was irritated, and Ferenczi deeply wounded. An exchange of blame and explanations followed, succeeding only in emphasising the differences in their respective goals.

Ferenczi seemed ready to take all the blame. On September 28, he wrote: "Still, I am sorry that you had in me a travel companion who is still so much in need of education. [...] I have begun to subject the events of our living together [...] to extensive self-criticism".

To which Freud replied on October 2nd:

"[...] I would like to have had you *different* in some respects. [...] you certainly expected to wallow in constant intellectual stimulation, whereas nothing is more repugnant to me than posing [...]. I would have wished for you to [...] take your place next to me as a companion with equal rights, which you did not succeed in doing".

Ferenczi accepted the criticism, but tried to defend his position. On October 3rd, he wrote: "I was longing for personal [...] companionship with you [...] and I felt [...] forced back into the infantile role. [...] I believed that *absolute* mutual openness [...] could be possible between two psychoanalytically-minded people [...]. But [...] you wanted nothing but to spend four weeks after a strenuous year of work in very well-earned rest in beautiful surroundings in the company of a compatible travelling companion. [...] I would [...] have been very grateful if you had said what you wrote in your letter while we were under way. [...] During the trip I played the ridiculous and certainly very repugnant role of one who is misunderstood [...]. If you had scolded me thoroughly instead of being eloquently silent!"

Freud also wanted to make himself clear. On October 6th he replied:

"Why didn't I scold you and in so doing open the way to an understanding? [...] it was a weakness on my part. [...] I no longer have any need for that full opening of my personality, but you have also understood it and correctly returned to its traumatic cause. [...] This need has been extinguished in me since Fliess's case, with the overcoming of which you just saw me occupied. A piece of homosexual investment has been withdrawn and utilized for the enlargement of my own ego. I have succeeded where the paranoiac fails".

Apparently, Ferenczi had trouble accepting this explanation, and sent the following answer on October 12th: "I still hold firm that it is not honesty but superfluous secrecy that is abnormal, although I do admit that the former can be overly emphasized by infantile influences".

The question the two men appear to be wrestling with is homosexuality. While Freud believes that he himself has solved this problem through an enlargement of his ego, he sees Ferenczi as experiencing it in an infantile mode. But to an outside observer, the relation between the two men is likely to resemble a love relation.

This "Palermo incident" remained a critical point of contention between them, and they referred back to it many times.

FERENCZI'S ROMANTIC AND MATRIMONIAL PROBLEMS

Freud played no small role in Ferenczi's love life. Of course, Ferenczi insistently invited him to do so, but Freud himself was too invovled to maintain a more neutral position.

The "Elma affair" started in January 1911. Since 1900, Ferenczi had been having a love affair with a married woman, Gizella Pálos, née Altschul, who was eight years older than him. She had two daughters, Elma and Magda. Gizella lived separated from her husband, Géza Pálos, who refused to divorce her, so that the affair had to stay more or less secret to keep up appearances.

Elma, the elder daughter, beautiful and very sought-after, suffered from great emotional instability and was unable to establish a stable relationship with any of the young men who courted her.

In February 1911, Gizella and Elma made a trip to Vienna in order for Elma to undergo surgery to correct a scar. The two women visited Freud. The latter liked Gizella immediately, but judged Elma harshly, seeing her as a superficial coquette, and even making a verbal diagnosis of *dementia praecox*, which would prove to be totally false. In fact, all her life Elma proved to possess a sharp mind, great sensitivity and exceptional moral integrity. One may think that Freud sensed the complications to come and incriminated Elma to release Ferenczi from blame.

Gizella asked Ferenczi to become Elma's analyst, which at the time did not constitute an error or a transgression, but Freud did warn Ferenczi about potential difficulties. The treatment started in July 1911, and the difficulties Freud foresaw soon showed themselves. A few months later, one of Elma's spurned lovers committed suicide. Elma responded with deepening depression and the therapy stalled. In December, Ferenczi's "analytic neutrality" gave way; he fell passionately in love with his patient. Greatly perturbed, he asked Freud for advice. The latter urged him to put an end to the analysis at once.

It was Freud who would become Elma's analyst, reluctantly, in response to Ferenczi's insistent request. This analysis was conducted in a very unorthodox manner: throughout its duration, the two men discussed with the greatest indiscretion everything that transpired in Elma's analysis, and in Ferenczi's personal relations with her. It was very much as if, for Ferenczi, this analysis was a sort of vicarious personal treatment.

For the next two years, Ferenczi was torn between his affection for his faithful friend and mistress Gizella, who understood him, shared his scientific interests and forgave everything; and Elma, beautiful, young and sensitive, and able to give him children, contrary to Gizella, who could no longer have children. Ferenczi's correspondence with Freud during this period took a more and more analytic turn. Yet, neither man ever mentions one of Elma's most remarkable qualities, apparent in her letters to Ferenczi and to her mother. These letters reveal the subtlety of her feelings, the elegance and sensitivity with which she bore these two trying years at the end of which she was the one who lost. Gizella showed Elma's letters to Ferenczi, who copied some passages to send to Freud, whole passages like the ones that follow. In January 1912: "[...] I am anxious about the future. My character is so unbalanced, [...] that it would be a risk for anyone to take me as a wife." And on February 18th: "If you and Sándor agree that you can't live without each other, tell me frankly. As long as you will feel his loss so deeply, he will not be able to tear himself away from you internally, and I will not be able to accept his love with a light heart." Indeed, the two women try to outdo each other in their love and devotion to Sándor, and their affection and abnegation one for the other, which ultimately makes the situation even more inextricable.

This period was also very trying for Freud; his advice was sought constantly, and he was often asked to intervene, while he was conducting an analysis with Elma. But he clearly took Gizella's side, either openly or through what we now call paradoxical injunctions. For instance, on February 13, 1912, he wrote to Ferenczi:

"[...] she [Elma] emphasized her love for you. [...] I am gradually getting used to the idea that you could take your summer trip with her instead of with me [...]. I would like to note that masochistic impulses very frequently take their course in an unfavorable marital choice. [...] Note that in saying this I am in no way taking sides against Elma".

Let us note in passing that here Freud positions himself as Elma's rival. We know that he was the one who won out in this situation. Freud never considered Gizella, whom he clearly preferred, a rival.

Ferenczi finally broke off his relationship with Elma and married Gizella, still regretting that he lost Elma, something for which he blamed Freud. To escape this painful emotional tangle, Elma rushed into an unhappy marriage with a Hungaro-American journalist, Hervé Laurvick, from whom she was soon separated. As for Gizella, she married Sándor as soon as she obtained her divorce from Pálos, but she remained torn between her love for Sándor and her love for her daughter. Eight years later, she still talked about the possibility of divorcing Sándor so that he could marry Elma, who was now divorced. Ferenczi had trouble accepting Gizella's age, which deprived him of the possibility of having children. Freud, the father of six children, did not consider paternity indispensable in a man's life; at least, he tried to convince Ferenczi of this.

Ferenczi's paternal transference to Freud became more and more pronounced. Freud drew attention to it by starting one of his letters with the salutation "Dear son". Ferenczi felt that he was trying to "extort a free analysis" by flooding Freud with self-analytic letters. The latter answered in a jocular tone: "Just try to extort something from me!"

THE ACTUAL ANALYSIS

It is in a letter dated December 28, 1912 that Ferenczi formulates a direct request for analysis: "It was and is in my intention [...] to go into analysis with you [...]". In 1913, this project becomes explicit, but Freud is reluctant. He is afraid the analysis will interfere with their relationship. His fear is well-founded. Of course, this relationship always had ups and downs; but the exposition to the "furnace of tranference", as Ferenczi called it, cannot take place without leaving some traces, and both men knew it.

Ferenczi himself showed some ambivalence, expressed through various forms of procrastination. But he reiterated his request regularly. Then, for nearly ten months, the question of analysis was never mentioned, although Ferenczi's letters became more and more self-analytic. He was troubled by this and complained that he had difficulty finding the right "tone" for his letters to Freud.

The First World War broke out at the end of July 1914. Under the pressure created by these events, Ferenczi wanted to use the time he had left before being inducted into the army, to start his analysis with Freud at long last. The latter, upset by this situation, was worried about his sons already on the front lines, and wanted to have his friend near him. He told Ferenczi he was anxious to see him in Vienna. Ferenczi had made up his mind, but was still ambivalent: "You know, of course, that I am suffering from the memory of the good father. Perhaps the bad one will loosen my tongue!", he wrote to Freud on August 24, 1914. On September 8th, he described a dream portraying Freud as a doctor who refuses to analyse him.

Finally, at the end of September 1914, Ferenczi decided to go to Vienna to start his analysis. He managed to make one more slip: he missed his train and could therefore only start his analysis on October 1st. The analysis was intensive, with two one-hour sessions a day. It was interrupted after fifteen days, when Ferenczi was called up to serve as a military physician. He found this interruption hard to bear and compensated by writing self-analytic letters once again. Freud tried to offer comfort: "The sudden interruption of the treatment [...] was very stupid. But it couldn't be helped". But he disapproved of the attempts at self-analysis, which, in his opinion, could only fail. After a a few weeks, Ferenczi gave them up. Concerning these weeks spent in analysis, on December 31st he wrote: "Despite their incompleteness, [...] you were nonetheless able to a certain extent to change my neurotic attitude, which has been evident for a number of years". All things considered, Ferenczi felt that this period of analysis was the most valuable experience he had in 1914.

His military service prevented him from pursuing his analysis in 1915. He was stationed in the city of Pápa, far from Gizella and Elma; he learned to ride horses and undertook to analyse his commanding officer while they were riding together. Being away from the usual sources of tension in his life was beneficial: he felt much better. He took time to outline the initial premises for his book *Thalassa*, which would be one of the works written by Ferenczi that Freud most admired. The latter did not abandon his friend while he had to be away: he visited him in Pápa. There is a photograph showing him with Ferenczi in uniform.

Finally, in 1916, Ferenczi was transferred back to Budapest, where he could take up his usual activities and his work as an analyst. He also went back to dealing with his usual problems: hesitation between Gizella and Elma, epistolary analysis and attacks of hypochondria. He considered continuing his analysis with Freud. The latter was starting to lose patience with his friend's endless hesitation and urged him to act and get married. Specifically, to marry Gizella, whom he always overtly preferred.

In order to make a decision, Ferenczi requested the continuation of his analysis, which he was disposed to pursue througout the month of June. Freud accepted, setting certain conditions: "[...] you should at least have one meal with us daily. Technique at least will require that nothing personal will be discussed outside the sessions". This flexibility of technique would not be accepted today.

The analysis continued, still with two sessions a day. Once he was back in Budapest, Ferenczi described his impressions to Freud:

> "[...] these three weeks were the decisive ones in my life and for my life. [...] Today I said to Gizella that I have become another person, one who is less interesting but more normal. I also admitted to her that something in me pities the old, somewhat unsettled man [...]. For the moment the break in our doctor-patient relations was too sudden not to have caused a certain shock effect".

The ambivalence present from the start in the relation between the two men is still there: Ferenczi admits that he finds it hard to feel gratitude towards his analyst, because the therapy deprived him of the pleasure that accompanied his symptoms, as well as of infantile irresponsibility, since it has transformed him into a responsible adult.

Ferenczi claimed to have learned a great deal in the course of his two-part analysis with Freud, about himself and about psychoanalytic technique, particularly the role of repetition. However, he remained just as undecided regarding his marital choice. The two men agreed that the work was not finished, and that it should be continued in September, during their vacation. They set aside two weeks for this purpose, planning to have two one-and-a-half-hour sessions a day. It was a short period, but the work would be intensive; Ferenczi would have liked to have a fourth hour each day, had he been bold enough to ask.

This last section of "concentrated" analysis took place between September 25th and October 9th, 1916. Ferenczi was deeply unsettled by it. Despite Freud's repeated refusals, he tried to continue the work through self-analytic letters. On October 24th Freud wrote him: "When I said the treatment was at an end, I did not mean it was terminated". He added that it was "at an end because it cannot be continued for at least six months and would thus place itself in the service of the neurotic intention"[19]. But Ferenczi could not recover from his emotional upheaval. On October 30th he wrote to Freud: "The effects unleashed by the treatment have been undulating up and down in me". Then, on November 13th: "I am going [...] through tormenting times".

On November 16, Freud tries to be very clear: "I consider your attempt at analysis finished, — finished, not terminated, but rather broken off because of unfavorable circumstances".

At last, Freud began to lose patience. On November 26th, he adopted a sterner tone: "[...] you are now using your analysis as a means of confusing your affairs". Ferenczi replied the very next day. He took note of the reproach, but explained: "It might be that I actually muddled up the situation... but I must also let work in me untroubled the hostile tendencies towards the father that certainly are existing in me. I am... fully aware of the tranferential character of my reaction [...]".

Thus, Ferenczi was perfectly aware of his ambivalence. But it would be reasonable to ask if this ambivalence was rooted only in the transference created in the analytic situation, or if it was an inherent aspect of the relation between the two men. These few lines express the criticism that Ferenczi was to address to Freud at the end of his life, namely that he neglected analysing his negative transference. Freud was still defending himself against this criticism ten years later, even after the death of his friend, in his article "Analysis Terminable and Interminable".

On December 24th, Christmas Eve, Ferenczi finally ended his attempts at extending his treatment through epistolary analysis. He wrote to Freud: "Let this sheet of paper be the proof that I have again attained a degree of normality. [...] I am happy to feel grateful once more".

In the seventeen years of correspondence which followed the end of this experience there are many references to Ferenczi's analysis with Freud. Many signs of

---

19 Translator's Note: Modified version of p.149, The *Correspondence of Sigmund Freud and Sándor Ferenczi: 1914-1919*, Falzeder, E. and Brabant, E. (Eds.), Harvard University Press, 1996.

clearly unresolved transference and countertransference punctuate the exchanges between the two men. As Freud so rightly remarked, the analysis was finished but not terminated.

Ferenczi was still unable to decide whether to marry Elma or Gizella. But Freud had already decided for him. On January 23, 1917, he wrote to her:

"Since I know you [...], it was an urgent wish on my part to see you united. I have worked on the realization of this wish with the most varied means, directly and indirectly, in friendly intercourse and through analysis [...]".

One could not be more honest or clear. The marriage finally took place in 1919 in tragic circumstances: Géza Pálos died of a heart attack while Sándor and Gizella were on their way to the registry office to get married.

GEORG GRODDECK AND GRODDECKIAN CONCEPTS

Georg Groddeck first comes on the scene in 1917. He writes to Freud, who is enthusiastic about his letter and forwards it to Ferenczi at once. But Ferenczi's reaction is much more guarded. Then, as Freud's interest in Groddeck gradually diminishes, Ferenczi's interest in him increases. Freud borrowed Groddeck's concept of the It, after which he paid no more attention to him.

Ferenczi and Groddeck shared a common objective: finding a way for analytic concepts to be of use in medicine, for analysis to be useful to the general practitioner. This project was to be carried out subsequently by Ferenczi's pupil Michael Balint, through the now widely known Balint Groups.

Finally, in 1921 Ferenczi met Groddeck when he visited his clinic in Baden-Baden. He wanted to study Groddeck's methods, and benefit from them personally as well. This therapeutic practice, which we would call psychosomatic today, seemed increasingly worthwhile to Ferenczi. The two men formed an immediate friendship. That same year, at Christmas, Ferenczi confided in his new friend in a long letter with self-analytic overtones in which he referred to his childhood, his relationship with Freud, his matrimonial dilemma and the role Freud played in it, in a much more free and spontaneous tone than that of his letters to Freud, about whom he wrote: "[for me] there was [...] too much the father".

Ferenczi and Groddeck entered into what might be viewed as an initial experiment with mutual analysis, which Ferenczi would undertake later with Elisabeth Severn. After this, Ferenczi went to Baden-Baden regularly for therapeutic holidays at Groddeck's clinic; he also sent some of his friends there, including Frédéric Kovács, the husband of his pupil and colleague Vilma, and Elma, the daughter of Gizella, who had been his wife since 1919.

THE BOOK CO-AUTHORED WITH OTTO RANK

The book whose English title is *The Development of Psycho-Analysis* was written in 1923 by Rank and Ferenczi, on the occasion of a contest proposed by Freud the previous year, dealing with the theme of the interdependence between psychoanalytic theory and technique. The manuscript was submitted to Freud, who initially showed great interest in it. Then, little by little, he became more critical. Ferenczi was upset. He tried to explain. Freud encouraged him to think independently, without seeking his approval at any cost. But Freud's tolerant attitude had its limits, as it became clear later, when Ferenczi's investigations took a direction Freud interpreted as a rift between them, almost a betrayal on his old friend's part.

This was perhaps the first true theoretical disagreement between Freud and Ferenczi, focusing on the respective importance of traumatic experiences and fantasy. Abraham and Jones were violently opposed to the ideas expressed in Ferenczi and Rank's book. Freud tried to avoid playing the role of mediator, and was able to quell the conflict to a degree. The 1924 Salzburg Psychoanalytical Congress proceeded relatively smoothly. However, it was Rank who paid the price for the reconciliation.

Afterwards, Freud and Ferenczi tried to reestablish the amiable relationship they had before. But the differences of character and of purpose that always existed between them became more and more pronounced. In 1926–27, Ferenczi spent seven months in the United States; Freud saw this as a possible parting of the ways. All his grievances against Americans resurfaced: their shocking customs for a European of the Old World like himself, the memory of his disappointment with Jung, Rank's desertion, and the controversy about lay analysis.

TECHNICAL PROBLEMS

Ferenczi, a physician above all, was always interested in the technical aspects of the work. He considered therapeutic success of primary importance. Freud, who for some time had only been considering analysis as a means of generating an income, was much more interested in theoretical research. He looked upon Ferenczi's experiments with skepticism, concerned about the inevitable errors and excesses associated with any experimentation.

After developing the so-called active technique, and then the principle of flexibility and indulgence, Ferenczi became more and more interested in searching for methods making it possible to treat cases considered at the time as unsuitable for analysis, that we would now call borderline cases or psychoses. As a result, he became the therapist who treated the desperate cases his colleagues sent him from all over the world, and particularly from the United States. This is how he came to treat two of the cases studied closely in his *Clinical Diary*, Elisabeth Severn and Clara Thompson.

At this time, Ferenczi's investigations focused on the deep layers of the psyche where the organic and the psychical intertwine, and on therapeutic methods which can exert an effect at this level. This is what led him to pursue his research on the respective importance of traumatic experience and fantasy. He felt that traditional analysis involves the risk of repeating the trauma, unless the necessary safeguards are taken. He insisted particularly on the need for tactfulness. This perspective was based on Ferenczi's clinical practice, as well as on certain experiences and events in his personal life.

Ferenczi always tended to respond to conflictual situations with somatic symptoms. During this period, around 1930, he was not in good health; he suffered from all sorts of ailments. But given his hypochondriacal tendencies, it was very difficult for his physicians, as well as for Freud, to indentify the problem precisely. Freud became impatient: he was older, he was fighting painful cancer of the jaw, and the younger man's complaints irritated him. The two men had been rivals in a strange competition for a long time: which one was more gravely ill, who was closer to death? Ferenczi got the better of Freud, so to speak, by dying first, although he was considerably younger.

We could surmise that when Ferenczi first described his hypochondriacal symptoms to Freud in detail, this was a call for help. But it was not the type of relation Freud wanted to have with him; in the end, he did reluctantly accept to become Ferenczi's analyst, but the analysis was fragmentary, brief, and finished without being terminated. As we know, at the end of his life Ferenczi rebuked Freud for not analysing his negative transference. Perhaps behind this reproach is hidden another: that of not having analysed the pregential level (or the psychotic core?), in other words, precisely this deep level where psyche and soma are intertwined. Certain passages in the *Clinical Diary* suggest the idea that if this level would have been analysed, Ferenczi might have avoided illness and death. His last experiments with analytic technique could be regarded as a last attempt to heal himself at the same time as his patients.

Ferenczi entertained the fervent wish that Freud accompany him on this experimental path. What he was asking for was encouragement, rather than Freud's agreement. But Freud could not encourage him; he saw the technical errors too clearly, and concluded that his friend's investigations were taking a wrong turn. Perhaps this orientation was making him feel ill at ease, since he rejected psychotics as being "too different" from him, and did not like them. Faced with Freud's criticism, Ferenczi provided explanations, then lapsed into long periods of silence, followed by more explanations. The malaise between them increased: Freud felt abandoned and betrayed, while Ferenczi felt misunderstood and treated like a child.

When the problem of the presidency of the International Psychoanalytical Association presented itself, it complicated this already difficult situation. Ferenczi, who, at Freud's prompting, proposed the foundation of the International Association, was its President for only a few weeks. Given Hungary's isolation at the end of the First World War, Ferenczi had to let Jones take over the position. He never occupied this position again, and was left with a certain bitterness on this account. It was Freud who insisted that he accept this role, because he felt burdened with age and illness, and wanted to leave his life's work in sure hands. This is just one more proof that he did not consider Ferenczi deviant or mentally ill. But the offer came too late. Ferenczi himself was in poor health and, what's more, involved in research that brought into question some important points of psychoanalytic theory and practice. Ferenczi did not feel he was in a position to act as the guardian of the status quo. Freud felt this refusal to be a dereliction of duty at a crucial moment. He had also hoped to "awaken" his friend by entrusting him with presidential functions, not realising how gravely ill he was.

Their misunderstanding probably reached its high point on the occasion of Ferenczi's last visit to Vienna, when he read to Freud his article "Confusion of Tongues Between Adults and the Child", that he planned to present at the 1932 Wiesbaden Congress. Very shocked, Freud left the room without even glancing at Ferenczi. It was the last time the two men saw each other.

The article plunged the whole psychoanalytic community in turmoil. Ferenczi had to be persuaded not to present his exposé. Freud asked him not to publish anything before understanding his errors. Ferenczi was deeply disturbed. Jones came to his rescue, in a roundabout way typical of him, by asserting that the text could be presented because it was too vague and insignificant to leave any particular impression, good or bad.

Between 1930 and May 1933, when Ferenczi died, the entire history of the Freud/Ferenczi relationship seems to be summarised in their correspondence. When Freud reproaches him with becoming less affectionate, Ferenczi replies, on January 17, 1930:

> "What happens in the relationship between you and me (at least in me) is an entanglement of various conflicts of emotions and positions. At first you were my revered mentor and unattainable model, for whom I nourished the feelings of a pupil — always somewhat mixed, as we know. Then you became my analyst, but as a result of unfortunate circumstances my analysis could not be completed. I particularly regretted that, in the course of the analysis, you did not perceive in me and bring to abreaction negative feelings and fantasies that were only partly transferred. It is well known that no analysand [...] could accomplish this without assistance. Painstaking self-analysis was therefore required, which I subsequently undertook [...]".

Freud defended himself:

> "You blame me for having neglected the foreseeable negative reactions in your analysis. Whereby you fail to consider that this analysis goes back fifteen years, and that at the time we were by no means so sure that these reactions could be expected in every case. At least, I wasn't. You yourself [should] consider how long this analysis would have had to last until inimical impulses in our excellent

relationship had succeeded in getting through".

It was Ferenczi who reinstated the friendly tone of their correspondence at the start of 1933, by sending greetings for the New Year. He referred to their long-standing friendship, and to his gratitude for it. But Freud was not ready to let bygones be bygones: he acknowledged their "intimate community of life, feeling, and interest", but regretted having to speak of it in the past, and attributed all the responsibility for the change in their relationship to Ferenczi.

On March 29, 1933, Ferenczi resumed contact with Freud, to inform him, first of all, about his state of health: "Perhaps you have heard from Dr. Lévy that in recent weeks I have endured a relapse of the symptoms of my previous illness (Anaem. pernic.), but this time less of a worsening of my blood count than as a sort of nervous breakdown from which I am only slowly recovering". The second reason for the letter was a warning: "[...] my pessimistic impression [of the threat represented by the Hitler regime] now includes Vienna and Budapest. Short and sweet: I advise you to make use of the time of the not yet immediately dangerously threatening situation and, with a few patients and your daughter Anna, to go to a more secure country, perhaps England. [...] Please take my warning seriously".

As soon as Freud understood how gravely ill his friend was, the tone of his reply became affectionate again. But he was not persuaded by Ferenczi's warning. On April 2, 1933 he wrote: "I am not considering leaving Vienna. [...] An emotional attitude naturally lies at the base of this decision, but there is also no lack of rationalizations. It is not certain that the Hitler regime will also overpower Austria. [...] There is certainly no personal danger for me".

Time would, of course, prove Ferenczi right. But for the moment he was still willing to admit that he may have panicked needlessly. On April 9th he wrote to Freud: "Your kind and understanding letter has made a deep and beneficial impression on me. My view about immediate necessary measures, which I presented to you, has been significantly ameloriated , [...] even though I am, perhaps, under the influence of still existing physical debility, much more inclined to panic than you". Ferenczi needed the support and affection of his old friend so much, that he was willing to set aside his own clear-sightedness in order to be in agreement with him.

A few weeks later, on May 4th, three weeks before he died, Ferenczi wrote to Freud again to wish him a happy birthday: "Only a few short lines to indicate to you that the date of your birthday is still in our memory. [...] I exert myself in giving credence to the optimistic statements of my doctors".

A VERY COMPLEX RELATIONSHIP

As I tried to illustrate using only a few brief quotes, the relationship between these two remarkable men was far more complex than people used to think based on available testimonies before the complete correspondence was published.

This intense, profound and fruitful relation was never entirely smooth, and at times was difficult to bear for one protagonist or another. The demands they placed on each other were impossible to satisfy and constantly led to dashed hopes. Freud seemed to look for a son in Ferenczi — a successor, a companion — a role none of his three sons could play. Freud would have liked Ferenczi to understand him completely, to follow his lead and appreciate the intricacies of his thinking; he wanted him to be independent and critical as well, but without deviating too much from the paths he himself was pursuing. Ferenczi tried to live up to these expectations, at first adopting an attitude of great admiration and total submission, and later through intellectual independence. But emotional independence would have been too painful for him.

What Ferenczi would have liked to find in Freud was a father, who would understand and forgive everything. "A superior, protective power", he wrote in his *Clinical Diary*. A mentor who would support him even when his research was hazardous, who would trust him. No doubt Freud tried to meet this expectation. But he was too preoccupied with the fate of his edifice, with the future of psychoanalysis, not to become frightened when his closest collaborators went off on paths completely foreign to him. Ferenczi's last experiments, those we consider today to have been the most fruitful, seemed totally mad to Freud.

These mutual expectations were, no doubt, intensified by Ferenczi's analysis with Freud. We are familiar with the complex effects of the interaction between transference and countertransference when the two people involved associate with each other and work together before, during and after the analysis, as it often happens in psychoanalytic associations. To undertake an exhaustive analysis of this exceptional relationship, one would have to take into account all the events — external and internal — in the lives of the two men, the structure of their families, their subjective place in these families, and many other factors. Only such an exhaustive description of the situation could explain the intensity of their bond, as well as the wounds they inflicted on each other.

GRODDECK BETWEEN FREUD AND FERENCZI

On May 27, 1917 Freud received an enthusiastic letter from Georg Groddeck. He replied to it on June 5th, saying: "[...] you are an analyst of the first order [...] [belonging] irrevocably to the 'Wild Hunt'". Ferenczi was more reserved: he found Groddeck's theories nebulous and his clinical accounts hard to believe.

Freud quickly realised that Groddeck was much too fond of his own independence and originality to join a group of any kind. Moreover, Freud was becoming irritated with Groddeck's fanciful ways, his public displays, in short, what he called his "nonsense". Little by little, he came to see Groddeck as a likeable clown, whom he treated with sympathy but kept at a distance. Despite Groddeck's repeated invitations, he never went for treatment to his clinic in Baden-Baden. Ferenczi, on the other hand, was very critical at the outset. After a vigorous and well-documented rejection of Groddeck's theories, he started to glimpse something that interested him in this strange, intense and sincere man. Finally, he suddenly decided to visit Groddeck at Baden-Baden, not only to study his methods, but also to be treated by him. Once he was there, a deep, immediate friendship was born between the two men. It was not only a meeting of minds based on theory; it was a personal relationship that lasted a lifetime.

Ferenczi sought help from Groddeck, the physician, not because the latter had convinced him of the accuracy of his theories, but because he had gained his trust. Afterwards, Ferenczi sent his family members and his friends to him.

After meeting Groddeck, Ferenczi became less and less disposed to tolerate the ironic, slightly impatient benevolence Freud showed his friend. Ferenczi attempted to win Freud over by assuring him of Groddeck's loyalty to the basic principles of psychoanalysis. He tried to diffuse Freud's foreseeable objections by bringing them up first. Eventually, he gave up these attempts and Groddeck was not mentioned again in their correspondence after 1927, although Ferenczi went for a holiday at Groddeck's clinic almost every year.

In the correspondence between Freud and Ferenczi, there are 54 letters which mention Groddeck. The first time, he is mentioned is in a letter written by Freud on June 3, 1917, where he is telling Ferenczi that he has received a "very interesting" letter from a German physician whose ideas are close to Ferenczi's concept of "pathoneurosis", and to the ideas they exchanged about Lamarck. Indeed, Freud and Ferenczi were planning to co-author a book about Antoine de Lamarck, but this project was never realised.

As I said earlier, Freud answered Groddeck on May 5, 1917 (the letter has been published), expressing his desire to "lay claim" to the "analyst of the first order" he saw in Groddeck, who asserted that his work was something independent of psychoanalysis. Then he forwarded Groddeck's letter to Ferenczi, who was much less enthusiastic. He sent the letter back to Freud, with severe and detailed criticism:

"Now to the extremely interesting letter of Dr. Groddeck [...]

Part of the things of which he informs us is, of course, known to us; I myself saw a case in which, for psychic reasons, pronounced swelling of parts of the face appeared from time to time. The remaining facts, even if they are for the most part within the realm of possibility, are in urgent need of review. I view with the skepticism the case with the Wassermann that became positive, then negative. Apart from the dubious value of this method of investigation, the way in which the unconscious could produce such a serological reaction is incomprehensible to me. One must assume that in the unconscious, *an image* of what is supposed to be produced in the body must be formed, to which the body then adapts itself (if the whole thing is true). In that way the occurrence of a syphiloid eruption or the occurrence of a hydrarthrosis, etc. is still explicable. But it is inconceivable how, upon the idea of a "negative Wassermann", the Wassermann could really become neative. The image [idea] "negative Wassermann" certainly has nothing in common with the, still unknown, processes in the blood. So Dr. Groddeck must — even if he does probably understand how to produce something new — still be a dreamer. But that speaks *in his favour*, to a certain extent. He is evidently not working with our psychoanalysis, but rather with the (to himself partly unconscious) transference, i.e., with suggestion in the old sense; only perhaps he suggests more successfully than others, since he has acquired psychoanalytic knowledge (evidently in a way that he doesn't want to remember). I will leave it open whether he also unconsciously uses other psychoanalytic powers (thought transference). — But what he says about *theory* (applicability of psychoanalytic principles to the somatic) is, of course, familiar to us. But his inclination toward sectarianism and mysticism expresses itself in the consistent use of the word "it" [*Es*] instead of "unconscious". A few examples are, to be sure, interesting (as is the case of scleroderma on the foot as a consequence of a fantasy about kicking the next-born child). So one should certainly make the man's acquaintance".

Freud responded to this critical reaction in his very next letter, on June 15th. He rebuked Ferenczi for his tendency to reject at the outset anything foreign to him. This reproach is surprising, considering Ferenczi's endless curiosity about new things. However, we must keep in mind that Ferenczi had had this type of reaction when he first read the *Interpretation of Dreams*. Freud had clearly not forgotten it. But it is also true that he blamed himself, on more than one occasion, for having the same kind of reaction. This is why, in 1924, he encouraged Ferenczi and Rank to pursue their own investigations despite his reluctance to join them.

On June 22, 1917, Freud sent Ferenczi the letter of reply he had received from Groddeck: "Enclosed the letter from Groddeck, which arrived today. You will certainly find, as I have, that it is somewhat tiring, [when he says] that the patient could have made things easier for the doctor if he had communicated the conclusions instead of the material, and that a good piece of complacency is required for this action. In the meantime, but the impression on the whole: *laudabiliter se subjecit*".

On October 9, 1917 Freud wrote Ferenczi to say that he would have "a little publication" of Groddeck's sent to him, to which Freud was asking him "to dedicate a detailed, benevolent review without much delay". Freud added: "I know and share your objections, but the heart of the matter coincides with your pathoneuroses and our Lamarck idea, and is certainly noteworthy. To what extent Groddeck's assertions are justified will be left to verification through suitable experience. Moreover, we have a personal interest in drawing him into the circle of our collaborators and to cultivate divergences from our way of thinking that are not fundamentally disruptive. In a letter today he also offered me contributions which I think I should accept".

Ferenczi wrote a review of "Psychic Conditioning and the Psychoanalytic Treatment of Organic Disorders", as Freud asked. But his own reservations were apparent in turns of phrase such as" "We have therefore no justification whatever for rejecting out of hand...", "statements which might startle us now", etc. Finally, he expressed the fear that the reader may be "put off by the extremely original but often fanciful approach" of the author. Gradually, in their letters, Freud and Ferenczi both start to identify in themselves and in their milieu processes they qualify as "typically Groddeckian".

On November 6, 1917, Freud described to Ferenczi an incident whose significance was to become apparent in light of Freud's subsequent cancer, diagnosed in 1923, six years later: "Yesterday I smoked away my last cigar, and since then I have been grumpy and tired, got heart palpitations and an increase in the painful swelling of my gums (carcinoma?), which has been noticeable since the meager days. Then a patient brought me fifty cigars, I lit one, became cheerful, and the gum irritation rapidly abated! I wouldn't have believed it, if it weren't so striking. Quite *à la* Groddeck!"

Should we go so far as to believe that if Freud had trusted Groddeck completely he would have been able to control the development of his cancer?

On November 18, 1917 Ferenczi reported his own "Groddeckian" symptom: a sore throat after a rendezvous with his friend Gizella, during which he was not very enterprising. A few days later, he reported to Freud some "Groddeckian" signs on Gizella's part.

Still, Ferenczi was not altogther convinced yet. On June 14, 1918 he wrote Freud:

"The enclosed letter from the crazy Swedish woman provides us with interesting insights into Dr. Groddeck's method of treatment. He must be a very uncritical man if he initiates a patient like this Swede into his correspondence with you. It strikes me altogether as more and more probable that Groddeck is not curing at all *with analysis*, but rather that with the aid of the transference he puts the plastic power of hysteria into the service of the organic tendency to heal. Precisely because he doesn't analyze but rather displaces the tendencies as a block, he is able to perform such feats. — Should I get the Swedish woman to give us further information?"

In early 1919, Ferenczi finally married his old friend Gizella. As they were on their way to the registry office, they learned about the death of Géza Pálos of a heart attack on the same day. In a letter dated March 4th, Freud spoke of "something demonic, in Groddeck's sense". On March 18th, Ferenczi was reporting that marriage had improved his state of health, saying: "So, also 'Groddeck' on my part!"

In the spring of 1921, Ferenczi wrote a review of Groddeck's novel *The Seeker of Souls: A Psychoanalytic Novel*. It was a sympathetic appraisal, but the Introduction preceding it expressed some hesitation: "It is impossible to say, for the moment, if what we are seeing is a brilliant new method of treatment, or the power of suggestion of a unique and exceptional medical personality [...]".

In August of the same year, Ferenczi decided to go to Baden-Baden in September, in the "hope of being able to study, with your permission, and at close quarters, how you apply psychoanalysis in the treatment of organic diseases", as he wrote Groddeck, but also in the hope that he himself could be helped by the treatment. Although Ferenczi seemed to think that "Groddeckian" symptoms would respond to Groddeckian magic, he was not ready to adopt Groddeck's theories. His stay at the clinic was, indeed, beneficial. But, above all, he discovered Groddeck to be a warm man whose unbridled imagination and freedom of spirit won him over. The two men developed an immediate friendship which was to last all their lives. On Christmas day of the same year, Ferenczi wrote Groddeck a long, intimate letter in which he was able to express everything he could not say to Freud, because "he was too big for me, there was too much the father", as he says in his letter.

As Ferenczi's friendship with Groddeck deepened, Freud grew more skeptical of Groddeck the theoretician. After a time, he only referred to Groddeck in his letters to make critical remarks in humourous, fiercely ironic tones, or to send greetings and birthday wishes.

March 30, 1922: "Tell her [Gizella] that I've recently read a number of old books by Groddeck (*A Child of the Earth, Tragedy or Comedy, Toward Divine Nature*), that are downright German and bad".

The last time Freud pays any particular attention to Groddeck is while writing *The Ego and the Id*, a project he describes to Ferenczi on July 22, 1922, saying: "I am occupied with something speculative, which is a continuation of "Beyond", and will either become a small book or nothing. I won't reveal the title to you yet, all I have to say is that it has to do with Groddeck".

Starting in 1921, Ferenczi and Gizella take regular therapeutic holidays in Baden-Baden. The friendship between the two couples deepens. On August 31, 1922, Ferenczi writes Freud that he is conducting self-analysis in Groddeck's presence and with his help. His initial judgment of Groddeck has softened; in his letter, he comments that Groddeck "sets about things very circumspectly and cautiously, and is true to the teachings of psychoanalysis in all essentials". After this, Ferenczi takes every opportunity to point out Groddeck's loyalty to the fundamental principles of psychoanalysis. In his September 24, 1922 letter: "He has always been true to psychoanalysis". In his August 10, 1925 letter: "He stands unshakably on the ground of psychoanalysis; in his November 23, 1925 letter: "He is a loyal disciple of psychoanalysis"; and on September 9, 1926: "He is true to us and our cause, even if he also goes his own way".

But Freud seems to remain skeptical. Groddeck annoys him and he says so, although he tries to spare Ferenczi's feelings by taking a friendly tone. On August 14, 1925: "[...] Sympathy is certainly the important thing, and I can tolerate the clever-foolish man very well, despite some dangerous nuances. Basically, he possibly doesn't belong with us after all..."

On December 1, 1925: "Personally, I like him very much, but scientifically, he is probably not usable; he overexerted himself with the unconscious influence on the organic and [with] the Id, and he is not the right man for working out an idea".

On March 25, 1927: "I gladly grant you your friend Groddeck, but lately he has been doing all too much trickery and nonsense, the "Id" has gone to his head".

On July 2, 1927: "His [Noah's] Ark fantasies are becoming less and less palatable to me. (Between us)."

On August 2, 1927, Freud asks Ferenczi to persuade Groddeck to "cease his agitation in the Ark for my Nobel Prize. It doesn't suit me."

Ferenczi made several more attempts to defend his friend or, at least, to soften Freud's criticisms by anticipating them.

On August 23, 1925, he wrote Freud: "My intercourse with Groddeck is very pleasant. He has a refreshing effect. On the other hand, I think I am exerting a moderating influence on his more artistic-intuitive manner of thinking and working, and I am facilitating his remaining within the scientific framework."

In a circular letter dated November 28, 1925:"Groddeck, whose intimations about a possible extension of psychoanalysis to the organic sphere are gradually attracting more attention, is an intuitive spirit. [...] his intercourse with me is suited to mitigate his, in a certain sense, also beneficial one-sidedness. (During two lectures given in Budapest): one had to recognize his merits, profit much from him, and both times one could determine the line of demarcation at which he overstepped the bounds of, in our opinion, still legitimate theoretical conclusions. [...] The medical members had to recognize in part the correctness of his main charge, that the organic-minded all too frequently neglect the personality of the patient, although almost all rejected certain exaggerations. [...] I, personally, learned something from [him], especially the art of occasionally forgetting the medicine that I have been taught."

And on September 27, 1926: "Even behind Groddeck's strange-sounding, occasionally confusing talks about illness, his "Id", etc., I could see things which may still have a future ahead of them. Only, his intuition would need to have an appropriate logical and scientific sorting out. Perhaps I will get a chance to accomplish part of this work."

After this, Ferenczi stopped trying to win Freud over to Groddeck's point of view. Particularly since he himself was not in full agreement with Groddeck's ideas; but beyond the theories, Ferenczi perceived that Groddeck intuited something important. Time proved him right. Ferenczi seemed to trust Groddeck's human qualities, which were reflected in his methods. At the theoretical level, the two men had numerous heated discussions, as witnessed by their correspondence[20]. Very likely, Ferenczi's perception of Groddeckian intuitions played an important role in the later developments of his own concepts. Of course, Ferenczi had never hesitated to explore new ideas, but we can imagine that Groddeck's independent spirit helped Ferenczi to withstand the often very harsh criticism coming from his colleagues and from Freud, and to pursue his research, whose great

---

20   Groddeck, G., *The Meaning of Illness: Selected Psychoanalytic Writings Including Correspondence with Sigmund Freud*, Karnac, 1988.

fecundity is only beginning to come to light today.

HUMOUR IN THE FREUD-FERENCZI CORRESPONDENCE

Humour — especially wit — and psychoanalysis have always gotten along well. After all, a witty remark often functions like an interpretation: it is a condensation, a summary, the shedding of a different light, in order to reveal a hidden meaning. Indeed, many analysts, including myself, have recourse to funny stories or wordplays as interpretations on occasion. Humour can take many forms: the comical, the burlesque, witty remarks or irony. Incidentally, in his *Clinical Diary* Ferenczi describes irony as the lowest form of humour, "a contemptible way of causing laughter", no doubt because it includes a large part of aggressivity.

Freud and Ferenczi made abundant use of humour in all kinds of situations. But more than this, Freud dedicated a book to the subject in 1905: *Jokes and Their Relation to the Unconscious*, that Ferenczi reviewed in his fashion in a 1911 article entitled "The Psychoanalysis of Wit and the Comical".

Of course, in their twenty-five-year correspondence, which has been compared to an epistolary analysis (reciprocal to some degree), they use humour freely as well. Most often, throughout the correspondence, Freud holds the position of analyst. But not always. There are also self-analytical passages: frequent, extensive and detailed in Ferenczi's case; more sporadic and reticent in Freud's. In the course of this epistolary pseudo-analysis, both men often use humour to make an interpretation or convey their thoughts and feelings.

Each man has his own particular style of humour. Freud's can sometimes be scathing, especially in regard to third parties. Freud's tone with Ferenczi is humourous, alowing him to express his thoughts with amused affection. He only adopts a sharper tone in the last years of their correspondence, when some of Ferenczi's ideas, particularly those about trauma and psychoanalytic technique, begin to diverge from his own theories. From that point on, Freud's style of humour gradually turns to bitter irony, while Ferenczi, distressed, no longer feels like laughing.

But although Freud maintained a generally friendly tone with Ferenczi, he did not spare his adversaries. For instance, on April 6, 1911, he wrote about Adler and

Stekel: "I am constantly annoyed about the two — Max and Moritz — who are also developing with great rapidity in a backward direction and will soon have arrived at denial of the unconsious. [...] Enemies are much more comfortable; you can at least ignore them". And on April 29, 1911, referring to Jung: "Rockefeller's daughter presented Jung with a gift of 360,000 francs for the construction of a casino, analytic institute, etc. So, Swiss ethics have finally made their sought-after contact with American money".

Freud did not hesitate to call one or the other of his enemies an ass or a pig. Ferenczi made one such attempt, calling someone a dog, but he instantly apologized — to dogs.

Ferenczi's style of humour was less harsh and rarely aggressive. He did not hesitate to use self-mockery — very characteristic of Jewish humour — , something Freud almost never did, given his concern with preserving his dignity. It is only in his correspondence with Fliess, to whose authority he is ready to submit, that Freud shows a degree of self-mockery: "I am looking forward to our congress [...]. I bring nothing but two open ears and one temporal lobe lubricated for reception. I foresee important things — I am that self-seeking — also for my purposes".

Both Freud and Ferenczi resorted to humour through style, slightly inappropriate words, unexpected expressions and double meanings (a nightmare for translators!). Thus, on November 26, 1908 Freud reassured Ferenczi, who feared he had been too hard on a colleague: "Misfortune doesn't come to him without justification". And he described his sister, who was in mourning, as "a virtuosa of despair". The two men also made unusual comparisons and used startling quotes in various languages: English, French, Spanish, Latin, Greek or Yiddish.

Their different styles of humour show the asymmetry of their respective positions. Freud is the master, the "Professor". Ferenczi is the pupil, sometimes the "son" whom Freud invites to act as an equal, without ever making this possible.

The two men share the same culture, and at times they only need to allude to a well-known traditional story to understand each other. For example, to speak of independence they may refer to the soldier Itzig, so poorly suited for army life that his superior officer advises him to buy his own cannon.

The two men discuss their health problems, the inevitable passing of time, ageing, death and illnesss. Humour allows them to deal with these difficult subjects with discretion and relative light-heartedness. When Freud speaks of his "poor Konrad", any cultured reader of the period understands that he is alluding to intestinal pain. Today, few people remember the novel *Imago*, by Karl Spitteler, who won the Nobel Prize for Literature in 1919 — the novel in which the expression originated.

Freud had some favourite targets for the full array of his malicious humour. The first of these were, without question, the Americans. Although he was given a very cordial welcome in America in 1909, Freud's antipathy for Americans was unremitting and based on prejudices he already harboured before his trip. For instance, on January 10, 1909, when he received the invitation to lecture at Clark University, he wrote Ferenczi: "I do find the presumption to sacrifice so much money in order to give lectures there much too 'American'. America should bring money, not cost money". Time did nothing to soften his resentment. In 1926 and 1927, when Ferenczi went to America, Freud was unhappy about his decision, fearing that Ferenczi might abandon him as he felt that Rank had, at the same period. The letter he sent Ferenczi before his departure, on September 19, 1926, starts: "Before you entrust yourself to the sea in search of the land of the dollar-barbarians...". On March 23, 1927, he congratulates Ferenczi for his work in the United States: "What fine work, what an achievement [...]. And unfortunately just for Americans, who don't know the true value of anything and on whom nothing makes an impression". He goes on to give "personal news from me that you don't need to tell to the savages over there". Still speaking of Americans, he says: "Psychoanalysis suits them like a white shirt suits a crow". He also refers to "Columbus' crime" of having discovered America. The only American he holds in great esteem is William Bullitt. And the only credit he grants America is that it introduced tobacco in Europe.

But the Americans are not the sole target of Freud's ironic wit. Women are also a favourite target. Especially — of course — American women. On October 23, 1926 he wrote about a woman physician, Dr. Powers: "Even among women and among doctors it's rare to find such stupidity, far above the human average". Of course, there were exceptions in this area as well, such as his daughter Anna, Marie Bonaparte and Lou Andreas-Salomé, about whom he nevertheless wrote in a letter dated March 20, 1913: "She is a highly significant woman, even though all the tracks around her go into the lion's den but none come out". Martha, whom he passionately courted during the five years of their engagement and respected throughout their marriage, was described in a 1936 conversation with Marie Bonaparte as "really not a bad solution of the marriage problem" — not a very romantic formulation.

But Freud's humour could also be more tender, as when he described Oskar Pfister as "a charming fellow... half Savior, half Pied Piper" (April 25, 1909).

Ferenczi was closer to his Jewish origins than Freud, who did his best to distance himself from them, not out of a desire to reject them, but for the good of psychoanalysis. He did not want psychoanalysis to be seen as a purely Jewish science, so as not to limit its scope. Some of Jung's assertions in particular clearly show that this concern was not merely imaginary. Ferenczi seems to have been less preoccupied with this question, and more at ease with his Jewish identity. His letters are strewn with Jewish stories serving to illustrate his impressions and feelings.

As I said earlier, these two men were preoccupied with illness and death throughout their lives; they often spoke of them, using a sort of understated humour. There was even a certain rivalry between them on this subject: who was going to be more seriously ill, more imminently threatened with death? Freud played this game more aggressively: he did not want the seriousness of his state underestimated, and wanted the distinction of dying first. But when Ferenczi won this deathly race, Freud forgave him and wrote a eulogy which praised him highly, calling him "a master of analysis" who "made all analysts into his pupils". Even after Ferenczi's death, Freud continued to converse with him, as he did in one of his last papers, "Analysis Terminable and Interminable".

The thought of dying was on Freud's mind even before his cancer of the jaw was discovered. On February 6, 1921, Freud the unbeliever wrote Ferenczi, speaking of Anton von Freund's widow, who was fantasising about being reunited with her husband after her death: "Explain to her that I, who am probably next in line for such a reunion, am prepared to convey greetings and undertake commissions".

Ferenczi broached the subject in his own humorous style; on July 24, 1921, he wrote: "I find that our friend Lajos [Lévy] — a former patient of mine! — is all too ready to emphasize the psychical; he clearly wants to pay me back in my own coin... [He] should above all know what is happening on the organic level, how I produce these attacks, in order wherever possible to take from my hands the weapons with which I (unconsciously) want to commit suicide". Freud answered at once: "I believe you are carrying on an 'unfair competition'. Because, in every letter to you, I write about the prospect of death [...], you take the hint and think you have to equal or outdo me". These few lines reveal a whole facet of their relationship. Freud has expressed on more than one occasion his irritation with Ferenczi's so-called infantile position in regard to himself, and has rebuked him, as he did after their trip to Palermo, for not treating him as an equal. At the same time, as the above lines reveal, Freud's desire is ambiguous. The scientist in him would like this equality, but the man has trouble accepting it.

Even small, unimportant complaints are reported in their letters by these two men who both have hypochondriacal tendencies. Freud is fully aware of this. On September 10, 1917, he writes: "Health quite uneven. He who has a talent for hypochondria can write all kinds of verses to it". Elsewhere, speaking of various ailments he is trying to treat in the mountains or at health resorts, he writes: "Seven organs are vying with one another for the honor of ending my life".

Ferenczi also complains constantly of a whole variety of ills. On August 24, 1914, he writes: "I, too, experienced a recurrence of massive slips of the tongue (which I, in the manner of the hypochondriac schooled in medicine, jokingly interpreted as incipient paralysis)". The following month, when he was called up for military service in the First World War, he wrote: "I learned that I would have to perform local duties. My unconscious seemed so gratified by this news that it immediately began substitutive gratification in the form of diarrhea". Ferenczi's various ills — respiratory or digestive problems, Grave's disease, suspected tuberculosis, etc. — ended up irritating Freud, who urged Ferenczi to forget all that and get down to work. Freud himself was worried about his age; I believe he covered over this anxiety by insisting on the prerogatives of age, the right of an "old man" to be tired and have countless little complaints, while a young man like Ferenczi shouldn't complain, since he has his youth.

When Freud's cancer was diagnosed, there was no more question of hypochondria. But Freud needed his humorous formulations that much more, since they helped him to cope. On September 16, 1930, after receiving the Goethe Prize, he wrote:

"The dreadful newspaper reports about my health must have reached you as well. [...] The reports are of course the reaction to the Goethe Prize and should warn us not to be fooled into thinking that the resistance to analysis has, in practice, eased up in any tangible way. The same reactionary attitude is shown in Bumke's speech [...], and also in the heightened activity among Adler's bunch of monkeys [...]. In short, the Goethe Prize will turn out to be costly for us".

On October 13th of the same year, he observed: "Living essentially for one's health has something unsatisfactory about it".

Starting in the early 1930s, disagreements between Freud and Ferenczi arise. Gradually, the uneasiness and tension between them become so pronounced that there is little room left for humour in their exchanges. One of the last occasions when Freud has recourse to humour — or more exactly fierce irony — is in the famous letter dated December 13, 1931, which discusses what Freud called "the kissing technique" that Ferenczi supposedly adopted. When Freud learned from gossiping patients at a party that Ferenczi might have kissed one of his patients (Clara Thompson), he wrote to him:

"You have made no secret of the fact that you kissed your women patients and let them kiss you [...]. Now, I'm certainly not one to outlaw such little erotic satisfactions out of prudishness or concern for bourgeois conventions. [...] Now, picture to yourself what will be the consequence of making your technique public... why stop with a kiss? [...] one will achieve still more if one adds 'pawing' [...]. Bolder ones... will take the further step of peeping and showing; soon we will have accepted into the technique of psychoanalysis the whole repertoire of demiviergerie [seductions] and petting parties, with the result being a great increase in analysis on the part of analysts and those who are being analyzed [...]".

Ferenczi was unable to use the same tone in answering this letter. There is complete misunderstanding between the two men about the nature of trauma and the method of treatment appropriate for seriously traumatised patients. The letters which follow are full of bitterness. Freud feels abandoned and Ferenczi, who tries in vain to plead his cause, feels misunderstood.

In the meantime, the health of both men is deteriorating, as is the state of the world around them. Ferenczi is aware of this and, in one of his last letters, he urges Freud to leave Vienna and go to England. But Freud interprets this as pessimism due to his friend's ill health.

In the last letters there is no more trace of humour, but there is no bitterness either. The old friendship resurfaces on both sides. Ferenczi died on May 22, 1933; Freud who had said he wanted no one but Ferenczi to write his eulogy, now wrote that of his friend. Gradually, Ferenczi's investigations which had at first seemed so shocking to him, now started to seem more interesting, as witnessed by Michael Balint, who had time to have Freud reread them near the end of his life.

I believe that we can describe these two men, and therefore their attitude to their undertakings, as follows: Ferenczi was a desperate optimist who, against all odds, hoped to take things in a favourable direction, find a way to cure all pathologies, bring out something good in every human being. Freud, on the other hand, could be called a "happy pessimist". Each time things took a wrong turn, when he saw that people didn't understand him, that his disciples were pursuing paths he considered worthless, he was pleased to comfort himself by confirming that once again things happen as he expected, given the iniquity of man's destiny.

THE "YOUNG SUICIDE": CRYPT OR PHANTOM?

My intention is to consider the story of a young woman who committed suicide, in light of the notions of "crypt" and "phantom" introduced by Nicolas Abraham and Maria Torok. The young woman was a patient Ferenczi described in 1929, several years after her death, to invite us to reflect on her case.

In France, the text "Mémoires d'une jeune suicidée" (Memoires of a Young Suicide) was published in 1987 in the Coq-Héron No. 104; this French version was translated from a German translation of the Hungarian original — the only version available to us. We know that the concepts of "crypt" and "phantom" are associated with various linguistic particularities. Therefore, it is a hazardous and uncertain enterprise to try to identify them in a translation made from another translation. In her Introduction to this autobiography — which she also formatted and provided with subheadings — Corinne Daubigny was asking the reader to keep in mind the numerous traumas accumulated in the young girl's short life, by pointing out, as Ferenczi did, that trauma becomes pathogenic above all when it is denied. She also pointed out that when Ferenczi published this story in 1929, he had just formulated the idea that the aim of therapy with traumatised patients was to provide them with the experience of a novel type of relationship, contrasting with the experience of their childhood. Corinne Daubigny uses the term "melancholic cryptophoria" to speak of this case. But let us go back to the girl's story.

FERENCZI'S PRESENTATION OF THE CASE AND POSTSCRIPT

One day, a beautiful young woman, 19 years old, employed in an office, came to see Ferenczi; she said she had decided to end her life, but wanted to talk with him about her decision first. He found her extremely likeable, very intelligent and cultured, with a highly developed moral sense and a great thirst for truth. She wanted to die because her childhood and her life had been too unhappy, and especially because she felt she was unable to love. This had caused her to reject a man who loved her and for whom she also had feelings. Ferenczi pointed out that her resolve to die could not spring solely from her present misfortunes, but must have deep roots, unknown to her, and that she must not take her life before exposing these roots.

But he was unable to start analysis with the young woman at once. The patient did not seem to be in a state of panic; she spoke calmly of her suicide plan, but also said that she wanted to think about it. As a result, Ferenczi did not feel she was in immediate danger. He suggested that she start to write the story of her life while she waited for her treatment to begin, and to come to see him from time to time until then. On these occasions, she seemed to be feeling better, until the day when she told him, very upset, that her brother-in-law had killed himself.

We have the account of the first ten years of the life of this young woman, whose name was Lisette. She also wrote the story of the second — and last — decade of her life. Ferenczi was able to read some passages of it, but this manuscript was not found. This second part of the young girl's life seems to have been richer, thanks to her access to nature, to art and to literature. But it was not a happy life, because the young woman lived in poverty, doing work that was hard and uninteresting. In addition, she lived with her older sister, an authoritarian woman whose mentally ill husband tried to rape her one day unexpectedly.

THE YOUNG GIRL'S STORY AND COMMENTS

The story of the young girl's life we have available recounts the first ten years of her life. Her subtlety, poetic sense and great sensitivity, obvious to Ferenczi, impress us as well. The first lines of her diary set the tone: "Inner life is like a sensitive instrument with a life of its own: the slightest touch of a string and the vibrations resonate through the whole scale, awakening the farthest sounds". Then she speaks of her feeling that she does not have the right to live. She attributes this feeling to weakness on her part. She feels as if she has a debt she can never repay. She says that she does nothing but receive, that she cannot accept what she receives and she can give nothing in return. I believe that it was precisely this feeling of being walled in, of impermeability to anything that could be a source of well-being, which drove her to suicide just when she could have started the treatment she had come to ask for.

The feeling of being guilty of something but not knowing what is a situation with which psychoanalysts are familiar. This feeling is often seen in children subjected to sexual abuse, as this young girl had been. But we may well ask if the "crime" in question is hers, that of her rapist — introjected by her through identification with the aggressor — , or a crime of unknown nature committed by one of her ancestors, about which we know nothing. We must remember that Lisette was kidnapped by a man when she was just a few months old, then left with an unknown woman, before her mother came to take her back the next day. We do not know what might have happened to her at an age before language development. The young girl's mother is described as loving, gentle, respectable, handling misfortune as best she could. Her father is a lazy drunkard who does not look after his family. Could it be that the prohibition to live comes from him, or could it come from the mother who, despite her devotion, doesn't know how to protect her children and provide for their needs? Out of desperation, this mother used to scold her daughter, telling her she was good for nothing. Lisette is filled with guilt for not being able to be of more help to her mother.

The young girl remembers that when she was very young she had to try to go unnoticed: unnoticed by her mother's employers, because it was important not to bother them; unnoticed by her drunk father who got into fits of rage and beat his children.

When she was 4 or 5, she was used for sexual satisfaction by a passer-by who gave Lisette's brother a few coins for the right to use her. The boy gave the money to their mother, who was delighted and didn't ask where it came from. The little girl didn't say anything and became very quiet and withdrawn from then on. This story illustrates perfectly the doubly traumatic situation described by Ferenczi, where the adult remains unaware of the trauma suffered by the child. Moreover, trauma of a sexual nature was frequent in the poor working-class environment in which the young girl lived: sexual games between children, exhibitionism, etc.

This case illustrates another Ferenczian notion: what he called "terrorism by suffering"; the gestures and cries of despair of the mother tortured the child. She thought that if she did not exist her mother's life would be easier.

Lisette's image of herself is not without contradictions: she has the impression of suffering more than other people, while she feels herself to be better than they are because she is more compassionate and more generous. At the same time, she feels worthless and not deserving to live. From the age of 5, the little girl started to express the desire to die. She describes in detail her father's brutality, and the way he would beat his children for any and every reason. He also stole from his own family any objects that could be of value, so that he could sell them to get drunk; and he invented pleasantries in bad taste to frighten his wife.

Lisette's story shows that her family, which belonged to the Hungarian urban lower class of the beginning of the 20th century, had known poverty and various kinds of trauma. Her narrative only describes two generations. There is no mention of any grandparent on either side. We do not know if they were dead, if members of the family lost touch with each other or broke off relations, nor in what circumstances the grandparents became absent. Neither do we know the reasons for the father's serious alcoholism. We can only surmise that the mother, whose sister lived in more comfortable circumstances, had come down the social scale by marrying this man. Although Lisette describes her mother as capable, loving and warm, the narrative shows that she burdens her children, and Lisette in particular, with complaints, lamentations and reproaches. Of course, she has many reasons to complain, but Lisette suffers terribly from her feeling of being helpless to solve the family's difficulties.

The diary mentions an older sister of Lisette's who works as a nanny in a bourgeois family; the mother admires her and she has a position of authority in the family. Lisette's brother, who is 4 or 5 years older, contributes greatly to the suffering of the little girl, but the latter is very attached to him, presumably as a sort of paternal substitute.

ANALYTICAL HYPOTHESIS

The child described here finds it impossible to create a coherent image of the world and of human relations. She can find no safety in the world that surrounds her, nor in her internal world.

In his postscript, Ferenczi speaks of this young girl's "unconscious need to suffer". A world that causes suffering is perhaps the only kind of world in which she finds some sense, some coherence — the only kind of world that confirms her expectations. What is more, her internal world is filled with hate, anger, jealousy and shame, feelings that are all painful and guilt-provoking, unless she succeeds in maintaining the conviction that they are perfectly justified. It is no doubt this impossibility to accept anything good, or very little, that life can offer — she ended an apparently satisfactory love relationship, as we said earlier — , and the need to prove that everything is denied her, which imprisons her in a hopeless situation and finally drives her to suicide. There is also, no doubt, a relation between her suicide and that of her brother-in-law, which took place a short time earlier. She killed herself with the same gun he did.

In the second half of her life, she lived for a time with her sister and this brother-in-law presented as mentally ill. Her autobiographical narrative reveals her resentment towards her sister, and we know that the brother-in-law once tried to have sexual relations with her, allegedly to see if she was still a virgin; but we do not know what they might have felt for each other. If we examine carefully all the elements available to us, what we have is:

a) **Early and repeated traumatic events**

When Lisette was a baby, the house had been plundered by one of her father's drinking buddies, who took not only the furniture, but also baby Lisette, whose mother only brought her back the next day. But the mother was now in an empty house with her children. We can imagine her panic and the feelings she transmitted to her children in this situation. Lisette drank in, with her mother's milk, her father's violence and her mother's constant anxiety.

Her mother said that she had been a well-behaved, silent child, afraid of her father, of the employers and of other children, and trying to go unnoticed. She liked nature, and particularly frogs and insects. My colleagues who are psychiatrists say that an interest in small, cold-blooded animals is often seen in people with schizoid personalities. In any case, her life situation was such that it could have led to depression, and even infantile psychosis in a sensitive child who, nevertheless, was able to develop a personality, albeit very fragile.

b) Sexual trauma and a split self

When she was about four years old, her brother took money from a man met on the street, to let him use her sexually. The man lay on top of her and ejaculated twice on her; it was not strictly speaking rape, since it seems that there was no penetration, but it was psychological rape, because the little girl, startled at first, was horrified, felt dirty and soiled, and burst out crying. The mother was happy to be given the money and did not try to find out what happened. The event was remembered consciously, as were the feelings and sensations associated with it, and the role played by the brother. Lisette also remembered the impossibility of talking to her mother, who was so overwhelmed by material problems that she welcomed money, no matter where it came from. The event remained a shameful secret she shared with her brother, who betrayed her, although she expresses no resentment towards him in her narrative.

Later, the sexual games of her cousins, and an encounter with an exhibitionist, reminded her of what she had experienced. She dreaded all men who drank and were depraved, but especially her father, who inspired fear and shame in her. Then there was a seduction attempt by a peasant who gave her a ride in his wagon one day when she was walking home carrying heavy packages. Another time, when she was out for a walk with her brother, while he went off to play with another boy, she was approached by a man who took liberties with her. This time she blamed her brother for abandoning her and betraying her. She wondered why these things were always happening to her. Was it because she was different? It never seemed to occur to her that her beauty might have something to do with it. She felt different, ashamed, stigmatised, and yet, as we said earlier, better than other people, more compassionate and generous.

She feared and mistrusted all adults, including her mother, whom she loved; she turned her repressed hate and revolt against teachers who took no real interest in the children entrusted to them and didn't understand them, especially the children of the poor. But she had feelings of compassion for an old drunkard like her father.

As we said, Lisette feels guilty for not being of more help to her mother, but every job she takes to earn some money — selling violets or funeral wreaths, delivering newspapers — ends in failure. She is ashamed of trying to sell something, of asking for money; she is also ashamed of not being able to do it.

The only pleasure of which she speaks in her account is the reading of stories. She devoured all the books of a little girl she is looking after. Once again, she failed at the task assigned to her. Instead of keeping the little girl entertained, she went off to read by herself. After this, she became interested in the New Testament and, from then on, she became totally devoted to Christ, and ultimately identified with him when he asked: "My God, my God, why have you forsaken me?" The guilt she felt for her sins was clearly overshadowed by shame: shame about her clothes, shame about her awkwardness, shame about her father, and no doubt shame for being ashamed.

There is no doubt that the initial sexual trauma is at the forefront of Lisette's awareness, as is sometimes the case, but she is completely unaware of the way in which some of these elements affect her reactions subsequently, in her childhood years and as a young woman. On the one hand, she knows what happened to her and she suffers when she remembers it; on the other hand, she is not aware how much this event continues to influence her behaviour. Her brother sold her innocence for a handful of coins; afterwards, she was unable to sell anything. She cannot even bring herself to demand what is owed to her. That man long ago told her to lie down and let him do what he wanted; from then on, she has been unable to give in to anyone or anything, she cannot show herself to her advantage to obtain what she needs, nor can she give in to shared desire.

Clearly, there is a splitting of the self between two positions: a position of passive suffering, and a position of rebellious pride, ultimately at her own expense. To love would be impossible for her, since that would require entrusting herself confidently to someone else and risking being betrayed, as she was by her brother, and as her mother was countless times by her father. As to the sexual act, it is associated with feeling soiled and ashamed. She is unable to realise that the adult woman she has become has means of defending herself which the little girl she once was didn't have. And any desire she feels or that someone else feels for her unconsciously awakens the trauma and causes her to break off the relationship.

It is difficult to say if analytic treatment with Ferenczi or a love affair with an infintely patient man could have eliminated the deathly contradiction between her moral ideal and her sexual desire, a contradiction created by her traumatic history.

c) The Brother-in-Law's Suicide

The young woman killed herself a few days after her brother-in-law did, with the pistol he used. We know that the suicide of a family member is likely to prompt the suicide of other people in the family. This is even more likely in the case of a person like Lisette, who had already announced her plan to end her life. In addition, we may ask what her true feelings were for her brother-in-law. She claimed she only felt hate towards him, as Ferenczi writes, but we can also imagine more ambivalent feelings for this man who had made advances towards her and who was the husband of an older sister she didn't like and was jealous of. Given her tendency to feel guilty and worthless, we can well ask if she did not consider herself responsible for the death of this man whose advances she rejected.

d) The Sphere of Phantoms

Lisette's mother is described as always protecting herself through recourse to little secrets, such as hiding her poverty from her wealthier sister. Thanks to the work of Serge Tisseron among others, we know that certain small secrets can hide greater secrets. As for Lisette's father, we know thanks to the work of Claude Nachin, Pascal Hachet and other authors, that alcoholism and drug addiction can hide either personal traumas or the transgenerational influence of unresolved traumas suffered by the patients' ancestors.

Let us note that an analyst who has been treating a patient who leaves or who dies, especially by suicide, without having revealed his secret, can be left feeling haunted by a ghostly presence; this impression fades with time, reflection, and sometimes revelation of the case. This could be one of the reasons that impelled Ferenczi to publish Lisette's story. I believe that this story made him uncomfortable for several reasons. He was unable to sufficiently sort out the young girl's problems, in the few encounters he had with her, to enable her to overcome the shock of her brother-in-law's suicide. And, giving in to his predilection for pretty women, as his correspondence with other analysts and particularly with Freud reveals, he once kissed the young patient, which in this case was certainly not advisable. In fact, it was during the period when he published the story that his discussions with Freud started about the gratifications allowed or not, needed or forbidden, with a certain type of patient. The famous "kissing technique" letter was written on December 13, 1931.

TO CONCLUDE

What, then, can we learn and understand about Lisette's story from this autobiography and the few impressions recorded by Ferenczi? This young girl who, through her account, appears to us to be sensitive and intelligent, remembers perfectly well traumas she suffered in her childhood and adolescence. But she has never been able to integrate their effects, which remain active and are revived whenever she confronts difficult situations in her life, revealing the fragility of her psychic structure.

And there has been no lack of difficult situations in her life: early kidnapping by a stranger, the sexual trauma when she was 4 or 5, her father's brutality and unpredictability, the anxiety and terror in which her mother lived, the ambiguous relationship with her brother-in-law, and everything else we don't know about.

We know nothing about the possible — and likely — phantoms of events her parents lived through in their own childhoods, since grandparents are never mentioned in the young woman's account, nor in Ferenczi's. We may have reason to think that the first sexual trauma experienced at the age of 4 or 5 could have led to the creation of a crypt in the girl's self. This story can also illustrate the functioning of a broken symbol whose fragments play a role in the young woman's behaviour when shame, the dominant feeling, is sometimes replaced by fierce opposition.

In addition, we know that, at the time, the Hungarian urban working class lived in extreme poverty, both moral and material. It is likely that under the influence of the Russian Revolution, attention began to be paid to this situation in Hungary, as witnessed by the literature of the period. Ferenczi, open to left-wing ideas, was certainly aware of all this when he became interested in Lisette.

FERENCZI'S VIEW OF TRANSFERENCE

In the book he co-authored with Otto Rank, *The Development of Psycho-Analysis*, Ferenczi insists on the fact that *theory must always be based on clinical observation.* Therefore, it seems reasonable to think that he constructed his perspective on transference based on his own clinical observations of his patients and of himself. This being so, I think it is not possible to discuss transference from Ferenczi's perspective without reference to his personal story and development, and especially the evolution of his relationship with Freud, because their mutual transference certainly played just as crucial a role in the identification and study of this phenomenon as the observations they made in the course of analyses.

Overall, Ferenczi's conception of transference does not differ from Freud's classic view, but he gives it a wider scope. Or more precisely, Ferenczi drew certain conclusions of which Freud was certainly not unaware, but which did not hold his interest. *Countertransference* is a case in point. Freud was the one who first drew attention to it, but he saw it chiefly as an obstacle, a source of difficulty that had to be controlled and neutralised as much as possible. For this reason, he did not recognise all of its effects, which later were revealed to be crucial and very productive in the development of psychoanalysis and psychoanalytic therapy.

From the earliest meetings between Freud and Ferenczi, their mutual transference was massive and immediate; it shaped the relationship that developed between them, and its future evolution. We can say that at first Freud, the older man and the master, was the object of Ferenczi's paternal transference, a situation which suited Freud very well and which he accepted almost too willingly. Afterwards, and quite early (let us remember the "Palermo incident" that occurred during their trip to Sicily), Ferenczi would have liked to develop a more maternal transference towards Freud as well. He was asking for an equal relationship, but above all for some indulgence and tenderness. But Freud was unwilling to accept this type of transference, as he clearly said on many occasions. Ferenczi was hurt by what he perceived as being relegated to an infantile role, despite Freud's largely accurate interpretation of this reaction. Indeed, we know than an interpretation must be given in a certain setting, at the right time and in the right manner. Freud's interpretation, as it appears in the correspondence between the two men, seems to be primarily defensive.

Thus, a certain degree of *negative transference* was present on Ferenczi's part from the beginning, in an otherwise very positive relationship. This tranference naturally triggered countertransferential reactions.

The first analysts often practised among themselves what we would now call "wild" analysis; but how could they avoid it, given the enthusiasm related to discovery, and the fact that they were so few in number? They analysed each other in every situation, in an atmosphere of widespread indiscretion which of course gave rise to resentments and conflicts. This no doubt had a profound influence on the way in which they conceived and developed various psychoanalytic concepts.

In 1909, only one year after meeting Freud, Ferenczi wrote an article about transference, entitled "Introjection and Transference". It is a somewhat disorganised article in which Ferenczi stumbles around in the dark, trying to bring to light the coherence between different psychoanalytic concepts. Several paragraphs are dedicated to defending psychoanalysis from its detractors, who were just as numerous at the time as they are today. Nevertheless, it is a particularly important article because it contains the preliminary sketch for a whole series of new ideas whose consequences would go beyond what Freud and Ferenczi could imagine at the time.

Among these ideas, one of the most important, I feel, is that transference is a universal human phemonenon, existing among neurotics and healthy people alike. Ferenczi wrote: "[We have] the knowledge that the fundamental differences, assumed before Freud's time, between normal and psychoneurotic do not exist. Freud showed us that 'the neuroses have no special psychical content that is peculiar to them and occurs only in them', and according to Jung's statement, neurotics suffer from complexes with which we all fight. The difference between the two is only quantitative and of practical import. The healthy person transfers his affects and identifies himself on the basis of 'aetiological claims' that have a much better motive than in the case of the neurotic, and thus does not dissipate his psychical energy so foolishly as the latter does".

Consequently, countertransference is also a universal phenomenon, a transference like any other. Therefore, countertransference is not solely a reaction provoked by the patient's pathology, but also includes what the analyst transfers to his interlocutor, depending on his own psychic characteristics.

Ferenczi wrote that in neurotics "[there are] very often 'reaction-formations', as an excessive accentuation in consciousness of a current feeling". Thus, transference in neurotics is seen as being of exaggerated intensity, and as constituting a special case of displacement.

Then Ferenczi introduces the concept of introjection, opposing it to that of projection. For example, psychotics project outside themselves painful affects, and as a result, find it hard to develop transferential relations, while neurotics introject them, so as to be able to transfer them later. Therefore, at the time when he wrote this article, Ferenczi already thought that transference is present in relationships of every kind, and even that it constitutes the very substance of these relations. This being so, what transpires between analyst and patient is, in fact, a relationship. Today, most analysts take this for granted. But in 1909, this was not seen as obvious. The analyst, often called "the doctor", was an observer who studied with indifference — not "neutrality", the term used by French translators — an object of study, the patient, to understand his functioning, and then help him to better understand his own internal world and the origin of his symptoms. This was done, if need be, by exposing him to fragments of psychoanalytic theory serving as explanations. It was Ferenczi who pointed out later, in The Development of Psycho-Analysis, that theoretical indoctrination of the patient had little therapeutic effect. I believe that this idea of "indifferent" listening had been conceived in an attempt to neutralise the effects of countertransference, which was seen as an obstacle rather than a useful tool. Of course, such an objective was totally unrealistic. This could be what caused one of Freud's first French translators, Anne Bermann, to choose the term neutralité (neutrality), which denotes, more than emotional uninvolvement, uninvolvement in the patient's life.

In this article, Ferenczi uses almost interchangeably the terms "transference", "introjection", "displacement" and "identification". All these phenomena play a role in every form of therapy, including hypnosis and suggestion, as well as in every form of neurosis. But these concepts are not identical; each one has its particularities, which Ferenczi gradually elucidated himself, before his followers, Michael Balint, Nicolas Abraham and Maria Torok among them, brought further clarifications. Specifically, the concept of introjection would be developed and refined later by Abraham and Torok, who drew very interesting conclusions pertaining to it, especially in relation to the mechanism of mourning, in their article "Mourning or Melancholia".

Another interesting idea suggested in this early article is that illnesses and neuroses are attempts to find a solution — albeit costly — , that deserves to be considered as a form of self-therapy. This is no doubt one of the sources of resistance encountered in every analysis: it is not easy to accept giving up a solution, no matter how imperfect, to replace it with a new solution one hopes will be better, but which is as yet unknown.

In his article, Ferenczi writes that "all later loving, hating, and fearing are only transferences, or, as Freud terms them, 'new editions' of currents of feeling that were acquired in the earliest childhood [...] and later repressed". He would subsequently clarify this definition, as we shall see, by noting that in addition to transferred affects, there are also current relationships with others, including the analyst. I think it is safe to say that one always uses known patterns to enter into a relationship, and that these patterns will be reshaped later, as the personality of the other person imposes itself more strongly.

"[...] an unconscious sexual element is at the basis of every sympathetic emotion", Ferenczi writes in his article. If censure intervenes creating a prohibition, what will result is antipathy or even repulsion.

Ferenczi's article makes a rather detailed study of *hypnosis* and *suggestion*, which function excusively through transference, and therefore only provide temporary results which do not outlast the relation with the hypnotist. In this article, Ferenczi introduces the idea of paternal hypnosis (through intimidation and injunctions), and maternal hypnosis (through tenderness and seduction). These concepts will be presented again in a famous article entitled "Taming of a Wild Horse".

Obeying the parent, says Ferenczi, becomes pleasurable once object-love, identification with the parent and his introjection have occurred. These mechanisms make transference possible. Then, this relation with the parent, the father, is transferred to teachers, leaders, superiors. In 1912, in "On the Definition of Introjection", Ferenczi gave a more detailed explanation of the functioning of transference and introjection.

Starting in 1912, he brought into question the usefulness of some scholarly interpretations widely used by analysts at that time. In "Transitory Symptom-Constructions during the Analysis", he observed that even the most relevant interpretations remain without effect if a sufficiently solid and positive transference is not present. But this is not all he has to say on the subject. The following year he deals with it again in "Belief, Disbelief and Conviction". He now seems to be certain that analytic treatment is not an intellectual process, although intelligence plays a part in it; but affectivity plays an essential role, by means of transference. Believing or not believing something depends mainly on the quality of the relationship, positive or negative, existing with the person who is the source of the information, rather than on the information itself.

Speaking of "fragmented analyses", analyses in several "sections" or interrupted by vacations, Ferenczi discusses termination of an analysis and what becomes of transference after an interruption, whether the analysis is terminated or not. When an analysis is interrupted without being truly terminated, the transference is not resolved and the patient remains dependent on the analyst. He will make contact again, either directly or through various signs (postcards, public praise of the analyst) if the transference is positive, or he will cut himself off from the analyst completely if the transference is negative. If the analysis is truly ended, he will simply lose interest in the analyst.

I believe this question of the possible permanence of transferential feelings deserves to be examined, particularly in the case of candidates who, once they are ready, become the colleagues of their former analysts. It is possible that Ferenczi displays his usual optimism when he thinks that an analysis can be truly terminated, and a transference altogether resolved. But he equates the end of transference with the acquisition of independence. This, I think, is the crux of the matter. Perhaps there is, in what he says, some confusion between infantile dependence that can result from transferring to the analyst one's early feelings for the parents, and the transference of more complex feelings which are part of all relationships. When one is ill or in a weakened state for any reason, there is a tendency to establish a child-parent transference, on the protected-protector model. But as the analysis advances, all kinds of feelings can be transferred to the analyst.

Further along in his article (in the discussion of the Bordeaux School), Ferenczi emphasises again that although establishing the transference is essential in an analysis, it is not sufficient. But in the 1910–1920 period, he does not yet seem to distinguish clearly what depends on transference, what depends on knowledge and interpretations, and what depends on the setting of the therapy. I wonder if even today all this is clear to us, given how intermingled these elements are.

One of the last articles of this period, written in 1919, deals with "Psychoanalytic Technique". In it, Ferenczi focuses particularly on countertransference. He seems fully aware that controlling the countertransference does not mean being indifferent. If the analyst has no feelings towards his patient, he cannot understand anything about him. He must allow himself to have feelings — which he will have in any case — , but he must not act on them. Another thing the article suggests, without stating it explicitly, is that countertransference, interpreted depending on the patient's pathology, is a valuable tool in the therapy.

We might imagine that the indifference recommended by Freud was, in fact, countertransference on the part of a man who saw himself as a scientist, entirely dedicated to his discovery, letting neither his private life, nor fatigue or illness distract him from it. He wanted to study emotions, not let them influence him. Yet, his writings and his correspondence clearly show that he was not immune to emotions, and even very passionate emotions. In fact, some of his emotional reactions caused him to ignore important ideas, such as those proposed by Ferenczi and Rank; but the timing of these ideas was not propicious, in terms of Freud's ability to accept them.

When Ferenczi introduced his so-called "active" technique at the start of the 1920s, he was forced to consider a number of psychoanalytic concepts from another point of view. He realised that although analysis starts with "passive" acceptance by the patient of his own association of ideas, and "passive" listening to them by the analyst, the latter's interpretation already constitutes an "activity". Then, transference to the analyst mobilises the libido, which is then withdrawn from the symptoms. After this, the patient tries to detach his libido from the new object, something he can only do thanks to the education of his ego by the analyst. The authority conferred to the analyst by the transference makes this active training possible. Thus, at that time, Ferenczi was already thinking that letting transference develop and then interpreting it was not enough; he planned to use the illusory authority associated with it to educate his patients. We know that after a time he criticised and abandoned the active technique. He also became increasingly cautious about the educational role of the analyst.

In one of the chapters he contributed to *The Development of Psychoanalysis*, co-authored with Otto Rank in 1923, Ferenczi reveals his acute awareness of the interdependence of transference and countertransference; he shows how the analyst's countertransference, in its turn, triggers transferential reactions in the patient; these could then be called "counter-countertransference". He points out how these cross-transferences make it difficult for negative transference to surface. Ferenczi knew from personal experience how important it was to allow negative transferential elements to manifest themselves. One of the things for which he blamed Freud after his three-part analysis with him in 1914 and 1916 was that Freud did not detect and did not analyse the negative aspect of his transference. Indeed, their correspondence clearly shows that, from the start, there were negative elements in this otherwise positive relationship.

In the same book, Ferenczi also explains that the analyst must submit everything he feels to self-criticism, and be fully aware of all his feelings; unless he does so, he won't understand what the patient wants to convey. Then Ferenczi goes on to warn his readers against considering any negative transference as a resistance, and reminds them that intensely positive transference can also act as a resistance.

Moreover, let it be said in passing that this concept of resistance deserves closer attention, as does the question of how to handle it. There was a time when what was recommended was to "attack" or "break" resistances. This period coincided with that of the active technique. Today, many analysts think that in the course of the analysis these resistances fall away on their own when the patient no longer needs them. Today it is considered preferable to use a circumvention technique.

Gradually, Ferenczi realised that the active technique did not promote the development of transference, and tended to reinforce resistances. For these reasons, he gave up this authoritarian technique, to try to establish a friendlier, more tolerant and more egalitarian atmosphere.

Thus, towards the end of the 1920s there was a significant change of direction in Ferenczi's research, as well as a change in his technique and in the nature of his transference to Freud. This also brought about a change in his attitude towards his patients, and consequently in their responses, as well as those of Freud. The first article in this last series of writings is entitled "The Adaptation of the Family to the Child", a title which might as well have been: "The Adaptation of the Analyst to the Patient".

Indeed, Ferenczi never stopped developing new techniques to solve the problems he encountered in his patients' treatment. It is while he was engaged in this process that he formulated explicitly that the analyst must find the means to help each patient, rather than selecting patients who could benefit from the traditional analytic treatment as it was practised.

In 1930, in "The Principle of Relaxation and Neocatharsis", Ferenczi engaged in serious criticism of the excesses of the frustration technique and of his own active technique, showing that they could create a type of tansference which makes the patient-analyst relation resemble more and more a pupil-teacher relation. This type of relationship makes it very difficult for the patient to express feelings of aggression or opposition, and very difficult for the analyst to admit his errors, or admit that he did not understand something, or misunderstood. Throughout the article, Ferenczi is pleading for greater flexibility of technique, more freedom concerning the rules, and an absence of theoretical dogmatism, since theory would naturally evolve with research and experience.

Here, we can see the consequences of the fact that Ferenczi's transference to Freud has evolved, that he no longer sees Freud as an infallible father, but rather as a brilliant researcher, open to new ideas, who does not prevent others from pursuing their own paths and helping psychoanalysis advance in new directions.

This was, in fact, what Freud would have liked to be, without always succeeding. Ferenczi's new attitude allowed him to prompt the re-examination of the traumatic origin of neurosis, which had been seriously questioned by Freud, but never entirely rejected. Careful not to be dogmatic himself, Ferenczi emphasised that he was speaking of a conceptualisation "not altogether clear" even to him.

A passage in "Confusion of Tongues Between the Adults and the Child" shows very clearly how he truly felt about his relationship with Freud: "Parents and adults, in the same way as we analysts, ought to learn to be constantly aware that behind the submissiveness or even the adoration, just as behind the transference of love, of our children, patients and pupils, there lies hidden an ardent desire to get rid of this oppressive love. If we can help the child, the patient or the pupil to give up the reaction of identification, and to ward off the over-burdening transference, then we may be said to have reached the goal of raising the personality to a higher level".

It is in his *Clinical Diary* that Ferenczi expresses most clearly the negative aspect of his transference to Freud. It is here that it becomes most difficult to sort out what should be considered transference (maternal or paternal for Ferenczi?), or a feeling inspired directly by the person of the analyst, in this case Freud.

Ferenczi is perhaps the one who has shown most clearly that every interpersonal relationship is derived from the first feelings of love and hate (in varying proportions), therefore on feelings transferred from what was felt for one of the parents, one of the siblings, or another significant person in one's childhood.

Ferenczi also showed that although in an analysis transference love is the most spectacular and vocal, negative transference is always present. He became aware of this through his own feelings towards Freud, described in the *Clinical Diary*[21]. As a result, he insisted that negative transference must be taken into consideration and analysed, that is, recognised, accepted and included as an element of every human relationship.

In conclusion, we can say that although Ferenczi defined transference in the most traditional Freudian manner, he identified several of its characteristics: its universal nature and the fact that it is very substance of any human relationship; the analyst's transference, that is, countertransference, and above all, the use of this countertransference to better understand the patient; the importance and omnipresent character of negative transference, the need to take it into account, accept it and analyse it; and even the importance of the analyst's negative countertransference, along with the need to be aware of it and deal with it.

FERENCZI'S VIEW OF TRAUMA: THEORETICAL DEVELOPMENT OR REGRESSION

In the psychoanalytic literature, just as in discussions among colleagues, Ferenczi and Freud are often opposed on the basis of certain ideas, or their personalities. Each of them has passionate disciples who want to promote the author they most admire, neglecting the others. This passionate attitude could be, in large part, a consequence of the trauma suffered by the psychoanalytic community as a result of the final conflict between Freud and Ferenczi, which emerged

in the 1930s but had been present in latent form for some time. Michael Balint describes this controversy in Chapter 23 of his book The Basic Fault, giving the history of the conflict:

---

21 Ferenczi, S., *The Clinical Diary of Sándor Ferenczi*, op. cit. See page 118 and pages 212-215, where Ferenczi analyses his relationship with Freud.

"The impact of this event was so painful that the first reaction of the analytic movement to it was denial and silence, broken only in recent years, since when all sorts of fictitious statements about Freud and Ferenczi have found their way into print: Freud was described as a ruthless autocrat, a dictator, and Ferenczi as a mean, cowardly schemer". (p. 149)

Such absolute judgments are also made about their respective theoretical positions, particularly concerning trauma. Some say Freud was convinced that most of the traumas described by his patients, especially hysterics, were in fact fantasies; while Ferenczi, blinded by his own pathology, came to believe all the stories his patients told him. On the contrary, some people contended that Freud, as a member of the bourgeoisie of his era, was unable to admit that such vile things could take place in "good families", while Ferenczi had the courage to confront the reality of these events.

These emotionally-charged attitudes indicate that the two men are closely linked in people's minds. And they were, in fact, close in reality: their correspondence testifies to their friendship, which was passionate, critical and ambivalent all at the same time.

Over the years, there were encounters of a personal, intellectual and professional nature, as well as conflicts, misunderstandings and disagreements, as is the case in any rich and profound relationship. The conflicts between the two men were due as much to the complexity of their relationship and their different personalities, as to differing standpoints on analytic theory and technique. Freud seems to indicate this in his letter dated January 20, 1930: "In reality, we should be content with determining that the theoretical differences between us also don't go any further than is unavoidable with two different workers when they don't have constant exchange of thoughts and along with that mutual influencing!" As we can see, Freud seems to blame the infrequency of their exchanges rather than their theoretical differences. In truth, at a certain point Ferenczi tried to free himself from the great influence Freudian thought had on him, feeling that his clinical experience and his research were taking him in a new direction. It was the overly passionate attitude of certain successors that was responsible for a simplistic presentation of the situation, although reality was much more complex.

In truth, the position of the two men, and particularly

Freud's, was more subtle. Freud never entirely rejected the traumatic aetiology of neuroses. Ferenczi, being more categorical, came to believe that all neuroses had traumatic origins which an analysis should be able to uncover before it can be considered terminated. But Ferenczi did not reject the notion of a pathogenic fantasy that could contribute to the process. The difference between the two concepts is therefore above all quantitative: Freud considered that a real trauma occurs more rarely than was believed, and Ferenczi was convinced that the role of pathogenic fantasy was less fundamental than Freud believed. Ferenczi thought that what patients say should be believed, even if not always literally, and that, in addition, trauma could be intense even when it does not take a spectacular form. Later, Masud Khan pointed out the pathogenic effect of small, repeated traumas, and Balint described the possible traumatic effect of the gap between what the child needs and what he is given by his entourage. Thus, Ferenczi introduced a wider view of what could constitute a trauma.

As is often the case, in this instance, instead of comparing two perspectives in order to eliminate one, it seemed more helpful to consider the possibility of pursuing two research paths, two ways of looking at the same phenomenon. Therefore, Ferenczi did not return to an outdated theory, but continued his research by picking up an abandoned thread of analytic theory that had not been followed to the end, to use his own description of the procedure.

Freud started by describing trauma as essentially sexual in nature, emerging in early childhood and reproduced later by an event during puberty, which will then produce the pathology. Then, little by little, as his hysterical patients narrated various events, the hypothesis of pathogenic fantasy took precedence over that of real trauma, without replacing it altogether. In *Introductory Lectures on Psycho-Analysis*, Freud wrote: "Here, then, we foresee [...] a greater wealth of determinants for the onset of illness; but we may also suspect that there is no need to abandon the traumatic line of approach as being erroneous; it must be possible to fit it in and subsume it somewhere else [in other types of cases]".

In his practice, which was much more flexible than the classical Freudian technique, Ferenczi encountered these other types of cases more and more often. This is what caused him to re-examine the question of the traumatic aetiology of neurosis, and to define trauma much more precisely. It was his work with patients we would call "borderline" today which enabled him to develop an understanding of the mechanics of trauma capable of generating neurosis.

Like Freud, Ferenczi identified several stages, but described them somewhat differently. Trauma in itself does not necessarily generate neurosis; if it is handled well by the child's entourage, it can even facilitate normal maturation. But it can trigger illness if it is followed by disavowal by important people in the child's life, particularly his mother. It is hypocrisy, making the child feel guilty, and rejection which can render the trauma pathogenic. The element of surprise, or repetition of the trauma, can also aggravate the situation. The secondary event according to Freud, an event which occurs during puberty, can sometimes coincide with Ferenczi's second stage: that of denial and shaming.

This is how Ferenczi describes the mechanism of action of trauma in his 1930 article "The Principles of Relaxation and Neocatharsis": "The recollections which neocatharsis evoked or corroborated lent an added significance to the original traumatic factor in our aetiological equations". And he goes on to say, alluding to his discussions with Freud: "The precautions of the hysteric and the avoidance of the obsessional neurotic may, it is true, have their explanation in purely mental fantasy-formations; nevertheless the first impetus towards abnormal lines of development has always been thought to originate from real psychic traumas and conflicts with the environment — the invariable precursors of the formation of nosogenic mental forces, for instance, of conscience".

Ferenczi shows how the technique of frustration used in analysis can, in some cases, reproduce the rigid authority of the parents and constitute a repetition of the original trauma; he writes that this trauma is often the result of "inadequate, capricious, tactless, even cruel" treatment, or of lack of understanding, disavowal or abandonment by important people in the child's life. Certain attitudes associated with the classical analytic technique can be experienced by the analysand as inadequate, tactless, or as abandonment.

Ferenczi insisted on the frequency of sexual trauma, even in the most puritanical families. Ingmar Bergman's largely autobiographical movie *Fanny and Alexander* provides a striking illustration of this. In other cases, Ferenczi stated, adults indulge in erotic games with the child, under the guise of a show of affection. The child responds enthusiastically, "more vehemently and far earlier" than is supposed. But what he seeks is play and tenderness. The adult, on the other hand, responds with a passion the child cannot understand. Feeling guilty, the adult may even scold and punish the child, getting rid of his guilt by placing it on the child. The suddenness of this reversal of attitude is one of the traumatic factors for the child. This is Ferenczi's concept of a "confusion of tongues", for which he was so severely criticised. Because he insisted on the fundamental innocence of the child, Ferenczi was accused of denying infantile sexuality. But Ferenczi was not saying that the child is "innocent" of sexual feelings, only that he experiences them without guilt unless an adult instills it in him as a way of freeing himself of his own guilt.

Trauma can also be the result of a lack of affection, a lack of stimulation or, on the contrary, excessive stimulation. While Freud speaks of a "congenital weakness" of the desire to live, Ferenczi prefers to speak of very early trauma, such as he describes in "The Unwelcome Child and His Death Instinct".

This is how Ferenczi describes the effect produced by trauma: the first reaction to shock is a transitory psychosis, a break with reality, followed by a psychotic splitting off and the destruction of the feeling of self and of the defences, even of form itself. The subject can then make himself malleable to withstand the shock better, or react with fragmentation or atomisation of the personality, especially when there is repeated trauma. Some fragments are killed, and become dead portions of the psyche, which the surviving portion will encyst, wall off, in a manner of speaking. Ferenczi insisted repeatedly on the sudden and unexpected nature of the shock. The subject is stunned, there is paralysis of all psychic processes, of motility, of perceptions, of thought; a state of passivity devoid of resistance emerges. The traumatised child, being physically and psychically weaker, cannot defend himself and has no choice but to identify with the aggressor, give in to all his desires, and even anticipate them. This kind of self-destruction can even include a pleasurable component: the pleasure of sacrificing oneself to superior powers, of sharing in some manner the power and greatness of the aggressor. The victim of the aggression may try to comfort himself with a feeling of his own wisdom and intellectual superiority. The aggressor is introjected and becomes intrapsychic. This is the only way to maintain a relationship of tenderness with an aggressor on whom the child is dependent, in a hallucinatory mode. But because the adult's guilt is also introjected, what was previously innocent play now becomes guilt and deserves to be punished. This leads to a split in the child: he is both innocent and guilty; as a result, he stops trusting his own senses. As for the aggressor, his sense of guilt causes him to deny the facts, increasing the child's guilt by showing extreme moral rigidity. If the child tries to tell someone close what has happened to him, especially his mother, he is often scolded for "talking silly" or lying. This is what happened to a 4-year-old boy who was the victim of sexual games inflicted on him by an adolescent cousin, when he wanted to tell his mother what happened. She was absorbed in the novel she was reading and pushed him away, not wanting to be disturbed by such "absurd stories". The child reacted by becoming almost entirely silent, and his future development was sufficiently disturbed to cause him to seek psychological help.

A child who suffered a trauma can also react with what Ferenczi called "precocious maturity". Suddenly, the child develops surprising intelligence and wisdom; he becomes the caregiver, or even the psychiatrist, of his parents. This is the *wise baby*, the one Ferenczi called a learned toddler, who takes it upon himself to deal with the problems of his inadequate parents. As a result of the split which took place, one part of the personality nurtures the other, becoming its "guardian angel", as it were. If a second trauma occurs, reinforcing the effects of the first, the guardian angel can be overwhelmed and the end result may be suicide. In his *Clinical Diary*, Ferenczi seems to interpret his pernicious anemia as a suicide attempt — successful, as we know — after the shock he experienced when he felt abandoned by Freud. This abandonment revived the trauma inflicted by his mother's coldness.

Thus, Ferenczi considered that this return to trauma theory was not a regression but, on the contrary, that it opened the way to research not yet conducted. A physician first and foremost, Ferenczi was interested from the start in the therapeutic consequences of this theory. He undertook to develop techniques allowing him to go as far back as the initial trauma; in this endeavour, he understood the therapeutic value of a process that had previously been seen as an obstacle to analysis: regression. The techniques he called "relaxation", "permissiveness" and "neocatharsis" were meant to facilitate regression, which could even deepen into a state of trance. In this state, the patient could relive the original trauma, and sometimes live it for the first time when he had remained unaware of it or had experienced it at an extremely early age. In such states, no recollection is possible and the original trauma remains inaccessible with use of the classical technique. Ferenczi hoped that reliving the trauma in a state of regression would allow it to emerge into memory and, as a result, become accessible to analysis. This would make better resolution possible. Ferenczi realised very quickly that in these states of profound regression the patient was extremely fragile; this required of the analyst that he exert close control over his countertransference and his own resistances, and use them in a measured way, so as not to lose control of the situation. While applying this process, Ferenczi had to report some setbacks: some patients went from repetition to repetition of the trauma, relieved each time but only briefly. Patients went back and forth between having emotions without understanding, and understanding without experiencing emotions, without actually reliving anything. In some cases, they sunk into states of frustration and despair that could cause them to put an end to the treatment.

Illness prevented Ferenczi from solving this problem. It was his friend and successor, Michael Balint, who continued this research, proposed a theory — that of the basic fault — to describe the process, and studied methods for helping patients emerge from this regression, which is nevertheless clearly useful.

It seems that Freud found this taking up of an abandoned thread very disquieting, even alarming. Although he never abandoned Ferenczi as a friend, he nevertheless refused to accompany him on this path. This research seemed like sheer madness to him, as he made clear in his letters to Jones and Eitingon. This also explains his extremely negative reaction when Ferenczi came to read him the text he planned to present at the 1932 Wiesbaden Congress, "Confusion of Tongues Between the Adults and the Child". It was even suggested that Ferenczi should be asked not to present the paper, and not to publish anything until he had reconsidered his erroneous thinking. Six years after Ferenczi's death, when Freud was nearing the end of his own life, he admitted to Michael Balint (personal communication) that in Ferenczi's last articles, including "Confusion of Tongues", there were many interesting points.

In heartbreaking terms, Ferenczi confesses in his *Clinical Diary* how much this situation made him suffer. With a few exceptions, Freud's reluctance blocked analytic evaluation of Ferenczi's ideas, as well as Rank's. A half a century had to pass before the analytic community rediscovered all the richness and all the new possibilities offered by Ferenczi's controversial investigations, and before these possibilities started to be explored, applied and pursued.

THE FREUD-FERENCZI CONFLICT: A VALUABLE INHERITANCE?

A chapter of Michael Balint's *The Basic Fault*[22] is dedicated to the disagreement between Freud and Ferenczi, described by Balint as a "trauma" for the psychoanalytic community. They say that hardship which does not kill you makes you stronger. Of course, there are many intermediary possibilities; the trauma produced by the misunderstanding between Freud and Ferenczi can be said to correspond to one of them. My intention here is to examine the repercussions of this trauma, and see if subsequent generations of analysts were able to benefit from this painful experience.

Although disagreements between Freud and Ferenczi were present from the beginning, their relationship was extremely positive. When Freud invited Ferenczi, the first year they met, to join his family on their summer vacation, his sympathy for the young man was obvious, although there was also the fear of being disturbed in his work (see correspondence). And this worry was not unfounded: Ferenczi never stopped disturbing him, since what he had to offer and to ask for touched upon subjects Freud was sensitive about. Ferenczi always tried to discover, in every person he met, the deepest and most authentic layer of

his personality. I believe Freud had the same desire, but could not bear it. He had weathered many storms in his life and had suffered greatly. When faced with his own strong emotions, he became defensive, although he had no problem facing such emotions in others. What he most wanted was to understand, to explore the deepest levels of ideas and people, but without risking his own emotional balance. Ferenczi, on the other hand, wanted to feel, to "feel with" (*mitfühlen*), to "feel inside" (*einfühlen*), as he said, risking his emotional balance every time.

Each man's theory and technique was deeply steeped in his attitude. Freud wanted to understand; Ferenczi wanted to heal. Everyone around them was perfectly aware of this difference: when people said "Professor", it was clear that they were referring to Freud. And when the "Doctor" was

22   Balint, M., *The Basic Fault*, op. cit.

mentioned, there was no need to specify that it was Ferenczi.

Analysts have always recognised the crucial importance of affects; those of the patient were studied, but those of the analyst were considered an obstacle to be ignored, a disturbance that had to be controlled. In fact, the patient was encouraged to express his emotions in a civilised manner only. The analytic setting and the conventions established in advance served this purpose, as did the interpretations, which sometimes degenerated into intellectual explanations.

Thus, Ferenczi did not introduce the interest in affectivity, in the analytic couple he formed with Freud, but he gave it the right to exist and recognised its essential role in the therapeutic process. The book co-authored with Otto Rank, The Development of Psycho-Analysis[23] testifies to this. Ferenczi did not see the analyst's countertransference and the patient's regression as obstacles, but rather as therapeutic tools. Balint, Ferenczi's pupil, friend and disciple, advised the analyst (as well as the physician) to intrepret his countertransference based on the patient's problems.

Today, most analysts (although we must avoid generalisation) are aware that they have to rely – not necessarily simultaneously — on intelligence, knowledge and affect. What is needed is to be open to the patient's problem, let a relationship develop and reinforce it, be willing to subject oneself to it no matter what affects it carries, involve one's whole being with meeting the other, become accessible, but without losing oneself. But in addition, it is just as important to understand, to make use of theory, or more accurately of theories, but certainly not a single theory that promises to explain everything coherently. Theories elevated to the status of dogma lock the analyst and the analysand into a rigid position, a framework that excludes whatever is personal to them.

Thus, the Freud-Ferenczi conflict is constantly reproduced by every analyst and in every analysis. Fear of failing to understand or of unleashing overly violent emotions can propel the analyst into the reassuring sphere of theory, causing him to make hasty interpretations serving to block what he fears he cannot control, instead of creating an opening for himself and for the patient. On the other hand, sinking into a state of incomprehension, inevitable at times in the course of an analysis, can cause the therapist

---

23   Ferenczi, S. and Rank, O., *The Development of Psycho-Analysis*, Nervous and Mental Disease Publishing Co., 1923.

to abandon any intellectual framework for a long time, and stay solely in the realm of emotions, even if it means "going under" with his patient. Indeed, analytic listening has become an increasingly complex activity. The various factors involved are sometimes complementary, often contradictory, escaping repeatedly the conscious control of the analyst, and coming under his control again from time to time.

Ferenczi reminds us that when we want to have complete control over events, we prevent the emergence of decisive fundamental factors. Freud warns us that the *laisser-faire* attempted by his pupil and friend Ferenczi can lead to a situation that escapes the control of both the analyst and the analysand, leaving them both powerless and in distress, particularly in cases of regression allowed to reach a state of trance. Here, we must turn once again to Balint, who offered theoretical and practical solutions to avoid such an outcome. In 1932, Ferenczi wrote: "Balint picked things up where I got stumped".

This disagreement and its repercussions give us a clearer undertanding of the inevitable and often fruitless conflicts, battles and debates which arise regularly in regard to the transmission of analysis. Attempts were made to submit this transmission to rules by means of "shaping" candidates. But is it possible to mould someone who practices an ever-changing occupation which must adapt to endless diversity? What I would prefer to propose is the greatest possible openness to knowledge and experience, the encouragement of adaptability, freedom of thought, critical thinking, and the courage to try, be wrong and admit it[24].

In conclusion, I would say that the disagreement (and difference) between Freud and Ferenczi has allowed us to become aware of the contradictory requirements arising in the course of an analysis: healing and research, conducted simultaneously or consecutively. Psychoanalysis has probably avoided the danger of becoming transformed into a rigid intellectual dogma, or of turning into a vague intuitive process, thanks to what this initial conflict brought to light, and what the followers of these courageous innovators have been able to construct. I know that the ideas I presented here somewhat naively are well-known and widely accepted. This leads me to conclude with a new question: what is this intense need, or this fragility, which makes it so difficult

---

24 See supra, section "Practicing Psychoanalysis", heading "Is Training a Utopia of Sorts?"

for human beings, including analysts, to live in the double sphere of that which they know and that which they don't know, of certainty and uncertainty?

A MULTIFACETED INHERITANCE: THE CLINICAL DIARY

"Be realistic, ask for the impossible!" This slogan of the French students who took part in the May 1968 revolt applies to Sándor Ferenczi perfectly. Faced with the real needs and the suffering of some of his patients, Ferenczi tried to meet them where they were, to enter the fog in which they stumbled, and to come out again bringing them with him. His desire to achieve this drove him to the limits of the impossible, and he paid a high personal price for it.

Sándor Ferenczi left us a substantial heritage: articles presenting his ideas and intuitions, an extensive correspondence that reveals the man behind the researcher, and finally a Diary.

This work, the *Clinical Diary*, written in 1932, holds a special place in Ferenczi's writings, and more generally in psychoanalytic literature. It is a unique work which provides today's psychoanalysts with many lessons learned on many levels. To be more precise, what the *Diary* transmits is not solely learning, but an education in the widest sense of the word, like that which parents give to their children, through their words and, above all, through example, both consciously and unconsciously. This *Clinical Diary* is the account, step by step, of Ferenczi's journey towards the impossible. He dared to undertake this dangerous voyage as long as he felt supported by Freud, if not in his experiments, at least in his person. When this support ran out, the journey ended in his death. Is it possible to resume things this way? I do not know. Michael Balint, Ferenczi's pupil and close friend, presents this version of things as a possibility.

The Clinical Diary contains many enlightening ideas originating in experience, and in experimentations whose successes, errors and failures are carefully recorded. But this work also illustrates Ferenczi's view of the very practice of psychoanalysis, and of the role of the analyst. He outlines what he believes to be the psychic functioning necessary for the practice of psychoanalysis. By exposing with rare, even unprecedented, frankness what he is doing, thinking and feeling, he reveals his manner of commitment. The reader has the impression that Ferenczi wants to avoid applying any censorship, and that he nearly succeeds. At least, this seems to be his goal. Only one area of censorship remains, with regard to future readers of the Diary. This exception was made by Ferenczi voluntarily, and was perfectly conscious and recognised. It is very probable that he did not intend, or at least hesitated, to publish the hand-written passages which concern his relationship with Freud. The passing of time made it possible to include them in the published version of the Journal.

While Ferenczi himself endeavoured to avoid any censorship as he was writing the *Clinical Diary* (1932), the successors entrusted with managing his inheritance did not follow his example. The account of events leading from the writing of the *Diary* to its publication clearly shows how difficult it was for the psychoanalytic community to follow in Ferenczi's footsteps in regard to eliminating censorship. Among Ferenczi's heirs, the one most faithful to his views was his literary agent, Michael Balint. The latter was determined to publish the *Diary*, but was perfectly aware of its explosive effects on the psychoanalytic community, which at that time considered Ferenczi to have mental problems and delusional ideas. Balint did not have time to carry out his project; he died in 1970. I took over the task of publishing the *Diary* at the end of 1970, after his death.

Once I had read the *Diary*, I felt certain that it had to be published. At first, Enid Balint wanted to submit the manuscript to two very reputable colleagues, Alexander and Margarete Mitscherlich[25], for their appraisal. They both thought that it could not be published.

The translation team of the *Coq-Héron*, which had just translated into French Volume IV of Ferenczi's *Oeuvres complètes*, as well as his correspondence with Groddeck, decided to translate the *Diary*. The French translation, published by Payot, was given a respectful and appreciative reception. Until then, no one had dared to be as frank as Ferenczi is in this exceptional text, and no one has been able to do it since. Should this surprise us?

The valuable inheritance contained in the *Clinical Diary* can be divided into three categories: ideas and intuitions, which complete the themes discussed in his published articles; technical experiments, particularly the last one, the most audacious — mutual analysis; and the account of the dangerous exposure of his own emotions in what he called "the furnace of transference", a two-way transference

---

25   Alexander Mitscherlich (Munich, Sept. 20, 1908–Frankfurt,

(transference and countertransference) requiring the analyst to be equally attentive to both components.

IDEAS AND INTUITIONS

For a number of years, Ferenczi had been focusing on the problem of trauma. What had first attracted his attention were the traumas suffered by soldiers in the First World War. After that, in the course of his clinical work in the 1920s, he came to understand more and more clearly the importance of early trauma. This is the theme of his last articles, including the most important and most controversial, "Confusion of Tongues between the Adults and the Child". The *Diary* also contains numerous notes on early trauma. Ferenczi's theoretical conclusions are rooted in the clinical observation of the last patients he treated in 1932, especially Elisabeth Severn (R.N.) and Clara Thompson (Dm).

This clinical work led him to conclude that any analysis taken back far enough can reach the "traumatic-hysterical basis of the illness". The reader discovers little by little the clinical observations and experiences which allowed Ferenczi to construct his views on splitting, and fragmentation and atomisation processes occurring after a trauma. Hypocrisy and lies that cause the traumatised person to doubt his own senses play an important part in these processes.

This is how parents — even well-intentioned parents — can plunge their children into confusion by denying the existence of what the child sees with his own eyes, or by asserting the existence of things the child knows do not exist. Social hypocrisy traumatises a mentally ill person. The analyst's professional hypocrisy, if his words or attitudes suggest that he feels something he does not feel, renew the patient's trauma. Ferenczi does not consider the analyst's honesty and sincerity with the patient a "technique", but a fundamental principle of psychoanalysis.

June 26, 1982) was a German psychoanalyst particularly interested in psychosomatic medicine. He is the author of numerous works, one of the best-known being *Society Without the Father*. Having left Germany during the Nazi period, he studied medicine in Zurich. One of his books, *Doctors of Infamy*, describes the practices of German physicians in the Nazi years. His third wife was Margaret Mitscherlich (Grasten, July 17, 1917–Frankfurt, June 12, 2012), a German psychoanalyst. In 1967, they co-authored *The Inability to Mourn*, a book about the repression of German guilt after the Nazi era. The book was not well-received when it was first published.

An error is certainly less harmful and less confusing than a lie, as long as it is recognised.

One of the consequences of this requirement of honesty between the analyst and the patient is that the analyst must consent to hear and analyse everything negative the patient may express towards him, without getting rid of this material at once by interpreting it to the patient as an effect of his transference. Indeed, this is one of the things with which Ferenczi reproached Freud: that he did not analyse the negative transference in the course of the three short sections of analysis he underwent with him. Freud defended himself, long after Ferenczi's death, in his well-known article "Analysis Terminable and Interminable", by saying that at the time nothing of a negative nature emerged in the analysis. But a careful reader of the correspondence between the two men can detect these obvious negative manifestations from the start of the relationship, with one of the earliest being the Palermo incident, which occurred during one of their first vacations together.

Rigid adherence to theory or to a standard behaviour blocks the patient. Throughout the *Diary*, Ferenczi draws attention to the importance of interaction, or more accurately to the collaboration between the physical and the psychical. These intuitions were no doubt what attracted him to Groddeck's ideas, and drove him to seek help from this German physician whose clinical work was rooted in the certainty that this collaboration exists.

Ferenczi asserts that traumas with the most serious consequences are those which were experienced in an unconscious state, either because they occurred at a very early age, or because the person was unconscious for another reason, such as the administration of a drug. To gain access to these traumas, a way must be found to allow the subject to experience them consciously for the first time.

Ferenczi also introduced the concept of "terrorism by suffering". The other, particularly a child in relation to his parent, becomes the servant and caregiver of the suffering person, letting himself be invaded by this foreign personality, which enters him and displaces a part of his personality.

A note written on March 10, 1932 seems particularly interesting given the development of psychoanalysis since its inception. Ferenczi realised that a process originally intended to be purely intellectual — understanding the sources of one's lack of well-being by removing the obstacles to this understanding — must gradually take into account all the affectivity that emerges during the analytic process. He also realised that in some states of regression, which he calls "deep relaxation", the intellect plays no role at all, any more than speech or reasoning. Later, Balint provided us with a better understanding of this situation through his "basic fault" concept. In the same Note, Ferenczi defended — albeit timidly — the legitimacy of his desire to "heal", for which he was often rebuked, being accused of *furor sanandi*.

A note written on April 5, 1932 discusses a problem whose serious and harmful consequences have been highlighted by recent historical events: the problem of hate, which Ferenczi describes by saying: "All hate is projection, in fact psychotic". He sees it as a successful attempt to be relieved of suffering by displacing it on the person believed to have caused it. Then the displacement can be extended "to a whole family, a whole nation, a whole species". Ferenczi believed that hate cannot be eliminated. This century and the one past can testify to that. He pleaded for the recognition of suffering, followed by mourning in the wake of horrific events, because mourning offers a way out.

It is not possible to describe here the depth of rich ideas and intuitions Ferenczi presents in the *Clinical Diary*. Every time one rereads it, one discovers new ones. And they are always preceded by the description of the process that led to them. For Ferenczi, each theoretical formulation is rooted in a clinical experience which involves his person profoundly, and is part of the affective dimension of the inheritance transmitted by the *Clinical Diary*.

TECHNIQUE

Ferenczi had a passionate interest in problems related to psychoanalytic technique. He believed that it was not up to analysis to select patients who could benefit from it just as it is, but rather that the analyst should adjust the analytic method and technique to each person who seeks help. The analyst must invent, he must invent something for each patient. Throughout his career as an analyst, Ferenczi carried out technical experiments: the active technique, the technique of indulgence and elasticity, and lastly the experiment with mutual analysis, described in detail in the Clinical Diary. That experiment never became a technique. Ferenczi soon noted all its disadvantages, even its impossibility, to say nothing of the painful situation in which it placed him personally. But this experiment was not an error, but rather an attempt to react to a real situation, such as the one we mentioned earlier, where the analysand is in a state of distress and confusion. This state creates hypersensitivity — without knowledge — to the analyst's emotions, and the patient needs to confirm the reality of what he feels, even when it is a complex or even hostile emotion. It is crucial not to deny what his sensitivity tells him, if we want to avoid repeating the trauma inflicted by the hypocrisy at the basis of the illness. The analysis of the analyst by the analysand (in this case R.N., a psychotherapist herself) attempts to give the analysand access to these essential points of reference. Thus, this unsatisfactory experiment has meaning. It is an impossible answer to a problem which, nevertheless, requires an answer. This is the situation which Michael Balint has unquestionably been able to unblock later.

Aside from this major experiment with mutual analysis, many observations concern the technical aspect of analysis.

Ferenczi discusses the limitations of free-floating attention, which is perfectly suited to situations where the end of the thread leading to the essential points is caught in a tangle that seems impossible to unravel, but which proves to be inadequate when the patient discusses the most sensitive spheres of his inner world.

The problems associated with regression are discussed extensively; Ferenczi did not wish to eliminate or shorten this phase. He felt that it was necessary to let the patient regress and even to facilitate this regression, a state giving the patient access to parts of his experience which had previously been inaccessible to him. But sometimes this situation leads to an impasse, and ends in separation, in an atmosphere of disappointment and despair. Thus, it was Balint who pursued this research, even while Ferenczi was still alive, so that the latter wrote in a note we mentioned earlier, written in Luchon in 1932: "Balint picked things up where I got stumped". Balint's last book, *The Basic Fault*, summarises all his work and describes his involvement with Ferenczi's investigations. One of the chapters of Balint's book, entirely dedicated to Ferenczi's relationship with Freud and its painful outcome, endeavours to reveal the underpinnings of their conflict, and its effects on the psychoanalytic community and the development of psychoanalysis.

Ferenczi was also very interested in another question at the frontier between theory and technique: the question of the end of analysis. I am not referring to an analysis interrupted by one or the other of the protagonists, but to treatment considered terminated by the analyst and the analysand. How is it determined whether an analysis is terminated? It is relatively easy to establish theoretical criteria. Identifying them in the course of the analysis is much more difficult. Can we say that all terminations of analysis are identical? Can we assert that the analysis is ended when all the problems are solved? What comes to mind here is the outstanding movie *The Snake Pit*, in which a long and difficult therapy ends with these words from the therapist: "Now you know where the light switch [is]. [...] you don't ever have to be afraid of being in the dark[26]."

EMOTIONAL INVOLVEMENT

The existence of this Diary is in itself an inheritance. It is perhaps the most important aspect of what we have inherited. It testifies to an attempt at honesty, a selflessness bordering on sacrifice, for the benefit of the analytic work with each patient — qualities which made Ferenczi the doctor of patients considered incurable, sent to him by colleagues all over the world.

Is this an example to follow? The question deserves to be raised. Some people think that this attempt to rid himself of all his defences contributed to Ferenczi's death. Yet, one of the essential duties of an analyst is to stay alive, despite all transferential attacks — be they from analysands or colleagues — that may be directed against him. The question might be asked whether the ease with which the analytic community accepted Jones's assertion that Ferenczi was mentally ill — a claim that deprived Ferenczi's last writings of their value — did not constitute a backing away in the face of the extremely demanding nature of the Ferenczian attitude. Of course, this attitude did not spring from any paranoid delusions, as Jones claimed, but it did denote an involvement beyond the usual limits. Ferenczi tried to compensate this excess by showing a degree of sincerity that was just as limitless. He was ready to admit the negative feelings a patient inspired in him, especially on the sexual level, so that neither of them would lose contact with reality.

---

26 The Snake Pit is a 1948 American movie directed by Anatole Litvak, with Olivia de Havilland, Mark Stevens, Robert Cunningham, etc., based on a novel by Mary Jane Ward, a writer who spent several years in a psychiatric hospital. It was one of the first movies showing the work of a psychoanalyst in a psychiatric hospital, 'Dr. Mark Kik', actually Dr. Gerard Charzanowski.

Ferenczi always pushed his experiments "to the absurd", as he himself said, even if this meant reconsidering afterwards and assessing more accurately where he should stop. But although this way of doing things is neither recommended nor possible for everyone, it nevertheless teaches us something essential: to fear nothing if we have good reason to believe that what we are doing contributes to advancing the treatment. No rule coming from a recognised and respected authority should prevent us from thinking for ourselves and taking full responsibility for what we are doing. The *Clinical Diary* also offers this valuable advice: never imitate anyone, not even Ferenczi. But this independence leaves each analyst "without cover", without any external protection. It is not by chance that Ferenczi never founded a "school", with the explicit desire of transmitting his ideas and his methods. It was up to his younger colleagues to select from everything he offered the things which could be useful to them.

The need to protect patients against incompetent practitioners and charlatans is used as justification for very rigid training and a structured programme, recommended by some analytic societies . A praiseworthy mission, but illusory. Charlatans are, by definition, uncontrollable. As to those who have received training and did not conclude that they are not made to be analysts, they are rarely incompetent. And if, exceptionally, an analyst is incompetent, it means that this incompetence was not detected by the person concerned, or by those responsible for his training. What is more likely is that an analyst may handle a situation inadequately, or that he shows blindness or weakness with respect to his own impulses. What training could claim to eliminate human frailty? The best way to ensure utmost safety for patients seems to be, after all, to encourage future analysts to think for themselves, to act based on their convictions, and to take full responsibility for the consequences, even if they are impressed by some theoretical constructions, or by the wisdom of a certain prestigious colleague. Total compliance with someone else's views, regardless of their worth or usefulness, when they have not been sifted through the awareness of a particular practitioner, places the latter in a precarious position. Any unforeseen event will prompt him to seek an answer in someone else's work, rather than in his own inner world. Ferenczi, who was in awe of Freud's genius, never abandoned his right to think and intuit independently.

Therefore, I believe that the best thing for an analyst to do is to act according to his best-founded convictions, and to deal with the consequences of the way he does things. Of course, prior to this, the analyst has to learn from experienced colleagues, from the available literature and, above all, from his own analysis. It is during what is called supervision, for which a better term would be, in my opinion, clinical discussion, that the analyst in training can acquire a wider view of the different ways of approaching a clinical situation. In terms of independence and the courage to take responsibility, few of us can expect to go as far as Ferenczi. But discovering one's limits and taking them into account is also part of the training required to become an analyst. All this is part of the valuable inheritance left by Ferenczi, specifically in his *Clinical Diary*. We all know how rare it is to hear someone relate exactly what he said and did in a session of analysis. First, this is very difficult, as one realises during the "clinical discussions" I mentioned. Even the most detailed accounts fail to reproduce all the gestures, expressions, ambient sounds, fleeting thoughts and impressions, and all the other elements that contribute to the atmosphere of a therapeutic encounter. The more precise the account one gives, the more exposed one is, and the greater the risk of being wounded. Ferenczi experienced all this.

Eighty years after his death, we are the ones who reap the benefits of his daring.

ON THE TRACES OF SÁNDOR FERENCZI OR SHERLOCK HOLMES IN MISKOLC[27]

We are in Miskolc, Sándor Ferenczi's birthplace, on November 2, 1987. Night is falling. At the invitation of the Hungarian Psychoanalytic Association, local and national dignitaries, and an international delegation of psychoanalysts from different countries are witnessing the unveiling of a commemorative plaque in memory of a native son of the city, now world-famous.

The site is surprising: the plaque is placed on the wall of a modern low-rent building of greyish hue, located in a remote suburb. In response to the surprise of those present, they are told that since the house where Ferenczi was born had been destroyed a few decades earlier, the plaque was being placed as close as possible to where the house had been. In fact, the address of Ferenczi's house was well known. It was the address of the famous bookstore, print

---

27 Based on an article co-authorized with Herbert Wachsberger after an investigative trip to Miskolc.

shop and concert agency of Bernát Ferenczi, Sándor's father. The family lived upstairs, above the store. The house was on the main street of the city, at 13 Széchényi Street. It was explained to the visitors that since the neighbourhood had been restructured, this street was the very one where the low-rent building they were admiring was located. The visitors were not the only ones who were surprised. The people living in the building were clustered at the windows, wondering what famous person could have been born in this house built only fifteen years earlier. After listening to the Hungarian national anthem played on a phonograph and to a few speeches, and then admiring some shrubbery recently planted in a hole drilled in the sidewalk, everyone went home.

Three years later, a small group of French psychoanalysts went to Miskolc to honour the memory of the illustrious forefather. None of the members of the group knew what the new name of Széchényi Street was, and they were therefore unable to find the house with the commemorative plaque. They were surprised to see that no one in the city could answer this question, and that those who were asked did not know who this supposedly famous Ferenczi was. But some of the oldest of them remembered the "Ferenczi house", a bookstore and stationery shop now torn down, and its last owner, Károly Ferenczi, who really was a celebrity in the city, and whose name was carved on the monument to the memory of those deported in 1944, that stood across from the synagogue. When the rabbi was consulted, he informed them that the Ferenczi bookstore was in the centre of town, the same centre as always, and that Széchényi Street, near the theatre, still had the same name. A kindly old gentleman wearing a bright orange silk kippa confirmed this: his classmate and friend, Friedmann, was employed in this bookstore. The members of the Jewish community were surprised to learn that Károly Ferenczi had a younger brother who had become an illustrious figure, at least abroad, and that they had not been invited to festivities organised in honour of one of their community members.

The owner of a used bookshop joined in the conversation: he said that on occasion he still saw books bearing the stamp of the famous Ferenczi bookstore. He confirmed the address and advised the small delegation to go to the municipal library to get more information.

The group hastened to the library. The librarian recognised Sándor Ferenczi's name. She produced a number of documents. Széchényi Street was still there, in the same place, bore the same name and appeared on city maps, both the present map and old maps. She told the little group that the Ferenczi house had been torn down in January 1957, since it was uninhabited and on the verge of collapse. It was the oldest house on the street, and the only one that was torn down. Its famous wrought-iron gate had been preserved, and was now in the city museum. In the place of this old house, unscrupulous architects had built a four-storey glass and steel building that housed a wholesale hardware store.

At the library, there were books and articles describing the important place held in the city by this bookstore and by its owner. There were articles describing the demolition of the bookstore, about which the authors of the articles expressed deep regret. A postcard showed the portion of the street with the bookstore that bore the inscription "Ferenczi" on the façade. The two houses on either side of the bookstore, seen on the postcard, were still there.

Of course, the plaque should have been placed on the glass wall of the hardware store. We can understand the reluctance of the organisers who preferred to resort to a trick rather than admit lack of respect for one of the few native sons of the city who acquired international fame.

But they wanted to preserve Ferenczi's memory by giving his name to a street in the city. To do this, they chose a street at the city limits: a short, narrow street located between some small houses and gardens on one side, and fields on the other. Of course, the French visitors were not in any position to take offence. One only has to go to Pré-Saint-Gervais, on the other side of the freeway, to see where Sigmund Freud Street is... But after all, Freud was not born in Paris.

The little French delegation took the opportunity to ask questions. But it encountered only silence and denial. The plaque has probably disappeared; in any case, no one has seen it again.

THE KOVACS FAMILY

Pann.20 Vilma Kovács   Fredéric et le chien Berci

Maison Naphegy. The house of the Kovàcs family where were also the clinical seminars of the Hungarian analytical society.

The office of Vilma Kovàcs

AS TIME GOES BY

THE BALINT FAMILY

Michael Balin
Photo by Ergy Landau

Alice Balint

John Balint with the
book about Michael
Bakint by Michelle
Moreau-Ricaud

AS TIME GOES BY
THE DORMANDI FAMILY

Olga Dormandi, botn Székely-Kovàcs, painter.
Photo by Ergy Landau

Ladislas Dormandi, writer and publisher

AS TIME GOES BY

THE FERENCZI FAMILY

Sàndor Ferenczi

Gizella Ferenczi,
born Altschul

Elma Pàlos,
Gizella's elder daughter

AS TIME GOES BY

THE DUPONT FAMILY

Judith Dupont in her office

Jacques Dupont

Pierre Dupont,
my son

Hélène Century, born
Dupont, my daughter

AS TIME GOES BY

COQ-HÉRON TEAM

Meeting of the Coq-Héron team

CHAPTER 3
ABOUT BALINT

MICHAEL BALINT (1896-1970)

To introduce Michael Balint to those who did not know him personally, one must speak of his powerful personality, which impressed anyone who knew him or worked with him. He could be described as "a man almost larger than life", to borrow the formula Thomas Mann uses to portray a character in *The Magic Mountain*. Willful, tenacious, ambitious, insatiable, endlessly curious, outspoken but tactful and tolerant when necessary, he was a man endowed with great sensitivity. In private conversation, he was a passionate interlocutor, tireless and ready to fight. He did not hesitate to be provocative and took pleasure in pushing his adversary as far as he could, even to the point of exasperation, to force him to reveal his deepest thoughts. In England, at the meetings of the British Psychoanalytical Society, where he felt at home, his central European forthrightness sometimes startled his English colleagues, who were used to Anglo-Saxon reserve. But elsewhere abroad, he had the reputation of being a calm, courteous and diplomatic speaker, appreciated in public debates for his moderation, tact and tolerance. But this did not prevent him from showing no indulgence for ideas that were confusing or evasive.

To sum up his career, he liked to say that he started out the son of a Jewish doctor with a modest family practice on the outskirts of Budapest, and became President of the British Psychoanalytical Society. He never attempted to hide his liking for success and honours.

Michael Balint was born on December 3rd 1896 in Budapest, the son of Dr. Bergsmann and his wife Margit, a simple, gentle and generous woman. His older sister Emmy had two classmates who were to play quite important roles in the history of psychoanalysis: Alice Székely- Kovács, who would become Alice Balint, and Margaret Schönberger, later known as Margaret Mahler. Balint did not get along with his father, whom he described as taciturn and withdrawn, but he felt very close to his mother.

After a solid secondary-level education, Balint undertook his university studies with his characteristic thirst for knowledge. He studied medicine, as well as biochemistry and physics, while taking courses in philosophy and mathematics. It was at this stage that one of his fellow students, Alice, who would later become his wife, lent him Freud's Totem and Taboo. He found the book so interesting that he went on to read Freud's other writings, particularly the Three Essays on the Theory of Sexuality, and then decided to focus his attention on psychoanalysis. In 1923 he and his wife Alice left for Berlin. They both wished to start psychoanalytic training with Hanns Sachs. While in Berlin, Balint worked as an assistant to Professor Otto Warburg, the future Nobel Prize winner, and introduced avant-garde psycho-somatic consultation in His and Zondek's department at the Charité Hospital.

Like many Hungarian Jews eager to show allegiance to this country, Balint changed his name from the German-sounding Bergsmann to Balint, a typically Hungarian name. But given the antisemitic policies in effect in that country, and the setting of an upper limit for the number of Jewish students admissible to an academic institution, Balint also changed his religion; he abandoned the Jewish faith, since he did not believe in it, adopting instead the most liberal form of the Protestant religion, Unitarianism. His father never forgave him for changing his surname and renouncing his religion, and refused to see him or his son John until just prior to their departure for England, when they met briefly. It was sweet-tempered Mrs. Bergsmann who stayed in touch will all the members of the family.

The Balint couple were not happy with their training analysis with Sachs, whose emphasis they found too intellectual. They went back to Budapest to continue their analysis, this time with Sándor Ferenczi. Their son John Alexander was born on February 11, 1925. He later became a physician as well, and had a successful academic career. Two years later, Alice's second pregnancy ended badly. The baby died in the womb, the fetal death was undetected, and severe septicemia developed, leading to endocarditis, which Alice survived. But she was left with an aneurysm of the aorta.

Between 1925 and 1939 the Balints were active members of the Hungarian Psychoanalytic Association. Each one had a private practice, but they also worked at the Psychoanalytic Clinic from its inception. They wrote numerous texts, developing their ideas in close cooperation. As Michael Balint would say later, it mattered little if they were published under one name or the other. Thus, in a work of collected articles published in England under the title *Primary Love and Psychoanalytic Technique*, Michael included the article "Love for the Mother and Mother Love", published earlier under Alice's name.

After having been his analysand and pupil, Michael Balint became Ferenczi's close collaborator. Both of them were interested, among other things, in finding a way to make it possible for physicians to utilise a psychoanalytic mode of listening. As early as 1923, Ferenczi had written an article on the subject. As for Balint, he stayed in touch with the medical world and published articles in medical journals; one of his articles concerned the organisation of the medical profession. After Ferenczi's death, Balint became Director of the Budapest psychoanalytic Clinic at 12 Mészáros Street, on the ground floor of the building in which he himself lived, and which belonged to his father-in-law, Frederic Kovács. Today, a commemorative plaque bearing the name Michael Balint can be seen on a wall of the building. Balint was also the one designated by Ferenczi's family to manage the legacy of his writings. This is how he came to be in possession of unpublished texts like *The Clinical Diary*, and of the complete correspondence between Freud and Ferenczi.

When the Germans invaded Austria in 1937, many Hungarians of the Jewish intelligentsia, particularly psychoanalysts, felt compelled to emigrate, since they now felt in great danger. The future proved them right, as we know. Hundreds of thousands of people were killed in that little country alone. Michael Balint's parents committed suicide when they were about to be arrested. The Balints immigrated to England in 1939, and settled in Manchester.

The day before the war was declared, Alice Balint died suddenly from a ruptured aneurysme caused by her endocarditis. Balint found himself alone, far from his family and friends, facing the hardships of wartime, having to integrate into a new country, and to bring up his 14-year-old son. He had to take all his examinations again in order to practice medicine in an institution, and had to acquire a private practice clientele to earn a living. He worked in several Child Guidance Clinics, where he conducted research on suckling rhythm, in the field of "babyology", as he called it. After a brief, unhappy marriage, at the end of the war Balint was at last able to settle in London. In 1949, he conducted a seminar for social workers at the Tavistock Clinic, with Mrs. Enid Eichholz, a young divorced psychoanalyst, the mother of two daughters. This was the beginning of what would later be called the "Balint groups", as well as the start of a third marriage, happy and long-lasting this time. With Enid, Balint recreated the same type of close cooperation he had had with Alice. He quickly gained respectable status in the British Psychoanalytical Society, without losing his "strange stranger" aura. He joined the "Middle Group", which mediated between the opposing camps of proponents of Anna Freud and of Melanie Klein — it was a hard school of diplomacy, tolerance, moderation and tact.

Michael Balint became a training analyst. He continued to use the method of the Budapest School: the first supervision of the candidate was conducted by his or her own analyst, in order to learn to identify and analyse countertransference reactions more easily.

Gradually, the Balint groups evolved and were fine-tuned. At first, they were organised for social workers, but Balint had always intended them mainly for family physicians. After these general practitioners, certain specialists became interested in them. Dermatologists were the first of these, since they were the most keenly aware of the presence of psychological factors in the pathologies they treated. Apparently, psychiatrists were the last to show any interest in this method.

Michael and Enid Balint travelled often. They were invited to give talks about the Balint groups. Every year, Michael gave courses, as guest professor, at the University of Cincinnati, in the Psychiatry Department, at long last. There was a Balint group in paediatrics in Paris, under the supervision of Ginette Raimbault. The Balints attended once every three months.

In 1970, Balint was elected President of the British Psychoanalytical Society, an honour which made him very happy. But he only exercised this function briefly. After recovering from a first heart attack, he was killed by a second attack on December 31, 1970. His ashes are buried in the Golders Green cemetery where Freud was laid to rest as well.

PSYCHOANALYTIC CONTRIBUTION

Balint's remarkably coherent work is presented extensively elsewhere in this volume.

In summary, Balint introduced the notion of primary love. After that, he studied the question of therapeutic regression: benign and temporary or malignant and lasting. He identified two extreme forms: ocnophilia and philobatism, explaining in detail these perplexing — or ultra-sophisticated — names he had chosen. He described the structure of the psychic apparatus as being composed of three levels; the oedipal level, the level of the basic fault and the level of creation. The Basic Fault is the title of his last work, which retraces the development of his theoretical perspective.

THE BALINT GROUP METHOD

As we saw earlier, Balint had always been interested in ways of making analytic discoveries useful for general practitioners. This interest was no doubt tied to the fact that his father was a family doctor to whom his son had many things to reproach. But it was in England, with his assistant — and later his wife — , Enid, that he developed the now well-known method of the Balint groups. Several of his writings describe the method, motivations and results of these "training cum research" groups. The first two are the best known: The Doctor, HisPatient and the Illness and Psychotherapeutic Techniques in Medicine. Other works followed, written by psychoanalysts or doctors. Little by little, the method was extended to people working in different fields; teachers and other professionals saw fit to improve the quality of their services thanks to a better understanding of the psychology of those in their charge. As is the case with all methods, some people, like Pierre Benoit, physician and analyst, continued to reflect on this method and to enrich it. There were also some misapplications: the method was transformed into a "pop psychology" technique, and there were attempts to teach it without involving a psychoanalyst. However, Balint Societies exist almost everywhere in the world. Of course, the Balint method is likely to remain confined to a limited circle of practitioners, since it requires time: time to speak with the patient, time to speak of oneself in the context of one's relation with the patient, and time to speak of the patient... But time is what doctors lack the most these days.

BALINT, FERENCZI'S LITERARY AGENT

This last function carried out by Balint deserves to be considered a task in itself. Gizella Ferenczi, Sándor's widow, entrusted Michael Balint with managing her husband's literary legacy. The writings had to be collected, from Gizella, from Anna Freud, who had Ferenczi's letters to Freud, and even from a Hungarian colleague, Ilona Felszeghy, who has picked up documents scattered on the ground after Ferenczi's house was destroyed in a Soviet bombardment during the Siege of Budapest. Then, the writings had to be sorted and indentified: finished articles as well as various notes, an almost undecipherable notebook, the 1932 clinical diary, poems to Gizella, correspondence. What was most difficult, and probably most painful for Balint, was to convince the psychoanalytic community that these writings were worth reading, that they were not the product of a sick mind, as certain rumours insinuated. These rumours had just found confirmation in the recently published Volume III of Ernest Jones' biography of Freud, in which Ferenczi was described as suffering from paranoid delusions.

Gradually, thanks to Balint, the tide turned. His most problematic task was the publication of the two major documents: The Clinical Diary and the Freud-Ferenczi correspondence. Balint knew that these two pieces of writing would come as a shock to the analytic community. This is why he wanted to publish them at the same time, thinking that each one provided an explanation for the other. His wish was to publish the correspondence in its entirety, with absolutely nothing censured, not a single passage. But this proved to be impossible in his lifetime. Anna Freud considered that the correspondence revealed too much of the intimate life of her family. As for the Clinical Diary, certain "elders" of the profession, deemed it clearly unpublishable. The translation team of the Coq-Héron did not agree. The Clinical Diary was translated and published; it was received with the respect and admiration such a unique text deserves. The Freud-Ferenczi correspondence could be published in unabridged form after Anna Freud's death. Balint was not able to see these works, but he had worked to prepare them. He had made an initial translation of the Diary into English, and had photocopied the correspondence.

To conclude, we can certainly say that Michael Balint was an original thinker. A pupil of Ferenczi, he pursued investigations in the same direction, but in his own way. Like Ferenczi, he never tried to surround himself with disciples or to found a "school". What he wanted was not disciples, but collaborators on an equal footing with him, responsible independent thinkers. Balint left a considerable heritage of writings known the world over in the medical field, and psychoanalytic works whose entire richness has probably not yet been sufficiently exploited.

MICHAEL BALINT, FERENCZI'S ANALYSAND, PUPIL, FRIEND AND SUCCESSOR

When Ferenczi died on May 22, 1933, the psychoanalytic community felt it had lost a very gifted colleague, whose capacities reached their peak in 1927 and 1928, but who afterwards wasted his time and his talents pursuing hazardous and fruitless experiments and research focusing on the technical aspects of psychoanalysis. Freud himself was deeply disturbed by the last contributions of his closest friend and favourite follower. In the eulogy he wrote at his friend's death, he spoke of "Thalassa, a Theory of Genitality" as being Ferenczi's most significant work, a text often misunderstood.

But a number of analysts, mostly Hungarian, had had the opportunity to work and to have discussions with Ferenczi in the last years of his life. They had thus been able to observe the genesis, development and application of his controversial ideas, and did not share the negative opinions concerning the research of his final years. Among these analysts we can cite Michael and Alice Balint, Imre Hermann and Vilma Kovács. They were all particularly interested in questions concerning object relations, and each of them conducted original individual research, not unrelated to that of the others.

When Ferenczi died, Balint took over as head of the Budapest Psychoanalytic Clinic. Gizella, Ferenczi's widow, named him executor of her husband's published work, a task he carried out with zeal and perseverance, and even with courage, given the reputation of "deviant" and victim of mental illness associated with the author he represented.

Balint's scientific work can be studied as three distinct research categories. First, there is his psychoanalytic work, which I shall present in the greatest detail. It is theoretical and clinical work, which Balint developed with remarkable steadiness. His thinking can be seen evolving from his first articles written in Budapest up to his last book published in London a short time before his death, The Basic Fault (1968). This book summarises his entire lifework, in a manner of speaking: his theoretical perspective, his view of the structure and development of the psyche, and their therapeutic implications. This is the aspect I wish to present here, showing how Balint's research is based on Ferenczi's most controversial articles, "Child-Analysis in the Analysis of Adults" (1931) and "Confusion of Tongues between the Adults and the Child" (1932).

Another aspect of Balint's work, probably the best-known, consists of the method he developed with Enid, his wife and companion during the last period of his life. This method was intended to help general practitioners use psychotherapeutic techniques and ways of understanding in general practice. Gradually, specialists became interested in the method as well. Today, "Balint Groups" exist all over the world; they are attended by family doctors, paediatricians and other specialists, as well as by non medical professionals like social workers, educators, teachers, nurses... Ferenczi had been the first to propose psychological training for general practitioners, in his 1923 article "Psychoanalysis in the Service of the General Practitioner". Michael Balint understood the value of the idea immediately, and was the one who put it into practice.

The third facet of Balint's work consisted in the management of Ferenczi's writings. He had to collect the texts, have them translated into different languages, particularly into English, and find publishers for them. A lengthy correspondence (unpublished) with Elma, Gizella's eldest daughter, makes it clear that this task required enormous time and effort. It is thanks to this enormous work that Ferenczi's contribution was brought back from oblivion, and now holds a predominant place in the field of psychoanalysis. It is Balint who prepared The Clinical Diary for publication, and insisted on the publication of the Freud-Ferenczi correspondence, although he did not see these projects realised. No doubt many obstacles had to be overcome along the way.

BALINT'S PSYCHOANALYTIC WORK

It would not be true to say that Balint simply pursued Ferenczi's ideas. A better way to put it is to say that his thinking "sprang up" from the soil of these ideas like a new plant. The same thing can be said about Hermann: he was nurtured by Ferenczi, but his ideas are his own and are based on his particular experience. Balint learned a great deal from Ferenczi, from his ideas, experiences, successes and failures. But he developed his own perspective, based on his clinical observations. His positioning vis-a-vis Ferenczi can be compared to that of Ferenczi vis-a-vis Freud. Both men received and tried out their mentor's ideas, but when their observations did not confirm these ideas in a satisfactory manner, they continued to search and reflect on their own.

Balint and Ferenczi share another common trait: the

method they proposed required a high degree of personal involvement on the part of the analyst, total honesty, great sensitivity and extreme modesty. These were harsh requirements; they seem obvious, but are more difficult to respect than one would think. This could explain, in part, why Ferenczi was neglected for so long, and why Balint's work is still not receiving the recognition it deserves — although he was never subjected to the same degree of rejection.

As I pointed out above, Balint's successive writings throughout his life construct a perfectly coherent picture of psychic structure and functioning. But he was not attempting to portray a closed system which could account for all the phenomena observed. Balint's primary concern was to raise questions, overturn certainties and create links with the theories of others, in order to shed light on a problem form several standpoints. He always pointed out the new questions raised by the answers he brought to previous questions. Without knowing it, he might have been confirming the saying that an idea which cannot be contradicted is undoubtedly a bad idea, because it puts an end to reflection instead of stimulating it.

As we said earlier, Balint learned a great deal from Ferenczi's mistakes and failures. The latter said many times, especially in his letters to Freud, that he could only work by going too far with his experiments, pushing them to the point of the absurd, and then backtracking in order to keep only the usable elements. Balint reacted by adopting the opposite attitude: extreme caution. He was not reticent in his thinking, but in his writing he was content to "propose", "suggest", "argue"; he also encouraged the severest evaluation of his proposals. Balint's ideas cannot be transposed in someone else's practice directly. To work like Balint means to make a personal investment, to use imagination, to be constantly aware of the needs of a particular patient, and to pay constant attention to one's own reactions. As Balint would say, it is a matter of interpreting one's own emotions in the context of the patient's pathology.

BALINT'S CONCEPTION OF PSYCHIC STRUCTURE AND FUNCTIONING

According to Balint, the most primitive state of the human psyche is not primary narcissism, which would mean withdrawal into oneself. As early as 1937, he questioned this theory, which he saw as born of pure speculation. It was not supported by clinical observation, and had been invented solely because logically this state seemed to reflect the simplest form of existence.

It is not possible to summarise here all of Balint's discussion on the subject. He has given a detailed account of his reasons for rejecting this notion (1937)[1]. He describes the evolution of this concept in Freud's thinking, underlining its inherent contradictions. He maintains that a primary relation exists between a developing human being and his environment. Everything we have learned since about intra-uterine life confirms Balint's perspective. Thus, future fathers are now encouraged to speak to the baby in the womb, so that their voices can become familiar to the unborn child. Haptonomy is based entirely on the possibility of communicating with the foetus.

Balint maintained that everything we actually observe points to an object relation, no matter how primitive. He calls this primitive relation primary love, a term he explains as follows: this primary relation is formed initially with very particular objects having no definite contour and offering no resistance. These objects are indestructible and entirely accessible to the subject. Instead of calling them objects, we could speak of pre-objects, like water and air. The foetus, and then the newborn, is in a sort of relation with what surrounds him. He needs his environment's capacity to adapt. Balint (1959) speaks of "harmonious mix-up through interpenetration". He gives other examples: there is a harmonious mix-up of this kind between us and the air we breathe. This air must be available to us, and it is impossible to determine if the air in our lungs or intestines is part of our body or part of the atmosphere around us, although the air and our bodies are not fused together. We do not realise that we "love" air unless there is a lack of it. It is the same thing for fish in the water and the placental villi attached to the uterine wall. To describe harmonious mix-up through interpenetration, Balint also uses the example of mayonnaise, where oil and egg yolk are mixed together, yet each one keeps its individuality. Every cook knows that the least mishap can mess up the mixing and separate the two ingredients.

This primary relation is akin to what Ferenczi called passive object-love (1933). He spoke of passivity to describe the manner in which the child receives what comes to him from the environment. But Balint rejects the idea of

---

[1] Balint, M., *Primary Love and Psycho-Analytic Technique*, Karnac Books, 1985.

passivity. He believes that the child, or the fetus, makes active use of everything he has at his disposal. Little by little, objects with definite contours emerge from pre-objects or substances. First, partial objects, and then whole objects.

Balint saw the mother-child relationship as being at the beginning a harmonious interdependence in which the two protagonists obtain what they need, since their interests converge to a large degree. Later, as the child's needs become more varied and complex, the interests of the two parties start to diverge, and do so more and more. As a result, the child encounters increasing resistance on the part of the mother. She gradually becomes an object with definite contours for the child, with her own desires, interests and will, an object with which the child has to negotiate. This is how active object-love, based on reciprocity, develops.

In Alice Balint's article "Love for the Mother and Mother Love" (1939), she writes that everything Ferenczi described in Thalassa concerning the man-woman relationship during intercourse applies to the mother-child relation as well. This article was published in Michael Balint's work Primary Love and Psychoanalytic Technique because it is the result of lengthy discussions they had together, which were formulated in writing by Alice. Indeed, neither of these relationships involves egoism or altruism, but both involve instinctual goals that are mutual and convergent. For instance, breastfeeding satisfies the needs of the mother as well as those of the baby. In the same way, in intercourse the two partners both find pleasure, albeit in somewhat different ways. In both cases, biological interdependence makes a certain naive egoism possible.

Between these two forms of interdependence — the early mother-child relationship and the man-woman relationship during intercourse — there is an intermediary stage: the development of the sense of reality, which will henceforth govern emotional life. The sense of reality is a secondary process implying tact, understanding, empathy, gratitude and tenderness. Balint's reasoning is based on Ferenczi's 1913 article "Stages is the Development of the Sense of Reality", describing the fact that, in order to satisfy his needs, the child must learn how to explore reality, evaluate it accurately and act upon it. In this process, the child goes through several stages: the unconditional omnipotence stage, the stage of magical-hallucinatory omnipotence, the stage of omnipotence through magic gestures, and the animistic stage described earlier in the chapter on Ferenczi.

The different stages of development correspond to Balint's description of how objects with definite contours emerge from primary substances. The child becomes aware of the particularities of these objects and of the fact that they have a will of their own; he then discovers more and more suitable methods of interacting with them.

Some of these objects are endowed, to some degree, with the positive and reassuring qualities of primary substances. They are felt to be very valuable and must satisfy great requirements: they must not have personal interests, desires or needs; they must identify completely with the subject's desires and needs, require nothing else and be indestructible. This is exactly what an infant expects of his caregivers; it is also what we see in people who are in a regressed state.

Other objects are perceived as obstacles to be negotiated using skills developed specifically for this purpose. Gradually, as we said, the subject becomes aware that objects have definite contours, their own desires, interests, needs and will, and that they can offer resistance. All these characteristics must be taken into account in order to develop a relationship with one of these objects. The object must be conquered.

Sometimes, significant problems arise at the start of this developmental process. In that case, the subject must invent various methods to face the situation. The method he invents at that stage will greatly influence his psychic structure and determine the form of his "basic fault", to use Balint's expression. This basic fault is a dynamic force of psychic life, but does not take the form of a conflict. It is, rather, something like a flaw in the structure; when it heals, it leaves a permanent scar with which the subject must learn to live.

Balint described the topical structure of the psyche as comprised of three levels:

The Oedipal level. This level is characterised by a relationship between three people. The dynamic force at work takes the form of conflict. The language used is conventional adult language, and the words have the same meaning for everyone.

The level of the basic fault. This level is characterised by a two-person relationship. The dynamic force operating takes the form of a fault, a flaw in the subject's structure. Adult conventional language is of no use at this level. We could call this a preverbal or pregenital level.

The level of creation. At this level, the subject is alone. He has disinvested all objects in the external world; he is attempting to produce another object — hopefully a better object — out of himself. What he produces may be a work of art, a theory, or even an illness. This is the level about which we know the least, which is the most difficult to explore, since the subject is alone here.

PRACTICAL AND TECHNICAL CONSEQUENCES

Having constructed this model of the human psyche based on his psychoanalytic practice, Balint tested it again in light of his practice. He attempted to incorporate the observations made in the course of his clinical work into his theoretical framework.

In the course of an analysis, there are always periods of regression rooted more or less deeply in the stages we just described. In some cases, the regression remains in the Oedipal area, making it possible to continue the analysis using association and interpretation, that is, to stay at the level of conventional adult language where words have the same meaning for both protagonists. Of course, non-verbal elements are always present, but verbal exchange predominates. These patients are able to undergo what is called classical psychoanalysis. For a long time, it was considered that only these subjects could be analysed. It was Ferenczi who introduced the idea that the method must adapt to the patient's needs, rather than the patient to the method. Balint followed the same line of thought.

Thus, there is another category of patients, that we would call "borderline" today. These patients may, at some point in the analysis, lose the ability to communicate in a conventional adult manner. While in this state, they can no longer perceive interpretations as having a precise meaning, but perceive only hostility or benevolence. In these patients, associations become repetitive empty words, devoid of any emotional charge, which prompt only empty interpretations. Balint compared this phenomenon to a scratched record (1968), with the needle stuck indefinitely in the same groove.

According to the precepts of classical technique, the analyst would try to bring the patient out of this state of regression as quickly as possible, and enable him to use adult language again. Doing this can lead to a partially successful analysis, which has not dealt with the deepest level of the patient's difficulties. In the past, a traditional psychoanalyst would have tried to dissuade this type of patient from continuing in analysis, recommending another form of therapy instead. But today this is no longer the usual way to proceed.

Like Ferenczi, Balint refused this kind of selection of patients. Ferenczi defended the idea that as long as a patient wanted to continue therapy, it was up to the analyst to find the techniques needed to help him. This is what explains his great interest in investigating analytic techniques. He explored extremely varied paths in this field; some of his technical proposals are now so commonly applied by most analysts that the latter consider them classical techniques, often not knowing that it was Ferenczi who introduced them (Balint, 1967).

Ferenczi was also the one who started to consider regression not as an obstacle to treatment, but as a phenomenon occurring regularly in analysis, to be considered an important therapeutic tool. He believed the same was true of countertransference, which had initially been considered as something to keep in check, rather than utilise. Balint was in total agreement with this point of view.

Balint observed that patients in a regressed state had to receive certain gratifications. But not any gratification. He had learned, once again from Ferenczi's mistakes, which the latter freely admitted, as he did in a note written in Luchon: "Balint took up things where I got stuck". Thus, Balint observed that the gratifications granted to the patient had to remain at the level of preliminary pleasure: allowing the patient to hold one of the analyst's fingers, granting an extra session, allowing him to telephone on a Sunday... However, gratifying impulsive demands could generate a form of malignant regression, an endless spiral of new demands after each gratification. This created a kind of addiction, comparable to drug addiction, and always led to despair on the part of both patient and therapist, and to the interruption of the treatment. It was Balint who identified these two types of regression, benign and malignant, and the techniques that could trigger one or the other.

The peaceful atmosphere, devoid of excessive pressure, which Balint strived to create, allowed the patient to find new solutions to the problem that had created the basic fault. Having done this, he could come out of his regression with new capabilities and new possibilities. Often, patients experience this as a rebirth and describe it as resembling coming out of a tunnel, coming back into the light, seeing a previously black-and-white environment in full colour. In 1932, Balint named this phenomenon a "new beginning". The patient is freed of his feelings of mistrust and recovers his ability to love without reserve. The basic fault is healed and the patient learns to live with the scar.

Balint had read and studied carefully all the observations described by Ferenczi in his last articles, his notes and The Clinical Diary. He also had access to the unpublished Freud-Ferenczi correspondence, in which Ferenczi repeatedly tried to explain to Freud the therapeutic objective of his experiments, which irritated his master so much. Balint added his own observations of patients who regressed beyond the Oedipal level, reaching the basic fault level where they attempted to attain a state of primary harmonious mix-up. He developed his theoretical perspective and technical proposals based on this clinical experience.

In effect, Balint came to identify two extreme forms of regression. The first is one where the patient looks for security in objects. His desire is to be held firmly by objects. But since he is not sure of their willingness to provide this holding, he is the one who holds on to them tightly. He can only advance from object to object, and experiences his distance from them as a space filled with unforeseeable dangers. Balint called this form of regression ocnophilia, from the Greek *okneo*, meaning attachment, hesitation, hollowness.

He called the other type of regressed patient a philobat, a term modeled on the word "acrobat", someone who wants to leave the ground. The philobat experiences objects as being potentially dangerous, and therefore best avoided. He only feels at ease in spaces free of any obstacles, and he develops all kinds of skills allowing him to manage potential obstacles as well as possible. To do so, he always equips himself with reliable devices he can carry with him. Balint stresses that both terms contain the root "phil", meaning "love", since these two extreme forms of regression have as their common source a love-hate ambivalence. In both forms, the sense of reality is disturbed by confusion between the external and the internal world. In practice, one generally encounters intermediary forms of these extremes.

A patient who has regressed to a stage of nostalgia for the serene state of harmonious mix-up becomes intolerant of any inopportune intervention. Balint tried to invent suitable techniques to deal with this situation, looking for solutions Ferenczi had been unable to find. The latter had identified this problem, and considered that the analysis of a traumatised patient could not be considered completed unless this level of regression had been reached. He perceived clearly that some aspect of the classical technique of abstinence and frustration had to be modified in this situation. But he was unable to find the right limit allowing the analytic work to continue.

It was in this context that Balint established that allowing, and even encouraging, this regression to take place, while sometimes necessary, could lead to a benign or malignant form of regression. One form allowed the patient to heal his wounds and to emerge from the regression; the other drew him into a spiral of endless demands, whose satisfaction only led to bitterness and disappointment. Therefore, the gratifications granted by the analyst had to remain within certain limits, those of preliminary pleasure, in order to allow the analytic work to continue.

Thus, Balint enabled patients considered "severely disturbed" to benefit from analytic therapy. Following in Ferenczi's footsteps, Balint considered that patients whose treatment could not be conducted from beginning to end at the Oedipal level of conventional adult language could nevertheless benefit from analysis, provided they are allowed to regress to the basic fault level and stay there long enough to arrive to a new beginning. What is needed at this stage of regression is to recognise the patient's needs and aspirations through suitable signals, rather than satisfy them.

It is clear that Balint understood perfectly well the essential lessons to be drawn from Ferenczi's theoretical and technical research: to always maintain critical awareness, even about the ideas of one's analyst, friend and respected teacher; never hesitate to question the most commonly accepted ideas, re-examine the theories of eminent authorities if they prove to be inefficient in practice or are shown to contain contradictions; always be attentive to what the patient says, whether what he says should be taken literally or not. This was what allowed Balint to benefit from both the successes and failures of his friend and teacher, as well as from his ideas and intuition. Balint then contributed, through his own original ideas, to the advancement of psychoanalytic theory and technique, without overlooking the work of others. He considered his own perspective as one possible way to look at a problem, but not the only one and not necessarily the best.

THE PSYCHOANALYTIC COMMUNITY TRAUMATISED

Passages from the Introduction to the Hebrew translation of *The Basic Fault*

The Basic Fault is Michael Balint' last book, written two years before his death. It is the culmination of his life's work. The book has a double structure:

Linear structure: Balint reviews all the themes he developed since the 1930s, showing how his vision of psychic life took shape gradually, from the first tentative ideas to this final work. I say "vision" of psychic life rather than theory because Balint always started with clinical observations he was trying to understand and put together in a coherent manner. Moreover, he did not hesitate, whenever possible, to "translate" his own conclusions into the language of other authors: Freud, Klein, Winnicott, etc., in an attempt to show that the facts observed are not simply the result of his personal technique. But he also explained why he preferred his own terminology. Let us review some of the essential stages in Balint's linear development: in 1932, introduction of the concept of "new beginning" in therapy; in 1937, elucidation of contradictions in the primary narcissism theory, of the purely speculative nature of the theory, and its replacement with the concept of primary love; in 1951, questioning the concept of primary hate, which Balint sees as always being a secon dary emotion; in 1958, the concept of three areas of the psychic apparatus; and the book Thrills and Regressions in 1959.

In addition to this linear structure, the book also presents a concentric structure: the focus would be chapter 23, entitled "The Disagreement between Freud and Ferenczi, and Its Repercussions". Balint considered this disagreement a veritable trauma for the psychoanalytic community. His entire theory of regression (the subtitle of his book is *Therapeutic Aspects of Regression*) is organised around trauma, the "basic fault" resulting from it, and the therapeutic use of regression in the analysis of patients with pathologies related to this fault.

Generally speaking, Balint always attempts to be clear in his writing. He wants to be understood. In this book, there is something almost provocative in the detailed explanations, the repetitions each time he discusses a new aspect of a subject introduced earlier, the references to the language such and such author would use to express the same idea... It is as if he was telling the reader: I want to avoid any misunderstanding that would change the meaning of what I am trying to say. All those who knew Michael Balint know that he was fond of provocation. But provocation in the noblest sense of the term: an incitement to reflection, real emotion, rigourous thinking, and the absolute refusal of any subterfuge and easy answers. The style of this book illustrates this type of provocation.

While Balint was ready to make concessions in order to save a relationship he valued, or to adapt to a milieu in which he wanted to live, he made no concessions when it came to scientific reasoning. Solid arguments would have been required to cause him to abandon one of his ideas.

Scientific reasoning had always been part of Balint's life. Right from adolescence, his father had introduced him to clinical reasoning by taking him along when he visited patients.

Balint submitted certain hypotheses of classical psychoanalytic theory to rigorous examination, and pointed out imprecision, and incoherent logic in reasoning or internal contradictions in certain cases. The purpose was not to uncover errors. Rather, Balint seems to have agreed with Maria Torok and Nicolas Rand who, in their book *Questions for Freud*, state that contradictions in a theory always indicate the fertile place from which it becomes possible to advance.

Balint also studied the relations between theory and technique, pointing out the diversity of techniques based on the same fundamental principles governing the psychic apparatus, and the difficulty of introducing a certain degree of precision.

Freud focused his research on pathologies in which the phenomena involved are internal for the most part, and external objects — including the analyst — only play a minor role. This is what prompted him to liken the analyst to a mere reflecting mirror. In other words, Freud concentrated on a single-person psychology, instead of taking into consideration the importance of the object relation. This state of affairs generated the myth of a "good technique", suitable in all cases. However, the psychoanalytic situation, due to its specific structure, is already inscribed in an object relation; each analyst/analysand couple has to create its own language, its own techniques; in short, it has to invent.

A considerable portion of the book is dedicated to the description of the basic fault level, its characteristics, therapeutic regression to this level and the appropriate therapeutic techniques to adopt.

Like Ferenczi, Balint chose not to select patients on the basis of their suitability for "classical" analysis. He believed that the technique had to adapt, as much as possible, to the needs of particular patients, just as child care must be adapted to each child's needs. Balint pointed out that adapting the technique was not something new. Analysts working with children had to do this. He cited Melanie Klein to illustrate, but criticised certain practices of the Kleinian school, such as maintaining a great inequality between analyst and patient, and imposing the analyst's language on analysands. In this context, he alluded to Ferenczi's notion of "intropressure" in the superego.

BALINT AND THE FREUD-FERENCZI DISAGREEMENT

Now let us look at the crucial chapter of the book dedicated to the disagreement between Freud and Ferenczi. Those who have had the opportunity to read the Correspondence of Sigmund Freud and Sándor Ferenczi were able to follow the evolution of this disagreement, practically from the start of the relationship between the two men. Ferenczi seemed to be desperately seeking a relationship on equal footing and devoid of hate, as described by Balint in his book, for which Freud was clearly not ready.

Their disagreement eventually became focused on the approach to regression. Freud had had too many bad experiences with regression to be able to acknowledge its therapeutic value (except in passing, in one article). In contrast, all of Ferenczi's experiences over the past few years confirmed that the inevitable — even necessary — regression occurring in analysis can be used to the patient's benefit. But Ferenczi had not been able to distinguish between benign and malignant regression. And Freud, who was already skeptical, had witnessed his failures.

Balint says, quite rightly, that this conflict constituted a trauma for the analytic community. But we have yet to understand why things took such a passionate and violent turn, why the entire analytic community was swept up in this dispute, and why the consequences lasted so long. Such a conflict between the two major figures of psychoanalysis can be a source of turmoil, but this does not explain the violence of the events that followed.

In fact, this trauma duplicated the previous trauma caused to the analytic community by Otto Rank's "revolt" and subsequent "defection". The Development of Psychoanalysis, co-authored by Ferenczi and Rank, and even more so Rank's The Trauma of Birth, triggered a veritable crisis within the psychoanalytic movement. Freud, who had initially been favourable to Rank's discovery, gradually liked it less and less. He realised that the emphasis on the crucial importance of events in the pre-Oedipal period — the area of the basic fault, according to Balint — and therefore on the role of the mother, brought into question the central and primordial place of the Oedipus complex, cornerstone of the Freudian edifice. This would then force him to reconsider the entire theory based on this complex. Apparently, Freud found this prospect unimaginable now that he was on the threshold of old age and had just learned that he had cancer. He preferred to accept a painful break with Rank, rather than undertake such a re-examination. At the time, Ferenczi had not been able to face the possibility of a disagreement with his analyst and teacher. He also preferred to break with Rank, despite their friendship and despite the fact that fundamentally he agreed with him.

But the clash with Freud was inevitable. For years Ferenczi's work had been taking a direction Freud found unacceptable. But Ferenczi's clinical practice kept pushing him in that direction.

I believe that what traumatised most of the analytic community so deeply was the distress of the founding father of psychoanalysis when faced with research whose pertinence was confirmed by clinical practice, and which brought into question certain points of theory that seemed to him firmly established. In order to be open to — and accept — Ferenczi's ideas, analysts would have had to admit that Freud had not understood or foreseen everything, that he could not provide an unshakeable and definitive theoretical corpus, or infallible and permanent guiding principles.

For most members of the analytic community, this was too much to ask for. They reacted by holding on "regressively" to the whole body of "classical" theory, in ocnophilic fashion, we might say. Any attempt on Ferenczi's part to be heard was met with clamorous and violent rejection. After his death, his work was shrouded in silence, until it was altogether swept away by Jones (along with Rank's work), who called both men mentally ill in Volume III of his monumental biography of Freud. It took much time and persistence on Balint's part, as well as on the part of all the other proponents of object relations, to bring Ferenczi's ideas back into the forefront, and for the research he started to be continued.

Balint did not have an easy task. He had to fight to have Ferenczi's work published in several languages. He had to conduct his research alone, or almost alone. And just as Ferenci in the past, he found himself disregarded forgotten and often devalued. Even today, many analysts consider that his major contribution consisted in providing general practitioners with useful psychotherapeutic techniques, and have only a vague idea of his psychoanalytic work. He is just now coming out of the shadows.

IMPRESSIONS UPON READING MICHAEL BALINT'S ARTICLE "THE ADOLESCENT'S FIGHT AGAINST MASTURBATION" (1926)

My first impression after reading this article was that customs and ways of thinking have changed so much since 1926 that the article is outdated. Between then and now, no doubt partly thanks to psychoanalysis, attitudes have changed, so that there is not so much associated guilt, and even the approach to the problem is somewhat different. In any case, guilt is always present, but is not necessarily the only factor playing a central role.

But on second thought, I had to temper my impression. Balint's analysis is convincing. The problem in this text is somewhere else.

In short, Balint's article tells us that masturbation in adolescents is accompanied by intense feelings of guilt and shame. Masturbation is strongly condemned by society. The reason for this condemnation, and for the feeling of guilt, is to be found in the fantasies associated with the act of masturbation, fantasies which are always ultimately incestuous. All the fantasy figures in the scenes imagined by masturbators represent, in more or less disguised form, the mother for the boy, or the father for the girl. But the prohibition of incest is a fundamental principle of our society. The act of masturbation and the fantasies associated with it signal the transition from infantile incestuous sexuality to adult sexuality with a partner of the opposite sex.

Overall, this analysis seems valid, to me at least, as it applies to adolescents.

But it does feel somewhat confining.

This way of restricting the question to the period of puberty leaves out a number of elements which seem to be closely tied to masturbation, and also have a role to play in adolescence.

In fact, masturbatory activity starts very early, in early childhood, as noted by numerous authors, including Freud, who worked as a paediatrician for ten years, as Carlo Bonomi reminds us in a fascinating article[2].

The "Subject Index" of Freud's writings, drawn up by Alain Delrieux[3], contains many references to masturbation. In a note written in 1910, he speaks of a normal masturbation period between the ages of 3 and 5. In 1912, he extended this period to infancy. Anyone can confirm the accuracy of this observation. Little children masturbate, without shame or guilt, until repression is introduced. At the time Balint wrote this paper, repression was practically the rule, and alluded to the risk of serious illness later in life, impotence, mental deficiency, etc. There were also threats, which ranged from castration, to reactions showing various

---

2   Bonomi, C., «Pourquoi avons-nous ignoré Freud le pédiatre», in *Le Coq-Héron*, No 134, 1994 : « Cent ans de psychanalyse », pp. 7-42.
3   Anthropos/Economica, Paris, 1997.

degrees of contempt and disgust. This was where fear, shame and guilt originated. Today, these types of threats seem to be more uncommon, but have not disappeared altogether. Sometimes the adults, at least the more enlightened among them, simply let the child know that such acts are private and should not be performed in public.

Of course, in our societies things like masturbation, answering the call of nature, or having intercourse are "not done" in front of others. One of the reasons for this might be that the witnesses might find such scenes too exciting. It is for this reason that these things constitute the theme of pornographic movies almost exclusively. These movies appeal more to men than to women. Is it because women feel more shame? Is it that women have less need of them? Or is it that these subjects are more exciting for men than for women, and that movies that would be exciting for women are yet to be invented?

Another well-known fact is that masturbation does not end after puberty. Even people with a rich and satisfying sex life may continue to indulge in this activity in some situations, sporadically or for a certain period of time, or even all the time, in parallel with their normal sex life. There could be many reasons for this. The partner may become temporarily or permanently unavailable for various reasons (absence, illness, age difference, etc.). Sometimes, people with a perfectly satisfying sex life masturbate from time to time for no particular reason other than a momentary mood. Freud himself noted in one of his letters that masturbation is the best sleeping potion.

All this leads us to think that masturbation is not simply a make-do substitute for normal sexual activity, but that it may also serve other functions. In fact, as far as the "make-do" notion is concerned, several authors including Freud consider that if masturbation is practised over too long a period, there is a risk of never finding a partner who will live up to the expectations established by the imaginary situation. This is tantamount to saying that solitary pleasure, with its unlimited freedom, could perhaps be better than the pleasure to be had in an object relation.

A closer look at the texts listed in the *Subject Index* shows that Freud never succeeded in formulating a clear opinion on this subject. At first, between 1893 and 1897, he believed, like most physicians of his era, that masturbation can cause all sorts of disorders: neurasthenia, melancholia, hysteria...

However, he always had doubts: in 1894, he wrote that when masturbation is stopped, anxiety neurosis appears. This would mean that masturbation can sometimes be an antidote to anxiety. In 1896, he noted that masturbation often follows seduction or sexual abuse by an adult. In 1897, he introduced the idea — later developed by Balint in his article — that drugs (tobacco, alcohol...) are substitutes to masturbation, with much more harmful effects than those of masturbation.

Gradually, Freud started to say that in addition to harmful effects (predisposing to neurosis or psychosis, subverting character, having bad somatic effects, etc.), masturbation also has favourable effects, because it provides consolation. In 1910, in the *Minutes of the Vienna Psychoanalytical Society*, he identified nine harmful effects and four useful effects of masturbation.

At last, he observed that masturbation is a generalised, normal practice in infants, and later in children between 3 and 5. In the latency period, masturbation reappears when parents administer routine care or make gestures of affection. According to Freud, these gestures are later remembered as having been attempts at seduction. We know that one of the points of disagreement between Freud and Ferenczi would later concern the more or less frequent occurrence of such seduction by the parents. In his famous 1968 article on trauma Balint added that parents can make such traumatising seductive gestures without any bad intentions, but simply through ignorance or awkwardness.

Finally, Freud admitted that masturbation is a universal practice in adolescence, and constitutes a passage between the autoeroticism of early childhood and object relations. (This is also what Balint affirmed in his 1926 article.) Freud even asked himself why guilt feelings are so persistent in people's recollections of this activity in adolescence. Elsewhere, Freud wrote that masturbation has no harmful effects at all if the mother and the father are not among the figures included in the associated fantasy. Balint disagreed on this point; he believed that the parental figures are always present, and that it is precisely this incestuous element which explains the intensity of the repression and the guilt feelings.

But in1933, in the *New Introductory Lectures on Psychoanalysis*, Freud no longer knew what to think of masturbation and admitted that he could give no advice to parents about the right reaction to have.

What did Ferenczi, another classical author whose follower Balint held himself to be, have to say on this subject? In 1912, during an extended forum on the subject organised by the Psychoanalytic Society, Ferenczi asserted, like almost everyone at the time, that masturbation was harmful and could cause neurotic disorders. But he argued that it was less harmful to engage in it than to repress it, as was customary at the time. He described some neurasthenia symptoms it could cause — but in some cases for one day only — tiredness, insomnia..., but he added that it was a helpful activity for falling asleep. Ferenczi believed that heterosexual intercourse with masturbatory fantasies amounts to masturbation by means of another body and leaves the person exhausted, while intercourse without fantasies is rather invigourating.

In this context, we might ask ourselves if masturbation and intercourse differ only in terms of intensity of pleasure (and we have seen that it is not clear which activity outweighs the other), or if there are other differences. In fact, two entirely different attitudes are involved: giving oneself some well-being when one feels the need for it, or engaging with another person in an act of love, welcoming his desire and being as mindful of his pleasure as of one's own. From this point of view, Ferenczi is no doubt right to equate loveless sexual relations with shared masturbation.

Strangely, in his article, Ferenczi referred to Fliess's theories, which claimed that there was a relation between the genital organs and the nose, and that masturbation caused inflammation of the nasal mucosae. We know that Ferenczi had problems with his nasal mucosae, and that their oedema seriously disturbed his sleep, so that he contemplated undergoing more and more invasive surgical procedures. We also know that he had admitted, in his letters to Freud, having masturbated a great deal when he was young. It is not unreasonable to wonder if guilt played a role in causing the nasal mucosae symptoms. But there is no evidence directly linking his onanistic activity to any physical symptoms whatever. Although Ferenczi was obviously an anxious, neurotic man, he certainly did not suffer from neurasthenia and he had a very active sex life.

What I learned from my own clinical experience is that all small children engage in masturbation at some time, in one manner or other. Sometimes, this serves to soothe unfamiliar sensations they are starting to experience. Afterwards, it is done to arouse these sensations and then calm them, because this is pleasant and soothing. Or they masturbate when they are distressed, or bored, or when they are afraid at night, alone in the dark in their beds. Or because they feel abandoned. A certain little boy I knew had a period of intense masturbation when he was 5 or 6, at a time when the fights between his parents were particularly frequent and violent. Both parents were very attached to their son and were distressed to see this reaction to the atmosphere in their home. But they remained discreet and reassured the child by showing him as best they could that the family would not break up. When the parents stopped fighting, masturbation on the child's part became sporadic and more discreet.

Most small children masturbate at night in their beds. It seems to be a way to relax, leave the outside world behind and turn their attention to themselves. I believe that unless someone interferes, there is no guilt attached to this activity at all. But when adults intervene, this is no longer the case. Many patients in analysis told me what a shock it was for them, in their childhood, to be discovered in these intimate moments by a parent and to be severely scolded. In my opinion, the sudden and brutal intrusion into this intimate space they had created was at least as traumatising as the words used to condemn their activity, and the threats that might have been made.

For adolescents, things are somewhat different. This is a difficult period when everything changes: the shape of the body, its sensations, the adolescent's goals, drives and their intensity, the expectations of the entourage, and their own ambitions, etc. I believe that for them masturbation, with the pleasure and discharge of tension it provides, is an answer to all these new tensions, pressures and excitement that suddenly appear in their lives, and whose satisfaction is never easy, and is sometimes impossible, in our kind of culture. An adolescent is not ready for the responsibility involved in having sexual relations with another person. When a girl who is a minor finds herself pregnant, the situation is hard to manage. The solutions available, such as prostitutes for boys, and even the use of contraception — the best answer, of course — , all have physical and/or psychological consequences.

For some adolescents and young adults, who are particularly anxious about their virility, masturbation serves to check that their "equipment" is in good working order. In this context, we might wonder if masturbation plays the same role for girls as it does for boys. In early childhood, the fact of having an organ that one could lose, or not having an organ that others have, no doubt has a role to play. In adolescence, the situation becomes even more asymmetrical. The internal pressures that incite girls and boys to masturbate are very likely not identical. In therapy, boys speak most often of their fear of not performing as expected during sexual relations, while girls speak of the pleasure they experience.

We might ask ourselves if the great sexual freedom society now grants to young people makes their lives easier or more complicated. Today, the sex life of adolescents starts very early and is often difficult and stormy. It may allow them to acquire a better "technique", but it does not seem to facilitate a more balanced love life later. Divorce is now more prevalent than ever. Of course, love and sexual practices are not necessarily synonymous. Perhaps too early and too easy satisfaction of sexual drives increases the gap between them.

Masturbation is the easiest way, and the one with the least consequences, to discharge excess tension so difficult to manage by other means. To illustrate, I can cite the case of a young woman who had been married for a few years and who, after experiencing a rich and varied sex life for a time, started analysis because she suffered from frigidity and infertility. At the age of 15, she had had her first, very satisfactory, sexual encounter with a boy of 16. She found herself pregnant and had an abortion; this was a very traumatising experience; she had to hide it from her parents and had to go abroad for the procedure. She was able to go through this ordeal with the complicity and financial help of her friends, but she was left with consuming guilt feelings. Despite her intense sex life, she no longer experienced the least pleasure and could not become pregnant. It might be supposed that she would have had an easier time if she had simply discharged excess sexual tension through masturbation.

As for adolescents who do just this, Balint's analysis is no doubt correct to a great extent. To explain their guilt feelings, we might add to Balint's list of reasons the possibility that they may feel uncomfortable knowing that they are avoiding something — adult sexuality — which they do not feel ready for.

In his article, Balint attaches great importance to the fantasies associated with the act of masturbation. Patients find it difficult to reveal them, even in analysis, and often refuse to do so. But, according to Balint, if patients can be persuaded to talk about these fantasies, much can be learned about their psychic life. I am inclined to wonder if the content of these fantasies is really so useful and revealing. In my experience, these fantasies vary little from one person to another; they often depict scenes resembling the situation in which erotic sensations were experienced for the first time, or in a particularly memorable manner. These fantasies tend to reveal certain events in the patient's history, rather than aspects of their psychic life. Similarly, although masturbatory activities vary greatly, their causes and effects are quite similar. Fantasies and practices seem less important to me than causes and effects. While Freud listed twice as many reasons to abstain from masturbation than to indulge in it, my advice would be the complete opposite.

Contrary to what the consensus used to be, I believe not only that masturbation is not an illness, or even a symptom of illness, but rather a remedy. It is a remedy for anxiety and loneliness in small children; a remedy for unbearable tension in adolescents, for whom finding other means is too difficult; and a substitute, sedative and soporific for adults. It might be a drug, but a soft drug, and an overdose — although not completely inconsequential — is not fatal.

Of course, negative effects cannot be eliminated altogether. Admittedly, if sexual tension is calmed too quickly, too often and too easily, there is not enough of it left to allow sexual relations to be truly satisfying. This is perhaps the case for people who have a low tolerance for pressure in general, and who, as soon as they face any tension, take tranquillisers, look for distractions, run to a psychotherapist, take drugs... or masturbate. All things considered, the last solution is certainly the least harmful and the least expensive[4].

WHAT IS GOOD HEALTH?
MICHAEL BALINT'S PERSPECTIVE

Everyone knows, or thinks he knows, what it means to be in "good health". But when one tries to define what good

---

4   Finally, let us note that masturbation also exists in the animal world. It is easy to see in cats and dogs. We don't know enough about the psychology of these animals to be able to analyse the phenomenon as we do in humans. But this fact indicates that this activity is more deeply rooted in biology than we thought.

health is, it becomes obvious that this apparently simple notion actually raises many questions. Is it the patient who determines whether he is in good health? Is it the doctor? (See Jules Romain's *Dr. Knock*). Is one's state of health determined by tests, X-rays, scans and other exams that keep being perfected? How is it that some healers obtain excellent results using whimsical methods that are far from scientific?

In fact, we are well aware that we do not know what exactly brings about a cure. For example, no one knows what the therapeutic agent is in homeopathic medicine, which is very helpful to some patients suffering from certain pathologies such as migraine. We can ask the same questions in reference to other "alternative" medicines as well.

To illustrate the complexity of the problem, let us consider this unkind story about psychoanalysis:

A man suffers from nocturnal enuresis. After having tried a multitude of medications, he consults a psychoanalyst. When he has been in analysis for three or four years, he runs into an old friend who asks him: "Have you been able to solve your problem?" And the man answers: "I am doing just fine. I still wet the bed, but now it doesn't bother me."

Has this man recovered from his illness?

It was with this question in mind that Michael Balint started to take an interest in the work of general practitioners and everything they are able to do for their patients. Everything, in fact, which they succeed in doing without knowing it. For as he writes in his book *The Doctor, His Patient and the Illness*, the most important remedy is the doctor himself. Consequently, Balint set out to study how to administer and make use of this remedy.

His interest in this problem went back to the time when his father would take him along on his visits to patients. The young Michael was very interested in everything he saw on these rounds, while being very critical of his father as a doctor, and as a father as well. As soon as he started to practise psychoanalysis, Balint began publishing articles about family medicine and general practitioners. During his analytic training in Berlin, he worked with general practitioners at the Charité Hospital; back in Budapest, while in analysis with Sándor Ferenczi, who was also very interested in this question, from 1926 on he published articles like "Psychoanalysis and Internal Medicine", in the Hungarian journal *Gyógyászat* (Therapeutics), on how psychoanalysis can help family doctors understand their patients better. Later that year, another article, "Psychoanalysis in the Service of the Medical Practitioner", was published in the Hungarian journal *Terápia* (Therapy). This article was translated into French by Michelle Moreau Ricaud, and included in her book *Michael Balint. Le renouveau de l'école de Budapest* (Michael Balint: The Comeback of the Budapest School)[5].

Balint also had a strong interest in the organisation of medical practice, a closely related topic, and published an article on the subject in 1930 in Gyógyászat: "Crisis in Medical Practice". This article, on a subject still highly relevant today, was published in French in Le Coq-Héron[6], in 1985.

Indeed, Balint always gave primary importance to the therapeutic function of psychoanalysis, agreeing with the position of Ferenczi, his master and friend, contrary to a number of analysts much more interested in theory, who were criticised, among others, by Ferenczi and Rank, in their book The Development of Psychoanalysis, for trying to force their patients to fit the theory instead of developing and changing the theory based on their clinical experience. These analysts responded by calling Ferenczi's therapeutic research a furor sanandi. It is for these reasons that Balint entitled his 1934 commemorative articles on Ferenczi, in Gyógyászat, "Sándor Ferenczi", the Doctor" (Le Coq-Héron, No. 98)[7].

Another article, published in 1949, confirms Balint's interest in the therapeutic aspects of psychoanalysis: "Changing Therapeutical Aims and Techniques in Psychoanalysis", included in Primary Love and Psychoanalytic Technique, a book bringing together his early papers, written before Balint's emigration to England.

During the war years, Balint was busy dealing with personal misfortunes and sorrows, so that he wrote very little between 1940 and 1945.

But he continued to think about the development of his theoretical system, as described above, as well as about

---

5   Moreau-Ricaud, M., Michael Balint. *Le renouveau de l'école de Budapest, op. cit.*, Érès, 2007.
6   Balint, M., "Crise de la pratique médicale", in Le Coq-Héron, No. 95, 1985.
7   Balint, M., "Sándor Ferenczi, le médecin", in *Le Coq-Héron*, No. 98), 1986.

a subject he had always held dear: the uses to which general practitioners could put psychological and psychoanalytic knowledge in their medical practice. Balint considered these two perspectives one and the same, as we shall see.

Balintian theory originated in Balint's long-standing opposition to the concept of primary narcissism, which holds that the fetus and then the infant exist as if in a bubble, isolated from any relations. His opposition was based on clinical observation. He wrote several articles specifically about the contradictions inherent in this concept. Among these, let us mention just two: "Critical Notes on the Theory of the Pregenital Organisation of the Libido" (1935) and "Early Developmental States of the Ego: Primary Object-love" (1937). Balint was convinced that as early as intrauterine

life there existed something akin to a relationship, which he called primary love, as distinct from primary narcissism. It could be described as a positive disposition towards the substances surrounding this developing being, the fetus: the amniotic fluid in which it is emersed, the warmth, the sounds he hears, and particularly his parents' voices, etc. We now know that modern science has validated Balint's ideas. Fathers who speak to their child still in the womb, haptonomy as a means of communicating with the fetus... all these presume that there is a being who, in his primitive manner, has contact with the outside world.

The idea of primary love and the states it creates, as well as Balint's analytic practice, caused him to take a particular interest in regressive phenomena. The question was how to use regression to obtain better therapeutic results. This is something which concerns both physicians and psychoanalysts, since regression can occur in all sorts of situations, from accidents to old age, as well as during an illness. Anyone working as a caregiver knows this without having to refer to any theory: when one hears them speaking to patients or to the elderly as if they were children, giving them pet names, most of them don't feel offended.

One of Balint's most important ideas, underlying all his psychoanalytic and medical work, is the concept of "whole-person medicine". He refused to split a human being into two parts: the body and the mind. For him, both refer to the same entity, the human being, and he believed that any therapeutic intervention must be directed to the "whole person", taking all his elements into account. Different approaches are possible, but it is always the whole person who must be treated. Balint used to say jokingly that even a broken leg can be cured with psychoanalysis, but it will heal faster with a cast.

As I described earlier, Balint identified three areas: the Oedipal area, the area of the basic fault and the area of creation. He calls them areas, not stages, because all three are present in the adult psyche. Thus, an adult whose behaviour is controlled primarily by the Oedipal area, can, in analysis, during an illness, under the influence of strong emotions or while in the arms of a lover, regress to the area of the basic fault.

Regression involves a certain risk, as Ferenczi discovered at some cost. Balint realised that it was the type of gratification granted which determined the outcome of the regression. Granting gratifications the patient could interpret as a promise of love and as permanent solicitude leads to what he called malignant regression. Hugging the patient, going to his home to conduct the session when he does not feel well enough to come to the analyst's office, having sessions that last several hours, are among the gratifications which could cause malignant regression. But when gratifications remain at the level of preliminary pleasure (holding the patient's hand, giving an extra session, allowing week-end telephone calls), the regression will take a benign form from which the patient will emerge in his own time and by his own means, in a state of well-being. This is what Balint called a "new beginning".

THE BIRTH OF THE "BALINT GROUPS"

In 1955, his first book about medical practice, The Doctor, His Patient and the Illness, was published. We have seen that his interest in the subject went back as far as his adolescence, and his early work. More directly, it resulted from his work sessions in England with general practitioners, which Balint called "research-cum-training" seminars, later known as "Balint groups". The aim was to study with the doctors themselves the effects of the "doctor-as-a-drug". A whole series of ideas and formulations emerged from these encounters, and are now part of the medico-psychoanalytic vocabulary.

Starting from the idea that "the doctor is the drug", Balint pointed out that consciously or unconsciously the doctor encounters the patient as a whole being. This had always been the case, but in general the doctor did not pay attention to this and did not use the phenomenon to see more clearly what was happening to his patient. A doctor's attitude towards his patients, including a total absence of interaction with them, is in itself a form of relationship with specific effects. Balint insisted on the fact that negative observations are important as well, and must be taken into account.

A caricatural example of this refusal of contact with the patient is the story of a woman who, after surgery for strangulated hernia, was recovering nicely. Each day, the surgeon and the nurse visited her in her room; without greeting her, the surgeon would look at the chart posted at the foot of the bed, exchange a few words with the nurse, and leave without looking at the patient or taking leave of her. The day before the patient was to be released, the surgeon entered her room without saying anything, as usual, but limping and with a cast on his leg. Concerned, the woman asked him what happened. For the first time, the doctor looked at her and recounted the whole incident in detail: how he slipped on the stairs in his building, how help arrived to take him to the hospital, and how the cast was placed on his leg. He even spoke of how upset his family had been. Then he gave the patient a charming smile and left the room. In fact, this doctor was afraid of contact with other people, and the patient had sensed his fear. This allowed her not to resent him, and "break the ice" when the occasion arose. Clearly, the doctor couldn't ask for more and gladly seized the opportunity.

When a doctor says to a patient: "Dear Sir, or dear Madam, you are not sick, your symptoms are psychological", he is addressing the whole person, but is conveying a message of rejection that could be formulated as follows: "The physical equipment is working as it should, this is what I am paid to look after; your existential problems don't interest me". Or he could be saying: "I know how to manage the ills of the body, it's my specialty; but I know nothing about the rest and these sorts of things scare me".

A number of British general practitioners were sufficiently aware of these problems to consent to participate in Balint's "research-cum-training" seminars. The groups met once a month and one of the doctors presented a case chosen at random. Then, there was a discussion about the doctor's attitude to the patient, the latter's reactions, what the doctor felt and how he could evaluate his feelings depending on the patient's personality and illness.

In these groups, Balint highlighted and asked the participants to examine what had taken place between the two protagonists, the doctor and the patient, as well as the effects of the interaction on each of them. For instance, the patient might find the doctor likeable, warm, friendly, or on the contrary, bad-tempered, bossy, indifferent or uncommunicative. The doctor may find the patient pleasant, open, reasonable, compliant, cooperative, or else mistrustful, reticent, aggressive, or calm, excited, anxious, etc. All these emotional perceptions and reactions are part of the atmosphere created between them, and will influence the therapeutic options the doctor offers, as well as the patient's reaction to the suggested treatment. In addition, these impressions will play a role in the doctor's ability to understand the patient's suffering as a whole person. Thus, Balint taught general practitioners to interpret their own feelings about the patient depending on the patient's illness. If the patient charms the doctor or moves him, or on the contrary bores him or irritates him, the doctor will ask himself what exactly in the patient arouses these emotions in him, and to what purpose. For we know that most often, if something we do or an attitude we have provokes a certain reaction on someone's part, this reaction was probably the goal we were seeking, consciously or unconsciously.

But Balint's aim was not to transform general practitioners into psychoanalysts. He never let these transferential and countertransferential interpretations turn into an analysis of the doctor's personality. If one of the doctors in the group started training to become an analyst, Balint took this as a failure. What he wanted was to give general practitioners the tools they needed to help patients attain a state of well-being; he believed that proper functioning of the somatic apparatus was not sufficient to provide this well-being, and that it may not even be absolutely necessary. A classic story that used to be told in the Paris Medical School concerns a cavalry officer who developed eczema on his inner thighs. His doctor treated the eczema successfully. But now the patient started to suffer from serious asthma attacks. Obviously, he needed an allergic reaction to express something that neither he nor his doctor was aware of, or able to take into account. As long as this "something" was not made apparent, he needed his symptom. And if one symptom was eliminated, he created another.

In 1961, Balint published a sequel to The Doctor, His Patient and the Illness, entitled Psychotherapeutic

Techniques in Medicine. In this book, Balint examined the psychotherapeutic techniques a doctor needs to understand a patient's condition. In his Introduction, however, he expressed a strange skepticism as to the reception the book might expect:

«*The status of psychotherapy in medicine is equivocal in more than one respect. Its enthusiasts claim that it is one of the most important therapeutic methods available; its enemies claim that is has no scientific justification whatsoever. Somewhere in between the two, medicine proper reluctantly admits that there may be some slender empirical basis to justify its use, especially if it is administered in conjunction with some other therapy, such as placebos, physiotherapy, etc. Psychoanalysis considers psychotherapy a poor substitute, really a kind of watered-down psycho-analysis. Academic psychiatry has very limited use for it in comparison with its interest in physical and chemical therapeutic methods*»

Balint's pessimistic assessment proved to be accurate and endured over time, with some rare exceptions. Today, attempts to regulate the profession of psychotherapist still reflect the heavy stigma inflicted by this perspective.

What about those Balint calls "repeat-prescription patients", who repeatedly ask for a prescription of the same drug, but do not want to see or speak to the doctor? This drug, or the idea they have of its efficiency, keeps them in "good health", and this is all they want. The doctor must not disturb the equilibrium they have established for themselves. This non-relation is nevertheless a form of relation, and it is important for the doctor to recognise and respect the request made by his patient. Experience has shown that if an appointment to see the doctor is suggested to such a patient, he disappears immediately and then enacts the same behaviour with another doctor.

A medical consultation which intends to take the whole person into consideration takes time. But time is what doctors lack the most. Balint calculated that a British doctor had about 6 minutes to see a patient. Therefore, he asked himself what can be provided to the whole person in these six minutes. He concluded that by using the proper techniques, what the doctor can do for the patient is not negligible, although it sometimes remains insufficient. For the patient as a whole person, a long appointment has to be proposed and scheduled, in order to look deeper into the patient's malaise.

The Balintian approach to treatment is rooted directly

in the theory of the "basic fault". To respond adequately to a person with a pathology of any kind, it seems indispensable to identify this flaw, this defect or fault that weakens him, and which he may attempt to compensate for in various ways. Physical symptoms and all kinds of lifestyle practices are manifestations of these attempts. They included dietary rules in order to lose or gain weight, improve digestion, prevent such or such dreaded health problem... Some people will not eat certain foods they "don't digest well", others must eat certain foods or drink specific beverages at each meal to feel safe. A woman I know could eat French fries with no problem, but her bowels resolutely refused boiled potatoes. Thus, a "healthy" diet varies considerably from one person to another.

To come back to our original question: does being in good health mean that all our organs function well, or does it mean experiencing a state of well-being? Better yet, is good health a balance between all the elements which constitute a human being?

All so-called psychosomatic diseases are spectacular illustrations of illness in general, with the added attribute of making the whole person particularly visible. In fact, could it not be the case that all diseases are psychosomatic, since humans are psychosomatic beings?

These considerations bring us to the question of preventive medicine, specifically in the form of routine medical exams. This very reasonable way of doing things has the same drawbacks as the "precautionary principle". Of course, it eliminates many dangers, or at least warns of them, but it causes people to live in constant fear of cancer, infections, car accidents, unhealthy food, impure air, etc. And this underlying anxiety about the dangers of living certainly has an effect on the quality of life of the whole person. In some cases, the precautionary measures, which have become obligations, are more constraining than the possible dangers to be avoided. Is it better to eliminate all unpasteurised milk cheeses, or to risk having gastroenteritis or even listeriosis once in a while? What is more harmful to the whole person: eating tasteless food or — perhaps — having a stomach ache occasionally? Some women are reassured by regular mammograms. Others live in fear in the interval between tests.

One may ask if all these precautionary measures, tests and guarantees are not, after all, attempts to escape the dangers of the disease called life, which no doctor can cure and which Groucho Marx — if I am not mistaken — described as a contagious disease, sexually transmitted and always fatal. Medicine, more than any other field of endeavour, deals with the problem of death, and we expect it to come up with a means of escaping it. But this is no doubt too much to ask for.

The only solution we can expect of medicine is to help us maintain a state of balance as long as we live.

All the things we just discussed are well-known to physicians. These practitioners are all familiar with what is called the "white coat effect", which can, for example, elevate blood pressure readings. But the expression indicates clearly that the doctor prefers attributing this effect to the white coat rather than to the one who wears it, that is, himself. Doctors don't always know how to handle human complexity, and try to work around it by focusing their attention on a single aspect. Medical schools do not provide instruction in these matters. It may also be that being responsible for the well-being of patients can sometimes be too great a burden. Indeed, it is a heavy burden. Therefore, many doctors send the patient to a psychotherapist, when his symptoms do not respond to suitable and reasonable treatment; and just as many psychotherapists send patients to doctors as soon as these patients complain of any physical pain. Of course, this is sometimes the right thing to do, but certainly not in every case. Again, this kind of decision requires good judgment and flexibility.

Some hospital departments, aware of these types of problems, have hired psychotherapists. An interesting experiment conducted in one of these departments has shown how a sensitive doctor, who had a good relationship with a young patient suffering from leukemia, saved his patient's life by discussing the case from time to time with one of the Department therapists, without forcing the young patient to enter into a second relationship with a new person, when he already had a very close relationship with his own doctor.

Michael Balint provided doctors with a number of tools serving to establish a better balance between the various components of a "whole person", and to manage situations with greater flexibility. But he did not succeed, and neither did his successors, in overcoming the resistance that prevents many doctors and professors of medicine from acknowledging the therapeutic importance of regarding the patient as a whole person. Many practitioners continue to treat their patients by relying solely on their human sensitivity, faring well and sometimes not so well, not knowing exactly what they are doing, or even wanting to know.

THE KOVÁCS-BALINT "DYNASTY"

To speak of a "dynasty" when referring to a mother, her daughter and her son-in-law might seem excessive, but I am tempted to use the term about these people because they had the same profession and were the analysands and pupils of the same analyst. I am speaking of three psychoanalysts: Vilma Kovács, her daughter Alice and Alice's husband, Michael Balint, all of them analysands, pupils, friends and proponents of Sándor Ferenczi.

Their story is part of a family saga I recounted earlier.

As we have seen, Vilma was a willful, decisive young woman who did everything unbecoming to a woman of her time: she was divorced, she had a profession and an income, she smoked and she learned to drive.

Alice, her oldest daughter, was as willful and decisive as her mother. It was thanks to her that Vilma' s children were reunited with their mother and brought up by a stepfather who gave them everything their father had been unable to give them.

And it was Vilma's agoraphobia which caused her to undertake analysis with Sándor Ferenczi, no doubt toward the end of the First World War.

The German author Christian Morgenstern, once made the humourous observation that psychoanalysis never cured anyone, but transformed many patients into analysts. Vilma Kovács at once confirms and invalidates this theory: cured of her neurosis, she nevertheless became an analyst.

As for Alice, she met Michael Bergsmann during her brilliant career as a student. He later adopted the more Hungarian-sounding name Balint. Alice and Michael became better acquainted at the Galileo Circle and at the university. Alice wanted to study anthropology, but since this subject was not taught at the University of Budapest, she opted for mathematics instead. It was in these courses that she met Michael and sparked his interest in psychoanalysis.

VILMA KOVÁCS

In the meantime, Vilma started to conduct analysis with patients under Ferenczi's supervision.

In 1921, in Berlin, where Alice and Michael, now married, were receiving training in psychoanalysis, Michael worked at the Charité Hospital, and Alice was finally able to study anthropology and take part in the meetings of the Berlin Psychoanalytic Society, where she even gave a talk on the application of psychoanalysis to an anthropological subject.

In the fourteen years that followed, the psychoanalytic movement took shape and developed actively in Hungary. A training Institute was created, and then a Polyclinic, on the ground floor at 12 Mészáros Street, in premises provided by Frédéric Kovács. The Hungarian group included several theoreticians and highly talented clinicians, some of whom, like Imre Hermann or Géza Róheim, were widely translated and are well-known.

Vilma Kovács was particularly interested in problems related to psychoanalytic training. She conducted the clinical seminar of the program and invented, with Ferenczi, the Hungarian training method, whose main particularity is that the candidate's control is carried out by his own analyst, in the analytic setting, with the candidate on the couch.

As for Alice, her main interest lay in education theory and pedagogical issues in general. But she could not call herself a child analyst because most of her patients were adults.

From the start, what distinguished Michael Balint was his great interest in analytic theory. He published many articles on theoretical subjects, in which he broached ideas he was to develop later, in England, in books like *Thrills and Regressions* and *The Basic Fault*. In addition, he was already searching, with his teacher Ferenczi, for ways to make psychoanalysis useful to general practitioners. At the same time, he had a busy practice. He was also Deputy Director of the Psychoanalytic Polyclinic, headed by Ferenczi. He took over the direction of the Polyclinic in 1933, after Ferenczi's death.

Vilma Kovács only published five articles throughout her life, but one of them, "Training Analysis and Control Analysis", is still pertinent today and has been translated in several languages.

Vilma Kovács' first article, "Analysis of a Case of Convulsive Tic", was published in the Internationale

Zeitschrift für Psychoanalyse in 1925. She had presented this case a year earlier to the Hungarian Psychoanalytic Association. The article describes the successful analysis of a 45-year-old woman using Ferenczi's active method. The author describes the conditions in which the tic appeared: narcissism, hypochondriac self-observation, homosexual tendency, etc. Vilma Kovács sheds light on the relation of the symptom to character formation. Her second article, published in Imago in 1926, was entitled "The Inheritance of Fortunatus". In this text, based on a folktale, she examines the role of testicles and the unconscious fantasies they evoke in the development of masculine genitality. Fortunatus wishes to seduce a princess. He has inherited a hat allowing him to be transported instantly wherever he wants to be, and a purse containing endless bounty. These two things, the penis-hat and the testicles-purse, must never be separated. However, Fortunatus wants to seduce the princess first by his wealth alone. This anal approach triggers an anal response: the princess steals the purse, identifying herself with the man in his role as provider; but the fear of a penis remains. Fortunatus then tries again, bringing the princess two apples, a good one and a harmful one. The harmful apple causes horns to grow on the princess' brow: an overcompensation for the missing penis. The good apple, given to her in exchange for the stolen purse, makes the horns disappear. This setting at the genital level makes it possible for things to go back to normal. The princess and Fortunatus are married, live happily and have many children. Based on this tale, Vilma Kovács analyses the development of the capacity for love, a subject taken up again and again by Alice and Michael Balint.

The third article, published in 1928 in *Internationale Zeitschrift*, is entitled «Examples of the Active Technique». In it, Vilma Kovács describes in detail her rigorous and precise application of this technique to three of her cases. This text is a superb illustration of the functioning and effects of this method.

The fourth article, «Tendency to Repeat and Character Formation», was published in *Internationale Zeitschrift* in 1931. Using a lengthy case history, the author shows how a young man was able to regain access, in analysis, to his desires, after an early traumatic experience cut off this access and initiated a long series of repetitions. In conclusion she writes: «...neurosis develops at the point where the unconscious tendency to repeat, that is, the tendency to live a life created by trauma, collides with the experiences of the conscious Ego».

Finally, «Training and Control Analysis», published in 1935 in *Internationale Zeitschrift*, is Vilma Kovács' best known article. In it, she explains the reasons which, at Ferenczi's initiative, caused the analytic community to require that the candidate undergo analysis as a prerequisite to the practice of psychoanalysis. She goes over the entire history of analytic training, from its inception. She points out the consequences of the analyst's countertransference for the patient, and examines different means of dealing with them.

Speaking of control analysis, the author describes and justifies the Hungarian system mentioned above. She insists on the need, for the analyst, to acquire the inner flexibility indispensable for working with patients whose character is entirely different from one's own. Finally, she discusses the unavoidable asymmetry of the analytic situation, which a candidate who is in analysis while conducting analysis with patients can identify more easily.

We may wonder why this Hungarian system has not been adopted by other training institutions. As we saw, this system bears Ferenczi's mark. Perhaps it gives rise to the same concerns and reservations as the whole of Ferenczi's work. In fact, this method places a great burden on the control analyst, much heavier than the burden he assumes elsewhere in the world. What is required of him is not simply to supervise the candidate's technical learning by drawing his attention, when necessary, to his own involvement. This method forces the control analyst to examine with the candidate the overall nature of his problems as they are revealed in the trying process that the analysis of a patient always represents. He must be able to manage all transferences and countertransferences inherent to this situation. This is, in fact, an almost superhuman task, like all those that Ferenczi tried to impose on analysts. The latter were given only two options: to live and work modestly with a permanent feeling of inadequacy — a way of doing things to which Ferenczi already attributed didactic value — , or to give up the practice of analysis.

The period when this article was published was perhaps the most intense and fertile in the life of the Hungarian Psychoanalytical Society. The Hungarian analysts worked, organised discussions, published. All of them contributed their time free of charge at the Psychoanalytic Polyclinic, to ensure its operation.

The rise of the Nazi Regime and the approach of the war put an abrupt end to the activities of the Hungarian Association, an interruption from which it would need years to recover.

In 1938, after the Annexation of Austria to Germany, the husbands of Vilma Kovács' two daughters felt that the situation had become too dangerous and decided to leave the country. Many analysts chose exile at that time. The Balints settled in Manchester. The Kovács briefly considered going to Paris, where their youngest daughter lived. They both died before the country was invaded by German troops. Michael Balint's parents were less fortunate: Dr. Bergsmann and his wife committed suicide when Arrow Cross men came to arrest them.

ALICE BALINT

Now, Alice Balint. An anthropology student, she turned her interest to psychoanalysis, married Michael Balint and, shortly after they returned from Berlin, gave birth to their son John, who was also given as a third name the Indian name Shotchipilli, in celebration of Alice's anthropological interests.

As we have said, Alice was particularly interested in pedagogical questions. She was education consultant for the journal Gyermeknevelés (Child Education). She answered letters from readers, as well as questions from parents participating in a seminar she conducted. Rather than give them advice, she provided them with a new perspective on the situation which caused them concern. She had learned a lesson of modesty from Ferenczi: she never presented herself as the one who knows. But this did not stop her from having convictions and principles which she applied continuously in her work.

As we said earlier, Alice was not a child analyst. She saw some children at the Polyclinic, but she learned about children, it seems, mostly from focusing on the child in the adults she treated, the child she herself had been, and no doubt her own child and other children around her.

Alice Balint's work is practically unknown outside of Hungary and not very well known even there. It is marked by very original and independent thinking. This is apparent when she discusses, in her very original manner, subjects as general as repression or the Superego. In this respect too she had learned from Ferenczi: never to imitate anyone, not even the most venerable teacher, but rather take from each one the elements that correspond to something in one's own personality, and use them after "fermenting" them in one's own inner laboratory.

The two Balints established a very close collaboration in their work. They discussed everything, sometimes in a heated manner, and elaborated their ideas together. As Michael Balint wrote in the Preface to Primary Love and Psychoanalytic Technique: «All our ideas — no matter in whose mind they had arisen — were enjoyed and then tested, probed and criticised in our endless discussions. Quite often it was just chance that decided which of us should publish a particular idea. [...] We published only one paper jointly, although almost all of them could have been printed under our joint names». This explains the fact that Alice's article «Love for the Mother and Mother Love» is included in his book. It was her last article, published in 1939. It represented an important stage in the work they had carried out together, and which Michael would pursue alone.

Alice Balint relied heavily on her anthropological knowledge in her psychoanalytic work and writing. She was aware of the crucial influence of the culture of a given society on the education of children. As a result, her articles on pedagogical issues never dispense general advice, of the type that could apply everywhere and in any era. In fact, her ideas are never presented in the form of advice, and always take into account the social and cultural context.

But she had strong convictions and expressed them freely. She insisted on the need to be honest with children, not to lie to them, not to hide from them the things that concern them (which does not mean telling them everything), and to respect them. Only in this way can they develop into aware, responsible adults.

Alice Balint's work comprises a general interest psychoanalytic child education book, and a series of articles, most of them published together posthumously, in 1940, under the title *Anya és Gyermek (*Mother and Child). Her book, entitled *The Psycho-analysis of the Nursery,* published by Routhledge and Kegan Paul, was translated into several languages.

At the time when Alice Balint was writing her book, psychoanalysis of children was in its very early stages. In her very personal manner, she formulated some basic concepts which remain of interest today. In addition, her anthropological perspective associated these concepts with socio-cultural considerations which psychoanalysis has perhaps not yet fully exploited. She insisted on the need to take into account social as well as psychological factors, in order to give a child the kind of upbringing that would enable him to feel at ease in his cultural milieu. We must keep in mind that living up to social expectations requires considerable effort on the part of the child. The task of psychology is to allow the child to make this effort with the smallest possible expense of energy.

Alice Balint's book, written in simple, easy to understand language, reviews problems related to impulse control, to the Oedipus complex (designated as the most dramatic episode of childhood), to the castration complex and to mechanisms of identification. Many examples are used to illustrate the different topics discussed.

In her conclusion, Alice Balint insists on certain points which remain, even today, little known by the general public and often misunderstood or underestimated by those who practice psychology and work in education. For instance, she points out that what makes an event pathogenic is the type of relation existing between the child and his entourage, especially his parents, rather than the content of the event itself. She also notes that lack of understanding on the part of educators springs less from ignorance than from the repression of what they know deep down. She considers that the psychological situation of children in modern society has worsened: they are more dependent in early childhood, and are more radically separated from the generation of their parents afterwards. Because the parents are the only element of stability and security for children living in cities in nuclear families, it is harder for them to overcome their Oedipus complex and castration complex than it was for children who lived in large rural families in the past.

This book, intended for a wide readership, made available to the general public all the knowledge psychoanalysis could contribute to child education. In addition, the author clarified all the misunderstandings and oversimplifications commonly observed in the application of analytic ideas to education.

Aside from this book, Alice Balint published about twenty articles. The first two constitute an application of psychoanalysis to anthropology; they were both published in *Imago*. One discusses Mexican war hyeroglyphs (1923), presenting and analysing all their components; the second, much more analytical in nature, entitled «The Father of the Family» (1926) analyses the role of the chief in different Indian cultures, in parallel with the role of the father in psychic life.

Alice Balint started to publish her major articles in 1932; some discussed psychoanalytic theory, others the mother-child relation and still others subjects of a more strictly speaking pedagogical nature. Thus, most of her work was written over a brief, seven-year period. Alice Balint died suddenly in August 1939 in Manchester, of a ruptured aneurysm.

Her first article on psychoanalytic theory was written for a collective work to be presented to Sándor Ferenczi for his sixtieth birthday: *Lélekelemzési tanulmànyok* (Psychoanalytic Studies). The article, entitled «Development of the Feeling of Love and of the Sense of Reality», attempted to show that "emotional life is modeled primarily on the relation of the Ego with the external world". It contained the initial formulations of the concept of primary love, which was subsequently taken up and developed by Michael Balint.

The second theoretical article, «The Handling of Transference on the Basis of Ferenczian Experiments», was presented at the first Four Nations Congress in Vienna. In it, the author discussed problems related to transference and countertransference, from a Ferenczian perspective, but in her own way. In fact, she pointed out that expressing one's own ideas is what makes one most Ferenczian, for Ferenczi had always encouraged his pupils and colleagues to follow their own research paths freely. Ferenczi knew the price of this independence. He himself had paid a high price when he finally allowed his reflection to deviate from that of Freud, and he also knew how painful it can be to incur the disapproval of a revered teacher.

The last two theoretical articles written by Alice Balint were both presented at the 1939 Psychoanalytic Seminar in Manchester. They were entitled «On the Ego» and «On Repression». She discussed these two classic concepts in an original fashion, lively and clear, giving useful clinical examples. Her presentation bore the mark of the anthropologist and the educator combined.

Three of her articles discuss the mother/child relationship. «A Specific Form of Infantile Fear » discusses the fear of being dropped, that is, of losing the mother's love, which she relates to Imre Hermann's famous theory of attachment. The article also contains the seeds of the theory that would lead Michael Balint to elaborate, a few decades later, his classification of regressed patients into ocnophils and philobats. The 1937 article «Reflections on Parental Love», a more pedagogical text, discusses the fact that loving one's child is not enough to solve all problems, because it is possible to love well or poorly. Alice Balint's best-known text, «Love for the Mother and Mother Love» (1939), was the last article she wrote. In it, she developed the themes introduced six years earlier, in «Development of the Feeling of Love and of the Sense of Reality». This text is included in Michael Balint's book Primary Love and Psychoanalytic Technique, which is a collection of articles. The theme of the article could be resumed by the following two quotes: "Maternal love is the almost perfect counterpart to love for the mother", and "The relation between mother and child is built upon the interdependence of the reciprocal instinctual aims" (1933).

Finally, a few articles and a series of shorter texts discuss pedagogical issues important to Alice. Two of these articles, «Forbidding and Allowing» (1932) and «The Bases of Our Educational System» (1937), were presented by her: the first at the International Psychoanalytical Congress in Wiesbaden, and the second at the second Four Nations Congress in Budapest. The shorter texts were all published in Gyermeknevelés (Child Education). They were, for the most part, answers to questions raised in seminars with parents, or in letters addressed to the journal. The titles included: «Thumbsucking», «Excessive Masturbation in Children», «The Problem of Informing Children», «Modesty», «When and What to Tell Children», and discussed many issues commonly encountered in families. The articles are easy and pleasant to read thanks to numerous clinical examples and to the author's sense of humour. As always, Alice Balint, faithful to Ferenczi's teaching, helps to reformulate questions in a more useful way, rather than providing ready-made answers.

MICHAEL BALINT

Michael Balint, whose biography and work I presented in detail earlier, was the best-known member of this « dynasty » of analysts. Contrary to Alice Balint, who died in 1939 at 40, and Vilma Kovács, who died in 1940 at 56, Michael Balint had time to develop his ideas and to see them become known through wide publication.

Throughout his life, Balint, Ferenczi's literary executor, worked to spread his teacher's ideas and have them accepted. Balint was convinced that these highly controversial ideas, often rejected or ignored, had simply been put forth fifty years too early, and that they would gradually be integrated into analytic thinking. Time proved him right. Today, Ferenczi's texts are translated in all languages, and conferences, seminars and study groups are dedicated to his ideas. This is in great part due to Balint, who deciphered his notes, his *Clinical Journal* and his correspondence with Freud.

I hope that I have shed light on the common elements present in the analytic work of Vilma Kovács, Alice Balint and Michael Balint, and that I have shown how all three of them are pupils and followers of Sándor Ferenczi. One of the key precepts they all adopted and applied was to always have the courage to pursue one's own original ideas. This may have caused them to share their teacher's fate in the sense that their work is not sufficiently known and is often considered outdated even before being read, studied thoroughly and applied.

CHAPTER 4
OTHER WRITINGS

FROM INFANTILE CURIOSITY TO SCIENCE
In Honour of Paul Roazen

In his beautiful speech at the congress on "One Hundred Years of Psychoanalysis", held in Geneva in September 1993[1], Olivier Flournoy expressed surprise at the inexhaustible curiosity of psychoanalysts about the private lives of their great ancestors. He noted, quite rightly, that psychoanalysis is the only science in which one encounters such an eagerness to know everything about the pioneers of the profession, to dissect every detail of their lives. Flournoy advised his colleagues to abandon these indescrete investigations and turn their interest to subjects more deserving of their attention.

Struck by the accuracy of his statements, I wondered if there were not, after all, some good reasons why analysts care so passionately about the personal qualities of those who founded their science. Of course, psychoanalysis has taught us how significant these intimate details are when it comes to the human psyche. In addition, there is no other science in which one works to such an extent with one's own personality, particularities, experiences, emotions, dreams, fantasies and desires — in short, one's own subjectivity. Therefore, it is not very far-fetched to suppose that psychoanalysis as it was passed down to us, with its theories and practice, is rooted in the innermost worlds and private lives of these pioneers, in the most secret recesses of their psyche. This makes it easier to understand the strong inclination of their heirs to look into the depths that are the source of the knowledge and the practice to which they themselves dedicate their lives. The very nature of their profession impels them to do so.

But was this curiosity not already present in them before this? Did it not contribute to the choice of their profession? This brings us to the frequently asked question of what deep motivation drives someone to become a psychoanalyst.

---

1   Flournoy, O., "Métapsychoanalyse", in *100 Years of Psychoanalysis*, special edition of the General Psychiatric Notebooks, published by Karnac Books, pp. 267–270; article published in *Le Coq-Héron*, No. 134, 1994: "Cent ans de psychanalyse".

The answers are numerous and vary from one person to another. But a few common elements seem to emerge. There is curiosity, of course: a motivation shared by all those who choose a field involving investigation of any kind. This is scientific curiosity, but with an underlayer of a more primitive nature: the curiosity of the child about the intimate lives of the adults around him, first of all his own parents. We could be right to think that every human being experiences this curiosity, and that in some ways it lasts a lifetime. What else could explain the success of books such as Anatole France en pantoufles[2] (Anatole France in Slippers), Monsieur Proust, narrated by his governess[3], or The Diary of Samuel Pepys[4] and other biographies and personal correspondence. The recent attack launched by the ex-mistress of a French political personality, which became such a success that the book sold hundreds of thousands of copies, is a case in point. To say nothing of gossip magazines and tabloids. These publications focus on the private lives of the rich and famous — royal families, world leaders, famous performers, artists, and other celebrities. In short, possible parental substitutes. And clearly the secrets which most interest the public are details about their sex lives. It seems that most human beings, in adulthood, are still holding on to an idealised image of what a "real adult" would be. Few people think that they have reached a real and complete state of maturity, whether it be in the professional or personal sphere. And those who try the hardest to appear mature are probably those who most doubt that they are; they will keep trying to discover how someone has to behave to feel truly and unquestionably like an adult. They think that following the example of "great men", or imitating them outright, might be a way to do it. I am tempted to say that those who stay in close touch with their own childhood have the best chance to become adults. Of course, psychoanalysts, or analyst candidates, are also subject to this universal motivation, although it is not the only one. Perhaps even more than in the case of other people, their curiosity — associated with each person's particular types of problems — is turned towards what takes place in the inner world, their own and that of others. Then, once they

---

2   Brousson, J.-J., *Anatole France en pantoufles*, Paris: Grès, G., 1924.

3   Albaret, C., *Monsieur Proust. Souvenirs recueillis par Georges Belmont*, Laffont, 2001.

4   Pepys, S., *The Diary of Samuel Pepys*, London: George Bell & Sons, 1893.

set out on the path of psychoanalytic training, everything combines to intensify this infantile curiosity about the "grown-ups" of this world. Naturally, any "apprentice" wants to acquire the knowledge, real or imagined, of his "masters". But psychoanalytic training begins in a very particular way, with individual analysis, whose goal is not to acquire knowledge, but rather to face one's own life experiences. The candidate is not with a mere teacher, but with someone who will acquire considerable importance in his life, someone who will play the most varied roles in his inner theatre: father, mother, friend or adversary, offering protection or constituting a threat. As a result, it is natural that this person's every act, gesture, word, public or private action, will be interpreted by his analysand as having a more or less direct connection with him. Nothing about his analyst leaves him indifferent; everything elicits an emotional reaction. This is the phenomenon of transference, which can reach great intensity, as we see in a letter sent by Ferenczi to Freud, after having been analysed briefly by the latter. In this letter, he uses the expression "the furnace of transference".

At some stage of his own analysis, the apprentice analyst starts to work. He now calls on an elder, called a supervisor, to talk about his clinical work, in the hope of receiving enlightening feedback. These supervisors, in turn, come to occupy a more or less prestigious place, and to inspire varying degrees of ambivalence, in the trainees' inner world. Finally, at the end of their training, the young analysts most often find themselves in the same circles as their supervisors, which does not facilitate the resolution — always difficult — of the transference... and its counterpart, the countertransference. It is probably the conjunction of these multiple transferences which produces the intense circulation of emotional reactions and gossip of all sorts in psychoanalytic milieus. Whether one participates in this or not depends on the strength of the defence set up to oppose one's primitive curiosity.

This transference onto the analyst or, to a lesser degree, onto the supervisor, is already present as transference towards these first analysts of the past who have remained present for their successors through their works and the organisations they founded. Some of their followers adopt their theories in whole or in part. They remain fiercely loyal to the school of the master they have chosen, they dissect his every word with deferential awe, reproducing faithfully their vocabulary and expressions, and sometimes even their ways of doing things. But the works of the ancestors can also be rejected, misunderstood, distorted, adopted in a falsified form, and even more or less deliberately ignored. The nature of transference can be very diverse.

Thus, infantile curiosity expresses itself not only with respect to those masters one personally met, but also with respect to the forerunners who analysed those who analysed these masters. The transference onto our analytic "ancestors" is kept alive by the impressions they have left on the analytic community through this filiation of analysed analysts, and everything they passed on through their professional, personal and private writing. Interest in these personal and private writings is so strong that once their works are published — and sometimes before — their correspondence, personal journals, notebooks, datebooks and miscellaneouos draft notes are published. Then there are the memoirs and other books of recollections written by their descendants, their close acquaintances, their physicians, their friends, colleagues, pupils, or even patients. Based on these avidly awaited texts, countless articles attempt to scrutinise the lives, origins, deeds, activities, words and inner lives of our fathers and mothers in the world of analysis. Some authors turn this scrutiny into works of great interest, such as the article by Carlo Bonomi, who tries to explain, based on some passages of Freud's biography, why Freud hid his experience in the pediatric field, to which he devoted ten years of his life[5]. Others, whose curiosity remains more primitive, attempt to discover the exact nature of Freud's relationship with his sister-in-law Minna Bernays, or the bounds of Ferenczi's involvement with Elma, the daughter of Gizella, his long-time mistress and future wife.

We must admit, then, that this curiosity about the private lives of the illustrious ancestors is deeply rooted in the human psyche, and that it manifests itself in an exceptionally powerful way in those who choose to become psychoanalysts, even before their training and the practice of their profession intensify this initial tendency.

Of course, one may ask what is the good of giving in to this infantile tendency, and insisting on going back to the deep internal sources that gave rise to the work of the famous ancestors, in an attempt to reconstitute the path

---

5   Bonomi, C., "Why Have We Ignored Freud the Pediatrician?", in *100 Years of Psychoanalysis*, special edition of Cahiers psychiatriques (Psychiatric Notebooks), op. cit., pp. 55–100.

they followed. Why not repress this curiosity and be content with the rich content of their works, in the form in which they left them to us?

Each one of us can then use these works as we see fit, depending on our personality and abilities. Or we can examine them critically and enrich them with our own discoveries. This work would be substantial enough. What, then, are the reasons for infantile curiosity to push the investigations into the private lives of "the great" to the limits of indiscretion, and even beyond? Why do we want to penetrate into the inner sanctums where ideas and inventions are concocted?

And yet, can we consider a work, be it literary, artistic or scientific, as being entirely separate from the personality of its author? Of course, sometimes we must do this, as for instance in cases where the authors of remarkable works are completely unknown to us, like the painters of prehistoric caves, or the authors of anonymous texts. But how triumphant we feel when we succeed in identifying one of them! And as soon as we know a little about them, we feel the need to analyse, to interpret what we have learned of their private lives, and to draw conclusions about their personalities. This is not, of course, the equivalent of a psychoanalysis, even when it is Freud who writes essays on Leonardo da Vinci, Goethe or Michelangelo. What he is writing could be called a psychological analysis essay. And the motivations might be somewhat different than those discussed above.

But if we examine more closely the motivations for these indiscreet intrusions into the private lives of our analyst ancestors, we find a whole variety of more or less contradictory sentiments: respect, recognition, sincere interest, even love, but also hate, jealousy and rivalry in some cases. Love, admiration and respect probably impel us to discover the personal depths from which the first analysts drew their inventions; to understand how Freud could conduct his autoanalysis, how he could go far enough to reach the constitutive elements of his own dreams; and how Ferenczi dared to confront and examine his own internal confusion, so as to write a work like the Clinical Diary. We would like to know what gave them the courage to accomplish these feats.

Sometimes, more ambivalent feelings could be involved in the motivation to explore the unexplored regions of the ancestors' inner world, regions they themselves were unable to explore: their weaknesses, their inadequacies and their blind spots. There may be a desire to show oneself more astute than they were. In some people, this can become outright aggressivity: they want to dethrone the great man, to kill him morally and scientifically, show that his discoveries had petty origins, or that he simply stole other people's ideas. We can suspect these iconoclasts of having all kinds of motivations, like jealousy, the need to compensate for a feeling of inferiority, or anxiety provoked by ideas which frighten them.

A negative reaction may also be provoked by the impression that the illustrious ancestors have discovered everything essential, and that their descendants can only develop and expand their ideas by making small additions. What comes to mind are certain heirs to large fortunes, who feel smothered by the wealth they suddenly inherit, manage it more or less poorly and without pleasure, or refuse it. Of course, in psychoanalysis like in the financial world, there are creative spirits who can innovate without turning their backs on what they inherited.

Another motivation — a positive one — may also be present: to give back to the great man, glorified and idealised by some, his human qualities, to depict him as a fellow man who can be understood and accepted in all his human complexity. This attitude eliminates the temptation to transform his ideas into a rigid doctrine and his texts into sacred writings, both of which neutralise thought and paralyse imagination.

But whatever the motivations, the attempt to intrude into the privacy of the pioneers of our science, or that of any other creator, constitutes a violation of their private lives and their secrets, because it goes beyond what they chose to reveal to us. This kind of investigation raises questions similar to those we had to answer when we wondered if opening Egyptian tombs, unwrapping mummies or dissecting corpses frozen for thousands of years was sacrilegious and showed lack of respect, or reflected a legitimate desire to acquire knowledge. What degree of invasion can we justify in the name of scientific research? Where are the limits imposed by the respect of the living and of the dead? How much time does it take to transform private lives into history? After how much time can we allow ourselves to subject objects, texts, even human bodies, to the extraordinary means of investigation available to us today for dissecting, analysing and exploring everything they can teach us?

Many researchers asked themselves these questions, but went beyond the limits they themselves established, because the desire to know and understand was stronger than all the rest.

I was part of a small group of people which translated into French the personal correspondence between Freud and Ferenczi, and had it published. One of the commentators, Ernst Falzeder, insisted on placing this epigraph in Volume 1, reproducing some lines from Heinrich Heine's *Memoirs*: "It is a forbidden and immoral act to publish even as little as a line by an author who had not him — or herself intended it for the public at large, and this applies particularly to letters addressed to private individuals. Anyone who publishes or commits them to print is guilty of a disloyalty which deserves our contempt".

Nonetheless, we went ahead and did this. Falzeder himself felt the need to add this comment:

"These letters which follow were not written for the greater public. They are nevertheless passed on for publication here; this, in the interest of psychoanalysis — which cannot be separated from personalities — and to provide access to historical truth[6]".

Paul Roazen, the historian to whom I pay tribute here, obviously shares with psychoanalysts — and many others — this primitive curiosity, given that he became a historian of psychoanalysis. When the time comes, his future biographers will have to uncover the roots of his deep interest in this field. Each of his numerous works forced him to study countless documents and interview all available witnesses. He then tried to explain the facts, understand the personality of the protagonists and establish the sequence of events.

His writings have aroused passion and controversy. He is undoubtedly a conscientious historian, who only presents well-documented facts; but his view of these facts is necessarily subjective. Just as subjective as the view his readers have of what he writes, particularly when they are psychoanalysts directly concerned by the people he describes in his works.

---

6   Freud, S., Ferenczi, S., *The Correspondence of Sigmund Freud and Sándor Ferenczi*, Vol 1, Harvard University Press, 1993.

Human curiosity — whether it focuses on science, psychoanalysis, history or the words and deeds of those around us — is limitless. Only time can tell where it has led us and where it will lead us. But it drives us forward unavoidably, in a direction we like to call — rightly or wrongly — progress.

WHAT IS LOVE ?[7]

"What is love?" Freud asks in a letter to Martha, quoting Shakespeare's *Twelfth Night*. There are as many answers as there are couples. As Freud wrote Ferenczi concerning Otto Rank's marriage: "[...] one certainly can't judge in these matters, not on behalf of another, either. In nothing is another so different[8]". The Freud couple is not exempt from this singularity.

Martha and Sigmund seem to have been an unexceptional couple, with no particular problems, as happy people are often described. But, in fact, their relationship might have surprised our contemporaries. The Freud couple seems to have constructed a happy life of sorts, but not what a present-day couple, or even every couple in their time, would consider happiness.

When Sigmund met Martha, a friend of his sisters, what he felt was love at first sight. Love at first sight implies that one projects on someone who is attractive and has pleasant manners everything one expects to find in a partner, without really knowing what is involved, or really knowing that person. Freud saw Martha as the only woman for him, and was determined to mould her into the woman he wanted, who would fit his image of a wife. The task did not prove too easy, as we can see when we read the letter Sigmund wrote to Martha on June 30, 1884, a letter in which he resumes the history of their relationship:

"To take a retrospective glance as you do is quite justified; I really think I have always loved you much more than you me, or more correctly [...], that I forced myself upon you and you accepted me without any great affection. I know it has finally changed and this success, which I

---

7   Revised version of the Introduction to Katja Behling's book *Martha Freud, la femme du génie*, Albin Michel, 2006.

8   Freud, S., Ferenczi, S., *The Correspondence of Sigmund Freud and Sándor Ferenczi*, op. cit., Vol 2, 1996.

CHAPTER 4: OTHER WRITINGS

wanted more than anything else, and the prolonged absence of which has been my greatest misery, gives me hope for the other successes which I still need.

Do you remember how you often used to tell me that I had a talent for repeatedly provoking your resistance? How we were always fighting, and you would never give in to me? We were two people who diverged in every detail of life and who were yet determined to love each other and did love each other. And then, after no hard words had been exchanged between us for a long time, I had to admit to myself that you were indeed my beloved, but so seldom took my side that no one would have realized from your behavior that you were preparing to share my life; and you admitted that I had no influence over you. I found you so fully matured and every corner in you occupied, and you were hard and reserved and I had no power over you. This resistance of yours only made you the more precious to me, but at the same time I was very unhappy [...]"[9]

Little by little, during the period when they were separated, and perhaps thanks to this separation (Freud lived in Vienna and Martha had gone back to her family in Wandsbeck, near Hamburg), things improved between them. Freud seems to say that although Martha's letters are not tender, they show that he is important to her: "[...] many wounds that went deeper than you know have been closed, and I feel within me a gaiety and a self-confidence which for a whole year had been unknown to me[10]". But he fears that Martha may lose her illusions about him during the time they spend together.

Freud's letters to Martha, which constitute over a third of the correspondence published under the title Letters of Sigmund Freud (1873–1939) by Basic Books, are an essential source of information for understanding what kind of relationship these two very different beings shared. What prevents us from understanding this relationship more fully is the fact that apparently none of Martha's letters have been preserved; the book only contains a number of Freud's letters, selected by their son Ernst. We know that on several occasions throughout his life Freud imposed a sentence of autodafé on various correspondence and notes. He liked to say that he wanted to complicate the task of his future biographers. But he said explicitly that he kept Martha's

---

9 Freud, S., *Letters of Sigmund Freud*, Freud, Ernst L. (Ed.), Basic Books, 1960, pp. 117–118.
10 ibid.

letters. Therefore, she must have destroyed them herself before she died. When he speaks in one of his letters of

"your [...] wisdom about love and life[11]", we can only regret not being able to read her letter. Indeed, we only glimpse Martha's desires and opinions through Freud's reaction to them.

Freud won Martha, despite her reticence, after a valiant struggle. But not by trying to hide from her what he was really like, or what he expected of her. He knew what he wanted and it seems that he was able to get part of it, but probably not everything. Incidentally, his expectations were somewhat contradictory. He had a certain idea of what women should be, and more specifically, THE woman, an expectation essentially consistent with the feminine model of his time. In fact, his ideal was a subtle mix of the conventional model and his own deep desires. On the one hand, he wanted a woman who would be his equal; in his letters, he wrote Martha at length about his work, his research, his patients. Unfortunately, there are no documents to let us know what her response might have been. But Katja Behling's biography describes her as having a firm character, solid intelligence and an independent turn of mind.

On the other hand, while he wanted to share his intellectual pursuits with Martha, Freud rejected the very modern vision of women presented, for instance, by Stuart Mill, a philosopher he admired and whose work he had even translated into German. Describing him to Martha, he wrote: "[...] he lacked the sense of the absurd, on several points, for instance in the emancipation of women [...]. I dare say we agree that housekeeping and the care and education of children claim the whole person and practically rule out any profession; even if simplified conditions relieve the woman [...]". And he goes on to say: "It seems a completely unrealistic notion to send women into the struggle for existence in the same way as men[12]".

Freud's vision of women did not progress much over the years. In his 1931 article entitled "Female Sexuality"[13], a very interesting article in many respects, there are passages such

---

11   Freud, S., *Letters of Sigmund Freud*, op. cit., p. 95. (Letter January 29, 1884).
12   ibid., pp. 75–76. (Letter November 15, 1883).
13   Freud, S. (1931) *Female Sexuality*, S.E. 21: 224–43, London: Hogarth.

as" "One thing that is left over in men from the influence of the Oedipus complex is a certain amount of disparagement in their attitude towards women, whom they regard as being castrated". And speaking of the woman, Freud says: "She acknowledges the fact of her castration, and with it, too, the superiority of the male and her own inferiority; but she rebels against this unwelcome state of affairs[14]". There are long passages about the way the little girl tries to manage her "deficiency", that is, her "biological inferiority". Strangely, the article does not mention the uterus, this "secret weapon" of women which gives them the power of life or death over all unborn children. Yet, the existence and function of this formidable organ determines an important element of the panoply of emotions which pervade the relationship between men and women, as the learned neurologist Paul J. Möbius acknowledged: "If woman was not physically and mentally weak, [...] she would be extremely dangerous[15]".

The ambivalence resulting from this state of affairs seems to be present in the Freud couple as well, judging by the voluminous correspondence between different members of the family. The habit of regarding women as inferior, encountered in exchanges between various people, as well as in psychoanalytic theory, is an expression of this ambivalence. The theory of penis envy in women is an example of this. It is not too far-fetched to think that women's social condition until recent times could, in and of itself, be almost sufficient to explain the existence of such penis envy. For we must remember that this enviable penis represented, at the time, a whole set of opportunities such as access to culture, the right to have and satisfy personal ambitions, the right to be a legal entity and the right to do business, and even to vote and participate in public life.

Clearly, progress in regard to women's social position did not eliminate this symptom, because the "penis" does not represent only the symbolic organ of masculine power. Maria Torok, who dedicated an article and a number of commentaries to the subject, and who recognises the socio-cultural legitimacy of this penis envy, has succeeded in untangling its deep psychic roots, its structure and its true object. Beyond the social aspect, Maria Torok has shown that "penis envy" was a ploy masking the desire of the

---

14   ibid., p. 229.
15   Möbius, P. J., *Über den physiologischen Schwachsinn des Weibes* (On the Physiological Idiocy of Women), Nabu Press, 2010.

girl — forbidden by her mother and her family — to use the relational possibilities of her body by receiving the penis of a man and experiencing pleasure. Torok concludes her article with these thoughts:

"[...] it is not obvious a priori that men should naturally want such a relationship of mastery. The falsity, the ambivalence, and the refusal of identifications it conceals should appear to him as so many snags on which his own full and authentic achievement comes to grief. And yet... who would doubt that in order to achieve his own interests in superiority man is almost universally the accomplice of woman's state of dependence and that he thrives in elevating all this into religious, metaphysical, or anthropological principles. What interest has he in giving in to his need to dominate the being through whom he could understand himself and who could understand him?[16]"

In other words, according to Maria Torok, women will always have to resolve possible penis envy, resulting from their relationship with the mother, but men would be well-advised not to involve themselves in this problem.

Nonetheless, when Freud speaks of the protection women need, and of the incongruity of exposing them to the need to work and earn a living, he is clearly seeing the situation exclusively from the perspective of the bourgeoisie — his own social class. But in fact, even in his time women of the working class worked, kept house and raised their children just as well as women of the bourgeoisie, who delegated most of these tasks to servants. Later, when a few women in his own milieu began to practice psychoanalysis and earn an income of their own, Freud probably modified his views to some extent. As Martha's fiancé, Freud was a passionate and romantic man. In his letters, he called Martha "My beloved girl", "My dearest treasure", "My sweet princess"... Once they were married, she became "My beloved Old Dear", or just "Beloved Old Dear", or sometimes "My dearest". And he would sign his letters "Sigmund", or "Papa".

In one of the letters, Freud let his future wife know what her life after marriage would be like. There would be no more romantic walks and declarations of affection. They would see each other less because Freud would be absorbed in his work and Martha would be kept busy by her housekeeping chores and the rearing of the children.

---

16   Abraham, N., Torok, M., *The Shell and the Kernel*, University of Chicago Press, 1994.

In the meantime, money problems are a constant worry for the young fiancé. He talks about it constantly in his letters to Martha. Buying a train ticket, a new hat or a gift for his future mother-in-law constitutes a serious difficulty. Indeed, most of the time Freud is struggling to survive, and the Bernays are not well-off either. This concern is no doubt also related to the fact that the Freud family, just like the Bernays family, has been hiding a stain on the family honour, a shameful event related to money. An uncle who was a counterfeiter, in Freud's case — the notorious Uncle Joseph — , and in the Bernays family, the fact that Martha's father served a prison sentence for bankruptcy fraud. In any event, both families agreed that there could be no marriage before the young suitor was able to support a family. For all these reasons, Freud considered it essential that professional success be accompanied by financial success.

In the end, Martha chose to comply entirely with her fiancé's desires, and then to those of her husband. It was not submission on her part, it was not that she was giving in. It seems to have been a deliberate choice, dictated by love, by duty and by the pleasure she took in things well done: a well-kept house, well-brought-up children, respect for the work and the requirements of the master of the house. As for Freud, it seems that he never neglected his duties as a husband and father either. The only question raised in this regard was the nature of his relations with Minna, Martha's sister, who was often his confidante and travel companion. Contrary to Martha, Minna had neither husband nor children, and no house to look after. Knowing the degree of intimacy reached by Freud's relationship with Minna presents no interest other than serving to understand more fully the very warm relationship between the two sisters, which was apparently cloudless and lasted until Minna's death. Could this relationship have included even the sharing of a man, or was it the case that the question never had to be raised?

Thus, Martha was a very controlled person, she showed perfect self-discipline, displaying level-headedness on numerous occasions, as we can see when we read Katja Behling's book. She always did everything to prevent tension in the family, she never complained and she never asked for anything. She witnessed her husband's passionate friendships with men without mixing in or showing any jealousy. With some rare exceptions. One of these exceptions is described in detail in a letter written by Freud on August 20, 1893 to his close friend Wilhelm Fliess:

"My beloved friend,

With anyone else I would, first of all, be embarrassed to cancel after I had definitely agreed to come and, second, give different reasons than those which I shall tell you in all frankness. Thus, the following piece of home psychology: I spent the 18th and 19th on a complicated tour around and on Mount Rax with my friend Rie, and yesterday sat in a cheerful mood in the new hut on the mountain when suddenly someone entered the room, completely flushed from the heat of the day, whom initially I stared at as at an apparition and then had to recognize as my wife. Martha has always maintained that climbing was impossible for her and that she did not enjoy staying on the mountain. But now she has followed me, had borne up well under the strain, and was enchanted by the view and the place. She expressed the wish to spend several days with me up here, where the accommodations are excellent, and I felt obliged to afford her this pleasure — which is possible, so to speak, without feeling remote from home, because from up here one can stay in touch with Reichenau by telephone and easily get down in two and a half hours. She had been looking forward to the trip to Csorba so very much. The events at home had shown her how difficult it is to make arrangements for leaving the children, and for the past six years, since child followed child, there has been little room for change and relaxation in her life. I do not believe I can deny her this wish. You can imagine what is behind it; gratitude, a feeling of coming back to life again of the woman who for the time being does not have to expect a child for a year because we are now living in abstinence; and you know the reasons for this as well. Now, this plan does not at all agree with my intention to visit you in Csorba[17]".

It seems that on this occasion Martha had wanted to accompany her husband on his visit to Fliess, but her family duties had prevented this. As a result, and altogether exceptionally, she arranged things so the visit would not take place, and her husband would spend some vacation time with her.

Martha was not in the habit of talking about her feelings, and therefore it is difficult to know what price she paid for being a supportive wife in all circumstances. But certain signs indicate, discreetly, that there might have been a price

---

17 Freud, S., *The Complete Letters of Sigmund Freud to Wilhelm Fliess*, Harvard University Press, 1985, pp. 53–54.

to pay. For instance, Martha was religious, while Freud was a convinced atheist. It was out of the question to carry out religious practices in his house. Martha adapted. She gave up Shabbat candles, Jewish holidays, kosher food. But eight days after Freud's death, she relit the Shabbat candles stored in a cupboard for fifty years. In addition, she had almost completely given up conjugal relations at the age of 34, since this was the only fool-proof contraceptive method available at the time (given that Freud refused to use condoms), and she had frequent, violent and unexplained migraines.

Martha seems not to have longed for any personal accomplishment other than her function in the family. She expressed her creativity through needlework, an activity she loved and practiced all her life. She liked to read (some good novels and historical works, according to Paula Fichtl, Freud's loyal servant); she rarely attended social events.

If we are to believe Esti, the wife of Freud's eldest son, Martin, Martha was somewhat looked down upon by Freud's students, who considered her dull and self-effacing. Gradually, it was Anna who replaced her mother as her father's companion. As we can imagine, this involved jealousy and suffering on both sides. The fact that Anna was analysed by her father created a close bond between them, as did her choice of a profession. As for Martha, she looked at psychoanalysis more or less as most people of her era did, with skepticism mixed with irony, as Esti confided to Paul Roazen in an interview.

To give a brief and possibly biased summary of attitudes in the Freud family, we could say that Freud loved psychoanalysis more than anything, including himself, while Martha loved an orderly life and peaceful family relations.

It would be difficult to imagine a present-day couple living like the Freuds. This is not only because of their respective personalities, but is also related to social life in their era, particularly that of the Viennese bourgeoisie.

Vienna during the reign of Emperor Franz Joseph was a major metropolis, the capital of a multi-ethnic empire, as described by the famous traveler of the 19th century, Victor Tissot. In Vienna, the Slavs, the Hungarians, the Italians and the Poles mixed with the Germanic population. In the cafés, there were newspapers in all these languages. Each ethnic group had its specialty: a majority of Czechs were government employees, while Hungarians held political positions. Tissot describes Vienna as a joyous city where much time was spent in amusement and where people worked little, except for Jews, many of them doctors and lawyers who were hard-working, and whom the population blamed for the consequences of its own frivolity.

Historian François Fejtö[18] described the city in these terms:

"[...] after surviving the 1873 financial crash, the first crisis of capitalism, followed by a cholera epidemic, Vienna (like all monarchies) became a city with two faces: the quasi provincial Vienna of the lower bourgeoisie, of traditionalist, anticapitalist tradesmen, with the Corso on the Ring swarming with "Süsse Mädel" (charming girls) — an expression invented by Arthur Schnitzler — and seductive officers; and the city of workers, engineers, employees, intellectuals and artists, where twenty languages were spoken[19]".

Fejtö also comments on the antisemitic reaction that followed the emancipation of the Jews and the liberal trend; Freud suffered the consequences of this reaction.

The situation was very different in Hamburg, the Bernays' hometown. Victor Tissot, the tireless traveler, visited Hamburg as well. Contrary to the Viennese, the residents of Hamburg, both rich and poor, worked hard. Money changed hands quickly, and people became overly confident. Fortunes were made and lost easily, only to be remade and lost again. We know that Martha's father did not escape this fate. But, unfortunately for the Bernays, he was unable to rebuild his wealth.

What kind of education did Martha receive as a child and young girl? In his book *The World of Yesterday*, Stefan Zweig describes at length the education system of the 19th century. But there is no mention anywhere of the education of girls. The only reference to young women is in a passage where Zweig describes student life in his circles:

"Every penny of our pocket money went on the theatre, concerts or books, and we did not feel it was important to appeal to girls when our minds were bent on impressing higher authorities. In fact, going out with girls seemed to us a waste of time, since in our intellectual arrogance we

---

18 François Fejtö (1909–2008), historian and journalist of Hungarian origin.
19 Fejtö, F., *Requiem pour un empire défunt. Histoire de la destruction de l'Autriche-Hongrie*, Lieu Commun, 1989.

regarded the opposite sex as intellectually inferior by their very nature, and we didn't want to spend our valuable time in idle chatter[20]".

Thus, we have only a vague idea of the education Martha might have received, first in Hamburg and then in Vienna. As Celia Bertin tells us: "In the culture created by men, girls were taught above all the traditional things allowing them to become women who accepted their fate willingly and without comment[21]". In school, they learned to read, write and count, and were taught a few rules of hygiene and morality. Sometimes they learned some history. But before 1904 no girls' school went as far as a secondary-school diploma, and there were no girls in universities. In 1907, a few universities opened their doors to girls, but the future psychoanalyst Helene Deutsh, for instance, had to enroll in Medical School because women were not admitted into the Law Faculty she wished to attend.

We know that Martha was a typical product of the education of her time. Katja Behling's book describes the life of this woman — wife of a man of genius — , a life which conformed to the model of the era, the life of a woman who chose to remain in the background in order to serve the needs and desires of her husband, and who did it knowingly, willingly, without complaint or recrimination. But given her strength of character and her intelligence, we may well ask what the life of the Freud couple would have been like if they had lived a half century later.

TRAUMAS

Some Theories Tested by Clinical Practice

The question of trauma is one of the oldest problems encountered by psychoanalysis. We know that Freud based his initial theory of hysteria on the existence of actual trauma, only to reconsider later and opt for a theory of pathogenic fantasy. According to others, like Ferenczi, there is a real trauma, or traumas, at the root of any neurosis.

In the early days of psychoanalysis, the main object of reflection was sexual trauma, particularly trauma to which young children were subjected by adults. Subsequent

---

20   Zweig, S., *The World of Yesterday*, University of Nebraska Press, 2013.
21   Bertin, C., *Marie Bonaparte: A Life*, Yale University Press, 1987.

events were thought to become pathogenic because they overlay these early infantile traumas. Then, little by little, especially due to the massive traumas inflicted by the two world wars on adults as well as on children, researchers were faced with increasingly complex questions. It was during the First World War that psychoanalysts first took an interest in these massive traumas, when they studied war neuroses. But their interest faded with the end of the war. It was the enormous number of people traumatised by the deportations, bombardments and massacres of the last sixty years that revived the interest of psychoanalysts in trauma-related problems.

However, the various psychic mechanisms involved in different kinds of trauma are far from being completely understood. The question I ask myself is whether the same theoretical tools can be applied to traumas as varied as the refusal to accept the birth of a sibling, abandonment, sexual aggression by an adult, deportation to a concentration camp, or the massacre of one's family in machete attacks? Are the differences only quantitative, or qualitative as well?

We know that no human being can avoid experiencing some traumatic situations in his lifetime, right from the start, no matter how loved, cared for, appreciated and protected he may be. Otto Rank has shown us that postnatal life even starts with a trauma — that of birth. Of course, we should study in depth the differences between the consequences of an easy or difficult birth, quick or extended, with or without forceps, or by Cesarian section. Advocates of birth without violence consider that checking procedures carried out at birth are needless traumas, and prefer to give precedence to emotional needs, to contact with the maternal odour, voice and body, which have been the reassuring universe of the baby, and leave the checks for later.

We know even less about traumas suffered *in utero*. Yet during its intrauterine life, the fetus can be subjected to all kinds of aggressions: deprivation or illness of the mother, blows, voluntary intoxication (alcohol, tobacco, various street drugs, medications), involuntary intoxication, etc. We are fairly well aware of the physical effects, but we know very little about the postnatal psychic consequences of such aggressions.

However, it has never been possible to establish with certainty what events or situations will produce traumatic effects. Moreover, the intensity of the pathogenic effect and that of the trauma are not necessarily equal. The same trauma can produce a more or less serious pathology in certain people, while other people only remember experiencing passing displeasure, or forget the event entirely. The following story illustrates this point. Two little girls, both about ten years old, had the experience of meeting an exhibitionist. The first was walking by a public toilet when a man came out with his fly wide open and called to her to "come and see". The little girl ran home screaming, her father jumped in his car and chased the man, but was unable to catch him. The family reported the incident to the police, and the child had to recount what happened. Later, discussing this event filled many sessions of the analysis the girl undertook as an adult. The second little girl found herself sitting across from an exhibitionist in the subway. When she got home, she told her parents that a man had wanted to show her his wee wee. She said: "When someone shows me something, I look. But it was really not very nice". Her parents explained that there are some unfortunate men in the world who can only feel pleased when they can frighten little girls. The child quickly forgot the incident. Clearly, sexual matters were not treated the same way in the two families, and this is what led to different reactions on the part of the two children subjected to the same aggression. The first girl was the youngest in a family of religious, conservative shopkeepers, who had to entrust their children to a nursemaid until they were old enough to go to school; this "abandonment" left the parents feeling somewhat guilty. People didn't talk much in this family, and especially not about sexual matters. The parents of the other little girl were cultured, liberal teachers. In their home, the adults talked about everything, in front of and with the children.

In some cases, not only is there no effect of a trauma, but the experience leads to developing additional strength, once it has been faced and overcome (see Ferenczi and, more recently, Boris Cyrulnik and many others). This resistance, or resilience as it is now called, can strengthen the personality for the rest of someone's life. But resisting trauma "too well" can also have pathogenic effects, especially the need to develop more or less rigid defences too early. We see this in the case of children whose faculties develop very quickly, to enable them to "care for", or at least neutralise, a psychotic parent. This mechanism allows some people to build a fortress that offers them protection, but also imprisons them. The resulting split cuts them off from more or less essential portions of their psyche and, consequently, from the external world. Such a situation is exemplified by the story of an eight-year-old boy living in a city in northern France. When France was occupied by the Germans, his parents, naturalised Latvian Jews, were arrested while the child was at school. His parents had explained to him many times what he should do if this ever happened: go see the bookshop owner two streets away, who had agreed to find the child a place to stay if needed. The child followed these instructions and everything went as his parents had planned. The latter never came back after the war. The family which had taken in the boy raised him. He was a very good student, became an engineer and went on to have a brilliant career. He developed a well-structured personality, but very rigid and intolerant, which caused him to have a chaotic personal life, marked by more than one divorce and by clashes with friends. He was very interested in psychology and psychotherapeutic techniques, but never felt the need to undergo treatment himself.

Rigidification is one possible defensive reaction to trauma. Another protective mechanism could be, on the contrary, to become extremely malleable, never showing any resistance at all. People who have adopted this mechanism absorb blows by letting themselves be pushed and pulled in all directions, thanks to a very yielding structure. They are easily influenced, willing to forfeit personal judgment and avoid any conflict they feel unable to face. In this context, it is important not to confuse malleability with flexibility. The latter allows a subject, who has a well-developed capacity to judge and a reliable ability to test reality, to assess the dangers correctly and adjust his reactions. The following case is a good illustration of malleability. The woman in question is in her thirties, and unmarried. She is the youngest, and only girl, in a family of five children. Her father, a military man stationed abroad, has often moved the family from one country to another. Each time, the children are torn away from familiar surroundings, from their friends, their school, the language spoken around them, the customs, the climate. All the children had a very strict upbringing, their father hit them and even used his belt to beat them. He also terrorised his wife, who submitted entirely to his authority, not daring to defend herself or her children. The boys rebelled after a while, left home and gradually forced their father to respect them. The girl was left alone at home. When she was 16 or 17, she tried to date boys but was quickly reprimanded and her father kept a close eye on her activities. Her childhood friends all eventually married and lost touch with her. The young girl took secretarial courses, went to church regularly and continued to live at home until she was offered a job in another city. She became an obedient employee, anxious and unimaginative, who called her father to ask for advice as soon as she encountered a problem. She divided her time between her office and her studio apartment, where she cut articles and pictures out of magazines to paste them in notebooks. Since she was not advancing in her work and was not meeting anyone in her personal life, she was advised to start psychotherapy. For months, she went to her sessions regularly and paid attention to everything her therapist said, without comment, until one day she ventured to give an opinion, shyly, and solved a minor problem without asking for advice. It can be considered great progress that during a recent vacation she went on a two-week camping trip organised by her parish, with a group of young people of both sexes.

Speaking of the effects of trauma, another scenario is that of pathological collapse after a sort of leap forward, an exceptional professional success, in the case of a person who did not receive sufficient emotional support to develop a solid psychic structure. I shall present here briefly two cases where social advancement created a veritable chasm between the parents' milieu and that which became their child's. One case involves a man, the other a woman. In both cases, a difficult and destabilising childhood was followed by a brilliant professional career which placed them in a very different world than that of their childhood; both were exceptionally intelligent people. The man, Antoine, was the only son of relatively well-off Breton farmers. His parents were religious, rugged, hard-working pig breeders. They considered shows of affection out of place, be it between the parents or towards the child. The mother showed her affection by dispensing invasive physical care, followed by blaming the child for giving her so much work. Each time a litter of piglets was born, the father gave one to the boy, encouraging him to give it a name and care for it. When the animal was old enough to be slaughtered, it was taken away from him. These repeated massacres affected this man for the rest of his life. The family lived in isolation; it didn't associate with anyone nearby because their farm was the most prosperous and they were afraid of arousing envy. The boy was a brilliant student. He was admitted to the prestigious École polytechnique and became a ministerial adviser in matters related to the oil industry. He lived alone all his life, desperately trying to maintain contact with his parents by making frequent visits to the village and providing all kinds of aid to the commune. He is now retired, having had no career advancement despite his capabilities. His interminable psychotherapy can be described as follows: he comes close to the core of his problems with great sensitivity, and then blocks the process by displaying his own intuitions using pseudo-logical arguments. His interminable treatment came to an abrupt end when he did not arrive for an appointment made after an absence of several weeks. Two letters asking what he intended to do were never answered.

The second case ended in tragedy. Louise, the daughter of agricultural workers, was exceptionally intelligent. The principal of her school persuaded her parents to let her continue her studies. Her father, a chronic alcoholic, was killed in an automobile accident when the young girl was about twelve. The village doctor became her legal guardian. When she was about 16, Louise developed a severe depression and her guardian sent her to have psychotherapy. She studied mathematics, obtained a doctorate and became a researcher and university professor. This difficult situation became inescapable when her guardian fell in love with her and eventually married her. They had a son. The young woman became increasingly ill. She resumed therapy, changed analysts, had delusions, underwent repeated treatment in a psychiatric hospital, and finally committed suicide, ending her child's life at the same time.

I believe that in both cases, in addition to the many traumas experienced in childhood in the harsh atmosphere of their families, the exceptional talents of these two people, which caused a break with the milieu from which they came, contributed to creating a traumatic situation.

I spoke earlier of collective trauma: deportations, massacres or various forms of rejection or contempt for entire groups of people. Even without organised violence, lack of respect, condescendence and daily offences inflicted on these groups can constitute repeated trauma. Here too, reactions vary greatly: some people show resignation or disavowal, hate themselves (they identify with the aggressor, as Ferenczi would say); others rebel or even overestimate themselves; or, in the best case, try to protect themselves by affirming their worth as complete human beings, even if their countrymen or the laws of the State deny them this worth.

All kinds of theories have tried to define these different

traumatic situations. Before going on to examine some of them, I would like to state what I think we can expect a theory to do. All the different theories attempt to describe and explain the same phenomenon. What we expect of them is that they be efficient, and explain the phenomenon to the greatest extent possible, without creating a closed system that leaves no opening for future research. These theories can sometimes complete each other, but they can also contradict each other. Incidentally, I think that contradiction is always particularly interesting, because it indicates the point where the pursuit of the research is likely to be the most fertile. This is what Maria Torok and Nicholas Rand highlight in their book *Questions for Freud*[22], in which they point out all the internal unresolved contradictions in Freud's theories, and show that it is precisely at these junctures that other theoreticians were able to make the research advance. In addition, the modes of expression of different patients prompt us to have recourse to one or another of these theories. Moreover, our own language and convictions, or our theoretical affinities, also influence what we are looking at and what we perceive. Thus, every theory is subject to many variables and is suffused with subjectivity.

Among the many authors who have dealt with the question of trauma, I shall focus on Ferenczi and on those who claim to be his direct disciples. But first, I would like to mention Freud's changing views.

Freud went from the theory of a real trauma in every case to the theory of pathogenic fantasy in most cases, a theory he developed concerning his hysterical patients. However, he continued to think about this question almost until the end of his life, including in his last work, *Moses and Monotheism*, in which he examines the similarity between the history of the Jewish religion and the genesis of neuroses: in both instances, there is an early traumatic event, subsequently forgotten, then a period of latency, and finally an unexpected and apparently inexplicable manifestation. According to Freud, the traumatic effect is produced in two stages: the more or less silent occurrence of the trauma (real or fantasised) in early childhood, and the pathological reaction in puberty. The case of the little girl traumatised by an exhibitionist could be interpreted based on this theory. Freud also took an interest in the particular form of trauma caused by the loss of a loved person or of

---

22   Rand, N. & Torok, M., *Questions for Freud*, Harvard University Press, 2000.

an ideal that held an important place in the subject's life. I will come back to his article "Mourning and Melancholia", in my discussion of the work of Nicolas Abraham and Maria Torok.

The first author to take an interest in the specific question of trauma was Sándor Ferenczi. He dedicated most of his work to it during the last years of his life. In his trauma theory, he included what he had observed during the First World War in regard to the war neuroses, that is, the shock and paralysis when the trauma first occurs, and the need to relive it over and over, until a better outcome can be achieved.

Ferenczi concluded that there was an actual trauma at the origin of all psychic illness. If the therapeutic process is sufficiently deepened, he wrote, one always finds a trauma at the root of the illness. But Ferenczi considered that it is not the traumatic event itself which is pathogenic, but the way this event is handled by the subject and his entourage. We could say that it is not the trauma, but the reaction to it, which is potentially pathogenic. If the entourage reacts appropriately, the trauma can even become a factor which facilitates psychic development. The case of the second little girl, who met the exhibitionist in the subway, could serve to illustrate this.

But if the entourage reacts ineptly, or ignores the event altogether, if the child is disavowed, disbelieved or even scolded, the illness can progress to a second stage. Ferenczi's two stages are not the same as those of Freud. But I for one see no major contradiction between the two viewpoints. Ferenczi considers that the second stage occurs immediately after the trauma, and that a possible pathological aftermath would be a third stage corresponding to Freud's second. This difference is coherent with the general orientation of the two authors: Freud gave priority to intrapsychic processes, while Ferenczi put the relationship first.

The story of little Nathalie could serve to illustrate this type of pathogenic effect in three stages. This little girl was raped at the age of six by a close friend of the family in the bathroom of her home, where she was changing clothes after returning from the swimming pool. The man threatened that there would be consequences if she told anyone. After the rape, the two of them, hand in hand, went out to join the family (father, mother and six brothers and sisters) in the garden, for a joyful birthday party. "What a nice little girl your Nathalie is!" the friend said. "Yes, Nathalie is a very nice little girl", her father answered. From that day on, Nathalie became grumpy and irritable; she was no longer a nice little girl. For several years, not a word was said about what happened. When Nathalie was about ten, her father was killed in a work accident, before she had time to tell him what happened to her. Then, when she was thirteen, she had her period for the first time and her mother, now a widow and very close to the rapist friend, explained to her what this means. Nathalie realised, as she later put it, that this man had tried to give her a child, and she finally told her mother about the rape. Her mother believed her, but could not decide to bring up the matter with this man whose support was valuable to her, and whom she continued to welcome into her home as if nothing had happened. This is when, little by little, Nathalie started to have more serious problems, which led her to seek analysis fifteen years later.

To describe the mechanism of trauma, Ferenczi speaks of a split, or a series of splits, leading to fragmentation, to the atomisation of the personality. The goal is to preserve a healthy portion that can function, by separating it from the dysfunctional portion which is split off and encysted. Nathalie lived more or less well until puberty, without thinking too much about the traumatic event. This would correspond to Freud's latency period. Then, the event suddenly emerged in her memory when her mother explained about a girl's periods. This corresponds to Freud's second stage of the trauma. Ferenczi might say that the mother's inadequate response at this second Freudian stage redoubled the original disavowal — albeit involuntarily — by the father when the trauma first occurred.

Ferenczi also describes the possibility of a progression of the trauma, which he compares to the too rapid ripening of a fruit bitten by a bird: the child reacts to a traumatic situation or action inflicted by his parents by maturing very early so that he can protect them or, in some cases, be the caregiver of a psychotic parent. Louise's case could, to some degree, correspond to this explanation, until the final tragic decompensation. But this traumatic progression can sometimes have a more favourable outcome. Paula, a young South American woman who is now 28, was the child of apparently infantile parents who both behaved in a quasi incestuous way with their daughter. Paula was the older of two children. The parents, wealthy and idle, were entirely preoccupied with appearances; the family must present a perfect front: there are no problems and they all love each other. Anything that might interfere with this picture is simply kept quiet or denied outright. Paula goes along with this: she is the perfect child, a model student, and clings to her parents like they cling to her. But underneath, she is a veritable volcano ready to explode. Up to the age of twenty-two, Paula lived with her parents, finished her studies with top grades and went no further. She played the violin, practised sports, participated in the activities of "good society" in the company of her parents, but never met a man who meant anything to her. Then, suddenly, when she was twenty-two, she decided to go to Europe and study science. She saw her parents a few weeks a year, and when she was with them she became the model child they so badly needed. She now had an interesting job and her sex life was more active, although she was not yet able to establish lasting relationships. From a very young age, Paula had developed great self-control, learned not to show her feelings or her true capacities, in order to spare her immature parents. All these "wise baby" efforts produced some damage, which led Paula to undertake psychoanalysis in France.

To understand some traumatic processes, Ferenczi introduced the important notion of identification with the aggressor (not the same as Anna Freud's concept bearing the same name; she used the term to designate the fact that the child becomes an aggressor himself in response to a minor aggression he endured, imagined or feared). Ferenczi was speaking of something much more devastating: the subject — usually a child — who is aggressed identifies with his aggressor to try to re-establish a semblance of harmony with an aggressor when the latter is someone he needs and depends on. The child does this in order to safeguard the love and protection of the aggressor, since they are indispensable to him. The one who is aggressed may also identify with his aggressor in order to at least be able to admire, and to some extent acquire, his strength; so as not to be a totally helpless victim; to try to understand him and make peace with his actions; to be able to accept, or even find some benefit in, what he cannot stop from happening. This brings to mind the frequent cases of mistreated children who defend their abusive parents, or the cases in which abused women refuse to denounce their husbands. Ferenczi speaks of identification with the aggressor and of introjection of the aggressor without making a difference between them. He sees introjection as an attempt to widen one's ego to include the impulses felt in relation to the aggressor. We shall see below how Nicolas Abraham and Maria Torok developed and clarified these concepts. In my own opinion, identification could be seen as an immediate reaction serving to deal with aggression and lessen its effects, while introjection of the aggressor is a process which structures and involves the subject, and is, therefore, probably more pathogenic.

It is not possible to summarise and illustrate here, using these clinical cases, all of Ferenczi's ideas relating to trauma. He also dedicated a large part of his writings to it, and particularly almost all of the *Clinical Diary*. His work served as a starting point for numerous investigations undertaken by his successors. Among them, I would mention first Michael Balint, his analysand, pupil, friend and, after his death, executor of his literary legacy.

MICHAEL BALINT AND TRAUMA

Michael Balint continued Ferenczi's research on trauma, and on regression during psychoanalysis, when this process is the only way to reach the level where the trauma was inscribed. Balint was able to solve certain difficulties that had tripped up Ferenczi, who sensed that his disciple was on the right path, as he indicated in a note written in Luchon in 1932.

Balint published many articles on trauma and therapeutic regression, and two of his books are almost entirely dedicated to these subjects: Thrills and Regressions and The Basic Fault, his last book, which summarises almost all his theoretical work, from the beginning. Then, he came back to the problem of trauma again, in his last article, published in the International Journal of Psychoanalysis in 1969, a year before he died. He remarked that all trauma theories he was aware of described a large proportion of the phenomena observed, but that none explain them all. Therefore, he presented his own model, which provided additional explanations. According to Balint, the most significant pathogenic traumatic experiences occur in early childhood. Based on his observations, Balint defines three stages in their constitution:

1) There is an intense relationship of love and dependence between a child and an adult, most often the parents or people entrusted with parental authority, such as teachers. Here, Balint emphasises the role of the mother, which he considers predominant, and which, for a long time, had not been sufficiently taken into

account in the early days of psychoanalysis.

2) The adult does something very exciting, painful or frightening, which startles the child, or which is repeated regularly. The child, who perceives that the adult has an acute need which impels him to act this way, would like to fulfill this need and comfort the adult. What follows is mutual seduction leading the two protagonists to perform passionate acts or causing the adult to feel guilty and reject the child's offer.

3) The child tries again, either in order to continue the exciting game or to end the rejection, which is unbearable when it comes from someone he depends on. The adult responds by denying what happened, or by discharging his guilt on the child. Balint seems not to take into account at all the second stage of the Freudian theory. This could be because, here, he is studying the mechanism of the trauma itself, and not yet that of its pathological consequences. Balint considers that the child participates actively, to some degree, to the traumatic situation. He agrees to play the exciting game sometimes or tries to comfort an adult carried away by his passion. This is not merely identification with the aggressor. It would be more accurate to speak of introjection, since in most cases we are dealing with the child's first objects of introjection.

Balint points out that the trauma inflicted is not always of a passionate nature, particularly when its source is the mother. At the beginning of life, it is sometimes very difficult to guess accurately the child's needs, and simple misunderstandings can have harmful effects. We can cite the case of a mother who believed in using suppositories as a cure-all and did so often, exciting and even irritating her son's anal area. His sex life in adulthood was seriously perturbed by this practice.

Paula's family, which I discussed earlier, is perhaps the best illustration of the three stages of Balint's model. In this close-knit tightly bonded family, the little girl had constant physical contact with her parents, and this contact had strong erotic overtones. The little girl and her father would close themselves up in his office, where she would sit on his knees while he told her stories; this went on until she was 13 or 14. In addition, Paula and her mother used to take their bath together, soaping each other down and rinsing each other. Both the child and her parents sought out these situations. This could be said to represent the first and second stages of the Balintian model. But after Paula reached the age of 12 or 13, each of her birthdays was a sad day for her parents, especially her father. He kept telling her that he did not want a daughter who was 13, 14, 15 and so on, and that she would never again be as attractive as she was at 12. Paula never stopped suffering from this rejection — the third stage of Balint's model — in this puritanical Protestant family belonging to a particularly strict domination, where it was unthinkable to talk about sexuality, and where the parents never exchanged the least gesture of affection but overwhelmed the child with such gestures.

The Balintian model was constructed based on situations where a child is seduced by an adult. But perhaps some aspects of the model can also be applied to the collective traumas mentioned earlier, inflicted on adults and children alike. I am referring to deportations, to work camps and concentration camps, where people suddenly found themselves without any emotional ties, in a state of almost total emotional frustration, and aggressed violently by those on whom they were entirely dependent. In this situation, some people let themselves be destroyed completely, like children mistreated in their families who become completely passive, physically and psychically. Other people tried to gain favour with their captors, to obtain their benevolence, to establish a semblance of trust, obtain some advantages, be appreciated by those who had power. Identification with the aggressor caused others to become kapos; still others were unable to bear the tension of a hostile situation and ended up adopting the cause of their aggressors. This has been called "Stockholm syndrome": the situation where hostages identify with their captors and end up joining their cause. In concentration camps, those who were best able to resist, apparently, were those who created friendships and ties of solidarity with other prisoners, could draw on a wealth of affection from their past life, or had the support of a shared ideology, be it political or religious. I could cite the example of a young Jewish girl, arrested because she was a member of the Resistance as well, who told me how one day, at Easter, they were given sausages, very exceptionally; but she refused hers, because it was pork. This shared orthodox religious position, on the part of a girl declaring herself to be agnostic, was no doubt more sustaining than the nourishment she would have gotten from the few calories she refused.

It is easier to bear a traumatic situation when the aggressor is recognised as such, than when the trauma is inflicted by someone who is considered a friend, a protector, someone who is expected to provide support, such as an adult in relation to a small child. But many modes of aggression are expertly designed to infantilise the victim, to place him in the position of a child entirely dependent on his aggressor for his physical or psychic survival.

LEONARD SHENGOLD

This situation was studied closely by an American psychoanalyst, Leonard Shengold. This author, steeped in literary culture, has used the works of Kipling, Dickens, Chekhov and Orwell to show the functioning of "soul murder" or "brainwashing", and how they can reduce an adult to infantile dependence on his aggressor. Soul murder consists of taking possession of the mind and personality of another person. A child is particularly vulnerable to this process because he is dependent. Some of Shengold's formulations are reminiscent of Ferenczi, whom he quotes as a source. He wrote, for example, that excessive stimulation has the same effect as great deprivation. The one who is aggressed defends himself by becoming insensitive; he comes to resemble an automaton. Inwardly, he experiences confusion, loss of confidence in his own senses, hate and rage. But despite his hatred and his rage, the child expects help to come from the abusive parent; consequently, he must create a mental image of a good parent, to prevent the disintegration of his personality. But this fight to avoid splitting also prevents him from distinguishing the good from the bad. Because the parent cannot be bad, it is the child who must be bad. He is unable to record and remember what actually happened. The parent implants in the child what he himself wants to have happened. Shengold, who likes literary examples, quotes George Orwell's *1984*[23]. Indeed, this book is also a perfect illustration of the Ferenczian model; Ferenczi could have written certain passages. The story can be resumed as follows: the action takes place in a nation crushed by the tyranny of a more or less mythical

---

23   Orwell, G., *1984*, Harcourt Brace Jovanovich, 1963.

Big Brother. People are forced to speak Newspeak, an extreme form of stereotypical language. The nation is supposedly constantly at war, to keep the population under the pressure of danger and hate, which takes up all their emotional energy. O'Brien, the future torturer of the hero, Winston, first establishes a relationship based on great trust with Winston. But Winston commits the serious crime of falling in love with Julia, and they are both arrested. O'Brien alternates torture with affectionate gestures, friendly words or pedagogical information: "You suffer from a defective memory. You are unable to remember real events, and you persuade yourself that you remember other events which never happened[24]". And later: "When finally you surrender to us, it must be of your own free will. We do not destroy the heretic because he resists us; so long as he resists us we never destroy him. We convert him, we capture his inner mind, we reshape him. [...] we bring him over to our side, not in appearance, but genuinely, heart and soul[25]". Still further, Winston thinks: "There was no idea that he had ever had, or could have, that O'Brien had not long ago known, examined, and rejected. [...] But in that case how could it be true that O'Brien was mad? It must be he, Winston, who was mad[26]". Later, O'Brien tells Winston: "Never again will you be capable of ordinary human feelings. Everything will be dead inside you. [...] You will be hollow. We shall squeeze you empty, and then we shall fill you with ourselves[27]".

Ferenczi speaks of superego "intropressure". This is the process that could explain the very surprising confessions at the Moscow Trials and elsewhere. Orwell writes that in Big Brother's world "Power is in tearing human minds to pieces and putting them together again in new shapes of your own choosing[28]". Ferenczi speaks of fragmentation, of splitting.

NICOLAS ABRAHAM AND MARIA TOROK

Finally, Nicolas Abraham and Maria Torok also drew inspiration from Ferenczi to formulate their theory of trauma. They dedicated a remarkable article to the particular form of trauma caused by the death of a loved one. The article is entitled "Mourning OR Melancholia",

---

24 Orwell, G., *1984*, op. cit., pp. 108-109.
25 ibid., pp. 112-113.
26 ibid., p. 113.
27 ibid.
28 ibid., p.118.

to refer to Freud's article "Mourning AND Melancholia". Freud describes mourning as the reaction to the loss of a loved being for whom one had strong feelings, that is, as a loss in the external world. As for melancholia, it is an internal loss, the loss of something in the ego. The person suffering from melancholia blames himself, feels unworthy and contemptible. In fact, feelings which would have been directed at the love object, now revert back to the ego itself. The investment taken back from the lost love object is not reinvested, but is used to establish the identification of the self with the object. Thus, the loss of the object becomes a loss of the ego. When the choice of the object was a narcissistic choice, there is fixation on the lost object and, in case of mourning, there is regression to primary narcissism. Here, identification precedes investment in the object. Freud called this phenomenon "incorporation", corresponding to the cannibalistic stage. In melancholia, there is regression to this cannibalistic stage. Freud defined melancholia as mourning that brings about regression. Mourning highlights the ambivalence of love relationships, he wrote. The subject blames himself for having wished the death of the loved one. The ego, narcissistically identified with the lost object, turns against itself the hate directed towards this object. The same phenomenon is seen in people with suicidal tendencies; Freud saw it as turning murderous impulses against oneself. The case of Béatrice might be a good example. She married an artist she admired greatly. After years of a stormy marriage spent with a depressed man considerably older than herself, he was killed in an airplane accident. After this, she dedicated her life to the idealised memory of the great man, acted as she supposed he would have liked her to act, and considered that her life was over, and nothing held any interest for her. She turned all the accumulated hate for her husband against herself and against her two daughters, whose lives she poisoned by endlessly decreeing what the daughters of such a father can and cannot allow themselves to do. This was accompanied by constant threats of suicide, and even some half-hearted attempts.

Nicolas Abraham and Maria Torok discussed the question of mourning and melancholia with reference to Ferenczi's concept of introjection. Strangely, Freud never used this notion, developed by Ferenczi in 1909, although he had shown great interest in it at first. In short, this concept states that the ego can only love itself. The ego's love of itself is extended to objects that are important for the subject. Thus, they are introjected in the self, producing a broadening of the ego. This brings to mind the biblical injunction: "Thou shall love thy neighbour as thyself". Transference also corresponds to an introjection, a broadening of the ego. Introjecting the analyst makes him a mediator in the process of reaching the unconscious. Nicolas Abraham and Maria Torok further developed and clarified this concept of introjection, contrasting it with the notion of incorporation.

According to them, normal mourning can take place when the lost object has been introjected: that is, it is not the object that is introjected, but the unconscious or repressed libido, "the sum total of the drives, and their vicissitudes as occasioned and mediated by the object", when a real relationship was established. The mourner grieves, but gradually becomes able to invest other objects once again, and to lead a full and normal life. The loss is not what causes introjection; on the contrary, the loss halts it if it occurs before introjection could take place. We can imagine that introjection of a person important to the subject can become problematic when the subject must, at the same time, protect himself from this person. This was the case for one of Béatrice's daughters: this mother, loving and protective, also exuded hate and dictated constraints, a situation that provoked complete emotional confusion in her oldest daughter.

When introjection could not be achieved, because the loss was that of a very young child, or because the process of introjection was interrupted by sudden abandonment or death while a relationship was being constructed, the only solution for the subject is to retain in himself the lost object, to compensate for the failed introjection through magic: through incorporation. The incorporation of an object occurs when the desires concerning it have not had a chance to be freed before the loss of the object; incorporation is used to deny the loss. Incorporation is a fantasy, contrary to introjection, which is a process. The loss acts as a prohibition and renders introjection impossible; the incorporation of the object sidesteps this prohibition without transgressing it, in the realm of fantasy. From then on, through the fantasy of incorporation, the object is transformed into an imago.

One of Béatrice's daughters incorporated the imago of her father, whom she lost when she was seven. The image she has of this man is both an unattainable ideal and a persecutor who prevents her from finding a suitable partner good enough for the daughter of such a man. She devalues her own scientific career, in comparison with her father's glory as an artist.

Introjection is gradual; incorporation is instantaneous and resembles a hallucinatory construction, a refusal of reality. It is a magical secret, contrary to introjection which works entirely in the open. Introjection puts an end to objectal dependency. Incorporation reinforces dependency. There are many legends that tell the story of people deeply attached to each other who are separated for a very long time and without losing their bond. But when this quality of relation could not be established, people stick to each other and cannot leave each other. Béatrice's older daughter feels she must call her mother every day and go to see her at least every second day. When she fails in her duty, she is terrified at the idea of what might have happened to her mother, or that she might have killed herself because of her "abandonment".

To describe incorporation, Nicolas Abraham and Maria Torok speak of a "commemorative monument [that] betokens the place, the date, and the circumstances in which desires were banished from introjection". It is a tomb in the ego.

These authors describe the mechanism of pathological mourning by explaining that, as a reaction to a death, there is a libidinal increase that can go as far as orgasm. It is an ultimate attempt at introjection. The death of the object allows its conquest through recourse to magic. This libidinal satisfaction is experienced both as surprising and guilt-provoking. It is regression to the hallucinatory satisfaction stage. The developed ego rejects this moment of regression, and the desire for the lost object is rigorously repressed. This repression excludes and preserves the lost object all at once. Nicolas Abraham and Maria Torok speak of the "exquisite corpse" and of the ego which continually looks for it in the hope of reviving it.

The imago created in case introjection fails functions as a prohibition of sexual desire. It is formed after a satisfaction was first consented to and then refused. This corresponds to Balint's description of trauma in general. A desire that is not introjected becomes reprehensible and unspeakable. When the object of desire, let us say an adult, accepts the child's budding desire which is also his own, there is introjection. But if the child's desire was accepted at first and rejected by the adult afterwards, along with his own desire, there will be fixation on the moment of satisfaction, and the child will try to recapture that moment, while suffering and feeling guilty.

IN CONCLUSION

All the authors I quoted above seem to agree on certain facts, confirmed by my own experience as well; they are that:

Life without trauma is not possible.

Not all traumas have pathological effects.

Some traumas can be integrated by the person without disturbing his psychic structure; they leave only a bad memory or are sometimes forgotten altogether.

It is not the actual intensity of the trauma that determines if there will be pathological effects. Events or situations that go unnoticed, or the repetition of a seemingly trivial trauma can have serious pathological consequences. We might remember Richard Hughes' novel A High Wind in Jamaica, in which a slight seismic tremor makes the cups in the kitchen shake. A little girl is deeply impressed by this experience. The event happens on the eve of her departure for England by boat. During the voyage, the ship is attacked by pirates, there are battles, people are killed, there is much violence. When, after countless adventures, she is finally reunited with her family and is asked to recount her adventures, the only thing she talks about is the earthquake.

Trauma occurs in several stages: two or three. In any case, something takes place which the psychic structure is unable to integrate. The occurrence stays there, in a split state, and can be reawakened by a subsequent event and cause a pathology. The initial event could have taken place in early childhood, at birth or before birth — all these scenarios are possible.

At one or the other of the stages, a model is constituted which we might call "basic fault", "scar" or "defect", as Balint did. This "fault" will determine a person's particular susceptibility to specific types of trauma in the future.

Thus, it is the psychic structure of the individual which renders him susceptible to certain traumas. It is reasonable to think that the more rudimentary this structure, the greater the risk of pathogenic trauma. This is why researchers started out by studying early trauma, often of a sexual nature. Of course, bombardments, imprisonment in concentration camps, the early loss of the parents and of all adult protectors — to which children in extreme situations are subjected —, can be seen as shocks involuntarily inflicted by the parents. In these situations, the children discover the powerlessness of these adults to protect them from certain dangers. I would like to temper this perspective by drawing attention to some cases I saw — as I said earlier — in which a very good relationship with the parents, lost early in violent circumstances, nevertheless protected the children later by preventing the development of pathological consequences.

ON AGING

Publishing a book about aging is not a trivial matter when it involves analysts who are still practicing. I think one must be careful about what he says and how he says it, keeping in mind that those who come to see us could be disturbed to discover their analyst talking about his experience of aging. People want their analyst to correspond to the image they need to have of him. In my case, I remember that when I started my training I needed a relatively young analyst; the one I chose had reached a certain age, but I saw him as being rather young. It suited me to see him this way. Revealing too much about oneself prevents people from imagining the other person and seeing him as they need him to be. For example, I remember someone who chose me as an analyst because he saw me as having Vietnamese features. Unbelievable but true! But it shows that we must take into account the possible effects of such a book on those who come to see us.

An American colleague, an excellent analyst, told me, when she was 70, that she had no more patients because people in America do not want to go into analysis with an old lady. Is there less fear of old people on the Old Continent?

When a new person wants to start therapy with me, I also think of my age. With certain people, I would be afraid to leave them unexpectedly, at any point in our work together, and perhaps at a time when they are fragile. I know that all my colleagues do not share this concern, because they feel that analysands can be trusted to know how to manage in any situation. Inversely, I have sometimes treated old people. Often, it is curiosity about a certain event in their life that awakens the desire or the need to better understand. But sometimes they undertake an analysis to deal with the fear of aging.

Some people come back to see an analyst who accompanied them earlier on their journey, at crucial moments in their lives: marriage or remarriage, pregnancy or adoption. Or when someone undertakes an emotionally charged activity, as was the case for a professor who was conducting research on the Shoah, and who needed to examine in analysis the feelings this aroused in him. In such cases, the fact that the analyst has aged in the meantime is irrelevant. Some of my analysands have expressed concern about my vulnerability given my age. After an accident that forced me to be away for quite a while, they talked about the possibility that they might lose me one day. But their confidence in my relative solidity soon got the better of their concern. In fact, this incident allowed us to discuss the problem of the mortality of human beings: mine as well as theirs.

My analysands, who are for the most part rather young, do not seem put off by my age. It is I who sometimes decides to send some people to a younger colleague when I have the impression that the therapy will take some time.

I have colleagues and friends who are very upset about having lost some of their physical abilities (walking, climbing, running...). Personally, these things don't bother me very much. There are enough things I can do to continue to find life interesting.

Some people ask themselves what they can do to age "well". In other words, they want to know how to experience enough pleasure for life to be worth living to the end. I think there is a good chance for a person to do this when he was given what he needed, especially as a child. The way those around you lived when they were old, the image they gave you of aging, also play a role. Of course, one's own state of health is important. One of the problems of aging is retirement. For some people, this brings relief at first, followed by boredom and depression afterwards. Other people continue to work, in their own field or in another. I am lucky enough to be part of this second category. Do intellectuals have an advantage? I do not know. Some people who are not intellectuals remain curious and interested in many things. I know a policeman who became a sculptor, and a lady who teaches French to refugees.

Indeed, old age also has secondary benefits: being pampered, having the right to complain, as long as one does not go overboard. A grumpy old person who complains about everything risks finding himself alone in short order.

Can old people claim to possess a certain wisdom thanks to their long life experience? Sometimes this is the case, but it is not a rule. Each one of us can only hope to benefit from this experience and let our entourage benefit from it, if our luck holds out long enough for that.

Analysts, like everyone else, have trouble dealing with this stage of life. We know that every one of us has to face it eventually, if he lives long enough. Growing old is a natural process and analysis does not change this, or only minimally. Contrary to my teacher Ferenczi, the hopeless optimist, I do not think that psychoanalysis can take care of everything.

In some respects, I see old age as a surrealist state: you are the same person you always were, you carry inside you the child, the adolescent, the adult, and even the infant and perhaps the fetus you were, and yet nothing is the same as before. There is an inevitable contradiction between the perception you have of yourself, and what you are able to do, given certain inescapable physical problems.

However, I have noticed that one can be old at any age, and even several times in one's life. The first time I felt old was the day after my eleventh birthday, when I woke up in the morning. I suddenly realised that my age would now be a two-figure number until the age of 99. Later, I felt a twinge when I turned 50, because this marked a half a century. And once again at 75, because we were in the year 2000, and I had always wondered if I would live that long. I once knew a woman, beautiful and youthful, who was seized by despair when she turned 40; she had the impression that her life was now over.

But there is also something more sinister in the experience of aging, which is difficult to put into words, although it is our common fate, or perhaps precisely because it is. This is the inevitable fear of the unknown shrouding death. We hesitate to share this anguish with people who have to face it themselves. It is an anguish that takes different forms, according to each person's beliefs and convictions. Some people are afraid of what there might be after death. Other people do not believe there is anything after death, but are afraid of the passage from life to death, of the moments just before death. People also worry about those they leave behind. Some worry about things they will no longer be able to control, and try to organise everything while they're still hale and hardy.

To conclude, I like to live, I am glad I can prolong this unique opportunity to observe the world around us. I like this work in which I engaged all my life, and which I would like to continue as long as I can.

FROM THE AMOEBA TO THE ROBOT

Two planets are chatting:

– Earth looks unwell, don't you think?

– You're right, she seems to be in very bad shape.

– Yes, they say she caught manitis.

– It's serious, but it goes away by itself...

Life started with unicellular creatures. The animal which is driven to try to dominate all other living beings, and even all of nature, also starts with two single-cell elements: the ovum and the sperm cell. For man, like for all other living beings, this is the origin of all the other building blocks of his whole body.

At first, the different humanoid species seem to have done nothing to differentiate themselves from the other animals. Then, at a certain point in his development, man started to consider that he was of a superior nature, a status he regarded as giving him divine rights over all of creation and all creatures. The biblical texts of all three religions of the book testify to this. Man lay claim to the right to use everything nature produced, be it in the animal, plant or mineral realm, as he saw fit. He grew them or exterminated them, ate them, forced them to work, made them suffer, removed their coats or their feathers, hunted them and killed them for profit or pleasure, without limit.

Once they claimed this superiority, human beings spent much time reflecting on what distinguishes them from all the other animals. Many criteria were submitted, but had to be abandoned one after the other. One of these criteria was proposed by the French writer Vercors (Jean Bruller)[29]. According to Vercors, the difference between men and animals is that one day man rebelled against nature and, from then on, has continually developed and perfected tools to escape its constraints. I had the privilege of knowing this exceptional man, and I remember a memorable discussion in which, pitting my adolescent abilities against Vercors' well-considered ideas, I tried to prove to him that nature always has the upper hand in the end. He replied, with reason, that this does not stop humans from persisting in their efforts to dominate nature. The conversation almost turned into

---

[29] Vercors, Plus ou moins homme, Albin Michel, 1950; Les Animaux dénaturés, Le Livre de Poche, 1978; Zoo, Magnard, 2004.

an argument, because each of us defended the portion of truth in what he was saying. Vercors saw nature as a foe who tries to counteract man's efforts to escape its laws. I saw it, and still see it, as an entity which exists, to which man belongs, and over which he has no power whatsoever. He can explore, acquire more knowledge and create better and better tools to improve his safety, his possibilities and his comfort. I see Vercors' perspective as illustrating above all man's boundless ambition, which goes hand in hand with his dream of superiority over all other living creatures.

Since that time, my own perspective has not changed. Man, with his vulnerability and his weakness, constantly invents and builds systems to protect and defend himself, to discover and understand, to accomplish what his physical and mental capacities alone would not enable him to accomplish without these means that are more efficient than he is, even though he invented them himself. Man flies in the sky, dives into the deep, communicates with other human beings anywhere in the world using sounds or images, or both. The machines he invented perform, in a few seconds, calculations it would take him decades to carry out if he had to do them himself. Man has even begun to know how to replace his own failing organs by almost indestructible machines, or to develop stem cells for the purpose of replacing specialised cells destroyed by illness or old age.

But there is a price to pay for all this. Not only do the best cared-for organisms die one day, since this is inscribed in their nature, but volcanic eruptions, earthquakes, tidal waves, floods, storms... can destroy in minutes all of these marvellous constructions. Man can prolong his life, but it would be disconcerting if he could prolong it indefinitely. Numerous inventions produce at least as many, or even more, disastrous effects as benefits. Nuclear power produces energy, but also provides means of destruction that now render possible the abolition of many forms of life on Earth, including human life. Greed has caused human beings to use nuclear power before they knew how to manage it. The first steam-powered vehicle was intended to pull canons. Later, automobiles and tractors were invented. But tractors can easily be transformed into tanks.

And then there is man's particular nature. The social environment he created fosters fear, selfishness and aggression. Humans compete for power and therefore turn their wonderful inventions against each other, instead of joining together and getting the most benefit from them with the least drawbacks. Man even has the particular talent of seeing clearly the destruction he will bring about, without being able to stop because the lure of immediate gain is too great, and the sense of solidarity with his fellow man is too weak. "Once I'm gone, come what may!"

Wonderful human inventions can also have slower and more surreptitious effects. As human beings continue to facilitate their lives by letting machines and robots perform the difficult tasks, they weaken their senses and their capacities, and dull their emotions. Many people, who have never been able to develop the capacity to love, are unable to establish deep emotional ties. They have hundreds of Facebook "friends", but no one with whom to share a relationship based on mutual trust. Indeed, these people feel so protected by the safety measures and systems installed to ensure their security, that they no longer develop any internal security — the one quality essential for handling the changing circumstances that are an inevitable part of life[30]. Such people are tempted to attribute all the flaws of their artificial armour to other people: they look for — and often find — someone to blame for their illness, for their everyday problems, even for floods or storms that someone should have foreseen and perhaps prevented.

The evolution of ideas in medicine deserves special consideration. The "whole person", to use Balint's expression, is constituted of body, consciousness and soul, integrated in a kind of entity whose nature is not yet clear to us. These elements function together as a whole. Our worries give us stomach pains, our problems give us headaches, frustration makes us break out in hives, love makes our heart beat faster, to say nothing of more complex and less well-known symptoms. How does this whole function when many of its components are replaced with artificial parts? How does an inner world take shape in test tube babies with undetermined parents? And what about children allowed to be born because they are of the desired gender and appear to have no abnormalities? This is another area in which humans want to control the situation. How will they deal with the consequences?

Humans are bombarded with information and entertainment, from morning 'til night. Fascinated by images, they experience superficial emotions and absorb prefabricated ideas (someone else's); many of them don't know how to read any more, are strangers to the pleasure

---

30   See Boris Cyrulnik's concept of resilience.

of learning and are unable to form a critical and responsible judgment about the various incitements competing for their attention. They have no time for this, and the social atmosphere in which they live does not encourage it, and even encourages the opposite.

We could dedicate a separate discussion to the accelerated rhythm we have introduced in all areas of life. Human beings no longer live at their own rhythm. When we look at our fellow creatures and see them eating when they are hungry, sleeping when they want to, and engaging in sexual activity at their pleasure (as long as we don't mix in), we become conscious of what we have lost in our frantic race towards progress. In fact, we know little about the animals around us. We can look at them, observe them, study them, know a great deal about their habits, and even love them, without being able to really communicate with them. To say nothing of some living beings so different from us that we can't even imagine a way of communicating with them. How can we have an exchange with a worm, a sardine or a microbe? The important thing in our attitude towards them is the respect we owe to all the rest of creation. Microorganisms, which do not have all our talents, can overpower us. What good are our marvellous inventions when we are facing a plague epidemic, an outbreak of the Spanish flu, or an AIDS pandemic?

Clearly, the only way for the human species to ensure its survival is to find its appropriate place among the other animal species again and remember how to live in harmony with nature. Not by regressing to an earlier stage in its development, but by inventing a new form of harmony or of solidarity among humans and with all other living beings. Will human nature be adaptable enough to allow this evolution? Man as he has become today, too greedy, too aggressive and too unrestrained, does not seem capable of inventing and instituting this kind of harmony. If nothing changes, the astronaut joke used as an epigraph above might well become a prophecy.

WHAT IS A VICTIM?

The victim is a fashionable figure. According to Pierre Nora[31], since we no longer have "saints, heroes or wise men, in other words, positive legendary figures, the victim now

---

31 See *Le Nouvel Observateur* magazine, August 14, 2008.

personifies the Good". That said, the figure of the victim is one in which countless internal and external processes come together. It is therefore very difficult to define what this means.

This is confirmed by the diversity of definitions given by *Le Petit Robert* dictionary:

1) living creature offered up as a sacrifice to the gods; 2) person subjected to the hate, torments, injustices of others; 3) person killed or injured; 4) person who dies in a natural disaster, an epidemic, an accident, or in an uprising or a war.

But the dictionary only mentions events which can befall a person from the outside. We might be tempted to resume this definition as "a person subjected to a traumatic event". Le Petit Robert only lists violent events, be they provoked by people or by natural phenomena.

The first meaning in the dictionary, "living creature offered up as a sacrifice to the gods", which may appear somewhat outdated today, is nevertheless very significant. A victim was offered as a sacrifice to a divinity in the hope of securing its favour as a compensation for the offering. This idea of compensation is still associated with the word "victim", even when it is not specifically mentioned. In the past, people had "misfortunes", and very rarely could anyone expect any compensation. Today, many people claim victim status and demand compensation. This explains the desperate search for someone to blame, someone responsible for the damages incurred by a person, someone from whom to demand compensation.

This situation can become almost absurd when, for example, the mayor of a town is sued because the gate of the school has collapsed. This man could then consider himself the victim of the victims of the fallen gate... or bring charges against the company which installed the gate, fifty years earlier perhaps. The idea of an accident is only accepted with great difficulty. Those who believe in the existence of a higher being can attribute the event to His will, which remains unknown to mankind. But the great numbers of people with little religious faith, or no faith at all, have trouble accepting that no one can be held responsible. Of course, this is not always what happens. Although accidents occur, there are also many intentional, or sometimes unintentional, aggressions.

But there is a troubling confusion here: in the case of a sacrifice, it is not the victim who asks for compensation, but the executioner of the sacrifical act. Of course, he sacrifices something — or someone — dear to him (emotionally or financially). When the Bible tells the story of Abraham's sacrifice of Isaac, Isaac is the intended victim, but clearly Abraham is also sacrificed, although he has the role of executioner. After this, the author of the story became frightened by the cruelty of his own imagination and negotiated replacing Isaac with a ram, which for Abraham is only a financial sacrifice.

Thus, it is possible to fall victim to one's own destructive, violent drives. Suffice it to remember the countless cases of emotional breakdown of French soldiers after the Algerian War, of American soldiers after the Vietnam War, of German soldiers after the war in Russia ... to say nothing of lesser-known events. In civilian life as well, there are repentant criminals who cannot accept what they did and are emotionally destroyed. Of course, there are situations which facilitate the explosion of savagery: war, tumultuous mass movement, the sight of comrades in arms killed by the enemy, group pressure, or even the laws in effect at a particular time. But those who fall victim to these situations suffer even more knowing that there are always a few strong individuals, with solid superegos, high conscientious inhibitions and well-integrated personalities, who resist, even if they put themselves at great risk.

Thus, executioners are also victims: victims of their impulses and their weaknesses, of the orders of their superiors which they don't dare disobey. However, some victims are innocent and others are guilty of various misdeeds. The innocent victims, or sometimes those who feel innocent even if they contributed to their misfortune (as we shall see later), are the ones who deserve compensation, whether they ask for it or not. Indeed, there are those who claim victim status forcefully (or with resignation), but there are others who feel diminished and humiliated by this position and refuse to be identified this way, even if this designation describes the reality of what they experienced; for them, asking for compensation is out of the question. This situation is illustrated by the well-known Hungarian mathematician Imre Toth, who suffered terrible persecution for both racial and political reasons. But when a friend dragged him to the office where claims for compensation were filed, he ran away at the sight of the waiting multitude, who looked to him like beggars. There was also the Hungarian landowner who had emigrated and who refused to ask for compensation for the house and the land the people in his village had stolen. In addition, it is a well-known fact that countless "victims" of the Nazi persecutions did not want, or could not, speak of what they had been through, and as a result, never asked for the least compensation.

Some people ask for something other than financial compensation. They only want the events that took place to be recognised. This recognition has aroused sufficient envy in some emotionally impoverished people to cause them to pretend to be victims themselves, especially of the Shoah, and to write false memoirs — sometimes captivating — in order to obtain recognition, more than to profit from what could be a bestseller.

But all these situations are associated with the idea of a sacrifice offered to a divinity, so well expressed in the English term "holocaust". This term applies perfectly to the fanaticised executioners, although they don't sacrifice anything of value to them (except their self-image), but not at all to the victims, who are simply subjected to a catastrophe without any metaphysical meaning. Still, some of these victims, among the most deeply religious, interpreted these events as divine punishment for possible "sins" of their whole community.

But the term "victim" does not apply only to people who suffered catastrophes like the Shoah. We must ask if it cannot be applied to any being subjected to a trauma or an aggression, whether it be a human being or an animal led to slaughter.

Can we not also speak of victims when the events are not spectacular, as is the case with the subtle mistreatment of children, that we might call simply pedagogical clumsiness; or with the lack of fit between what the child asks for and how the adults in charge respond? Aggression takes so many forms that it is difficult to formulate a coherent definition of a victim based on this. For example, a woman I know twisted her ankle when she stepped in a hole in a New York sidewalk; she was awarded substantial damages by the city and used the money to repaint her apartment — a job long overdue. But she is, nevertheless, a victim. The peasant in Bangladesh whose house was destroyed by an earthquake, and who lost his family as well as his meagre possessions is a victim too, just like the innocent man in an American jail, waiting to be executed unless a good investigative journalist takes an interest in his case. And of course, there are those who were victims of the Nazi concentration camps.

The subjective aspect, that is, what happens in the

psyche of the trauma victim, complicates things even more. Subjective reactions range from seeking recognition, compensation or only financial benefits, as we saw in the case of the lady in New York, to complete mental and physical breakdown. Breakdowns vary in degree of severity; some people recover, alone or with help, and other people don't. There are also people who recover for a time. We are reminded of the suicides of former concentration camp prisoners — Primo Levi, Jean Améry, Bruno Bettelheim and many others — years after they returned, and after a desperate attempt, even largely successful in some cases, to go on with life.

To complicate things even more, the intensity of the victim's reaction is not proportional with the severity of the trauma. Some people are virtually destroyed by events which others would barely notice, while other people overcome, with more or less effort, spectacular traumas.

The legal definition is not at all helpful: a victim is anyone who can provide proof of a prejudice he suffered. The loss of a limb in a war or accident brings an indemnity of such and such value, regardless of the way in which the person bears the loss. A specific sum of money is set to compensate someone for the death of a loved one, the theft of a television set, as well as an irreplaceable family memento.

We must mention one other instance of victimisation which concerns humanity as a whole. Little by little, human beings are becoming aware of the more or less irreversible damage that their activities inflict on the planet they inhabit. Incidentally, the Earth will recover very well and continue to spin. But humanity risks destroying — at least, it has the means to destroy — its own environment to the point where human life on the planet will become impossible. Humanity could become its own victim. This situation is brilliantly illustrated by Cormac McCarthy in his novel The Road[32].

Thus, victimhood seems to be such a multifaceted phenomenon that it is impossible to make a complete study of it. To address the subject, one must try to identify a category of traumatising events, or a victim category, or a category of reactions. Those whose profession is to understand the human psyche, will probably see this last category as the best way to approach the subject, in order to untangle this complex web.

---

32 McCarthy, C., *The Road*, Picador, 2009.

In recent years, Boris Cyrulnik has focused his interest on people who are able to regain their balance after a trauma. He called this ability "resilience", using a term coined by two American school psychologists, Emmy Werner and Ruth Smith who, over a period of about 30 years, observed children traumatised in the 1939–1945 war years; the term was also used by John Bowlby in his writings on attachment. The saying "What doesn't kill you makes you stronger" refers to people who have this quality. A whole series of circumstances and characteristics, innate or acquired thanks to these circumstances, can contribute to build resilience. I think that perhaps the most important of these circumstances is starting life in a loving, reliable and secure environment. This experience teaches that such an environment can exist, and makes it possible to build reserves that reinforce resilience. An elderly lady I know, who lost her whole family due to a series of serious illnesses, expressed it beautifully when she said that the fifteen years of happiness she had with her husband constituted "reserves you can draw on to live". In addition, in her childhood, this lady had had a special relationship with her father. And then, there is also lucky happenstance. An emotionally fragile person in certain areas may only experience traumas affecting the stronger aspects of his personality, which he can withstand. For example, a man decorated several times for acts of courage in the First World War refused to hide property belonging to a Jewish family who were his friends, during the Occupation, because the idea of possibly being arrested and taken away between two gendarmes, before all his neighbours, was literally unbearable to him. His physical courage was his strong point; his moral courage was more fragile.

But many people lack the internal equipment and the secure past which could have prepared them for displaying resilience when misfortune (or another human being) strikes. Or when they suffer a trauma affecting them where they are weakest.

The shock can destroy them, destabilise them, plunge them into internal chaos, or make them lose touch with reality. Or, more insidiously, cause, afterwards, a pathology whose traumatic origin will only be able to be exposed through psychological work, which might allow the person to emerge from it.

Sándor Ferenczi considered that all psychic illness had an external traumatic origin, and that if the analytic work was pursued far enough, a so-called "real" trauma would be found, in truth, at the root of every pathogenic fantasy. Indeed, we can say that in any more or less healthy family, a little girl is attracted to her father at some point. But for her to fantasise that her father raped her, something must have happened to her that could trigger such a fantasy.

Those who suffered something clearly identifiable, a known misfortune, an aggression in circumstances of which they are aware, may find the trauma difficult to live with, and the shock difficult to overcome. But they know how to approach the problem and they have a chance — although not the certainty — to recover sufficiently to live a worthwhile life. And there are also people who are permanent victims. They are hurt by the slightest things, and they always have bad luck, no matter what they do... or don't do. Nothing can help them, everything they touch goes wrong.

There was a young woman who was charming, beautiful, talented, touching, and constantly besieged by misfortune. She worked in theatre. Her colleagues bent over backwards to help her, find her work, an apartment, contacts... but nothing ever worked. She had a talent for making people feel that they were not going about things the right way, that their help was clumsy and unwelcome, that their good intentions couldn't lead anywhere. She succeeded in discouraging everyone, convincing all those who wanted to help that they were powerless and would inevitably fail. Finally, she was rejected by all those who had tried to help her and who could no longer bear the unavoidable failure of all their efforts. She ended up destitute, and the people who had cared about her lost track of her.

There was also the lady who worked as a civil servant in a provincial town, who was rejected by her colleagues, persecuted by her superiors, tyrannised by her widowed mother whom she had taken in, who came looking for help in analysis. The analysis was long and difficult but succeeded in unearthing many difficult situations she had lived through, although she rejected all the interpretations offered, finding them mistaken or hurtful. But, little by little, the patient, who continued to be besieged in every way, became better able to cope, to make the best of a bad situation, to manage her mother's demands better and to introduce some satisfaction in her personal and professional life. She had always been very reticent to pay for her sessions, since she considered that psychological help was something every person owed to his fellow man, without charging for it. She decided to end the analysis when her life became bearable and even somewhat pleasurable. She left her analyst saying: "I am stopping now, since you took away everything, even my symptoms..."

These two people, and particularly the first, represent a specific category of victims. We might say that the status of victim is a language for them. It is a way of saying that the problem is elsewhere, they know not where, that they don't know what it is about and that, therefore, neither they nor anyone else can do anything about it. They even report each new misfortune with some satisfaction, because it confirms and emphasises what they are trying to make those around them understand — indeed, understand themselves. This allows them to live, or rather survive, and to obtain the only kind of satisfaction they can. Their constant complaining, often justified, makes those close to them believe that they want help. This is true, but only to prove again and again that this help is useless and that, often, it makes the situation even worse. And they are right. All help in response to taking her request at face value will fail to solve the problem. Because they are unable to define the problem.

Helping these people effectively is an arduous task, because often they find it difficult to ask for and accept help that can give concrete results. They draw nourishment from their misfortunes alone, and to solve their problems they would have to reconstruct their image completely. They would have to give up everything that constitutes their identity, the substance of their life, the meaning of the universe, in exchange for something they don't know yet, and they would have to construct a new image of the world.

If those who are victims of a certain type could be grouped together in a category, it could be these people: those who are not conscious of the ways in which they are damaged, and who sometimes cannot become aware of this. These people are born with a gap in their history, an empty space they can't locate and certainly not fill.

This is the case of the woman who knows that her maternal grandmother had an affair considered shameful with a man rejected by society, who abandoned her with the little girl they had together. No one ever speaks of this grandfather, what she knows about him does not explain the rejection, and this whole branch of her lineage is completely unknown to her. Her mother is prey to bouts of depression, but nothing is ever discussed in this rather cold family in which all three children have emotional problems. The oldest daughter is unhappy in her marriage, the son has repeated stays in a psychiatric hospital, and the youngest daughter is unable to establish a stable romantic relationship, despite her strong desire to have a family. Each time she meets someone new, she thinks, very quickly, that her unbearable solitude is over; then she starts to have doubts, to suspect that her much desired companion has all sorts of faults. Eventually, the latter leaves her, when he senses the suspicion and mistrust behind her smiling, seductive air. This woman finally sought help in psychotherapy but came up against a dull and obscure image of her life, in which no event seems significant or critical to her. Her sparse memories are cut off from the emotions associated with what she remembers. She seems suspended in timelessness, with no past and no concrete plans for the future.

Often, the only way to decipher these lives is through the concepts of Nicolas Abraham and Maria Torok. In these lives, persistent exploration can uncover what these authors call crypts[33], phantoms[34] and transgenerational consequences[35].

Not all traumatic effects can be overcome. The case of survivors of the Shoah who committed suicide after fighting these effects for years is significant enough to force us to admit this. But despite the ultimate failure, their situation is entirely different than that of the people dedicated to unhappiness we described above, who live only through their suffering and misfortunes. The former fought, were able to build a life that was rich and full but could not sustain it until its natural end. The latter are simply unable to fight, because their identity is built on their victimhood. Their only hope is to be dislodged from this position by an unforeseen event or by intervention from the outside.

All this points to the fact that throughout our existence all of us are, on occasion or constantly, willingly or unwillingly, conscious or unconscious victims of numerous more or less serious traumas inflicted on us by life. And all of us have to learn to live with the final trauma that casts its shadow on

---

33 "The crypt can be seen as an inclusion in the self, whose effect is preservative repression, functioning as the place in the psychic apparatus where the secret is buried."
34 "The phantom, an invention of the living, is meant to objectify in a hallucinatory mode, individual or collective, the gap produced in us by the concealment of some part of a loved object's life."
35 When descendants are burdened with the effects of family secrets never revealed to them.

every human life. We are victims of the human condition. But the suffering ensuing from this is not evenly distributed. Some victims are more victims than others, either because their traumas are more violent, more numerous and repeated, or due to their own inherent weaknesses. These people can sometimes find help provided they have the strength, or the good fortune, to take the first step in that direction.

ABOUT RACISM

Racism is a difficult concept to define, whose meaning has been further obscured by the common usage of the word. One definition could be: the perception of real or presumed — even imagined — differences, in any area, in other groups of people. This would make it a universal human trait, present in all individuals. Perceiving such a difference can produce liking as well as animosity. For instance, the Indians of South America saw the Spanish invaders as superior beings. We know that, in that particular case, this was a tragic error. Other people admire Americans for their practical sense, Italians for their warmth and their musical talent, Spaniards for their sense of honour, the Chinese for their inventiveness and their capacity for work, and so on. Negative characteristics are just as widely attributed to a whole nation. Thus, there may be a benign and a malignant form of racism, depending on one's way of reacting to these supposed differences. It appears to be a universal human trait to want to divide people into "we" and "they", the same as us and different from us, and to classify differences into real or imaginary, into positive and — especially — negative.

Indeed, in common usage, the malignant connotation predominates: rejection, contempt, hate, fear, verbal or physical aggression which can go as far as murder, or even genocide.

Imagination plays a significant role in the phenomenon of racism. The differences themselves are often totally imaginary, and therefore their harmful effects are also imagined.

A racist reaction can be provoked by the most varied factors: skin colour, religion, culture, sexual orientation, or even occupation, food and eating habits in general, social position, opinions, belonging to an ethic group or a nation... in short, all the situations in which a whole category of human beings is collectively imputed with certain characteristics felt by the racist to represent a danger or potential harm for himself and those he considers his fellow beings.

In truth, in many cases, the racist reaction seems to be a response to a need: the need to distinguish at a glance the friend from the foe. Racism can also be an attempt to boost low self-esteem. It is not the only way to achieve this, of course. A witty lady I knew described her companion's grandiose and sometimes outrageous undertakings by saying that he was building a skyscraper to hide a hole in his sock. Leonardo da Vinci insisted repeatedly in his notebooks on his desire that the work he leaves behind be significant enough not to fade from memory like the foam of sea waves. Some people think that Freud decided, in adolescence, to become a great man, and that he created the major edifice of psychoanalysis, in order to repair the "injury" caused to the family by the uncle who was a forger. To achieve their ambitions, these men did not hesitate to give of themselves, to pay a high price — that is, produce an unprecedented body of work.

Other people look for an easy way to improve their self-esteem: they make others pay a high price. Racists belong to this category. Intelligent, cultured people can succumb to the temptation of racism. Some become aware of it. For instance, a young teacher who was in analysis started to make antisemitic remarks during a session with his analyst. A little surprised, the analyst asked him what a Jew was, in his view. The young man thought for a long time and suddenly burst out laughing: "Well, for me a Jew is someone to whom I can feel superior without having to do anything — I, who am so inept and insignificant." Not only was this man instantly cured of his antisemitism, but it turned out that he subsequently found more worthy ways to improve his self-image, since a few decades later he was a renowned university professor whose books were translated into several languages.

INTERNAL MECHANISMS AT WORK IN RACISM

Thus, racism is a human phenomenon rooted in human affects, impulses, anxieties and fantasies. The tools it uses are projection and splitting.

The mechanism of projection can serve to displace on the rejected object everything one dislikes in oneself and in those of one's own kind, the character traits which escape one's control, and the threatening character of feared but unidentified entities. Those who speak of the miserliness of Jews or the violence of Arabs, for example, would be well-advised, if they are able, to take a look at themselves. In the schoolyard, children use clear and simple words to enact this process. When they shower one of their playmates with insults, the victim says: "The one who says it is what he calls me." Often, this wisdom is lost by the time the children in the schoolyard become adults.

Those who are too distressed by life's difficulties may feel comforted by the idea that these problems could have a specific, identifiable cause, in the shape of an evil-doing group of people who can be stopped from causing harm.

Projection usually focuses on unfamiliar human groups among which, preferably, one doesn't know anybody personally. This precludes the need to verify one's preconceived ideas, and protects one from guilt of any kind. But some people manage to avoid even this stumbling block, by convincing themselves that the members of the hated group they know personally are exceptions.

This method of self-protection has certain advantages, but some serious disadvantages as well. The human group to which everything vile, unpleasant and despicable is attributed becomes a hostile and potentially threatening enemy. Its members are regarded with fear and disgust; they are a threat to the "purity" of the racist's group, which must therefore protect itself from them by stopping them from doing harm, as a preventative measure. This vicious internal cycle set in motion in the racist's mind can lead him to murder, and even mass murder, committed with a clear conscience. Or almost. Indeed, the racist often has a secret feeling that something "is not right". The Nazi and Rwandan executioners, like other murderers, all tried to hide the traces of their deeds, and to deny that they participated in them.

The notion of "purity" plays a major role in the phenomenon of racism; it is one of the qualities the racist believes himself to have and feels obligated to protect at all costs from any "blemish" that the rejected group might inflict. Mixed marriage is the worst attack on purity, but living together, being acquainted or simply being neighbours is bad enough.

An internal splitting mechanism can help the racist maintain a positive image of himself despite the verbal or physical violence he may unleash against the object of his hate. With those closest to him, he is human, considerate and affectionate. Members of the rejected group are inferior and harmful; they must be made to disappear. One can be a loving husband and father while commanding a death camp.

Many Nazi officials who participated actively in the extermination of Jews and Gypsies, to say nothing of the massacre of entire Polish, Russian and other villages, lived peaceful, normal lives afterwards, exercising ordinary occupations. We can see the same thing in Rwanda, where victims and assassins now live as neighbours . . . harbouring mixed feelings, no doubt.

Another universal human trait is at work here as well: the certainty of the human species that it has the right to dominate all of creation and, therefore, the right to correct all that exists as it sees fit. Mankind feels authorised to eliminate everything it objects to, and develop limitlessly everything it finds beneficial. This is how the human race comes to exterminate entire species, both animal and vegetable, that are part of its universe, disrupting balances without giving any thought to the consequences. This primitive impulse to eliminate any physically or emotionally disturbing element, be it mosquitoes, weeds or human groups on whom negative qualities are projected, is one of the factors involved in the phenomenon of racism.

While the mechanisms underlying racism are universal, the forms taken by racism are not: situations vary depending on the targets and on quantitative factors. The power that an isolated racist has to do harm cannot be compared with the power of a group or a population in the grip of a collective racist delusion. Each of the major racist historical events mankind has known had particular characteristics. I will look more closely at two events which continue to weigh on human conscience, but which are far from being the only ones.

Racism targeting Blacks is based on a prejudice that portrays them as primitive savages, lazy and stupid, in short, an inferior race. This prejudice is not rooted only in total ignorance of African cultures, blithely destroyed by colonisers; it is also motivated by desire for material profit. The racist society feels entitled to exploit the riches belonging to these so-called savages, and use these people themselves as free labour[36]. But fear and jealousy are also present: Blacks are thought to possess a very enviable,

---

36   Of course, slavery existed without a racist component. It was practised mainly for profit, but without disdain or disgust. The slave had inferior status, but was not considered subhuman.

even frightening superiority, specifically in the sexual sphere. Now that members of this "savage" race teach in universities all over the world and practice every profession, it becomes increasingly difficult to maintain the fiction of an inferior race; what remains is the black skin and the sexual threat. In some societies, and not only in North America, racism against Blacks persists and can even lead to murder. Although racist murderers are isolated individuals, most often they remain unpunished; this makes the whole society guilty of the crime, because it tolerates these murders, even if it does not explicitly authorise them.

Indeed, individual racism is a latent threat for those targeted by it. But collective racism is of a different nature. It sweeps up not only those who share the delusional views in question, but also all those who are unable to resist the pressure of the majority, who are afraid to stand out or to have problems if they don't chant the slogans with the rest of the crowd. They are more afraid of the racists they've joined than of those they target, and participate in the repression of the latter more or less willingly. Thus, it's possible to join a racist movement through cowardice, and not based on any conviction. But once you participate in racist acts of aggression, what happens to your self-image? Very few people are able to judge their own acts clearly, and many feel obligated to adopt beliefs they did not have previously, to avoid admitting that they are cowardly and barbaric.

Racism directed against Jews, which has been labeled antisemitism relatively recently, has its own particularities. First, its long history: it is the oldest and most durable form of racism. Racists consider the Jew, like the Black, subhuman; he is to be feared because of his various capacities: he acquires all the wealth, has secret powers over the whole world, and has been able to obtain fraudulently the most prestigious, interesting and lucrative positions. Neither the poverty of the shtetls and ghettos in Poland and Russia, nor the modest living conditions of Jewish craftsmen has been able to shake this belief. But antisemitism has an even older religious component, which has its basis in fact. Judaism is at the origin of the two other monotheistic religions, Christianity and Islam. Both have incorporated entire segments of Judaism and have laid claim to many of its founding myths. This created the need to find a way to eliminate the bothersome ancestor, in order to claim the status of sole representative of the true faith. Even Jesus has been dispossessed of his Jewish identity, to better separate the new religion from its origins. Although antisemitism fosters racial fiction, the religious dimension develops on its own and generates conflicts between proponents of different faiths. This is no longer racism, but the mechanisms involved are the same and produce the same effects. This religious precedence — difficult to dispute — and its consequences, dating back to the birth of Christianity, probably explain why the Jews were among the first peoples to be persecuted, and in recent history, to be made the object of an attempt at total, industrial extermination, sanctioned by the laws of a State.

In order to strengthen their position, and based on their prejudices, certain racist groups which need to put down other groups of people to feel superior (as explained by the young teacher mentioned above) develop a veritable pseudo-scientific delusional theory. Thus, we have seen so-called scientists using various measurements to try to define the traits characteristic of a Jewish race. The attempt could only fail, of course, since there is no such thing as a Jewish race; it is a myth. What there is, is Judaism and its traditions, and some people adopt this culture or are adopted by it. Among those who consider themselves Jews, there are the descendants of different peoples of the Middle East, which included the Jews; descendants of Slavic people converted to Judaism, the descendants of mixed populations which included the Jews; Jews descending from Jews converted to factions of Christianity or other religions; as well as Jews originating from a Szekler (Székely) village in Transylvania, whose entire population adopted the Jewish faith and traditions.[37]

Given these facts, any scientific theory which uses them to define a human group or a special bloodline can only be a delusion. Latent racist feelings in certain people can spread and flare up when a society faces difficulties, be they economic, psychological, or existential. In other words, when a society or group of people, finding no solution to their problems, starts to look for an external culprit whose elimination could put an end to seemingly insurmountable difficulties. There are innumerable examples of this in

---

37   Szàvai, Géza, La Jérusalem sicule, Pont, 2011. The village of Bözödújfalu (Bezidul Nou) was called the Szekler Jerusalem because a large segment of the Hungarian minority living there had chosen the Jewish religion. These Hungarians had no blood ties with Jews, but they had become "Jews in the soul". This spiritual and religious conversion, which took place in the 16th century, is unique in the history of the Christian faith. These villagers were exterminated in the Second World War with other Jews.

ancient, recent and current history.

Those who harbour racist feelings, individually or collectively, look for a target in an attempt to eliminate a difficulty, thereby creating a difficulty for an entire group of people. Indeed, being the target of racism is a confusing and problematic situation in many ways. Not only is there constant physical danger, which is tormenting enough. In addition, the targeted group must also face delirious accusations which nevertheless have concrete effects, belittling and contempt, social rejection and exclusion from a whole range of fields. How can a person maintain a high enough degree of narcissism to grant himself all the human rights a racist society denies him?

To resist, to survive, to protect one's family, much strength of character and self-assurance are needed; not everyone has this strength. Some people let themselves be crushed, others try to discard the identity that endangers them. Still others choose pride and self-respect over safety, and may pay for this attitude with their life and the lives of their families. Some people, who cannot bear conflict, identify with the aggressor and accept the inferior status, seeing it as justified in reality. All those who were born or spent their childhood in a racist environment that rejected them asked themselves, at one time or other, if there was not, after all, some particular trait they possessed which explained this rejection. In any case, being the target of a racist process forces one to carry out painstaking, arduous internal work, which will necessarily affect one's internal world and produce consequences with which the person is left to cope.

The way in which the target of racism reacts to the situation in which he has been placed also produces effects on the racist. Most often, the result is a standoff which tends to worsen the emotional state of the two protagonists. It is extremely difficult for each of them to regain any lucidity about what he is and what the other is. But some reassuring stories show that this can come about sometimes. I can give the example if a young Jewish painter who spent a few months every year in a women's residence in Montparnasse. There, she was reunited every time with a beautiful and charming red-haired young woman with whom she had made friends. One day, this woman started talking about her disgust for Jews, saying she could smell their unpleasant odour fifty yards away. The young painter felt compelled to answer that she could smell nothing, even at two feet, because she was

Jewish herself. The beautiful redhead was dumbfounded: "So then, Jews are like you? I have never known any personally; so this means they are very fine people, and very interesting!" She became curious about who Jews really were, learned Hebrew, started reading everything she could find about Judaism, opened a bookstore specialising in Jewish history and culture, and became known as an expert in the field. This story shows that one should never consider a situation hopeless.

Indeed, racists vary considerably in their way of thinking and, as a result, in the way they act. In the case of the young teacher and the beautiful redhead, they needed to solve an internal problem, in which the object of their rejection played no role at all. In the case of the white Alabama men who threw a grenade into the room where Black little girls were attending Sunday school, what was at work was cruelty founded on hate. In the case of Nazi officials, or the officials of the countries invaded by the Nazis, who did not act themselves but signed documents sending entire populations to death, what appears to be present is a split. Some people can take their aggression as far as insults and humiliation, but stop short of physical violence. There have been true antisemites who saved the lives of Jews, because for them certain limits could not be crossed.

In conclusion, we might ask ourselves if the racist phenomenon should not be considered a neurosis, or even a psychosis, located in a particular area of the psyche, an individual or social illness which involves a delusional conviction. If this were the case, racism, like all mental illnesses, would be an attempt to solve a personal or societal problem. But, like in all mental illnesses, racism as a solution would be very costly for all those involved, the racists as well as their targets. Societal mental illness is as difficult to treat as individual mental illness; it is rooted in deep traits of the human psyche. Thus, racism would appear to be more closely associated with pathology than with criminality, although it can sometimes lead to criminal acts on a massive scale. Of course, these crimes must be prevented whenever possible, and must be punished when they are committed. But it must be kept in mind that they are pathological phenomena. This pathology occurs in human beings who, in most cases, are not mentally ill and are, therefore, completely responsible for their actions.

THE DEAD AMONG THE LIVING[38]
Inheritance and Transmission

The relation of the living to the dead is fundamentally ambivalent. This ambivalence is clear as soon as we raise the question of the place held by the dead in the minds of the living. But not only in their mind: the dead are also present in their body, from the moment of conception and at the moment of birth. Life is a period of reprieve before dying, and this is probably what makes the living ambivalent.

We, the living — all species of the living, animal and vegetable, are all descendants of living creatures from long ago, who are now dead, and we carry their legacy. The first unicellular organism that appeared on the planet (we don't really know how...) left its traces in us. This inheritance, outside the realm of what psychologists and psychoanalysts can clarify, must be left for scientists to elucidate. Psychology can only start to explore this inheritance, this presence of the dead in the midst of the transient fringe represented by the living, from the time when the human species appeared on Earth, and from the start of the historic era.

PRESENCE OF THE DEAD

The presence of the dead amid — and in — the living manifests itself in many ways. For instance, through direct, material presence: life moves from structure to structure, between animal and vegetable species, using various mechanisms. It passes through chromosomes, which ensure the mixing of origins, through genes, and through DNA passed on from generation to generation.

In a more subtle way, the dead are also present in the memory of the living, of those who knew them or who heard about them. They are present in their works, from the simplest to the most noble, from cut flint to the most exquisite works of art. They are present through their ideas, which the living take up, reshape, develop, and perhaps deflect from their intended course. The dead are also present in a more subtle way when someone shows a characteristic that cannot be explained in any other way than as coming from an ancestor, about whom the person in question may know absolutely nothing: a gesture, a facial expression, a sensitivity, or a talent. Some of the dead

---
38 Article written in response to a discussion proposed by Fabio Landa.

remain present as individuals, because they have acquired personal fame through their works, their actions or simply their personality. People like Cleopatra, Archimedes, Augustus, Leonardo da Vinci, Johann Sebastian Bach and Napoleon exist for all humanity, which knows them through their achievements, their stories, their historical context. People can try to imagine their character and their inner being. This presence invariably elicits the ambivalence mentioned above. The living admire them, envy them, love them, hate them and idolise them, often all at the same time. The various feelings generated by Freud constitute a good example of such ambivalent reactions. Some people hate him because they envy the importance of a man they see as having many flaws and who nevertheless deeply marked his era. Others idolise him and perhaps love him, especially since some of these positive emotions reflect back on them, his disciples.

THE DEAD IN THE IMAGINARY SPHERE

The dead also hold a significant place in the imagination of the living, once again with ambivalent overtones. The former are portrayed in countless stories, legends, various beliefs and superstitions. Entire libraries are filled with books about their lives and destinies. For, in fact, we are afraid of them but also invoke their help. We try to win their favour by offering gifts and signs of respect. We try desperately to imagine their condition, for we must not forget that they illustrate our future, which remains an unsolved mystery. The only thing we cannot imagine is nonexistence, the absence of any "condition". Human beings have always tried to construct a representation of things they cannot gasp through knowledge. And the hope of continuing a personal existence in some form or other has never left them. They can, if they must, give up the idea of preserving their bodies — while playing with the notion of a possible resurrection at the end of time — but they have trouble with the idea of giving up their soul, their mind, their conscience, everything that constitutes their personality. Belief in a sort of immortality of the soul is part of almost all religions.

But if it is true that nothing is lost and nothing is created, then no one and nothing disappears without leaving some residue which influences the functioning of the universe in some way. And if this is true in the material world, could it not also apply to the immaterial sphere? Moreover, how do we know that the immaterial is not rooted in some part of the material world? We still have a great deal to learn about what our genes and our DNA carry. There are still too many things in the world in which we live that we can neither perceive or explain.

THE DEATH OF THOSE CLOSE TO US

A whole chapter could be dedicated to the deceased we knew personally, or who were close to people we know. We remember them, or remember the stories told about them by those who remember them. Whether these remembrances are true, fragmented or reconstructed, they bespeak of a personal relation.

Then there are the people we loved, and who died. In their case, any ambivalence we felt towards them when they were alive tends to disappear. We take them into ourselves, as it were, we carry them inside us. When we remember their characteristics, the ones we liked and the ones we found irritating, everything about them becomes endearing and everything serves to keep them alive inside us. We can talk to them, we ask ourselves what they would have thought of a certain event, or a certain opinion. Their presence in our thoughts, in our psyche, gives us strength and a feeling of security. These deceased, what we pass on of them to our descendants, create more than a transgenerational effect; they create a conscious personal awareness.

More indirectly, but in the same context, there are the memories of those who have heard about a person from others, who also heard stories about them and remember these stories. This is how family legends are born. In a certain French family, people still mention an ancestor bearing the splendid name Petrus Jacobus, a soldier in Napoleon's army, who came back alive from the Russian Campaign, but whom, of course, no one has known personally for several generations. The story even recounts how one evening after dark he knocked on the window of his family's house, surprising everyone and creating a great stir. Could it be pure chance that the father and son who are still here to tell the story are called Jacques and Pierre?

Other people who have died remain present through their works or through actions that have marked history. Very distant events, which grow more distant with each generation, can determine the present of the living who have come after them. Sometimes centuries pass between the action of a distant figure and an event which results from it in the present. This situation is illustrated, for instance, by the time separating the founders of a religion from those who practice this religion now, or more precisely, what they have made of it. The divinities introduced by these religions are regarded with the same ambivalence as the dead. These divinities are malicious or benevolent towards humans depending on whether or not the latter offer them the gifts and sacrifices they demand, and show them the respect and submission to which they are entitled. Could they be, to some extent, the representatives of our dead ancestors?

TRANSGENERATIONAL EFFECTS

There are also some deceased whom their descendants know about or come to recognise, who signal their presence in a more subtle manner, more difficult to define, and whose influence on the lives of the living can remain completely unknown to those who are affected by it. These are transgenerational effects, which we recognise more and more often now in our psychoanalytic practice, without knowing yet how they are transmitted. They are felt at the psychic as well as the physical level, and we might ask if they are not, like human structure itself, always necessarily psychosomatic in nature. We are just beginning to understand the extent to which the experiences of previous generations can influence our destiny in strange ways. Family secrets exert their influence this way. An event considered shameful is shrouded in silence, the descendants know nothing about it, but they sense there is an uncomfortable gap in the family history. These transmissions of elusive events exert an influence on successive generations. This is so even when we don't know what life experience we are reacting to. If we can identify it, we can sometimes deal with its effects better. But how far back can we go to identify such an unknown legacy whose origin is sometimes very difficult to determine? Let us take the case of the man who could not eat any red-coloured vegetables (cabbage, beets, etc.) because he ascribes to them (without ever having checked) a metallic taste identical to that described by H. G. Wells in his novel The War of the Worlds as being the taste of the food eaten by Martians. Is this man reacting to Wells' imagination? Or to something on which the author's imagination was founded? Or possibly to something connected with his own ancestors, or those of the person who gave him the book as a gift?

THE DEAD IN DREAMS

The dead also signal their presence in our lives by appearing in our dreams. They appear at our invitation, of course, since the dreams are ours. They can seem vengeful or outright hostile or, on the contrary, benevolent, as they are in all other circumstances. A young woman who had just lost her father, whom she loved very much, recounted this dream: I was walking in a corridor full of twists and turns, in an apartment where I had once lived with my parents. Suddenly, around a corner, I came face to face with my father. It was so wonderful, I could hardly believe it. Filled with joy, I exclaimed: "It's not possible!" He took me in his arms and said, "But you see, it's possible, since I'm here". Other dreams involving the dead are less comforting and can even turn into nightmares. Of course, interpretations vary depending on the context.

DEATH, GHOSTS AND PHANTOMS

Death itself is often portrayed as a benevolent, even tender character, as in the poem *Death and the Maiden* by Matthias Claudius, set to music by Shubert, or as a strange and sinister character, like the one in Ingmar Bergman's movie *The Seventh Seal*.

In general, the dead are frightening when we refer to them as "ghosts" or "phantoms". But not always. They also have the ambivalent character mentioned above. Ghosts of loved ones can be perceived as friendly and protective. I will illustrate by telling the story of a lady, a friend of Sándor Ferenczi, who was talking about the occult with an acquaintance whose portrait she was painting. She spoke of Ferenczi's research on the subject, and of her joy if he were to send a sign of his presence from "the beyond". At that very moment, her easel suddenly made a considerable leap forward. Without really believing it, she hoped that it was Ferenczi signaling his presence, rather than attributing the event to the vibrations caused by passing subway trains under the building.

THE WORSHIP OF ANCESTORS

The memory of loved ones who died, especially if we had a very close relationship with them, holds a very important place in our lives. We imagine them, remember their words, their gestures, the things that happened to them. We keep photographs of them. Most often, ambivalent feelings make us remember only their good qualities and their successes; they may be annoyed if we remember negative things about them. We speak of them to people who did not know them, and some people have a way of telling their stories so vividly that even those who never knew them acquire a feeling of familiarity with them. This was the case for an elderly lady with a rich internal life who seemed literally surrounded by those she had loved and lost. She had loved them well enough just as they were not to need to embellish them. She remembered the good things and bad things about them without fearing that this would anger them; she talked about them as naturally, and at times even joyfully, as if they were actually there. And indeed, those who listened could feel their presence.

This place held by those we lost is rooted in the love and respect we had for them, or perhaps by a sense of duty. Worship of the ancestors exists, in various forms, sacred or not, in all corners of the globe. It helps to maintain the link between the world of the living and that of the dead; this is essential for the living, who know that one day they will join the world of the dead. Whether this tradition is overtly religious or strictly secular, it is always permeated with religiosity, that is, with beliefs. In some cultures, an altar is built for the ancestors, and special ceremonies are dedicated to them. In Western culture, there is the Day of the Dead, on the first of November, when people visit cemeteries to place flowers on the graves of their loved ones. Certain flowers are specifically chosen for this occasion. Contrary to the anonymous dead who are often malicious, ancestors are perceived as keepers of our conscience, entrusted with rewarding good deeds, and condemning or even punishing bad deeds.

Volumes could be written about the manner in which the bodies of the deceased are treated. These bodies must be respected, but made to disappear as quickly as possible. Huge monuments like the pyramids can be built to house them, but the bodies must be out of sight. Whatever the means of burial may be, they are intended to keep alive the memory of the dead. It must be added that cemeteries are not ready to welcome anybody. There are separate cemeteries for Jews, Muslims and Christians, and all Christians are not welcome in the cemeteries reserved for them — for instance, if they died by suicide. Hostilities between human factions also extend to the dead: acts of desecration are committed in "enemy" cemeteries, and sometimes even upon the corpses buried there.

RELICS

Objects which belonged to deceased loved ones or to famous people now dead acquire particular value. Various relics are stored piously in churches. Some people spend fortunes on relics such as the last shirt worn by Napoleon on Saint Helen's Island. It is said that the Goethe Museum must keep a reserve of Goethe's quills so as to replace at once the ones stolen by certain of the poet's admirers. And then there is the young woman who never used a cigarette case, and who started to use her uncle's bulky silver case, presented to her ceremoniously, although she had not known this uncle who died in concentration camp. We have only to remember Lamartine's poem: "Objects, do you have a soul which attaches itself to ours and forces to love?"

AMBIVALENT FEELINGS

How can we explain this power — beneficial or malicious — of those who are now completely powerless?

As is almost always the case, the answer is no doubt complex. Hope, guilt, love and hate are all mixed together, and combined with the fear of an unknown which has remained totally inscrutable. We cannot imagine nonexistence. The phrase "So and so is dead", with its inherent contradiction, illustrates this inability perfectly. Nonexistence is unimaginable for the living.

Cultivating the memory of ancestors confers on the dead the status of deities. There can be doubt about their existence, but they are nevertheless all-power. We need them and we fear them. We expect something of them, without really believing it possible. We ascribe to them an existence beyond death that we hope for ourselves, with no possible certainty.

CONCLUSION

To come back to our unicellular ancestor, successive generations have determined what we are today, and will lead to what our species — and all other species — will become in the future. The dead are everywhere, before us, around us, inside us. The fate of the living is to become the dead. But the dead no longer exist in the world accessible to us. It is their legacy that continues to exist and is transmitted from one generation to another, in three ways we know about: the double modality of the psychosomatic, and the memories and works left by those who came before us. But many things in our universe are inaccessible to us, and some will certainly remain so for a long time to come, if not forever.

EDUCATING PARENTS

I once wrote a book entitled *Instruction Manual for Children with Difficult Parents*.[39] This is how the idea came to me. I was working as a psychotechnical demonstrator at the Palais de la découverte, the oldest science museum in Paris, and I had been asked to give lectures on all kinds of problem children: children who lie, who steal, who have this or that bad behaviour.

After a while, doing this started to irritate me. I realised that we were not looking at the origins of these problems. Children are not born liars or thieves. They discover the world gradually, through the people in their entourage, by seeing how they live. The children's attempt to adjust to the world of these adults is what can lead them to lie or to steal. They most often love the people in their world, are loved by them and depend on them.

Everything these people do, their way of being, has great importance for them; they define themselves in relation to these people. This is the environment to which they must adapt, accepting it as it is, because in the beginning they are powerless. They can neither assess nor modify their entourage. Therefore, they have to develop all sorts of strategies to make themselves a place in their environment and be able to express some of their needs and desires.

At first, the means they use to do this are very primitive, and therefore difficult to understand at times. An infant, or a fetus in the womb, can only take chances with its health, or risk its life by developing all kinds of physical symptoms, some of which could be serious. This does not necessarily mean that their parents are bad parents, or are doing something wrong. It only means that there are internal or external factors which impede good development. Some of these obstacles can be identified and eliminated, while others cannot. With the exception of obvious accidents, no one has ever understood why some babies die in the womb, or what causes crib death.

---

39   Van den Brouck, Jeanne (Judith Dupont's pseudonym), *Manuel à l'usage des enfants qui ont des parents difficiles*, Preface by François Dolto, Paris, Seuil, 1988.

CHAPTER 4: OTHER WRITINGS

Later, the child can express himself by other means: cries, tears, anorexia or bulimia...

We might think that everything becomes easier with speech. But this is not at all clear. Words are not always to be understood literally; sometimes they can even mean the opposite of what they say.

A five-year-old little girl was admiring with longing the pink dresses with flounces, lace and little flowers hanging before the shop of a travelling merchant. Her mother, noticing her covetous look, asked her if she would like to have one. But the little girl had often heard her parents talking about what is in good taste and what is in bad taste. These dresses she so much wanted were definitely to be considered in bad taste. So she answered: "Oh, no!" And, of course, her mother did not insist.

The child adapts to the world in which he has arrived; he can do this in one of two ways: 1) change in order to satisfy the explicit and implicit demands of his entourage; or 2) try to change this entourage using all kinds of means, mostly indirect, because, as I said earlier, the balance of power is not in his favour.

This second method is what constitutes the "education" children give their parents and their entourage. They say that "truth comes out of the mouths of babes". I would say, rather, that children speak truths, because, most often, there is more than one. A French saying sums this up succinctly: "To each his own truth". And there is also the so-called objective truth, and inner truth, which are not necessarily the same. Most truths spoken by children are closer to inner truth. Here are some examples:

A mother is driving, while her 8-year-old son, sitting beside her in the car, is making a racket, distracting her. Being a good mother, and patient, she controls herself, and in the calmest tone possible, tells him several times, without raising her voice, to quiet down because what he is doing can put them both in danger. The child finally answers: "Mom, stop shouting." "But I'm not shouting!" , says the mother who has tried so hard to be patient. "You're not," says the boy, "but you really want to!" He couldn't have said it better.

Another story is about a 5-year-old boy. His mother has just scolded him or refused to give him something he wanted. Red with rage, he stormed out of the room, shouting: "I don't love you anymore!" Two minutes later, he peeked through the door saying, "I love you anyways, but not right now!"

One day someone asked Freud why children lie; he answered that it's because they are imitating adults. Indeed, to adults certain lies seem so legitimate, even advisable, that they don't really consider them lies, but polite phrases or "good excuses" to use for saying "no" without hurting anyone's feelings. But children see very clearly that adults are not telling the truth. So why should they hesitate to pretend that they did their homework when they didn't, if only to protect the adults' peace of mind and the tranquility of the household?

At the same time, children allow themselves to express freely objective realities in situations where adults would probably try to find a "good excuse":

Little Sara comes running to her mother, crying: "Samy pushed me". The mother asks Samy: "Why did you push your sister?" Samy answers: "Because I really felt like it…"

Children tend to express their inner reality even more than adults. The following story is a good example: a little boy comes running home from school and throws himself in his mother's arms:

- Mommy, I was chased by a lion!

- How can you tell such stories, his mother answered. When you say your prayers tonight, you are going and ask God to forgive you for telling such a silly lie.

The next day, the mother asked the boy if he had prayed and asked for forgiveness.

- Yes, said the boy. And God told me: "Don't worry about it, little one; anyone would have been afraid of such a big dog…"

These stories are enough to teach adults two things: first, that it's not necessary to be hypocritical with a child, because usually his sensitivity will allow him detect the real feelings we are trying to hide. If he trusts an adult, he will tell him what he feels; otherwise, he won't say anything, but will form an opinion about the lack of reliability of that adult, or of adults in general.

The story of the big dog teaches us not to always take what children say literally. In fact, this is also true about what adults say. When we say that we waited for a bus for hours, we are probably talking about fifteen or twenty minutes. But it would not be possible to convey all our impatience and irritation if we said just fifteen minutes.

Once we understand that children never talk just for the sake of talking, we realise that they can remind adults of things they may have forgotten in their eagerness to become really adult and leave behind childish things. Children have more spontaneous contact with their feelings than adults, and adults are the ones who teach them not to always express their feelings, or even to deny them or constrain their expression to the point of reversing them or no longer being aware of feeling them.

For example, children are taught that they should love their parents, and that not to love them is a serious offence, even something unnatural. Yet even the famous Ten Commandments that are the foundation of most religions do not ask us to love our parents; they speak of honouring and respecting them. In fact, it would be more accurate to say that it is great good fortune to be able to love one's parents and, luckily, situations where one cannot love them at all are relatively rare. But there are parents who truly cannot be loved. Jules Renard's story Poil de Carotte provides a classic example. And even when parents are loved, they are not necessarily loved 24 hours a day, as the little boy we mentioned above explained so well.

What children say always means something, contains a message, sometimes literal but very often to be taken figuratively. If the adult can decipher the message, he always learns something important or interesting. And the child is given proof that he can communicate with that adult.

As we have said, even very young babies are able to convey many important things through their cries and various sounds they make, but they are only superficially understood, if at all. This leads to frequent misunderstandings and some traumas inflicted, unintentionally of course, by this mismatch between the need expressed and the response, which, nevertheless produces undesirable consequences.

Children react to everything that happens around them, and notice all the inconsistencies in the adults' words and behaviour. They don't do this to criticise the adults — they don't have the tools for that — , but rather to try to understand the essential meaning of what adults say and do, and to try to learn how one should behave with adults and in the adult world.

Every adult begins life as a child. The more closely he stays in touch with the feelings and impressions of childhood, the better he will understand his own children, and the more he will be able to profit from the things they teach him. Children are the ones who teach adults how to be parents. One can only become a parent by having children, and any preparation always proves fruitless. Once they are there, children educate their parents through their comments, their questions and their distress, their expectations and their demands, that are sometimes contradictory or impossible to fulfill:

They ask their parents to be all-powerful and all-knowing, but when they come to realise that this is not the case, they are only angry if their parents try to deny it. Because they are never fooled. To illustrate, one grey morning a little girl asked her father: "Daddy, turn on the sun!" And she was not angry with him when he answered: "I would if I could."

Children enter a universe they discover little by little. At first, everything is a problem for them. They stumble in the dark and ask questions. We are all familiar with the "why?" stage, useful to a child not only to learn things, but to assess the reliability of the answers he receives. Indeed, very often, when a child asks a question, he already has a more or less vague idea of the answer, or of the impossibility of an answer.

For instance, one day when he was with his mother and 6-year-old brother at the market, a 4-year-old boy suddenly asked: "Who is God?" While his mother was scratching her head and trying to come up with an answer to this thorny question, the older brother beat her to it, saying: "It's someone who died a very long time ago!" For the moment, this Nietzschean answer seemed to satisfy his younger brother. The question would no doubt come up again, more than once...

Children try to devise all sorts of means to deal with the weaknesses, even faults of their parents. They develop all kinds of skills in order to be able to survive the most aberrant and sometimes the most difficult family situations. As anyone faced with a problem would do, they try to remedy the dysfunction of the adults in their entourage. If this proves to be impossible, they adapt; but this adaptation could be very costly.

One of the worst problems children face with adults is, indeed, that adults lie to them. They lie about Santa Claus, about all kinds of family secrets, about sexuality, about the origins of adopted children, even though the children see or sense that what they hear is false, that the stories they are told are lame. Examples of this abound. For instance, there is the story about the little boy whose mother explains very scientifically that his little brother is in her belly and, when the time is right, he will come out through a natural pathway. When the little boy asks how his little brother came to be in her belly, the mother, suddenly embarrassed, answers that it was Baby Jesus who put him there. The child asks at once: "And daddy wasn't angry?"

Of course, it's best to say things at the right time, and in the appropriate manner.

In the 1930's, a couple, who were psychoanalysts and parents, learned this from direct experience: they wanted to explain to their little girl everything about the way babies are born. They chose what they felt was an opportune moment, spoke of the little seed from the father, the other little seed from the mother, and their encounter…A few days later, the little girl came home from school very angry: "What is this ridiculous story about little seeds that you told me? The teacher explained everything, now I know it's the stork that brings babies!" It's clear then that it is best to wait for questions before offering answers. Another little boy, who was informed by chance when he overheard the explanations given to his older brother about the two half-grains ("demi grains", in French) and their meeting, passed on the information to his kindergarten friend: daddy and mommy have a migraine together and that makes a baby.

A particularly difficult stage in parental education comes at adolescence. The adolescent wants to be independent and protected at the same time, free but accompanied. He feels his body changing and tries desperately to keep control of it; he is able to engage in more and more activities, but has trouble identifying his limits and deciding how much responsibility he can carry. He wants his parents to provide security, to take care of him, but without mixing into his affairs; he wants them to be there, but doesn't want to be under their scrutiny. In short, what he asks of them is simply impossible to provide.

But there is a message to be heard in his excessive, contradictory demands and injunctions: that parents must recognise his contradictory needs, and also become aware of their own limitations. Their adolescent children need to encounter them in their full humanity, with their successes and errors, admire them for what they have actually accomplished, and regard them with a degree of indulgence for their weaknesses and failures. They want their parents to recognise that they have moods too, that they can be unfair at times and later admit their shortcomings. But they want their parents to play their parental role despite everything; they want to be able to count on their love, on their sense of responsibility. They want their parents to set down firm rules, even if they can't always enforce them. I think that what adolescents would like to teach their parents is how much they need to acquire inner security based on solid attitudes that can serve as reference points. What is allowed or not allowed varies to a certain extent from one family to another. The important thing is for these rules to exist, and for young people to know where they stand in relation to them, and find their bearings in the world in which they live.

They may not adopt all of their parents' principles because the world is changing and each generation is different. But they know since early childhood that they need rules and principles to serve as guidelines in their lives. They may break the rules, but it is important for them to be aware of what they are doing and why. And they expect the same clarity from adults.

Some children complain of their parents' laxist attitude, which they perceive as abandonment. As if these parents were leaving them without any support. Of course, this does not prevent them from rebelling against their authority at the same time. It is up to the adults to manage these contradictory reactions.

Children and adolescents do not need to have all their desires satisfied, even though they constantly multiply their claims and demands. They need to know that their personal desires and aspirations are heard, recognised and respected, even if the parents lack the means, or the ability, or simply the desire, to satisfy them. Finally, when they leave childhood behind, they leave their family and teach their parents that it is crucial for them to take charge of their own lives responsibly, and strive to have full and interesting lives without making their children their only reason to live. And also teach them that instead of trying to keep their children in a position of inferiority in order to hold on to a power that has become illusory, they should be ready to relate welcome them as equals when the time comes.

CHAPTER 5
BRIEF NOTES

THE PROBLEM OF THE "MODEL CHILD"

The best development one can wish a child is to evolve from a position of total emotional and material dependence at birth, to a position of material and emotional independence as complete as possible in adulthood. Clearly, emotional independence does not mean absence of affection or a lack of need for affection. What it does mean is sufficient redirection of emotional dependence to be able to form other ties, to distance oneself physically from one's family without losing contact, and to invest energy in one's work and various interests.

Psychoanalysts Nicolas Abraham and Maria Torok, following in the footsteps of Sándor Ferenczi, have called this successful "introjection". This means that the child has internalised those he loves sufficiently to feel that they are close even when they are not actually there.

The process leading to this is long and intricate, involving many familial, social and cultural factors. The earliest and most direct role is no doubt played by the family. As is the case with all intricate processes, all kinds of snags and incidents can occur during a child's development. They are of many different types and take the form of very diverse syndromes.

One of the most disconcerting syndromes, and the most difficult to interpret, is that of the "model child". This is the child who doesn't give anyone any trouble, obeys, succeeds, fills all expectations — expectations which correspond perfectly to the child the parents had imagined at the moment of his conception.

This is the child described by the expression "as good as gold": a child who doesn't stand out, doesn't shout, doesn't cry, doesn't speak, doesn't move and doesn't hear what goes on around him. This is the child the parents can take anywhere and leave sitting in a chair, knowing he won't bother anyone while those around him discuss other things, including him, as if he was not there. In truth, he is not there, because he isn't anywhere. Or, in the best case, because he pretends that he is not there. He senses that in order to be accepted, he must not bother anyone, and must act as if he doesn't exist. Because a child needs to be loved and accepted, he will do whatever he must to be loved, including becoming nonexistent. The methods he can use vary: he can become autistic, mentally retarded (truly or seemingly), or simply fearful; he will have no personal desires and will find it extremely difficult to become an open-minded adult, active and able to love.

But this extreme form of adaptation can also manifest itself in other ways. For instance, a very intelligent child may succeed brilliantly in school. In these cases, the child has excellent grades in all subjects, but is not passionately interested in anything. His focus on good grades leaves him no time or energy for other things. Often, after obtaining the last in a series of diplomas — with honors — , he does not know what he should do, what profession to choose, what career to embark on; he may then break down and sink into depression.

Another possible situation, remarkably described, once again, by Ferenczi, is that of the child who senses the fragility of one of his parents or both, who feels that they are in distress, that they are overwhelmed by the obligations of daily life, and that they lack the strength to face them. He reacts by becoming the nurse, the caregiver of his parents, because he needs them. He cannot let the ship he is in sink. To describe this situation, Ferenczi spoke of "terrorism by suffering", whose effects can be the same as those of mistreatment. The parents' constant complaining forces the child to mature quickly and to take on too early responsibilities that are too heavy for him.

Parents who inflict this sort of situation on their children — unwittingly, since they are not conscious of doing it, illustrate perfectly the often mocked position of the one who is "responsible but not guilty". Of course, every person is responsible for what he thinks and does. But these parents are unable to act differently, unless they realise that there is something wrong with the functioning of the family, and seek help. There are reasons for their weaknesses, and there could be remedies. Often, the upbringing they themselves received impels them to force their children into the same mould that was imposed on them.

They don't realise that by doing this they stifle their child's personality, his critical faculty, his sense of personal responsibility, his awareness of his own desires, as well as his curiosity, his ability to act and his ability to take calculated risks.

There have been recent models of child education whose primarily objective was to teach obedience and discipline.

This does, in fact, produce obedient and disciplined adults, ready to do anything, including the worst atrocities, with a clear conscience, as long as they're ordered to do so. Clearly, this social model also has serious consequences on a child's development.

Finally, we must not forget that education goes both ways. It is the children who teach adults to become parents. And "grown-ups" who know how to listen to children, and don't always hear them only literally, can benefit greatly in ways that will help them and their children. These adults will be able to detect, behind the façade of the model child, the distress, fear and lack of confidence in himself he is hiding.

READING

Calculated Risk or Incalculable Danger

It is generally believed — and rarely contested — that reading is an enriching activity eagerly sought by the reader, who asks for nothing better than to receive the ideas and emotions transmitted by the text. But, on closer look, readers can have other reasons for wanting to read. For many readers, the main objective is to find an effective means of protecting himself from the ideas and emotions the text is setting forth. There is even real delight, no doubt, in opposing the arguments presented and in refusing to be moved by the emotion expressed by the author. These readers see the text as an offensive weapon, a sort of infernal machine the author attempts to sneak into the internal world of the unwary reader, in order to produce mental and emotional changes that escape the reader's critical assessment.

We might object that the best defense would be not to read the work in question. It's a simple, direct and inexpensive solution available to everyone. Still, this text exists, spreads widely, and its contents reach those who abstain from reading it through hearsay, often in a distorted, simplified form; its power is increased by apparent consensus, which also increases its harmful effect. The reader absorbs the work unwittingly.

Despite its proven lack of reliability, this method has been widely used. It constitutes the basis of all censure and blacklisting. Countless works have been burned or destroyed in hope of stopping the spread of their contents and protecting from their impact minds considered too fragile and impressionable. For instance, in order to deprive the Maya of their civilisation, considered impious, the European invaders destroyed their libraries containing thousands of texts, only four of which survive today. This mass extermination of a culture seemed to have succeeded. But hundreds of years later, a few stubbornly curious individuals took on the task of deciphering the four remaining books and have apparently been successful.

Censure is prevalent in the private sphere as well. Some parents want to protect their children from reading material they consider dangerous for their minds or emotions, by placing these works, liable to disturb them, under lock and key, or by gluing together the pages containing subversive or disturbing passages. These parents who choose censure instead of trusting their children's own defenses often forget that by discussing their concerns with them, they reinforce their children's critical thinking and strengthen their character, which will allow them to choose themselves what they want to read and when. Not doing this is likely to produce the same results as those brought about by the amiable country priest who took the praiseworthy initiative of showing a movie every Sunday in a barn in his village. But in order to protect young souls from overly suggestive amorous scenes, he would cover the projector with his hat at critical moments. Then he would remove it, but always too soon. So he would quickly put it back again, and leave it a little longer. The result was that the audience ended up seeing only what he had intended to hide. Worse still: their attention was focused precisely on what the good father wanted to shield them from. In the same way, parents who try to hide certain books from their children only attract their attention to them, and "force them", as it were, to read them secretly even before they truly want to, in an attempt to uncover secrets that are being kept from them. These parents do not realise that it is always best to stimulate curiosity and satisfy it, even if it is not by giving a literal answer. One well-advised father understood this. He gave his child access to his entire book collection, saying: "If it interests you, it means it's for you; if it doesn't interest you, it's not for you."

Blacklisting, official or unofficial, is another form of censure. It functions in a covert way and exists in the most varied spheres, religious or professional. A certain author is called "outdated", "boring", "not serious", "deviationist", "unintelligible", "crazy"...In short, reserved for well-informed readers. That is to say, readers who have already set up all the necessary defences to avoid being influenced by harmful ideas. More sensitive readers are sometimes provided with expurgated versions. Even the Bible has undergone this process.

It is a process psychoanalysts know well. Generations of analysts excluded Sándor Ferenczi's work, labeling him deviationist and mentally ill, although his works were published and available to them. This state of affairs persisted until, little by little, thanks to the efforts of a few more clear-sighted professionals, these works were brought into the forefront, since they are essential for understanding phenomena encountered daily, as well as therapeutic situations which might have remained unresolved without Ferenczi's contribution.

Thus, the radical means employed to cut off access to writings considered dangerous by social or familial authorities are not completely effective. Forbidden ideas, good or bad, always make their way into people's awareness, and exert their influence for better or worse.

Different readers create different personal defenses when they read. One of these defences is to read the text without understanding it. The reader blames the opacity of the writing, or his own incapacities, which he considers insurmountable. An even better defence is to read the text and misunderstand it. This is like storing something in a compartment not suitable for it. Finding it again will be impossible, so it will be replaced by a false memory. Other people recognise, sometimes without any justification, their own ideas in a text, and then invoke the authority of the writer to legitimate these ideas. The best way to do this is to fragment a text. Everyone remembers Michel Rocard's half sentence, used over and over by all those who oppose immigration from poor countries: "France cannot take in all the misery in the world", forgetting to quote the rest of the sentence: "but it must do its part honourably." This method is widely used to defame, distort, deviate, or invert the author's intention.

Sometimes, pointing to an imprecision, a mistake, even minimal, can suffice to eliminate a whole text which could have disturbing effects.

Some readers can, if need be, completely separate intellectual understanding from any emotional reaction. They read texts, understand them, analyse them, apply them to their own thinking, but are not affected by them: what they read has no effect on them. They understand, but their feelings are not involved. Some of these readers become veritable encyclopedias, able to remember an impressive quantity of facts, but without being personally affected. They juggle with ideas like in a question-and-answer game show in which one scores points regardless of the subject the question deals with.

Contrary to these "armoured" readers, there are readers whose sensitivity makes them absorb everything like a sponge. What they read disturbs them, causes them to act, and can transform them into dangerous fanatics with unshakeable convictions which allow them to overstep the limits of the law, of morality or simply of humanity. In their case, what is lacking is the critical faculty, even when their intelligence remains fully effective.

Finally, there are happy readers, or particularly suitable periods for reading, when a text is discovered at the right time, presented in the right form, and read in the right context so that it penetrates into the depths of the reader's inner world. When this happens, something latent in the reader is awakened, doors that were closed open, and permanent personality changes can occur.

Of course, even for particularly receptive, open-minded readers, this kind of effect cannot be expected every time. These are exceptional events in a person's life. But these extreme effects clearly show that reading is not a neutral activity. Its effects can range from indifference to the total disruption of someone's life. Writing is a powerful means of transmitting ideas that would have remained confidential otherwise. And ideas in motion trigger emotions, and sometimes passions, action or paralysis — with consequences that can become uncontrollable. No one can predict how far the consequences of a new idea can go, when this idea is spread complacently in writing and read by people with very diverse perspectives.

THE ARTS IN THEIR ERA

All forms of art evolve with time, so much that we sometimes have trouble recognising that we are dealing with the same category of creation. Where is the similarity between the prehistoric drawings in the Lascaux Cave and the paintings of Fra Angelico, Claude Monet or Andy Warhol? Between a statue in a "Pardon" in Brittany, Michael Angelo and an "installation"? Between a medieval castle, Haussmann-style architecture and the Pompidou Centre? To say nothing of the differences between Couperin,

CHAPTER 1: BRIEF NOTES

Schubert, Bartók and Pierre Boulez. Or, Ronsard, Balzac, the Dadaists and René Char. And I'm only speaking of artists of the Western culture.

Regardless of their differences, all these artists reveal something of the human, and something of their era. Human beings don't change, or very little. They always express their emotions through the various forms of art they create, but in different ways and through different means.

What societal phenomena are reflected by these forms of art, painting, music, whose evolution over centuries is so disconcerting for successive generations, and then gradually accepted, at least to a degree?

Present-day societies, at least our Western-style societies, are in a state of chaos and disorientation. Many social systems that were relatively stable but costly in human terms were undermined and eventually overturned by discontent and revolt among the members of a particular group whose situation has become untenable. Often, these social systems were, in fact, unjust, intolerant of any difference, of any new idea, of any changes in social status. Today, many barriers have been removed — intrapsychic as well as external barriers. But having lost these barriers, societies and their members have often lost their points of reference as well. A human being who is lost and disoriented becomes easily afraid. He attributes his fear to some real or imagined cause, placing the blame on this or that group of people, and turning his aggression and hate towards this group and its members. Our era abounds with examples of this. It is a time of the most murderous wars, of exterminations of entire populations, whether they be genocidal in nature or mass murders with no distinction between categories of people. The effects of human savagery are greatly increased by technical advances; the resulting excesses of cruelty and brutality further contribute to blunting sensitivity in people.

The arts of our era reflect all this. Social and moral rules, no matter how imperfect, provided people with a frame of reference; their loss leaves people somewhat confused. In parallel, the rules and conventions of different forms of art have been set aside, even rejected and held in contempt. It has become alright to paint on anything, and with anything. Even to place any objects on any material serving as support. It is no longer necessary to know how to draw, or to know the rules of composition, to consider and call oneself a painter and be accepted as such. Similarly, one can make music which mixes classical instruments with any object that can produce noise. This absence of rules exists to some degree in all the arts. This loss of guidance, this deconstruction, leaves artists disoriented and causes a sort of headlong rushing ahead: to feel creative, one must do something nobody did before, no matter what that is. The emphasis is gradually shifting from the work of art to the artists. The latter feels free to express himself in any way he wishes, and to use any materials, especially those no one else has thought of using before. The result of an experiment, interesting in itself, is sometimes presented as a finished work of art.

This process involves a considerable degree of aggression. There are works that attempt to shock, to disturb, to make the spectator ill at ease. This is not a side effect, such as that often produced by works of art, but a primary, deliberate intention. As the arts evolved over time, certain works created a stir, disturbed people's thinking and sensibilities. This was the effect they produced, but this effect was unintended. This is not the case for contemporary art. For many artists, disturbing and shocking people has become the primary aim. They want to invent something completely original, no matter what it is. A play by Sophocles presented with actors in bathing suits, a concert where the musician smashes his instrument at the end of the show, a "painting" which is a blank canvas...The artist becomes more important than his work, and signatures also become larger and larger.

This also reveals something about the society in which we live. Elders are no longer considered to have wisdom and to have something to pass on. They are helpless to deal with new inventions. Their grandchildren have to adjust their portable phones and repair their computers, provided they have ventured to acquire such devices. In short, they can be disposed of, along with their rules and their knowledge.

One other thing is worth examining. Our numbers are growing, and as a result we are losing individuality and becoming less attentive to each other. Intimacy becomes a rare luxury, often replaced by affective solitude in the midst of a multitude. For instance, recently the body of a man was found in an apartment; he had apparently died alone a year earlier, without anyone noticing. Understandably then, everyone is looking for a way to be noticed. In order to be noticed and to assert the unique quality of their personality, those who have artistic talent, or simply an affinity for a form of art, try to produce a work unlike any work ever done before. Those without talent will resort to setting fire to cars. The most insane will shoot people at random, on the street, in a school or anywhere. There are also more and more autobiographies written. People display their lives on the Internet and give their advice to others about everything.

Strangely, this individualistic quest for visibility is associated with extreme conformism. On the one hand, one is free to dress as one likes; on the other hand, clothing is becoming more and more uniform. Everyone — that is, the majority of people, but of course not all — wants to own the same object, made by the same manufacturer, and wants access to the same entertainment, in the same places. Could this striving for originality be also a kind of uniformisation of the sought-after objective?

Man's natural curiosity has impelled him to discover and understand the meaning and functioning of the universe which surrounds him, so that he can utilise them to increase his well-being. This search for well-being is limitless and does not take long-term effects into account. The expectation is to obtain everything right away. This search for well-being, or what appears to be well-being, inevitably produced despair. Because the search is endless, there is never real satisfaction, and the quest for something better leaves no time to enjoy what one has. This has always been so, but now the process is speeding up. No one can predict what tomorrow will be like. But in today's conditions, who would take fifteen years to complete a painting, the way Leonardo da Vinci did when he painted the Mona Lisa?

Today, one must "save time", even in art. And people say that "time is money". Artists must produce quickly and sell quickly, or else be content to remain amateurs. Once a book is published, it must sell quickly; if not, a few years later it is turned into pulp. It's not that publishers are greedy; if they don't sell enough, they go bankrupt. Today, a reader enjoys the books he reads, then resells them or gives them to other people. Only rarely does anyone have his favourite books bound, so he can take them up at will and go through them again, to reread the passages he most enjoyed. To say nothing of today's practice of reading books on screen, which has made the object itself, its smell, the texture of the paper, the beauty of the print, obsolete. And does an author write the same way when he knows that in order to be published the book must be sellable, and quickly?

Only time will tell what will become of the enormous artistic production of our time. For in fact, there is no lack of talented artists. But the public, even when it is well-informed, and art experts themselves, are not always able to distinguish them from among the multitude of "art makers" who are so prevalent.

The works which will survive will no doubt also testify to the aggressivity and even to a certain small-minded cruelty of our era. The acceleration of change, which does not bring about only progress, clearly influences the state of mind and sensitivity of human beings, and therefore artistic production in all areas, the attitude transmitted by this production, and the very objectives of artistic creation.

CAN THE EFFECTS OF PSYCHOANALYSIS BE ASSESSED?[1]

Such a question presupposes the existence of measurement tools. The disappearance of symptoms could be considered a valid measurement. But we know that a symptom is not an isolated phenomenon, but is always a sign of something: a signal, like pain, for example; and we know it is unwise to simply put and end to the pain without finding its cause.

I can illustrate by speaking of a particularly intelligent and sensitive patient who undertook analysis for a problem of premature ejaculation. After three or four weeks, he was happy to tell me that his symptoms had disappeared, that his attention was no longer focused solely on this problem and its consequences, and that the analysis could now advance further.

Thus, eliminating the symptoms, without trying to discover what they point to, is like closing the mouth of someone who wants to express a complaint. Of course, we will not have to hear him, but he will be left with his suffering. Or, to use a comparison made by Freud: a fool blows on an electric lamp as if it were a candle. "When we deal directly with the symptom, we are acting like this man. What we must do is find the switch." Since I can think of no objective means making it possible to measure the effects of psychoanalytic treatment, let us consider some subjective criteria.

Most people who undertake an analysis know, or soon discover, that beneath the symptom there is a deeper

---

1   Text intended to explain to the public how psychoanalysis functions.

malaise, harder to identify, which the symptom expresses. These patients feel restricted, blocked in their love life and in their work, their development, the use of their talents, their ability to enjoy what is enjoyable, and their ability to deal with hardships. The reasons are of many kinds, and often numerous.

When these people enter analysis, they try to formulate what they feel, what they think, in a setting in which they relate to a person who gives them the time they need to do this. But, above all, this other person does not act on the emotions aroused in him by the narration he hears, but gives his emotions and those of the patient the time to develop and become clear.

The patient builds this relationship, which we could call protected, on the model of the early relationships he had in his life; in other words, he relies on his experience. We call this transference on the relation with the analyst of feelings experienced in the past. Let us note in passing that transference is a common phenomenon, which is the basis of all relationships. The difference is that the analytic setting, with its protected character, encourages transference to develop and to be discussed.

As for the analyst, he feels the emotions the patient usually triggers in others, and which repeatedly cause him problems. But instead of answering with an action, as people do in ordinary circumstances, he uses these emotions to help the patient realise what is happening between them. This makes it possible for the patient to become aware of the process he initiates, of its repetitive nature, and often of its causes and the early experiences which have given rise to the way he acts.

This being said, the past cannot be changed and the scars it left cannot be erased. But we can create a situation, thanks to the protected analytic relation, which provides the patient with the safety and support he needs to be able to invent a better way to manage his past and his old injuries, without paying such a high price. Because neurosis is itself a way of managing. We might even say that neurosis is the normal state of balance of a human being. But this state always demands a price to be paid. The price could be minimal, it could offer an optimal price-quality ratio, or in some cases it could seriously damage the person's ability to live and enjoy life.

I could go back to the story — somewhat unflattering for psychoanalysis — which nevertheless illustrates the process quite well: the story of the enuretic patient mentioned earlier.

Incidentally, speaking of the enuresis symptom, very widespread particularly in children, I have made an interesting observation which underscores its value as a sign. In some children, the symptom disappears right at the start of the therapy, which is then pursued until the deep causes are uncovered. Other children continue to wet the bed until the last session, fearing that their parents will stop the therapy as soon as their goal — stopping the bedwetting — is reached.

And so, how can we evaluate the effects of psychoanalysis? We can consider that treatment has been successful when a person who has been solitary and uncommunicative starts to create relationships and to enjoy the things that give people pleasure in life; when a man or woman who has never been able to have a lasting relationship can establish a couple relationship; when a person who was withdrawn and anxious starts to care about the well-being of those around him; when a person who has suffered repeated failures thrives in his work...

Sometimes the goal is attained completely, or in great part, or only somewhat. And sometimes not at all. This is so with any therapeutic intervention.

But we must not forget that psychoanalysis is not only a therapy. Therapy is one of its applications. But many people enter into it with the idea that an in-depth examination of their way of being and of functioning will help them to do their work better, for instance, to take greater interest in their activities. I have seen this type of motivation in teachers, doctors, social workers...and even in nuns. Only these persons themselves could assess to what extent they obtained what they were looking for. I have met people for whom this was obvious. In some people, the beneficial effects appeared some time after the end of the analysis. Other people went off to live their lives and I never knew what their analytic experience had meant to them.

FRUITFUL TRANSGRESSIONS

A certain number of psychoanalytic practices are described in one of two ways: "orthodox" or on the contrary, "deviant" or "transgressive". The first type of practice is expected to respect scrupulously the rules defined by the founder of psychoanalysis, even if they are not always completely clear; or the rules set by the founders of subsequent schools such as Melanie Klein's or Lacan's, among others. The second type of practice is regarded with suspicion, even hostility, by many analysts and by all psychoanalytic societies, starting with the International Psychoanalytic Association. Of course, it is the duty of psychoanalytic associations to ensure the proper training of practitioners, and the quality of their services. It is not desirable for just anything to be practiced and called psychoanalysis. The task of orthodox analysts can be useful. But there is a high risk of transforming theory into dogma, of replacing the judicious application of a method with blind obedience to masters, and personal experience with belief.

This way of deviating is not particular to psychoanalysis. It is particular to certain human personalities. These include disciplined people who are very respectful of the laws and the rules in effect in their social milieu; rigid personalities who have decided once and for all what is good and what is bad and will not change their minds; as well as fearful and timid people who feel more secure when they obey recognised and respected authorities. These people do not like to take risks and often become diligent plodders, avoiding as much as possible all unexpected and unusual situations. By limiting themselves to typical situations, they can even attain resounding success in certain circumstances.

But there are other types of people. The undisciplined, the disobedient, as well as the curious, those who will look into corners where others say there is nothing to see, those who accept and even seek challenges, unsolved problems, unexplored territory.

These are often the people who are criticised, rejected, sometimes excluded from official groups, considered a danger for their profession and the scientific field in question. They disturb the smooth functioning of institutions, bring into question the teaching of the profession, creating disorder in the hierarchical structure. They take risks and force others to do so. They sometimes stumble into blind alleys, encounter failures, change direction. But they are also the ones who most often bring about progress, open new perspectives, new areas of investigation for their science; the ones who discover new methods and ways of approaching problems. The adventurous spirit of these innovators does not make their life easy. Only their determination to constantly pursue their research allows them to bear the doubts and worries they experience, as well as their colleagues' impatience and lack of understanding. Transgression is not their objective; they overstep the boundaries in an attempt to resolve problematic situations they encounter in their practice, situations missed by "orthodox" practitioners who rely on well-regulated methods.

We are greatly indebted to those who "transgress": they cause some distractions, but also bring about most of the progress in various practices and fields of knowledge.

AUTHORITY, AUTHORITARIANISM
A personal experience

We are in the 1950s, in the month of October, at the Faculty of Medicine in Paris. The auditorium is full: all the second-year students want to attend their first lecture, a lecture in biology. It's noisy, people are talking, changing places, meeting friends, calling out to each other.

The dean is the one giving this lecture. He is a tall man, imposing, sure of himself and self-important. He comes in and steps in front of the blackboard with a regal demeanour; his haughty gaze encompasses the whole room. Instantly, the noise becomes chaos. Animal cries ring out, some students have trumpets and alarm clocks that go off everywhere. Paper airplanes criss-cross the space overhead, coins wrapped in paper land on the professor's desk. He lifts his arms to demand silence, then tries to shout over the noise in the room. Finally, he gives up; furious, he writes on the blackboard: "You're nothing but savages", which is true, and then leaves the room.

A half hour passes, while the noise diminishes by a few decibels, but remains impressive, nonetheless.

The chemistry professor comes in: a slender man of small stature, with white hair, a remarkable teacher known for the contagious enthusiasm he feels for his field of science. He sits down, pushes aside the paper airplanes and other objects cluttering his desk, and looks through his notes. A few minutes later he looks up at the audience and says softly: "Are we ready to start?" Instantly, there is complete silence. Pen and paper appear on the desks, and attentive eyes follow the professor's fingers as he writes the title of the first lecture on the board, after erasing the previous inscription.

I, who was to become a psychoanalyst, never forgot this impressive display of the power of what would later be called "quiet strength", this respect expected and also shown to others, and this passionate interest in the subject one teaches.

CLINICAL NOTE
An illustration of Winnicott's notion of the false self

Winnicott named "false self" a defensive organisation of the ego set in place early by the latter to protect itself from trauma. Thus, the false self serves to protect the true self, but sometimes the true self can be completely silenced by the false self, and becomes almost inaccessible.

This notion seems to find a perfect illustration in this case of a 25-year-old man. In the course of his psychoanalytic sessions, this young man displayed two modes of relation: either he spoke easily and coherently, expressing well-structured content that remained totally inaccessible to any intervention by the analyst; or he remained silent, in a state of intense anxiety. If the analyst did not attempt to interrupt this silence, the analysand was left, at the end of the session, in a state of extreme anxiety, and presenting a physical symptom that varied: headache, dizziness, stomach ache...If the analyst commented in any way, the anxiety disappeared at once, and was replaced by the easy flow of words whose content was inaccessible.

The young man was perfectly aware of this double process, which he described by saying that he had a tape player inside him. When the analyst makes a sound, it is as if he is pushing the start button of the tape player. Everything that the patient says then is perfectly true and sincere, but as if it had been recorded in advance: it cannot be acted on or modified in any way. If the analyst does not turn the tape player on, the patient is confronted with a part of himself which experiences intense feelings, but does not have the ability to speak. The tape player would be the equivalent of the defensive organisation of the false self, as Winnicott defines it, sheltering the fragile true self, intensely alive but mute, so effectively that it renders it — at least temporarily — inaccessible.

AN UNUSUAL REQUEST FOR ANALYSIS

I received a telephone call from a gentleman who expressed himself courteously and with refinement. He said he heard about me from someone whose name I didn't recognise. He wanted to meet with me to discuss entering into analysis. We set a date for his appointment.

The man who arrived at my office looked like a vagrant: disheveled, unkempt, unshaven, unwashed. But still just as distinguished and courteous. He was very cultured, well versed in literature and in the psychoanalytic sphere. He said he was self-educated. His questions were mostly of a philosophical nature; he was careful not to reveal anything about his personal history, saying that "we would talk about that in the analysis."

Somewhat disconcerted, I tried to gain time before suggesting anything. I asked how he planned to deal with the practical aspects of undergoing analysis: the schedule, paying for the sessions...He said he had already thought about these things, and this is what he suggested: he would like three sessions a week, they could be scheduled at my convenience, since his time was his own, given that he was unemployed; as for paying me, since he had practically no income, he planned to pay me in kind: do odd jobs in my house, or clean, do food shopping and even prepare meals, since he was skilled in these areas. He considered this arrangement to be mutually beneficial, and did not see any of its disadvantages. Of course, I remembered the episode where one of Freud's patients, who arrived a little too early, sat down in the garden with Mrs. Freud and helped her to peel vegetables. But I was not ready for such an unusual experience, despite the illustrious precedent.

I therefore chose to give this unusual client the address of a public clinic where he could enter into analysis and, at the same time, meet with a social worker who could help with the practical aspects of his life. I asked him to call me to tell me if this worked out. If not, we would look for another solution.

The man, still courteous and reliable as he had appeared to me from the start, called some time later to tell me that he had started analysis at the clinic I suggested, and was very pleased with it.

This incident, although seemingly resolved, left me somewhat uneasy. To have undertaken analysis on the terms suggested would not have been acceptable, of course, but the problem embodied by this man has never been looked at closely. I should perhaps have had the courage to suggest to him that he should first acquire the means to enter analysis and then come back, while accepting to meet with him from time to time in the interim. Perhaps this would have given him the strength to get himself out of the position of someone receiving state assistance. Instead, I sent him into the arms of a social worker. In short, I eluded the problem of this worthy person, instead of trying to help him solve it.

AN ANALYSIS IN THE LONG TERM

A young man, about 25, came to see me. His problem was that he was unable to pursue studies, to keep any kind of job, or to stay in a relationship. His father was a philosophy professor, his mother looked after the house...quite badly, in his opinion.

The young man started an intensive psychotherapy, for which he paid out of his salary, working as a dishwasher in a restaurant. After a few sessions, he disappeared without keeping his last appointment. I waited for a while, and then stopped reserving time for his sessions. Two years later, I received a phone call: the young man reappeared saying he had not forgotten that he owed me money for the missed session. And he wanted to continue his psychotherapy.

When he saw me, he said that he had taken accounting courses and had been working in a publishing house for the past year. He was dating a young woman who seemed to appreciate him. Before leaving, he paid for the missed session and for the one we just had, and made another appointment.

During his next session, we agreed on the days and times of the therapy that was to follow. But the young man did not come to the next session, and I had no more news of him. Given what had happened two years earlier, I did not recontact him.

This time, he had to let three years pass before showing up again. He told me he remembered that he had missed a session without cancelling, and wanted to come and pay for it. We made an appointment, he came, paid for the session he missed three years earlier, and told me he now had an executive position at the publishing house, that he had married the young woman he had told me about, and that they just had twin girls.

He wanted to see me the following week and we made an appointment. This time, I was not surprised that he did not come. He would only need a few months to complete his strange "therapy". The next time I heard from him was when he sent a note of apology and a check for the missed session, by mail. I would never hear from him again.

What can I say about this experience, unique in my practice? It was as if this young man was using his debt, repeatedly renewed, to stay in contact with his therapist and his therapy. We might think that this young man, discredited by his father and overshadowed by two brilliant older brothers, wanted to experience a relation in which he was trusted, so that he could prove this trust was justified, that he could fulfill his commitments and shape his own life. However, what remains a total mystery is how he conducted his therapeutic process, that he could not, or did not want to, share with his analyst.

WHERE IS PSYCHOANALYSIS GOING?

This is a question which I am tempted to answer by saying that I really don't know. Formulating the question this way seems to suggest that there is a point of arrival, which I do not believe. I would prefer to ask: how will psychoanalysis continue?

I am certain that psychoanalysis will progress. This has, indeed, been the case until now. Almost everywhere in the world psychoanalysts emerge, with new ideas based on new experiences. The analyst's store of knowledge changes, techniques are enhanced, and pathologies change as well. In fact, each analysis is a new experience because it involves a particular analysand working with a particular analyst, necessarily creating a unique situation. In other words, each analysis is unique, different than all others, and likely to open new perspectives. The psychoanalyst's working tool is himself, his character, his sensitivity. In the immediacy of the session, he works much more with these than with his intelligence and knowledge. Both of these are also needed, of course, but in the analytic process itself they only play an indirect role, once they have been "metabolised" by the analyst and integrated into his emotional universe. This, then, is a source of constant renewal.

Psychoanalysis has progressed considerably since Freud. He was the one who laid its foundations, formulated the theories and invented the techniques. To achieve this, he invested everything he had and everything he was. He called upon his intelligence and his curiosity, as well as his clearly stated ambition to become someone important, in the scientific domain as well as socially. He also wanted to repair all that had gone wrong in his family, to avenge himself on fate, as it were. Psychoanalysis was born of all these elements, but afterwards it integrated ideas and practices Freud would have mistrusted or simply rejected. As he rejected Ferenczi and Rank, whose ideas emerged at a time when they could not be heard by Freud, or by most psychoanalysts. What happened was the same as what takes place when an interpretation is given at the wrong time: even if it is right, it cannot be used by the analysand.

Today, Ferenczi and Rank are considered classic authors of psychoanalysis. Since their time, other creative minds have experienced this kind of lack of understanding, Nicolas Abraham and Maria Torok, to mention just two. And, to a lesser extent, analysts like Winnicott and Balint, whose work, although accepted, has long been regarded with a certain reserve in the analytic community. I wonder if we should not include Jung somewhere in this list. His research certainly deserves something other than the total disregard shown to it by many analysts.

Although the constant progress of psychoanalysis seems undeniable, it encounters a number of obstacles. I don't know if we should see these obstacles as slowing its progress, or rather as adapting it to the pace of human beings when they are faced with the necessity to revise their ideas, their convictions and even their beliefs. The community of analysts, like all other human groups, needs to preserve a sense of security through different means: by trying to safeguard all that it considers worthwhile, precious — everything that serves to define the identity of its members. This tends to make a community intolerant of any kind of change, mistrustful of any kind of experimentation. Psychoanalytic societies, created to protect the principles of the profession and the quality of practitioners, tend to let their well-established practices become static, and to invent training methods that will reproduce existing standards as closely as possible. When this is the mission, innovators are necessarily seen as disquieting trouble-makers, or even as suffering from some kind of mental problem.

This phenomenon of advancement followed by stagnation, wanting things to stay as they are, and then starting to innovate again, is seen in all the sciences. But psychoanalysis is in a particularly difficult position because, given its nature, it cannot produce tangible, unquestionable and reproducible proof of results. The results it brings about only appear in the long term. This makes psychoanalysis vulnerable to criticism and attacks.

I am convinced that there is no need to defend psychoanalysis — an almost impossible task in any case, given the intense passions it awakens. I believe psychoanalysis defends itself quite well. Those whose personality makes it possible for them to make use of it are well aware of its benefits, and they will continue to use the analyst's couch and produce the new experiences that are the source of all progress.

HAGIOGRAPHERS AND ICONOCLASTS[2]

It's an observable fact: some great men (not all) elicit in a number of their followers the irresistible desire to transform them into legendary heroes; they try to hide everything that seems to them — rightly or wrongly — susceptible of tarnishing the image of the great man, and might even invent some stories that show him in a favourable light, as if his actual merit was not enough. All these "improvements" are, of course, made in conformity with the social values existing in a certain era.

Other people, on the contrary, have an equally irresistible desire to find fault with such and such a great man, who has become their target for one reason or another (their greatness being, perhaps, the only reason), and to show that he also had weaknesses, that his works are not perfect, or even unreliable, or outdated, or plagiarised.

Impelled by their passions, both the former and the latter risk deforming history and making it confusing and incoherent.

Hagiographers can have a number of motives, separately or together; the desire to be able to rely on a totally trustworthy guide whose viewpoint can ensure that one is always on the safe side; the possibility of basking in the aura of the esteemed figure; the creation of an object on which to project one's desire for absolute love, that even the most loved of the people close to them do not merit; and other more personal motives that one or the other of them may have.

Iconoclasts could be irritated by the grandeur or celebrity of a great man, to such a degree that they feel impelled to smash the idols they are presented with.

---

2 Modified passage from the Introduction co-authored with Fabio Landa in Le Coq-Héron No. 207, dedicated to historian Paul Roazen.

CHAPTER 1: BRIEF NOTES

Refusing to have Gods and masters, they fiercely protect their independent judgment. There may be a rival to eliminate, or a thinker whose ideas seem intolerable. Or an authority figure in their personal world, whom they combat in the person of any great man. As with hagiographers, all kinds of targets can elicit positive or negative projections.

I consider hagiographers more dangerous. Their concealments and their lies are always discovered sooner or later. Through the attempt to conceal, in itself, the characteristics or facts that they want to hide become exaggerated, overblown, and risk discrediting the person, and sometimes even his work, unjustly. We have seen how Freud's expurgated correspondence, which was in circulation long before complete editions were available, served to nurture the most diverse suspicions. Freud was accused of being involved in a ménage à trois with his sister-in-law Minna, of having abandoned his four sisters to the Nazis, of having written his work by plagiarising a whole series of earlier authors, and of many other things. The monumental biography Ernest Jones wrote, at the expense of some of his closest companions, also did Freud a disservice. It was when he could be seen in all his humanity that Freud regained his full status.

As for iconoclasts, they sometimes make a useful contribution by debunking myths about self-proclaimed figures, or about a pseudo scientist like the infamous Trofim Lissenko. But they also attack famous people who have produced truly important work, which for some reason triggers their hostility, disturbs them, makes them feel ill at ease. But they do less damage than hagiographers. I say this because I believe that a truly valuable work, and its author, can withstand their attacks. Perhaps not at the moment it happens, perhaps not in all milieus, but over time, as the rejected ideas prove their efficacy and usefulness. In truth, there is no need to defend them; the way they approach the most fundamental truths defends them better than any discourse coming from supporters. Sooner or later, we end up admitting: "And yet it moves." There is no need to hide the imperfections, errors, and weaknesses of these creative, original thinkers. They only reveal the paths taken to arrive at their inventions, and the fact that they were human. The criticism to which they are exposed does not diminish in any way the respect they deserve.

Freud the man aroused the enthusiasm of hagiographers as much as the anger of iconoclasts. Surrounded by admiring followers afraid that the least flaw could tarnish the value of Freud's work, they tried, and continue to try, to protect both the man and the work from dangers which, in reality, have no power to harm them. Among these followers, there are some whose greatest fear is that if their hero is not flawless, they themselves, their position, even their means of earning a living, will suffer the consequences. This is what creates legends that turn the figure of Freud into a marvelous being, undoubtedly, but impossible to understand as simply human.

The need for coherence and truth causes historians, like Paul Roazen, to search through archives, question witnesses, look into "forbidden" corners. And they always end up revealing the facts that others attempted to obliterate. Some people, like Roazen himself, experience the satisfaction of restoring the historical truth, the logic of events and the coherence of the historical figures involved. In general, the great man and his work come out looking just as great, but more believable. Other people, seeing that they have been duped, sink into complete disillusionment. They no longer give any credence to the great man or to his work, suspecting some new trick behind every fact, every testimony, every story. They dedicate, and sometimes lose, a great deal of energy trying to demythify the object of veneration presented to them, and they run the risk of missing out on work of great value.

Thus, we have to conclude, sadly, that iconoclasts only deprive themselves of something enriching, while loyal, devoted followers, who seek to improve and enhance the image of their hero through any means, do him a disservice. Instead of perfecting someone who has no need of it, they discredit him.

www.ingramcontent.com/pod-product-compliance
Lightning Source LLC
Chambersburg PA
CBHW071300110526
44591CB00010B/726